P9-CFG-260

Exploring Christian Heritage

Exploring Christian Heritage

A Reader in History and Theology
Second Edition

C. Douglas Weaver
Rady Roldán-Figueroa
Editors

BAYLOR UNIVERSITY PRESS

© 2017 Baylor University Press
Waco, Texas 76798-7363

All Rights Reserved. No part of this publication may be reproduced, stored in a retrieval system, or transmitted, in any form or by any means, electronic, mechanical, photocopying, recording or otherwise, without the prior permission in writing of Baylor University Press.

Cover Design by Stephanie Milanowski
Cover Image: Rublev, Andrei (1360–c. 1430). *Saint Paul.* Location: Russian State Museum, St. Petersburg, Russia. Photo Credit: Scala / Art Resource, NY

The Library of Congress has cataloged this book
with the ISBN 978-1-4813-0698-0.

Printed in the United States of America on acid-free paper with a minimum of 30 percent recycled content.

TABLE OF CONTENTS

PREFACE TO THE SECOND EDITION

The idea of a "Christian heritage" may seem to assume a monolithic, monochromic, and monotone understanding of Christianity. However, the notion of "Christian heritage" upon which this text is predicated describes the intellectual history of Christian thinkers, movements, and ecclesiastical bodies as they sought to respond to their historical contexts. The variety of traditions, locations, and movements that are represented in this anthology of primary source materials demonstrates the intellectual dynamism and vitality of different forms and expressions of Christianity. Ideas are never floating in thin air. Ideas are always embodied in practices, inscribed in material culture, and transmitted and appropriated through thick networks of social interaction. The present collection offers the reader many windows from which to contemplate the Christian heritage.

There are several features of this collection that are noteworthy. While the collection is organized in chronological order, it is not bogged down by punctilious concerns with chronological detail. Selections are meant to flow smoothly and to illustrate the general direction of change in Christian intellectual history. Short introductions are intended to facilitate access to these highly contextualized texts. Major periods in the history of Western Christianity are well represented. Readers should be able to grasp the general contours of Christian intellectual discourses during the early, medieval, Reformation, and modern periods.

Moreover, the editors have endeavored to offer the reader a collection that is gender inclusive. Texts have not been edited to reflect inclusive language. Instead, historical usage has been preserved. However, the editors have resisted a construct of "Christian heritage" that has historically privileged male voices. The collection offers in this way a window, modest as it may be, to women's responses to social and intellectual challenges.

Lastly, the editors are grateful to the many people who made this second edition possible. Special thanks are due to Dr. Carey Newman and the skillful and talented staff of Baylor University Press for their commitment to this project. In particular, Jordan Rowan Fannin played a critical role in bringing the second edition to fruition. We want to recognize Brandon Frick, who coedited the first edition. Other people who contributed with suggestions and recommendations include Malcolm Foley and Joshua Smith. Also, in his years as chair of the department of religion at Baylor University, Dr. William Bellinger has been responsible for creating a friendly and joyous academic environment in which ideas can flourish and intellectual curiosity can be cultivated. In closing, Rady Roldán-Figueroa is grateful for his friendship with Dr. Douglas Weaver. Their friendship, which crystallized during the Reformation Studies Colloquium held at the University of St Andrews in 2010, has endured in spite of the geographical distance that stands between them.

C. Douglas Weaver
Rady Roldán-Figueroa
April 2017

PREFACE TO THE FIRST EDITION

Exploring Christian Heritage will take its readers on a journey through the significant traditions of the Christian faith. The book, a compilation of primary source excerpts, is designed for students taking courses in Christian Heritage, Church History, and Christian Theology. Anyone with an interest in the Christian tradition—the varied practices and beliefs of Christians throughout the centuries—will benefit from reading the texts.

The readings are organized chronologically and cover the journey of Christianity from the second century to the present. Expected classic readings (e.g., Augustine, Aquinas, Luther, and Calvin), largely unknown figures (e.g., Anne Askew, William B. Riley), and cutting edge contemporary writers (e.g., John Howard Yoder, Rosemary Radford Ruether) are all included. Readings come from early, medieval, Reformation, and modern periods in the history of Western Christianity. While not exclusively so, modern readings give special attention to Christianity in the United States.

Given the historical nature of the documents, the editors have not updated them with inclusive language. Each reading is introduced with a brief description of the author of the excerpt. Following each reading, a source citation is listed. Publishers who have graciously allowed inclusion of their copyrighted material are acknowledged in this bibliographical note.

The editors of this volume wish to thank the staff of Baylor University Press and its director, Dr. Carey Newman, for their work and for recognizing the value of a new primary source collection for students and other readers. We also wish to thank Dr. William Bellinger, chair of the department of religion, for his strong support of the project. The editors are grateful to faculty members of Baylor's department of religion (especially Dr. Daniel Williams and Dr. Joe Coker) for their input regarding figures to be included in the book. We are grateful for assistance from Baylor graduate students Courtney Lyons, Scott Prather, Jamey Gorman, Jeremy Stirm, David Nydegger, Ginny

Brewer-Boydston, Will Williams, and Myles Werntz. We are especially grateful to Michelle McCaig, administrative associate in the department of religion, for the many and varied tasks she completed.

To all students, but especially students at Baylor University, we hope that this primary source reader will enhance your study of the Christian faith.

C. Douglas Weaver
Rady Roldán-Figueroa
May 2011

1

IGNATIUS OF ANTIOCH

IGNATIUS, BISHOP OF ANTIOCH (ca. 35–107), is known as one of the "Apostolic Fathers" of the second century. His extant writings include seven letters written on his journey from Antioch to Rome while under arrest for his Christian faith. The letters reveal Ignatius' warnings against docetism (the belief that Christ only appeared to have human flesh) and affirmations of the importance of the eucharist as Christ's body and blood and the centrality of the bishop (monarchical episcopate) for the unity of the faith. Ignatius' letters also reveal his intense desire to be a martyr—an ultimate witness to the faith—and later Christians affirm that he was martyred.

Docetism, Eucharist, and Christ

I give glory to Jesus Christ the God, who has given you such wisdom. For I have perceived that you are firmly settled in unwavering faith, being nailed, as it were, to the Cross of the Lord Jesus Christ in flesh and spirit, and firmly planted in love in the blood of Christ, being fully convinced as touching our Lord that He is truly of the race of David according to the flesh, and Son of God after the Divine will and power, truly born of a virgin, baptized by John, that all righteousness might be fulfilled by Him, under Pontius Pilate and Herod the Tetrarch, truly nailed for us in the flesh (of whose fruit we are, of His most blessed Passion); that He might raise up an ensign to the ages through His resurrection, for His saints and believers, whether among Jews or Gentiles, in one body of His Church.

For all these sufferings He endured for our sakes that we might be saved. And He truly suffered, as also He truly raised Himself up. Nor is it the case, as some unbelievers affirm, that He suffered in semblance—it is they who are in semblance. And according to their opinions, so shall it happen unto them, for they are without body and demon-like. For I know and believe that He was in the flesh even after the resurrection. And when He came to Peter and those who were with him, and said to them, "Take, handle me and see that I am not a spirit without body" (Luke 24:39) . . .

Mark those who hold strange doctrine with regard to the grace of Jesus Christ, which came to us, how opposed they are to the mind of God. They have no thought for love, nor for the widow, the orphan, the afflicted, the prisoner, the hungry nor the thirsty. They withhold themselves from eucharist and prayer, because they do not confess that the eucharist is the flesh of our Savior Jesus Christ, whose flesh suffered for our sins, and the Father in His loving-kindness raised up . . .

Avoid divisions, as the beginning of evil. Follow, all of you, the bishop, as Jesus Christ followed the Father; and follow the presbytery as the Apostles. Moreover, reverence the deacons as the commandment of God. Let no man do anything pertaining to the Church apart from the bishop. Let that eucharist be considered valid which is under the bishop or him to whom he commits it. Wherever the bishop appears, there let the people be, even as wherever Christ Jesus is, there is the catholic [*universal*] Church. It is not lawful apart from the bishop either to baptize or to hold a love-feast. But whatsoever he approves, this is also well-pleasing to God, that everything which you do may be secure and valid.

It is reasonable then that we should awake and live soberly, while we have opportunity to repent and turn to God. It is good to acknowledge God and the bishop. He that honors the bishop is honored of God. He that does anything without the knowledge of the bishop serves the Devil . . .

Martyrdom

I write to all the churches, and charge them all to know that I die willingly for God, if you do not hinder me. I entreat you, do not unseasonably befriend me. Allow me to belong to the wild beasts, through whom I may attain unto God. I am God's wheat, and I am ground by the teeth of wild beasts, that I may be found pure bread [of Christ]. Rather, entice the wild beasts to become my tomb and to leave nothing of my body, that I may not when I have died, prove a burden to anyone. Then shall I truly be a disciple of Jesus Christ, when the world shall not even see my body. Entreat the Lord for me, that by these instruments I may be found a sacrifice unto God. I do not order you in the manner of Peter and Paul. They were Apostles, I am a condemned man. They were free, I, until this moment, am a slave. But if I suffer, I am Jesus Christ's freedman, and in Him I shall arise free. Now in my bonds I am learning to give up all desires . . .

The furthest bounds of the universe and the kingdoms of this world shall profit me nothing. It is better for me to die for the sake of Jesus Christ than to reign over the boundaries of the earth. I seek Him who died for us. I desire Him, who rose [for our sake]. My travail-pains are upon me. Forgive me, brethren. Do not hinder me from entering into life; desire not my death. Bestow not upon the world one who desires to be God's; nor tempt me with the things of this life. Allow me to receive pure light. When I come there then shall I be a man. Allow me to be an imitator of the passion of my God. If anyone has Him dwelling in him, let him understand what I desire, and have empathy with me, knowing what constrains me.

SOURCE: J. H. Srawley, *The Epistles of St. Ignatius, Bishop of Antioch* (London: Society for Promoting Christian Knowledge, 1919). "Docetism, Eucharist, Christ" section from "The Epistle to the Smyrnaeans," 91–93, 95–98. "Martyrdom" section from "The Epistle to the Romans," 74–75, 77.

2

THE *DIDACHE*

THE *DIDACHE* (*The Teaching of the Twelve Apostles*; although the actual title, if there was one, is unknown)—now included in the writings of the "Apostolic Fathers"—was a church handbook of Christian ethics and liturgy most likely compiled in the early second century. It often quotes from the Gospel of Matthew, which is usually associated with Antioch and Jewish Christianity. The first part of the *Didache* begins with the "Two Ways" (common in Jewish wisdom literature and found in the Qumran texts, and other "Apostolic Fathers," the *Epistle of Barnabas* and the *Shepherd of Hermas*, and later works). Authorship of the second part is unknown, though scholars suggest Syria for its place of final compilation.

Two Ways

There are two ways, one of life and one of death, and the difference is great between the two ways. Now the way of life is this—first, you shall love the God who made you, secondly, your neighbor as yourself, and all things that you would not have done to you, do not to another . . . But the second commandment of the teaching is this. You shall not murder; you shall not commit adultery; you shall not corrupt youth; you shall not commit fornication; you shall not steal; you shall not use magic; you shall not practice sorcery; you shall not procure abortion, nor commit infanticide; you shall not covet the goods of your neighbor . . . My child, do not be an observer of omens, since it leads to idolatry; nor a user of spells, nor an astrologer, nor a magician, nor wish to see these things, for from all these things idolatry arises . . .

But the way of death is this: First of all, it is evil and full of cursing; there are found murders, adulteries, lusts, fornications, thefts, idolatries, witch-crafts, sorceries, robberies, false witnessings, hypocrisies, double mindedness, fraud, pride, malice, self-will, covetousness, filthy talking, jealousy, audacity, arrogance . . . See that no one makes you to err from this way of doctrine, for he teaches you without God. If you are able to bear the whole yoke of the Lord, you will be perfect, but if you are not able, do what you can.

Other Instructions

Baptism, Fasting, and Prayer. But concerning baptism, baptize thus: having first recited all these precepts, baptize, in the Name of the Father and of the Son and of the Holy Spirit, in running water; but if you have no running water; baptize in some other water, and if you cannot baptize in cold, then in warm water. But if you have neither, pour water three times on the head, in the Name of the Father, Son, and Holy Spirit. But before the baptism, let him who baptizes and him who is to be baptized fast, and any others who may be able. And you shall command him who is baptized to fast one or two days before.

But as for your fasts, let them not be with the hypocrites, for they fast on Mondays and Thursdays, but do your fasts on Wednesdays and Fridays. Neither do you pray as the hypocrites, but as the Lord has commanded in his Gospel, pray: "Our Father in Heaven, hallowed be thy Name. Your kingdom come. Your will be done as in Heaven so on earth. Give us this day our daily bread. And forgive us our debts as we also forgive our debtors. And lead us not into temptation, but deliver us from the evil: for yours is the power and the glory forever." Pray three times a day in this fashion.

Eucharist. But concerning the Eucharist, after this fashion give thanks. First, concerning the cup. We thank you our Father, for the holy vine, David your Son, which you have made known to us through Jesus Christ your Son; to you be the glory forever. And concerning the broken Bread. We thank you, our Father, for the life and knowledge which you have made known to us through Jesus your Son. To you be the glory forever. As this broken bread was once scattered upon the mountains, and after it had been brought together became one, so may your Church be gathered together from the ends of the earth into your Kingdom, for yours is the glory, and the power, through Jesus Christ, forever. And let none eat or drink of your Eucharist but such as have been baptized into the name of the Lord, for of a truth the Lord has said concerning this, "give not that which is holy to the dogs" (Matt. 7:6) . . .

Prophets. Whosoever, therefore, shall come and teach you all these things, receive him; but if the teacher himself turns and teaches another doctrine with a view to subvert you, do not listen to him, but if he comes to add to your righteousness, and the knowledge of the Lord, receive him as the Lord. But concerning the apostles and prophets, thus do according to the doctrine of the Gospel. Let every apostle who comes to you be received as the Lord. He will remain one day, and if it be necessary, a second; but if he remains three days, he is a false prophet. And let the apostle when departing take nothing but bread until he arrives at his resting-place; but if he asks for money, he is a false prophet. And you shall not attempt or dispute with any prophet who speaks in the spirit; for every sin shall be forgiven, but this sin shall not be forgiven. But not everyone who seeks in the spirit is a prophet, but he is so who has the disposition of the Lord; by their disposition they therefore shall be known, the false prophet and the prophet . . . and every prophet who teaches the truth, if he does not what he teaches is a false prophet.

SOURCE: Charles H. Hoole, *The Didache, or Teaching of the Twelve Apostles* (London: David Nutt, 1894), 75–85.

3

JUSTIN MARTYR

JUSTIN MARTYR (ca. 100–165) was a Roman philosopher who converted to Christianity. He is known as one of early Christianity's most prominent apologists who defended the faith against pagan criticisms. Rather than attempting to separate from Greek culture, Justin attempted to make Christianity and elements of Greek culture compatible. He argued that Christianity was the ultimate true philosophy. Justin, whose best known works include his *First/Second Apology* (ca. 147–161) and the later *Dialogue with Trypho*, is known for his emphasis on Jesus Christ as the Logos. He was martyred under the Roman Emperor Aurelius.

Pagan Criticisms

But first, I cannot but take notice that though we hold some opinions like those of the Greeks, yet the name of Christ is the only thing we are hated for, and though innocent, yet we are dragged to execution like criminals; while others in other places have the liberty of worshipping trees, and rivers, and mice, and cats, and crocodiles, and many other such silly animals. Nor are the same things considered deities everywhere, but different countries have different gods; so that they charge each other with irreligion for not worshipping the same deities; and yet, in fact, the only thing you accuse us for is for not worshipping the same gods, for not offering libations, and the scents of fat, and plaited garlands, and victims to departed spirits. You need not be told that the same deities are not acknowledged everywhere, for what serves some for a god serves others for a sacrifice.

Logos/Reason

But lest men of perverse minds, attempting to mislead Christian converts should contend, that we assert that Christ was born a hundred and fifty years ago, in the time of Cyrenius, and that He taught during the time of Pontius Pilate; and thus claim (that we suggest) that all mankind before the birth of Christ must have been innocent, I shall by way of prevention solve this doubt. One article of our faith then is, that Christ is the First-begotten of God, and we have already proved Him to be the very Logos, or universal Reason, of which all mankind are partakers; and therefore those who live by reason are in some sort Christians, notwithstanding they may pass with you for atheists. Such among the Greeks were Socrates and Heraclitus, and the like and such among the barbarians were Abraham, and Elias, and Hanniah, Mishael and Azariah, and many others, whose actions, nay, whose very names, I know, would be tedious to relate, and therefore shall pass them over; so, on the other side, those who have lived in defiance of reason, were unchristian, and enemies to the Logos, and such as lived according to Him; but they who make reason the rule of their actions are Christians, men of undaunted courage and untroubled consciences, for whose sake the Logos, by the will of God, the Father and Lord of all, was by the very power of Himself made man in the womb of a virgin, and was named Jesus, and was crucified, and died, and rose again from the dead, and went again into heaven; all which I have proved at large, and is very intelligible to any person of honest understanding . . .

And whereas Plato, in his *Timaeus,* philosophizing about the Son of God, says, "He placed Him in the universe in the figure of the letter X"; he evidently took the hint from Moses; for in the Mosaic writings it is related that after the Israelites went out of Egypt and were in the desert, they were set upon and destroyed by venomous beasts, vipers, asps, and all sorts of serpents. Moses then, by particular inspiration from God, took brass and made the sign of the cross, and placed it by the holy tabernacle, and declared that "if people would look upon that cross, and believe, they should be saved" (Num. 21:9) upon which he writes that the serpents died, and by this means the people were saved. Plato upon reading this passage, not knowing it to be a type of the cross, and having only the idea of the letter X in his mind, said that the next power to the Supreme God was figured in the shape of an X upon the universe. And Plato, reading in Moses "that the Spirit of God moved upon the face of the waters" (Gen. 1:2), likewise mentions a third, for he gives the second place to the Logos of God crossed upon the world; and the third place he assigns to the Spirit, which is said to "move upon the face of the waters," thus expressing himself, "The third about the third." And hear how the prophetic Spirit has foretold the general conflagration by the mouth of Moses; you may perceive from these words: "An everlasting fire shall descend and burn unto the lowest hell" (Deut. 32:22). It is not therefore we who take our opinions from others, but others take theirs from us; for you may hear and learn these things from [believers] among us who cannot read; rude and barbarous in speech, but in mind wise and faithful, and some of them lame and blind; and thus you might plainly see that Christianity is not owing to human wisdom, but to the power of God.

SOURCE: Justin Martyr, *The First Apology of Justin Martyr*, ed. John Kaye (Edinburgh: John Grant, 1912), 31–32, 56–58, 72–73.

4

THE EPISTLE TO DIOGNETUS

*T*HE EPISTLE TO DIOGNETUS is one of a collection of early Christian writings known as the "Apostolic Fathers," which date from the first centuries of the Christian era. The letter was discovered in the Middle Ages when a monk saved it from being used to wrap fish. Scholars think that it was written sometime around 150–200 for the purpose of either making Christianity sound appealing or defending Christianity as a religion. It is unclear whether the addressee, Diognetus, was an actual person or a rhetorical figure. The letter, most of which is produced below (some argue chapters 10–12 were added later), highlights the moral excellence of Christians and contrasts the God of Christianity and his Son with the lifeless idols of the Greek gods.

The Folly of Greek and Jew

Chapter 1

Since I see, most excellent Diognetus, that thou art exceedingly anxious to understand the religion of the Christians, and that thy enquiries respecting them are distinctly and carefully made, as to what God they trust and how they worship Him, that they all disregard the world and despise death, and take no account of those who are regarded as gods by the Greeks, neither observe the superstition of the Jews, and as to the nature of the affection which they entertain one to another, and of this new development or interest, which has entered into men's lives now and not before: I gladly welcome this zeal in thee, and I ask of God, Who supplieth both the speaking and the hearing to us, that it may be granted to myself to speak in such a way that thou mayest be made better by the hearing, and to thee that thou mayest so listen that I the speaker may not be disappointed.

Chapter 2

Come then, clear thyself of all the prepossessions which occupy thy mind, and throw off the habit which leadeth thee astray, and become a new man, as it were, from the beginning, as one who would listen to a new story, even as thou thyself didst confess. See not only with thine eyes, but with thine intellect also, of what substance or of what form they chance to be whom ye call and regard as gods. Is not one of them stone, like that which we tread under foot, and another bronze, no better than the vessels which are forged for our use, and another wood, which has already become rotten, and another silver, which needs a man to guard it lest it be stolen, and another iron, which is corroded with rust, and another earthenware, not a whit more comely than that which is supplied for the most dishonorable service? Are not all these of perishable matter? . . . Are not they all deaf and blind, are they not soulless, senseless, motionless? Do they not all rot and decay? These things ye call gods, to these ye are slaves, these ye worship; and ye end by becoming altogether like unto them. Therefore ye hate the Christians, because they do not consider these to be gods. For do not ye yourselves, who now regard and worship them, much more despise them? Do ye not much rather mock and insult them, worshipping those that are of stone and earthenware unguarded, but shutting up those that are of silver and gold by night, and setting guards over them by day, to prevent their being stolen? . . . Well, I could say much besides concerning the Christians not being enslaved to such gods as these; but if any one should think what has been said insufficient, I hold it superfluous to say more.

Chapter 3

In the next place, I fancy that thou art chiefly anxious to hear about their not practising their religion in the same way as the Jews. The Jews then, so far as they abstain from the mode of worship described above, do well in claiming to reverence one God of the universe and to regard Him as Master; but so far as they offer Him this worship in methods similar to those already mentioned, they are altogether at fault. For whereas the Greeks, by offering these things to senseless and deaf images, make an exhibition of stupidity, the Jews considering that they are presenting them to God, as if He were in need of them, ought in all reason to count it folly and not religious worship. For He that made the heaven and the earth and all things that are therein, and furnisheth us all with what we need, cannot Himself need any of these things which He Himself supplieth to them that imagine they are giving them to Him. But those who think to perform sacrifices to Him with blood and fat and whole burnt offerings, and to honour Him with such honors, seem to me in no way different from those who show the same respect towards deaf images; for the one class think fit to make offerings to things unable to participate in the honor, the other class to One Who is in need of nothing. . . .

The Role of the Christian in the World

Chapter 5

For Christians are not distinguished from the rest of mankind either in locality or in speech or in customs. For they dwell not somewhere in cities of their own, neither do they use some different language, nor practise an extraordinary kind of life. Nor again do they possess any invention discovered by any intelligence or study of ingenious men, nor are they masters of any human dogma as some are. But while they dwell in cities of Greeks and barbarians as the lot of each is cast, and follow the native customs in dress and food and the other arrangements of life, yet the constitution of their own citizenship, which they set forth, is marvellous, and confessedly contradicts expectation. They dwell in their own countries, but only as sojourners; they bear their share in all things as citizens, and they endure all hardships as strangers. Every foreign country is a fatherland to them, and every fatherland is foreign. They marry like all other men and they beget children; but they do not cast away their offspring. They have their meals in common, but not their wives. They find themselves in the flesh, and yet they live not after the flesh. Their existence is on earth, but their citizenship is in heaven. They obey the established laws, and they surpass the laws in their own lives. They love all men, and they are persecuted by all. They are ignored, and yet they are condemned. They are put to death, and yet they are endued with life. They are in beggary, and yet they make many rich. They are in want of all things, and yet they abound in all things. They are dishonored, and yet they are glorified in their dishonor. They are evil spoken of, and yet they are vindicated. They are reviled, and they bless; they are insulted, and they respect. Doing good they are punished as evil-doers; being punished they rejoice, as if they were thereby quickened by life. War is waged against them as aliens by the Jews, and persecution is carried on against them by the Greeks, and yet those that hate them cannot tell the reason of their hostility.

Chapter 6

In a word, what the soul is in a body, this the Christians are in the world. The soul is spread through all the members of the body, and Christians through the diverse cities of the world. The soul hath its abode in the body, and yet it is not of the body. So Christians have their abode in the world, and yet they are not of the world. The soul which is invisible is guarded in the body which is visible: so Christians are recognised as being in the world, and yet their religion remaineth invisible. . . . The soul though itself immortal dwelleth in a mortal tabernacle; so Christians sojourn amidst perishable things, while they look for the imperishability which is in the heavens. The soul when hardly treated in the matter of meats and drinks is improved; and so Christians when punished increase more and more daily. So great is the office for which God hath appointed them, and which it is not lawful for them to decline.

The Incarnate God

Chapter 7

For it is no earthly discovery, as I said, which was committed to them, neither do they care to guard so carefully any mortal invention, nor have they entrusted to them the dispensation of human mysteries. But truly the Almighty Creator of the Universe, the Invisible God Himself from heaven planted among men the truth and the holy teaching which surpasseth the wit of man, and fixed it firmly in their hearts, not as any man might imagine, by sending (to mankind) a subaltern, or angel, or ruler, or one of those that direct the affairs of earth, or one of those who have been entrusted with the dispensations in heaven, but the very Artificer and Creator of the Universe Himself . . . Him He sent unto them. . . .

Chapter 8

For what man at all had any knowledge what God was, before He came? Or dost thou accept the empty and nonsensical statements of those pretentious philosophers: of whom some said that God was fire (they call that God, whereunto they themselves shall go), and others water, and others some other of the elements which were created by God? And yet if any of these statements is worthy of acceptance, any one other created thing might just as well be made out to be God. Nay, all this is the quackery and deceit of the magicians; and no man has either seen or recognised Him, but He revealed Himself. . . .

Chapter 9

Having thus planned everything already in His mind with His Son, He permitted us during the former time to be borne along by disorderly impulses as we desired, led astray by pleasures and lusts, not at all because He took delight in our sins, but because He bore with us, not because He approved of the past season of iniquity, but because He was creating the present season of righteousness, that, being convicted in the past time by our own deeds as unworthy of life, we might now be made deserving by the goodness of God, and having made clear our inability to enter into the kingdom of God of ourselves, might be enabled by the ability of God. And when our iniquity had been fully accomplished, and it had been made perfectly manifest that punishment and death were expected as its recompense, and the season came which God had ordained, when henceforth He should manifest His goodness and power (O the exceeding great kindness and love of God), He hated us not, neither rejected us, nor bore us malice, but was long-suffering and patient, and in pity for us took upon Himself our sins, and Himself parted with His own Son as a ransom for us, the holy for the lawless, the guileless for the evil, the just for the unjust, the incorruptible for the corruptible, the immortal for the mortal. For what else but His righteousness would have covered our sins? In whom was it possible for us lawless and ungodly men to have been justified, save only in the Son of God? O the sweet exchange, O the inscrutable creation, O the unexpected benefits; that the iniquity of many should be concealed in One Righteous Man, and the righteousness of One should justify many that are iniquitous! Having then in the former time demonstrated the inability of our nature to obtain life, and having now revealed a Savior able to save even creatures which have no ability, He willed that for both reasons we should believe in His goodness and should regard Him as nurse, father, teacher, counsellor, physician, mind, light, honor, glory, strength, and life.

The Pursuit of Full Knowledge

Chapter 10

This faith if thou also desirest, apprehend first full knowledge of the Father. For God loved men for whose sake He made the world, to whom He subjected all things that are in the earth, to whom He gave reason and mind, whom alone He permitted to look up to heaven, whom He created after His own image, to whom He sent His only begotten Son, to whom He promised the kingdom which is in heaven, and will give it to those that have loved Him. And when thou hast attained to this full knowledge, with what joy thinkest thou that thou wilt be filled, or how wilt thou love Him that so loved thee before? And loving Him thou wilt be an imitator of His goodness. And marvel not that a man can be an imitator of God. He can, if God willeth it. For happiness consisteth not in lordship over one's neighbors, nor in desiring to have more than weaker men, nor in possessing wealth and using force to inferiors; neither can any one imitate God in these matters; nay, these lie outside His greatness. But whosoever taketh upon himself the burden of his neighbor, whosoever desireth to benefit one that is worse off in that in which he himself is superior, whosoever by supplying to those that are in want possessions which he received from God becomes a God to those who receive them from him, he is an imitator of God. . . .

Chapter 11

Mine are no strange discourses nor perverse questionings, but having been a disciple of Apostles I come forward as a teacher of the Gentiles, ministering worthily to them, as they present themselves disciples of the truth, the lessons which have been handed down. For who that has been rightly taught and has entered into friendship with the Word does not seek to learn distinctly the lessons revealed openly by the Word to the disciples; to whom the Word appeared and declared them, speaking plainly, not perceived by the unbelieving, but relating them to disciples who being reckoned faithful by Him were taught the mysteries of the Father? For which cause He sent forth the Word, that He might appear unto the world . . . For in all things, that by the will of the commanding Word we were moved to utter with much pains, we become sharers with you, through love of the things revealed unto us.

Chapter 12

Confronted with these truths and listening to them with attention, ye shall know how much God bestoweth on those that love (Him) rightly, who become a Paradise of delight, a tree bearing all manner of fruits and flourishing, growing up in themselves and adorned with various fruits. For in this garden a tree of knowledge and a tree of life hath been planted; yet the tree of knowledge does not kill, but disobedience kills; for the Scriptures state clearly how God from the beginning planted a tree [of knowledge and a tree] of life in the midst of Paradise, revealing life through knowledge . . . Let your heart be knowledge, and your life true reason, duly comprehended. Whereof if thou bear the tree and pluck the fruit, thou shalt ever gather the harvest which God looks for, which serpent toucheth not, nor deceit infecteth, neither is Eve corrupted, but is believed on as a virgin, and salvation is set forth, and the Apostles are filled with understanding, and the passover of the Lord goes forward, and the congregations are gathered together, and [all things] are arranged in order, and as He teacheth the saints the Word is gladdened, through Whom the Father is glorified, to Whom be glory for ever and ever. Amen.

SOURCE: *The Apostolic Fathers: Revised Texts*, ed. J. R. Harmer, trans. J. B. Lightfoot (London: MacMillan and Co., 1898), 503–11.

5

PERPETUA

BEFORE THE ROMAN EMPIRE granted toleration to Christians in the early fourth century, Christianity was illegal, and believers could be persecuted. Stories of martyrdom gave testimony to the "ultimate witness" of faith. Perpetua (181–203), a noblewoman from North Africa along with her slave, Felicitas, were martyred in Carthage during Emperor Severus' persecution of Christians. While it is generally accepted that the work was edited by Tertullian of Carthage, her account remains the earliest extant text known to have been authored by a Christian woman.

Martyrdom

The young catechumens, Revocatus and his fellow-servant Felicitas, Saturninus and Secundulus, were apprehended. And among them was Vivia Perpetua, respectfully born, liberally educated, married, having a father and mother and two brothers, one of whom, like herself, was a catechumen, and an infant son being nursed. She was about twenty-two years of age. From this point, she shall herself narrate the whole course of her martyrdom, as she left it described by her own hand and with her own mind.

"While," says she, "we were still with the persecutors, my father, for the sake of his affection for me, persistently sought to turn me away, and to cast me down from the faith. 'Father,' I said, 'do you see, let us say, this vessel lying here to be a little pitcher, or something else?' And he said, 'I see it to be so.' And I replied to him, 'Can it be called by any other name than what it is?' And he said, 'No.' 'Neither can I call myself anything else than what I am, a Christian.' Then my father, provoked at this saying, threw himself upon me, as if he would tear my eyes out. But he only distressed me, and went away overcome by the devil's arguments . . .

"Another day, while we were at dinner, we were suddenly taken away to be heard, and we arrived at the town-hall . . . We mounted the platform. The rest were interrogated, and confessed. Then they came to me, and my father immediately appeared with my boy, and withdrew me from the step, and said in a supplicating tone, 'Have pity on your baby.' And Hilarianus the procurator . . . said, 'Spare the grey hairs of your father, spare the infancy of your boy, offer sacrifice for the emperor's well-being.' And I replied, 'I will not do so.' Hilarianus said, 'Are you a Christian?' And I replied, 'I am a Christian' . . . The procurator then delivered judgment on all of us and condemned us to the wild beasts, and we went down cheerfully to the dungeon. Then, because my child was nursing and was usually staying with me in the prison, I sent Pomponius the deacon to my father to ask for the infant, but my father would not give the child to him. And even as God willed it, the child no longer desired to nurse, nor were my breasts in pain. Consequently, I was not tormented by anxiety for my child or by pain in my breasts . . .

"After a few days, while we were all praying, there came to me a word (vision). I saw Dinocrates going out from a gloomy place . . . and he was parched and very thirsty, with a filthy appearance and poor color, and he still had the wound on his face which he had when he died. Dinocrates was my brother who died when he was seven years old from a miserable disease. His face was so eaten with cancer that his death caused repugnance to everyone. I prayed for him but there was a large gap between us so that neither of us could approach the other. In the same place where Dinocrates was, there was a pool full of water, but its top was higher than the boy's height. Dinocrates raised himself up as if to drink. I was grieved that, although that pool held water, on account of the height to its brink, he could not drink. I knew that my brother was suffering, and I trusted that my prayer would bring help to his suffering . . . It was revealed to me that Dinocrates had a clean well-dressed body and was finding refreshment. Where there had been a wound I saw a scar. And that pool which I had seen before, I saw now with its margin lowered even to the boy's waist. Water was overflowing and there was a golden bowl full of water. Dinocrates drank from the bowl and it remained full of water . . . And when he was satisfied, he went away from the water to play happily, after the manner of children, and I awoke. Then I understood that he was freed from the place of punishment . . .

"The day before we were to fight, I saw in a vision . . . we arrived breathless at the amphitheater . . . Then there came forth against me a certain horrible looking Egyptian, along with his fighters, to fight with me. And there came to me, as my helpers and encouragers, handsome youths, and I was stripped of my clothes, and I became a man. . . . And we drew near to one another, and began to fight. He sought to lay hold of my feet, while I struck at his face with my heels; and I was lifted up in the air, and began to attack him as if I could stay in the air . . . I grabbed his head, and he fell on his face, and I stepped upon his head. And the people began to shout, and my helpers yelled victory . . . Then I awoke, and perceived that I was not to fight with beasts, but against the devil. Still I knew that the victory was awaiting me . . ."

But respecting Felicitas . . . she was now eight months pregnant (she was pregnant when she was apprehended). As the day of the exhibition drew near, she was in great grief because her martyrdom could be delayed by her pregnancy—because pregnant women were not allowed to be publicly punished . . . also, her fellow-martyrs were painfully saddened that they might have to leave so excellent a friend alone (to travel) in the path of the same hope. Therefore, joining together in grief they poured forth their prayer to the Lord three days before the exhibition. Immediately after their prayer labor pains came upon her, and when, with the difficulty that accompanied an eight months' delivery, one of the servants said to her, "You who are in such suffering now, what will you do when you are thrown to the beasts, which you despised when you refused to sacrifice?" And she replied, "Now it is I that suffer what I suffer; but then there will be another in me, who will suffer for me, because I also am about to suffer for Him." Thus she gave birth to a little girl, which a certain sister brought up as her daughter . . .

The day of their victory came and they marched from the prison to the arena like they were traveling to heaven . . . Perpetua was first led in. She was tossed and fell on her back; and when she saw her tunic torn from her side, she drew it over her as a veil for her thighs, more concerned for her modesty than her suffering. Then she was called for again, and bound up her disheveled hair; for it was not becoming for a martyr to suffer with disheveled hair, lest she should appear to be mourning in her time of glory. So she rose up; and when she saw Felicitas badly hurt, she approached and gave her her hand, and lifted her up. And both of them stood together; and the brutality of the populace being appeased, they were recalled to the Sanavivarian gate. Then Perpetua was helped by a catechumen, Rusticus, who kept close to her; and she, as if aroused from sleep, so deeply had she been immersed in the Spirit and in an ecstasy, began to look round her, and to say to the amazement of all, "I cannot tell when we are to be led out to that cow." And when she had heard what had already happened, she did not believe it until she had seen certain signs of injury in her body and on her clothes . . . Afterwards she addressed the catechumen and her brother, saying, "Stand fast in the faith, and love one another, all of you, and do not let my sufferings hurt your faith" . . .

And when the people demanded to see killings by the sword that they might make their eyes partners in the murder, the prisoners rose up of their own accord, and went to where the crowd wished; but they first kissed one another that they might consummate their martyrdom with the kiss of peace . . . Perpetua, that she might taste some pain, being pierced between the ribs, cried out loudly, and she herself placed the wavering right hand of the youthful gladiator to her throat. Possibly such a woman could not have been slain unless she herself had willed it, because she was feared by the impure spirit. O most brave and blessed martyrs! O truly called and chosen to give the glory to our Lord Jesus Christ!

SOURCE: "The Passion of Perpetua and Felicitas," in *The Ante-Nicene Fathers: Translations of the Writings of the Fathers down to A.D. 325*, vol. 3, *Latin Christianity: Its Founder, Tertullian*, American reprint of the Edinburgh edition, ed. Rev. Alexander Roberts and James Donaldson (New York: Charles Scribner's Sons, 1908), 699–705.

6

IRENAEUS OF LYONS

IRENAEUS OF LYONS (ca. 125–202) was an early Christian theologian and bishop. As a former student of Polycarp (an "Apostolic Father" who was said to be a student of the Apostle John), Irenaeus claimed to be part of the developing tradition of "apostolic succession." His five-volume *Against Heresies* (ca. 180) and its defense of the faith against Gnosticism helped to define early Christian orthodoxy. His recapitulation theory, included below, highlights the themes of incarnation and atonement in the Christian faith.

Recapitulation

The Lord, having redeemed us with His own blood, and given His soul for our souls, and His own Flesh for our flesh, and pouring out the Spirit of the Father for the union and communion of God and man—both bringing down God to man by the Spirit, and again bringing man to God by his Incarnation, in might and in truth, by His coming bestowing upon us incorruption, by our communion with Him—all the doctrines of heretics come to nothing.

Thus, they are vain who say that He only appeared to be human. For these things took place, not in make-believe, but in substance of truth. But if, not being Man, He appeared Man, he did not continue that which He was in reality, a Divine Spirit (because the Spirit is invisible). Nor was there any truth in Him, for He was not those things which He appeared to be . . .

And we have shown that it is the same thing to say that He appeared but in fancy, and that He took nothing of Mary. For He could not have had flesh and blood in reality, (whereby He redeemed us), except by recapitulating unto Himself that old creation of Adam. Vain therefore are they of Valentinus' group, who hold this doctrine, that they may cast out the life of the flesh, and cast away the creation of God . . .

Evidently the coming of the Lord to His own . . . and the summing up which He made of the disobedience at the former tree by the obedience at the present tree, and His undoing the perversion, the evil perversion of Eve, that Virgin now espoused to a man: all this news was well and truly preached by the Angel to the Virgin Mary, now under a husband. For as the former was led astray by the Angel's discourse to fly from God after transgressing His Word, so the latter by an Angel's discourse had the gospel preached to her, that she might bear God, obeying His Word. And if the former had disobeyed God, yet the other was persuaded to obey God; so that the Virgin Mary might become an Advocate for the Virgin Eve. And as mankind was bound unto death through a Virgin, it is saved through a Virgin; by the obedience of a virgin the disobedience of a virgin is compensated. For while the sin of the First-made man is yet receiving correction by the rebuke of the First-born, the Serpent's craft being overcome by the simplicity of the Dove, we are freed from those chains whereby we had been bound to death . . .

Thus gathering all into one, he was Himself gathered into one—both stirring up warfare against our enemy, and forcing him out, who at first had led us captive in Adam, and trampling his head: as God said to the Serpent in Genesis, "I will put enmity between you and the woman, and between your seed and her seed: he shall mark your head, and you shall mark his heel" (Gen. 3:15). About Him who had to be born of a Virgin woman in the likeness of Adam, it [her seed] was announced as "marking the Serpent's head" . . . For the enemy would not have been properly overcome, had not this conqueror been a man born of a woman. For by a woman he ruled over man from the beginning, when he set himself against mankind. For this cause the Lord also confesses Himself the Son of Man; gathering up into himself that original man, of whom the formation of the woman took place: that as by a conquered man our race went down to death, so by a conquering Man again we might go up into life.

SOURCE: Irenaeus, *Against Heresies* (Oxford: James Parker & Co., 1872), 450–51, 494, 497.

7

TERTULLIAN OF CARTHAGE

TERTULLIAN (ca. 160–ca. 220), a North African apologist, converted to Christianity from paganism around 190. Like Irenaeus, Tertullian was an influential theologian who helped define the developing orthodoxy of the Church. He was the first Christian thinker to use *trinitas* (Trinity) to describe God as Father, Son, and Holy Spirit. Tertullian attacked the teachings of Marcion and the modalism of Praxeas. Tertullian was a strict ascetic; he also viewed pagan culture and Christianity to be incompatible, and he eventually joined the strict sect of Montanism. Often referred to as the "father of Latin Christianity," Tertullian's writings heavily influenced Cyprian of Carthage. The selections below reveal Tertullian's attitude toward pagan culture and his influential understanding of the Trinity and Jesus Christ.

Attitude toward Pagan Philosophy

These are "the doctrines" of men and "of demons" produced for itching ears of the spirit of this world's wisdom. This the Lord called "foolishness," and "chose the foolish things of the world" (1 Cor. 1:27) to confound even philosophy itself. For philosophy is the material of the world's wisdom, the rash interpreter of the nature and the dispensations of God. Indeed heresies are themselves instigated by philosophy. From this source came the aeons . . . of Valentinus, who was of Plato's school. From the same source came Marcion's better god, with all his tranquility; he came of the Stoics. Then again, the opinion that the soul dies is held by the Epicureans; while the denial of the restoration of the body is taken from the aggregate school of all the philosophers . . . From all these, when the apostle would restrain us, he expressly names philosophy as that which he would have us be on our guard against. Writing to the Colossians, he says, "See that no one deceives you through philosophy and vain deceit, after the tradition of men, and contrary to the wisdom of the Holy Spirit" (Col. 2:8). He had been at Athens, and had in his interviews (with its philosophers) become acquainted with that human wisdom which pretends to know the truth, while it only corrupts it, and is itself divided into its own manifold heresies, by the variety of its mutually repugnant sects. What has Athens to do with Jerusalem? What harmony is there between the Academy and the Church? What between heretics and Christians? Our instruction comes from "the porch of Solomon," who had himself taught that "the Lord should be sought in simplicity of heart." Away with all attempts to produce a mottled Christianity of Stoic, Platonic, and dialectic composition! We want no curious disputation after possessing Christ Jesus, no inquiry after enjoying the gospel! With our faith, we desire no further belief.

Rule of Faith

Now, with regard to this rule of faith—that we may from this point acknowledge what it is which we defend—it is, you must know, that which prescribes the belief that there is one only God, and that He is none other than the Creator of the world, who produced all things out of nothing through His own Word, first of all sent forth; that this Word is called His Son, and, under the name of God, was seen "in diverse ways" by the patriarchs, heard at all times in the prophets, at last brought down by the Spirit and Power of the Father into the Virgin Mary, was made flesh in her womb, and, being born of her, went forth as Jesus Christ; thereafter He preached the new law and the new promise of the kingdom of heaven, worked miracles; having been crucified, He rose again the third day; (then) having ascended into the heavens, He sat at the right hand of the Father; sent instead of Himself the Power of the Holy Spirit to lead such as believe; will come with glory to take the saints to the enjoyment of everlasting life and of the heavenly promises, and to condemn the wicked to everlasting fire, after the resurrection of both these classes shall have happened, together with the restoration of their flesh. This rule, as it will be proved, was taught by Christ, and raises among ourselves no other questions than those which heresies introduce, and which make men heretics.

Trinity

For God sent forth the Word, as the Paraclete also declares, just as the root puts forth the tree, and the fountain the river, and the sun the ray. For these are emanations of the substances from which they proceed . . . the tree is not severed from the root, nor the river from the fountain, nor the ray from the sun; nor is the Word separated from God. Following, therefore, the form of these analogies, I confess that I call God and His Word—the Father and His Son—two. For the root and the tree are distinctly two things, but correlatively joined; the fountain and the river are also two forms, but indivisible; so likewise the sun and the ray are two forms, but coherent ones. Everything which proceeds from something else must be second to that from which it proceeds, without being on that account separated. Where, however, there is a second, there must be two; and where there is a third, there must be three. Now the Spirit is third from God and the Son; just as the fruit of the tree is third from the root, or as the stream out of the river is third from the fountain, or as the apex of the ray is third from the sun. Nothing, however, is alien from that original source from where it derives its own properties. In like manner the Trinity, flowing down from the Father through intertwined and connected steps, does not at all disturb the *Monarchy*, while it at the same time guards the state of the *Economy*.

Concerning Christ . . . the property of each nature is so wholly preserved, that the Spirit on the one hand did all things in Jesus suitable to itself, such as miracles, and mighty deeds, and wonders; and the Flesh, on the other hand, exhibited the affections which belong to it. It was hungry under the devil's temptation, thirsty with the Samaritan woman, wept over Lazarus, was troubled even unto death, and at last actually died. If, however, it was only a *tertium quid* [*third thing*], some composite essence formed out of the two substances . . . there would be no distinct proofs apparent of either nature . . . In one Person they no doubt are well able to be coexistent. Of them Jesus consists—Man, of the flesh; of the Spirit, God.

SOURCE: *Latin Christianity: Its Founder, Tertullian. The Ante-Nicene Fathers: Translations of the Writings of the Fathers down to A.D. 325*, vol. 3, ed. Rev. Alexander Roberts and James Donaldson (New York: Charles Scribner's Sons, 1908), 246–47, 249, 602–3, 624–25. Sections on pagan philosophy and the apostolic tradition are from *The Prescription Against Heretics*; section on the Trinity is from *Against Praxeas*.

$$\underset{8}{\underbrace{}}$$

CYPRIAN OF CARTHAGE

CYPRIAN (ca. 208–258), Bishop of Carthage, North Africa, was heavily influenced by his predecessor, Tertullian, and continued the North African tradition of stringent, rigorist faith. Despite hiding during the Decian persecution, Cyprian was an influential church leader who defended the faith against the schismatic Novatianists (i.e., Cyprian regarded sacraments invalid if they were administered outside the church; thus he insisted on the rebaptism of schismatics). The excerpt below is from Cyprian's most famous writing, *On the Unity of the Church* (251), which asserts the exclusive claim that there is no salvation outside the church. Cyprian ultimately was executed during Emperor Valerian I's persecution of Christian clerics.

The Church and Salvation

And therefore you have acted advisedly and with vigor, dear brother, in excommunicating the deacon who has often stayed with a virgin; and, moreover, the others who had slept with virgins. But if they have repented of this unlawful lying together, and have mutually withdrawn from one another . . . But if any one of them be found to be corrupted [*i.e., not virgins*], let her abundantly repent, because she who has been guilty of this crime is an adulteress, not against a husband, but against Christ; and therefore, a due time being appointed, let her afterwards, when confession has been made, return to the Church. But if they obstinately persevere, and do not mutually separate themselves . . . they can never be admitted by us into the Church, lest they should begin to set an example to others to go to ruin by their crimes. Nor let them think that the way of life or of salvation is still open to them, if they have refused to obey the bishops and priests, since in Deuteronomy the Lord God says, "And the man that will do arrogantly, and will not listen to the priest or judge, whoever he shall be in those days, that man shall die, and all the people shall hear and be afraid, and no longer act arrogantly" (Deut. 17:12-13). God commanded those who did not obey His priest to be killed, and those who did not listen to His judges who were appointed for the time. Indeed they were killed with the sword, when the circumcision of the flesh was yet in force. But now that circumcision has begun to be of the spirit among God's faithful servants, the proud and rebellious are slain with the sword of the Spirit, in that they are cast out of the Church. For they cannot live out of it, since the house of God is one, and there can be no salvation to any except in the Church.

Unity of the Church

The Church also is one, which is spread abroad far and wide into a multitude by an increase of fruitfulness. As there are many rays of the sun, but one light; and many branches of a tree, but one strength based in its tenacious root . . . separate a ray of the sun from its body of light, its unity does not allow a division of light, break a branch from a tree—when broken, it will not be able to bud . . . the Church, shone over with the light of the Lord, sheds forth her rays over the whole world . . . She [the Church] is one mother, plentiful in the results of fruitfulness; from her womb we are born, by her milk we are nourished, by her spirit we are animated.

The spouse of Christ cannot be adulterous; she is uncorrupted and pure. She knows one home; she guards with chaste modesty the sanctity of one couch. She keeps us for God . . . Whoever is separated from the Church and is joined to an adulteress, is separated from the promises of the Church; nor can he who forsakes the Church of Christ attain to the rewards of Christ. He is a stranger; he is profane; he is an enemy. He can no longer have God for his Father who has not the Church for his mother. If anyone could escape who was outside the ark of Noah, then he also may escape who shall be outside of the Church . . . He who breaks the peace and the concord of Christ does so in opposition to Christ; he who gathers elsewhere than in the Church scatters the Church of Christ . . . He who does not hold this unity does not hold God's law, does not hold the faith of the Father and the Son, does not hold life and salvation.

Source: First selection is from "Epistle 61"; second selection is from *On the Unity of the Church*, in *The Ante-Nicene Fathers: Translations of the Writings of the Fathers down to A.D. 325*, vol. 5, *Fathers of the Third Century: Hippolytus, Cyprian, Caius, Novatian, Appendix*, American reprint of the Edinburgh edition, ed. Rev. Alexander Roberts and James Donaldson (Buffalo, N.Y.: The Christian Literature Co., 1888), 358, 422–23.

9

ORIGEN OF ALEXANDRIA

ORIGEN OF ALEXANDRIA (185–254), theologian and biblical scholar of the influential school at Alexandria, Egypt, was one of the most prolific writers of the ancient world. His writings included *On First Principles*, which is considered the first systematic treatment of Christian theology. Although Origen professed commitment to the apostolic faith, several of his teachings were later deemed heretical. The selections below include his explanation of a threefold interpretation of Scripture as well as speculative ideas later rejected by the Church.

Consummation of the World

Let us now see what is meant by the "freedom of the creation" and its "deliverance from bondage." (When at the end and consummation of the world souls and rational creatures have been released as it were from their bars and prisons by the Lord, some of them by reason of indolence will move but slowly, while others by earnest effort will speed along in brisk flight. And since all have free will and of their own accord can acquire either virtues or vices, the former will be in a much worse condition than they are now, while the latter will arrive at a better state. For differences of movement and will in either direction will lead to different states; that is, angels may become men or demons, and on the other hand demons may become men or angels.) When Christ "shall have delivered up the kingdom of God, even the Father" (1 Cor. 15:24), then those living beings, because they have before this been made part of Christ's kingdom, shall also be delivered up along with the whole of that kingdom to the rule of the Father; so that, when "God shall be in all" (1 Cor. 15:28), they also, since they are a part of all, may have God even in themselves, as he is in all things.

Transmigration of Souls

Whole nations of souls are stored away somewhere in a realm of their own, with an existence comparable to our bodily life, but in consequence of the fineness and mobility of their nature they are carried round with the whirl of the universe. There the representations of evil and of virtue are set before them; and so long as a soul continues to abide in the good it has no experience of union with a body. But by some inclination towards evil these souls lose their wings and come into bodies, first of men; then through their association with the irrational passions, after the allotted span of human life they are changed into beasts; from which they sink to a level of inanimate nature. Thus that which is by nature fine and mobile, namely the soul, first becomes heavy and weighed down, and because of its wickedness comes to dwell in a human body; after that, when the faculty of reason is extinguished, it lives the life of an irrational animal; and finally even the gracious gift of sensation is withdrawn and it changes into the insensate life of a plant. From this condition it rises again through the same stages and is restored to its heavenly place. On earth by means of virtue souls grow wings and soar aloft, but when in heaven their wings fall off through evil and they sink down and become earthbound and are mingled with gross nature of matter.

Scripture

But, as we had begun to say, the right way, as it appears to us, of understanding the Ccriptures and investigating their meaning, is the following; for we are taught out of scripture itself how we ought to think of it. We find some such rule as this laid down in the Proverbs of Solomon concerning the examination of divine Scripture. "Do you," it says, "portray these things to yourself threefold in counsel and knowledge, so that you may answer words of truth to those who question you" (Prov. 22:20-21).

Each one must therefore portray the meaning of the divine writings in a threefold way upon his own soul; that is, so that the simple may be edified by what we may call the body of the Scriptures (for such is the name we may give to the common and literal interpretation); while those who have begun to make a little progress and are able to perceive something more than that may be edified by the soul of Scripture; and those who are perfect and like the men of whom the apostle says: "We speak of wisdom among the perfect; yet a wisdom not of this world, nor of the rulers of this world, which are coming to nothing; but we speak God's wisdom hidden in a mystery, the wisdom which God foreordained before the worlds unto our glory" (1 Cor. 2:6-7)— such as these may be edified by that spiritual law, which has "shadow of the good thing to come," (Heb. 10:1) as if by the Spirit. Just as man, therefore, is said to consist of body, soul and spirit, so also does the holy Scripture, which has been bestowed by the divine bounty for man's salvation . . .

But in order to learn the truth of what we say from the facts themselves, let us now examine the actual passages of Scripture. What man of intelligence, I ask, will consider it a reasonable statement that the first and the second and the third day, in which there are said to be both morning and evening, existed without sun and moon and stars, while the first day was even without a heaven? And who could be found so silly as to believe that God, after the manner of a farmer, "planted trees in a paradise eastward in Eden" (Gen. 2:8), and so therein a "tree of life," that is, a visible and palpable tree of wood, of such a sort that anyone who ate of this tree with bodily teeth would gain life; and again that anyone who ate of another tree would get a knowledge of "good and evil"? And further, when God is said to "walk in the paradise in the evening" (Gen. 3:8) and Adam to hide himself behind a tree, I do not think anyone will doubt that these statements are made by Scripture in a figurative manner in order that through them certain mystical truths may be indicated.

Again, when Cain "goes out from the face of God" (Gen. 4:14), the statement clearly impels a thoughtful reader to inquire what the "face of God" is, and how anyone can "go out" from it. But not to extend unduly the work we have in hand, it is quite easy for anyone who wills to collect from the holy Scriptures instances that are recorded as actual events, but which it would be inappropriate and unreasonable to believe could possibly have happened in history . . .

For our contention with regard to the whole of divine Scripture is that it all has a spiritual meaning, but not all a bodily meaning; for the bodily meaning is often proved to be an impossibility. Consequently the man who reads the divine books reverently, believing them to be divine writings, must exercise great care.

SOURCE: Origen, *On First Principles*, trans. G. W. Butterworth (Gloucester, Mass.: Peter Smith, 1973; New York: Harper & Row, 1966), 65, 72–73, 275–76, 288–89, 297. This is a reprint from the 1936 edition published by the Society for Promoting Christian Knowledge, London. Used by permission from SPCK.

10

EDICT OF MILAN

Following the Diocletian persecution of Christians, Emperor Constantine, along with Emperor Licinius, issued the Edict of Milan (313), declaring religious toleration for all in the Roman Empire. After believing that his vision, in which Christ led his army to victory, had been fulfilled, Constantine established religious toleration toward all religions, and explicitly Christianity. The Edict is considered the turning point in the cessation of persecution of Christians and the beginning of a favored status for Christianity in the Roman Empire.

Toleration of Christianity

Whereas both I, Constantine the Emperor, and I, Licinius the Emperor, had a very successful meeting at Milan, in which we treated all things that related to the welfare and safety of the public; among other matters we thought that nothing could be of greater advantage to our people, or concern ourselves more, than the settling of those matters, in which the worship of the Deity consisted; and therefore we judged it right to allow to all Christians and others, free liberty to follow that religion which they should like best; by this means that Supreme Deity, who dwells on high, might be gracious and favorable to us, and to all our subjects. Therefore upon due deliberation and weighty reasons, we have thought fit, that no man might be denied the liberty of professing either the Christian religion, or any other, as he shall judge it best; that so the great God, whom we worship with free minds, may in all things bless us with his gracious favor and protection. Therefore we will have you to know, that we have thought fit to annul all those restrictions, that might seem to be in our former edict addressed to you, relating to the Christians: and we do now ordain that every one that is disposed to adhere to that religion may be allowed to continue in it with all freedom, and without any hindrance: and we have explained this the more copiously to you, that so you might understand that we have given a free and absolute liberty to the said Christians to profess their religion. And since we have allowed this liberty to them, you will likewise understand that we allow the like free and full liberty to all those who profess any other religion . . . With relation to the Christians, we have thought it fit likewise to add this particular; that the places in which they used to hold their assemblies, and concerning which there were some rules set in a former edict addressed to you, that have been purchased either from our treasurer, or from some particular persons, shall be restored to them, without any excuses or delays; and without either asking or taking any money from them upon that account. We order likewise restitution to be made by all owners; and that all such as may have either purchased them, or owned them, shall in order to their being compensated by us for their loss, go to some magistrate, that so we, according to our mercy, may relieve them . . . And we will be hereby assured, that the divine favor, of which we have already enjoyed, shall always watch over us, and that we ourselves shall be always successful, as well as the public happy . . .

SOURCE: Lactantius, *A Relation of the Death of the Primitive Persecutors*, trans. Gilbert Burnet (Glasgow: Robert & Andrew Foulis, 1766), 185–88.

11

PROCEEDINGS BEFORE THE CONSUL ZENOPHILUS

THE "PROCEEDINGS BEFORE THE CONSUL ZENOPHILUS" are the official court record of a trial which took place in 320 in Cirta, now Constantine, Algeria. Despite the dry formality of its language, the Proceedings provide a glimpse of what would come to be known as the Donatist controversy. When the Roman Emperor Diocletian outlawed Christianity in 303, government officials confiscated copies of Scripture from Christian leaders. When the persecution ended a few years later, a North African group called the Donatists thought any church leaders who had cooperated with the confiscations should be disqualified from leadership. The selection below is a mayor's record of the confiscations in his city, which was read in the trial before Roman Consul Zenophilus as evidence against Silvanus, a bishop who cooperated with the confiscation while a subdeacon.

Confiscation of Christian Texts

In the consulate of Diocletian the Eighth, and Maximinian the Seventh, on the nineteenth of May, from the Acts of Munatius Felix the perpetual flamen [mayor], the guardian of the colony at Cirta.

When they came to the house in which the Christians were accustomed to assemble, Felix the flamen and guardian of the state said to Paul the Bishop:

"Bring out the Scriptures of the Law, and anything else that you may have here, as has been commanded, that you may obey the order." Paul the Bishop said: "The lectors have the Scriptures. But we surrender what we have here."

Felix the perpetual flamen and guardian of the state said to Paul the Bishop: "Show us the lectors [readers] or send to them."

Paul the Bishop said: "You all know them."

Felix the perpetual flamen and guardian of the state said: "We do not know them."

Paul the Bishop said: "The public officers know them—that is Edusius and Junius, the notaries."

Felix the perpetual flamen and guardian of the state said: "Let the matter of the lectors stand over. They will be pointed out by the public officers. Do you surrender what you have."

In the presence of Paul the Bishop (who remained seated), of Montanus and Victor of Deusatelium, and Memorius priests, Mars and Helius the deacons, Marcuclius, Catullinus, Silvanus, and Carosus the subdeacons standing by with Januarius, Meraclus, Fructuosus, Migginis, Saturninus, Victor, and the rest of the grave-diggers, Victor of Aufidus made this brief inventory against them:

"*Two golden chalices, also six silver chalices, six silver pots, a silver chafing vessel, seven silver lamps, two torches, seven short brass candlesticks with their lamps, also eleven brass candlesticks with their chains, eighty-two women's garments, thirty-eight veils, sixteen men's garments, thirteen pair of men's shoes, forty-seven pair of women's shoes, eighteen pattens for the country.*"

Felix the perpetual flamen and guardian of the state said to Marcuclius, Silvanus and Carosus the grave-diggers: "Bring forth whatever you have."

Silvanus, and Carosus said: "All that was here we have thrown out."

Felix the perpetual flamen and guardian of the state said to Marcuclius, Silvanus, and Carosus: "Your answer is set down in the Acts."

After the cupboards in the bookcases had been found to be empty, Silvanus brought forth a silver casket and a silver candlestick, for he said that he had found them behind a jug.

Victor of Aufidus said to Silvanus: "Had you not found these things, you were a dead man."

Felix the perpetual flamen and guardian of the state said to Silvanus: "Search more carefully, lest anything else should have been left behind."

Silvanus said: "Nothing has been left behind. This is all—what we have thrown out."

And when the dining-room was opened, there were found in it four casks and six jugs.

Felix the perpetual flamen and life-guardian of the state said: "Bring forth whatever Scriptures you have, that we may obey the precepts and commands of the Emperors."

Catullinus brought forth one very large codex.

Felix the perpetual flamen and guardian of the state said to Marcuclius and Silvanus: "Why have you given us only one codex? Bring forth the Scriptures which you have."

Catullinus and Marcuclius said: "We have no more, for we are sub-deacons, but the lectors have the codices."

Felix the perpetual flamen and guardian of the state said to Marcuclius and Catullinus: "Show us the lectors."

Marcuclius and Catullinus said: "We do not know where they live."

Felix the perpetual flamen and guardian of the state said to Catullinus and Marcuclius: "If you do not know where they are living, tell us their names."

Catullinus and Marcuclius said: "We are not traitors, behold we are here. Order us to be killed."

Felix the perpetual flamen and guardian of the state said: "Let them be taken into custody."

And when they came to the house of Eugenius, Felix the perpetual flamen and guardian of the state said to Eugenius: "Bring forth the Scriptures which you have, that you may obey the decree."

And he brought forth four codices.

Felix the perpetual flamen and guardian of the state said to Silvanus and Carosus: "Show us the other lectors."

Silvanus and Carosus said: "The Bishop has already told you that the notaries Edusius and Junius know them all. Let them point out their houses to you."

Edusius and Junius said: "We will point them out to you, my lord."

And when they came to the house of Felix, the worker in marbles, he brought forth five codices. And when they came to the house of Victorinus, he brought forth eight codices. And when they came to the house of Projectus, he brought forth five large and two small codices.

And when they came to the house of Victor the Grammarian, Felix the perpetual flamen and guardian of the state said to him: "Bring forth whatever Scriptures you have, that you may obey the decree."

Victor the Grammarian brought forth two codices, and four quinions [a gathering of five manuscript leaves]. Felix the perpetual flamen and guardian of the state said to Victor: "Bring forth the Scriptures. You have more."

Victor the Grammarian said: "If I had more, I would have given them."

And when they came to the house of Euticius of Caesarea, Felix the perpetual flamen and guardian of the state said to Euticius: "Bring forth the Scriptures which you have, that you may obey the decree."

Euticius said: "I have none."

Felix the perpetual flamen and guardian of the state said to Euticius: "Your statement is set down in the Acts."

And when they came to the house of Coddeo, his wife brought forth six codices.

Felix the perpetual flamen and guardian of the state then said: "Look and see whether you have not got more. Bring them forth."

The woman said: "I have no more."

Felix the perpetual flamen and guardian of the state said to Bos the public official: "Go in and search whether she has not any more."

The public official said: "I have searched and have not found anything else."

Felix the perpetual flamen and guardian of the state said to Victorinus, Silvanus, and Carosus: "If anything has been kept back, the danger is yours."

Source: *The Work of St. Optatus, Bishop of Miletus, against the Donatists*, ed. and trans. O. R. Vassall-Phillips (London: Longmans, Green, & Co., 1917), 346–81.

∿

12

ARIUS OF ALEXANDRIA

A RIUS (250–336) was a schismatic priest from Alexandria whose teaching on the creaturely character of the Son of God was deemed heretical by the Council of Nicaea in 325. Initially he was excommunicated by Peter, Bishop of Alexandria, only to be later reconciled to the church and made a presbyter in 313. Arius' teachings, known as Arianism, claimed that the Son of God was not eternal but was created by God the Father, making the Son distinct from, and subordinate to, the Father. The Council of Nicaea (325) affirmed the full divinity of Jesus Christ. The selection below is from Arius' correspondence with a prominent bishop who sympathized with his views of God.

Arianism: Christology

(1) To a most longed-for lord, a faithful man of God, orthodox Eusebius; Arius, who is unjustly persecuted by Pope Alexander on account of the all-prevailing truth which you also protect, sends greetings in the Lord.

(2) Since my father Ammonius was coming into Nicomedia, it appeared to me reasonable and fitting to address you through him and in like manner to remind your innate love and disposition, which you have toward the brothers because of God and his Christ, that the bishop greatly pillages us and persecutes us, and invoking all things moves against us, so that he might drive us as godless men from the city. All this is because we do not agree with him when he states in public, "Always God always Son," "At the same time Father, at the same time Son," "The Son ingenerably coexists with God," "Ever-begotten, ungenerated-created, neither in thought nor in some moment of time does God proceed the Son," "Always God always Son," "The Son is from God himself."

(3) And since Eusebius, your brother in Caesarea, and Theodotus, Paulinus, Athanasius, Gregory, Aetius, and all the bishops throughout the East, say that God without beginning exists before the Son, an anathema was pronounced against them—except Philogonius, Hellanicus, and Macareius—heretical and ignorant men, who speak about the Son. Some of them say that he is a belching, others an emanation, and still others alike-ingenerate.

(4) If the heretics should threaten us with myriads of deaths, we are not able even to hear these impieties.

But what do we say and think? What have we taught and what do we teach? That the Son is not unbegotten or a portion of the unbegotten in any manner or from any substratum, but that by the will and counsel of the Father he subsisted before times and ages, full of grace and truth, God, only-begotten, unchangeable.

(5) And before he was begotten or created or defined or established, he was not. For he was not unbegotten. But we are persecuted because we say, "The Son has a beginning, but God is without beginning." Because of this we are persecuted because we say, "The Son has a beginning, but God is without beginning." We are persecuted because we say, "He is from nothing." But we speak thus inasmuch as he is neither part of God nor from any substratum. On account of this we are persecuted. You know the rest. I pray that you are strong in the Lord, recalling our afflictions, fellow pupil of Lucian, truly "Eusebius."

SOURCE: "Arius's Letter to Eusebius of Nicodemia," in *The Trinitarian Controversy*, ed. William G. Rusch (Philadelphia: Fortress, 1980), 29–30. Used by permission.

13

ANTHONY OF EGYPT

SAINT ANTHONY (ca. 251–356) is considered the "father" of Christian monasticism. He practiced a life of stringent asceticism and isolation in the Egyptian desert. He eventually attracted many disciples. His biography, written by Athanasius, is one of the significant "lives of the saints" that contributed to the genre of Christian hagiography. The following selection highlights Anthony's calling and elements common in early monasticism regarding intentional poverty, temptation, and spiritual warfare.

Monasticism

Anthony was an Egyptian and came from a family of considerable wealth. He was raised in a Christian family, attended church with his parents and was attentive to what he heard, keeping in his heart the things that were profitable. He was an obedient child and never bothered his parents for luxuries.

After the death of his father and mother he was left alone with one little sister. He was about eighteen or twenty, but now he had to care for both his home and his sister. Less than six months after the death of his parents, after attending church as he regularly did, he began reflecting as he walked how the Apostles left all and followed the Savior. He thought about how in Acts they sold their possessions and brought and laid them at the Apostles' feet for distribution to the needy, and how great a hope was laid up for them in heaven. Pondering over these things he entered the church while the Gospel was being read, and he heard the passage where the Lord said to the rich man, "If you would be perfect, go and sell all that you have and give to the poor; and come follow Me and you shall have treasure in heaven" (Matt. 19:21). Anthony, believing that the passage had been read on his account, went out immediately from the church, and gave the inheritance of his family to the villagers . . . having collected much money he gave it to the poor, reserving a little for his sister's sake.

And again as he went into the church, hearing the Lord say in the Gospel, "be not anxious for tomorrow" (Matt. 6:34), he could stay no longer, but went out and also gave those things to the poor. He committed his sister to some well-known and faithful virgins and put her in a convent to be raised. He then devoted himself outside his house to [ascetic] discipline, taking care of himself and training himself with patience . . . He worked with his hands, having heard, "he who is idle let him not eat" (2 Thess. 3:10), and he spent part of his money on bread and part he gave to the needy. He was also constant in prayer, knowing that a man ought to pray in secret without ceasing (1 Thess. 5:17). He had paid attention to what he had read and what he had heard [from the Scriptures] . . .

The devil, who hates and envies what is good, could not endure to see such commitment in a youth, so he attempted to trap Anthony as he was accustomed to doing to others. First, the devil tried to lead him away from the [ascetic] discipline, whispering to him to remember his wealth, [the responsibility of] caring for his sister, claims of family, love of money, love of glory, the various pleasures of food and the other relaxations of life, and at last the difficulty of virtue and the hard work it required. He suggested also the infirmity of the body [that characterized the ascetical lifestyle] . . . The devil one night even took upon him the shape of a woman and imitated all her acts simply to beguile Anthony. But he, his mind filled with Christ and . . . filled with rage and grief turned his thoughts to the threatened fire and the gnawing worm [of hell], and . . . passed through the temptation unscathed. All this was a source of shame to his foe. For he [the devil], deeming himself like God, was now mocked by a young man; and he who boasted himself against flesh and blood was being put to flight by a man in the flesh.

For the Lord was working with Anthony—the Lord who for our sake took flesh and gave the body victory over the devil, so that all who truly fight can say "not I but the grace of God which was with me" (1 Cor. 15:10).

He [continued to] keep vigil to such an extent that he often went without sleep. He ate once a day, after sunset, sometimes once in two days, and often even once every four days. His food was bread and salt, his drink, water only. It is needless to even speak of meat and wine since none of the other serious ascetics did this. He had a rush mat to sleep on, but for the most part he lay upon the bare ground. He would not anoint himself with oil, saying it was proper for young men to be earnest in training and not to seek what would enervate the body. They must make their bodies get used to labor, remembering the Apostle's words, "when I am weak, then am I strong" (1 Cor. 12:10). For, Anthony said, "the fiber of the soul is strong when the pleasures of the body are diminished" . . .

Anthony departed to the tombs which were not close to the village. He asked one of his acquaintances to bring him bread at intervals several days apart. He entered one of the tombs, and after the acquaintance shut the door on him, Anthony remained within by himself. The enemy could not endure it and was even fearful that in a short time Anthony would fill the desert with his discipline. Coming one night with a multitude of demons, the devil cut him with stripes [which made him] lay on the ground speechless from the excessive pain. He affirmed that the torture had been so excessive that no blows inflicted by man could ever have caused him such torment . . .

The Lord did not forget Anthony's wrestling, but was there to help him. Looking up he saw the roof as it opened, and a ray of light descended to him. The demons suddenly vanished, the pain of his body ceased immediately, and the building was whole again. But Anthony, feeling the help, getting his breath again, and being freed from pain, sought the vision which had appeared to him, and said, "Where were you? Why did you not appear at the beginning to stop my pains?" And a voice came to him, "Anthony, I was here, but I waited to see your fight; because you have endured, and have not been defeated, I will always be a help to you, and will make your name known everywhere." Having heard this, Anthony arose and prayed, and received such strength that he perceived that he had more power in his body than before. He was then about thirty-five years old.

SOURCE: "Life of St. Anthony," in *A Select Library of Nicene and Post-Nicene Fathers of the Christian Church*, vol. 4, second series, *St. Athanasius: Select Works and Letters*, ed. Philip Schaff and Henry Wace (New York: The Christian Literature Co., 1892), 195–99.

ೱೢ

14

ATHANASIUS OF ALEXANDRIA

ATHANASIUS (296–373), Bishop of Alexandria, was the foremost opponent of Arianism in the debate between the schools of Antioch and Alexandria. He was exiled at least five times—leading to the expression "Athanasius against the World"—during which time he wrote his various apologies and orations. Athanasius was eventually restored to his episcopal see (366), where he defended the definitions of trinitarian orthodoxy decided at Nicaea in 325. The first selection below is from his *On the Incarnation of the Word* (ca. 318) a significant work in early Christology on the incarnation and the divinity of Jesus Christ. In another selection, Athanasius' Easter Letter of 367, he was the first Christian leader to list the twenty-seven books now recognized as the New Testament canon.

On the Incarnation

Therefore, the Word of God, being incorporeal, incorruptible, and devoid of matter, came into our domain. Beforehand He was not far from it; for no part of creation had ever been left void of Him, but, being together with His Father, He filled all things everywhere. He came descending of his own loving-kindness and voluntary manifestation to us; both seeing the rational race [*i.e., humankind*], perishing, and death reigning over them by corruption . . . He also saw the excessive depravity of men, and that little by little it increased so against themselves, that it could no longer be borne. When, lastly He saw the condemnation of all men to death, pitying our race and our infirmity, moved by our corruption, and not bearing the tyranny of death, in order that what was made might not perish, and the work of His Father in forming man might not be vain, He took a body for Himself, not dissimilar to ours. He did not wish to be simply incarnate, nor only to be visible; for if He had wished only to be visible, He could have made a divine manifestation by some more excellent body. But he took our body, and that not in the abstract, but of a spotless and stainless Virgin, knowing not a man—a body, pure, and truly unsullied by any intercourse with man. For He, being all powerful and the Creator of the universe, built a temple for Himself [*i.e., a body*] in the Virgin, and made it, as it were, an instrument proper to Himself, making Himself known in it, and dwelling in it. Taking a body like ours—because of all of us being subject to the corruption of death—and surrendering it to death in the place of us all, He offered it to the Father of His own good-will. He did this so that all might die in Him, and that the law of corruption might be destroyed; since its force had been already spent on the Lord's body, it no longer had any place against humanity. He did this so that He might restore people again to incorruption who had turned back to corruption, and from death might restore them to life, by the assumption of the body, and by the grace of resurrection, making death to vanish before them as a reed before the fire . . .

It was not the part of any one else to change that which is corrupt into incorruption but the Savior Himself, who at the beginning made all things out of nothing. Likewise, it was not the part of any other to teach men about the Father and to overthrow the worship of idols, but of the Word who orders all things and who alone is the true Only-begotten Son of the Father.

But further still, because it was necessary to pay what was due from all—for it was due that all should die, as I have said before, for which cause especially He came on earth—that He, after the proofs of His divinity by His works also offered up a sacrifice for all, surrendering His own temple to death in the place of all so that He might make all men upright and free from the old transgression. In this He showed Himself stronger than death and His own body to be incorrupt, the first-fruits of the resurrection of all . . .

Now His body, since it had the substance common to all men (for it was a human body), though by a new miracle it was formed of a virgin alone, nevertheless being mortal, like other bodies, also died. Yet by the entrance of the Word into it, it was no longer corruptible in accordance with its own nature, because of its union with the Word of God, it became free from corruption. Both these things marvelously happened to come to pass in the same body: the death of all was fulfilled in the Lord's body, and death and corruption were annihilated by the indwelling Word. For there was need of death, and it was necessary that there should be a death on behalf of all, in order that what was due from all might be paid. Thus, as I have said, the Word, since it was not possible for Him to die (for He was immortal), assumed a body which was able to die, that He might offer it as His own instead of all humans; and that He Himself, suffering for all by reason of His entrance into it, "might destroy him that had the power of death, that is, the devil; and deliver them who through fear of death were all their lifetime subject to bondage" (Heb. 2:14).

Biblical Canon

I shall adopt, to commend my undertaking, the pattern of Luke the Evangelist, saying on my own account, "Forasmuch as some have taken in hand, to reduce into order for themselves the books termed apocryphal, and to mix them up with the divinely inspired Scripture, concerning which we have been fully persuaded, as they who from the beginning were eyewitnesses and ministers of the Word, delivered to the fathers; it seemed good to me also, having been urged by true brothers, and having learned from the beginning, to set before you the books included in the Canon, handed down and accredited as divine; to the end that anyone who has fallen into error may condemn those who have led him astray; and that he who has continued steadfast in purity may again rejoice, having these things brought to his memory."

There are, then, the Old Testament [ed: *Esther is omitted here in his listing*] . . . and the New Testament [ed: *gospels are listed first, then general epistles, then Paul's letters (14). With the exception of mentioning the general epistles before Paul's, the twenty-seven books are listed in the order found in Bibles today*].

These are the fountains of salvation, that they who thirst may be satisfied with the living words they contain. In these alone is proclaimed the doctrine of godliness. Let no man add to these, neither let him take anything from them. For concerning these, the Lord put to shame the Sadducees, and said, "You err, not knowing the Scriptures" (Matt. 22:29). And He reproved the Jews, saying "Search the Scriptures, for these are they that testify of Me" (John 5:39).

But for greater exactness I must add the following; that there are other books besides these not included in the Canon, but appointed by the Fathers to be read by those who newly join us, and who wish for instruction in the word of godliness. The *Wisdom of Solomon*, and the *Wisdom of Sirach*, and *Esther*, and *Judith*, and *Tobit*, and that which is called the *Teaching of the Apostles* [*Didache*], and the *Shepherd* [*Shepherd of Hermas*]. But the former, my brothers, are included in the Canon, the latter being [merely] read; nor is there in any place a mention of apocryphal writings. But they are an invention of heretics, who write them when they choose, bestowing upon them their approval and assigning to them a date, so that using them as ancient writings, they may find occasion to lead the simple astray.

SOURCE: Selection on the Incarnation is in Athanasius, *A Discourse of S. Athanasius on the Incarnation of the Word of God*, trans. James Ridgway (London: James Parker & Co., 1880), 27–31, 71–75. Selection on the biblical canon is in Athanasius, "Letter 39, for 367," in *A Select Library of Nicene and Post-Nicene Fathers of the Christian Church*, vol. 4, second series, *St. Athanasius: Select Works and Letters*, ed. Philip Schaff and Henry Wace (New York: The Christian Literature Co., 1892), 551–52.

15

GREGORY OF NYSSA

GREGORY, BISHOP OF NYSSA (330–395), was one of the Cappadocian Fathers (along with his brother, Basil the Great, and friend, Gregory of Nazianzus) who contributed significantly to the defense of Nicene theology and the doctrine of the Trinity in opposition to Arianism. Gregory was well versed in Platonic and Neoplatonic philosophy and worked to make Christian theology superior to Greek philosophy. In the selections below Gregory addresses the Trinity in "On Not Three Gods" and the ransom theory of the atonement. His "fishhook" illustration was a popular way of explaining the concept of ransom, one of the dominant interpretations of the cross in early Christianity.

Trinity

Most people think that the word "Godhead" is used in a unique way to describe God's nature; and just as the heaven, or the sun, or any other of the parts of the universe are denoted by proper names which describe their subjects, so people say that in the case of the Supreme and Divine nature, the word "Godhead" is fitly adapted to that which it represents to us, as a kind of special name. We, on the other hand, following the suggestions of Scripture, have learned that God's nature is unnameable and unspeakable, and we say that every term invented by human custom or handed down to us by the Scriptures, explains our concepts of the Divine Nature, but does not signify the nature itself . . . It is clear that none of the terms we use actually signify the divine nature, but some characteristic is made known. For we say, it may be that the Deity is incorruptible, or powerful, or whatever else we are used to saying about Him. But in each of these terms we find a specific sense, fit to be understood or asserted of the divine nature, yet not expressing the essence of the nature . . .

In the case of the divine nature, we do not learn that the Father does anything by Himself in which the Son does not work conjointly, or again that the Son has any special operation apart from the Holy Spirit. But every operation which extends from God to the creation . . . has its origin from the Father, proceeds through the Son, and is completed in the Holy Spirit. For this reason the name derived from the operation is not divided with regard to the number of those who fulfill it, because the action of each concerning anything is not separate and unique, but whatever happens in terms of God's providence for us or in the government and constitution of the universe, happens by the action of the Three, yet what does happen is not three things . . .

When we inquire where this good gift (life) came to us, we find by the guidance of the Scriptures that it was from the Father, Son, and Holy Spirit. Yet although we set forth Three Persons and three names, we do not consider that we have had given to us three lives, one from each person separately. But the same life is given us by the Father, prepared by the Son and depends on the will of the Holy Spirit . . . We do not call those whose operation gives one life three Givers of life, neither do we call all those who are contemplated in one goodness three Good beings . . . so neither can we call those who exercise this divine power and operation toward us and all creation, conjointly and inseparably by their mutual action, three Gods.

The Ransom Theory of the Atonement

For as they who have bartered away their freedom for money are the slaves of those who have purchased them (for they have constituted themselves their own sellers, and it is not allowable either for themselves or anyone else on their behalf to call freedom to their aid, not even though those who have thus reduced themselves to this sad state are of noble birth. If any one out of regard for the person who has so sold himself should use violence against him who has bought him, he will clearly be acting unjustly in thus arbitrarily rescuing one who has been legally purchased as a slave. Whereas, if he wishes to pay a price to get such a one away, there is no law to prevent that). On the same principle, now that we had voluntarily bartered away our freedom, it was required that no arbitrary method of recovery, but the one consonant with justice should be devised by Him Who in His goodness had undertaken our rescue. Now this method is in a measure this; to make over to the master of the slave whatever ransom he may agree to accept for the person in his possession.

What, then, was it likely that the master of the slave would choose to receive in his stead? . . . What would he accept in exchange for the thing which he held, but something, to be sure, higher and better, in the way of ransom, that thus, by receiving a gain in the exchange, he might foster even more his own special passion of pride? . . . The Enemy, therefore, beholding in Him such power, saw also in Him an opportunity for an advance, in the exchange, upon the value of what he held. For this reason he chooses Him as a ransom for those who were shut up in the prison of death. But it was out of his power to look on the unclouded aspect of God; he must see in Him some portion of that fleshly nature which through sin he had so long held in bondage. Therefore it was that the Deity was invested with the flesh in order, that is, to secure that he, by looking upon something congenial and kindred to himself, might have no fears in approaching that supereminent power; and might yet by perceiving that power gradually showing more and more splendor in the miracles, deem what was seen an object of desire rather than of fear.

. . . It was not in the nature of the opposing power to come in contact with the undiluted presence of God, and to undergo His unclouded manifestation, therefore, in order to secure that the ransom in our behalf might be easily accepted by him who required it, the Deity was hidden under the veil of our nature, that so, as with ravenous fish, the hook of the Deity might be gulped down along with the bait of flesh, and thus, life being introduced into the house of death, and light shining in darkness, that which is diametrically opposed to light and life might vanish; for it is not in the nature of darkness to remain when light is present, or of death to exist when life is active.

SOURCE: Atonement selection in chapters 22–24, *The Great Catechism*; "Trinity" section from "On Not Three Gods," in *Gregory of Nyssa: Dogmatic Treatises*, in *A Select Library of Nicene and Post-Nicene Fathers of The Christian Church*, vol. 5, second series, ed. Philip Schaff and Henry Wace (New York: The Christian Literature Co., 1893), 332–34, 492–94.

16

EARLY CHRISTIAN CREEDS

THE APOSTLES' CREED is an early Christian statement of belief that is widely used today across Christian faith traditions. While its current wording dates to the eighth century, the Apostles' Creed reflects earlier summaries of belief (e.g., the Old Roman Symbol) from the second and third centuries. These summaries were called the "rule of faith" and often served to define orthodox belief over against movements like Gnosticism that were deemed heretical. The Symbol of Chalcedon was the confessional statement of early Christianity approved at the fourth ecumenical church council—Council of Chalcedon (451)—that provided a definitive orthodox statement regarding the Trinity and the relationship between the divine and human natures of Jesus Christ. Its language clearly opposed movements—Arianism, Apollinarianism, Nestorianism, and Eutychianism—judged to be heretical. Like the Apostles' Creed, the Symbol of Chalcedon is still used in Christian worship today.

Apostles' Creed

I BELIEVE in God the Father Almighty, Maker of heaven and earth,

And in Jesus Christ his only Son our Lord; who was conceived by the Holy Ghost, born of the Virgin Mary, suffered under Pontius Pilate, was crucified, dead, and buried; he descended into hell; the third day he rose again from the dead; he ascended into heaven, and sitteth on the right hand of God the Father Almighty; from thence he shall come to judge the quick and the dead.

I believe in the Holy Ghost; the holy catholic Church; the communion of saints; the forgiveness of sins; the resurrection of the body; and the life everlasting. Amen.

SOURCE: "Apostles' Creed," in *The Book of Confessions* (PCUSA) (Louisville, Ky.: Office of the General Assembly, 2002), 7. Reprinted with permission of the Office of the General Assembly, PC (USA).

Symbol of Chalcedon

We, then, following the holy Fathers, all with one consent, teach men to confess one and the same Son, our Lord Jesus Christ, the same perfect in Godhead and also perfect in manhood; truly God and truly man, of a reasonable [rational] soul and body; consubstantial [coessential] with the Father according to the Godhead, and consubstantial with us according to Manhood; in all things like unto us, without sin; begotten before all ages of the Father according to the Godhead, and in these latter days, for us and for our salvation, born of the Virgin Mary, the Mother of God, according to the Manhood; one and the same Christ, Son, Lord, Only-begotten to be acknowledged in two natures, without confusion, without change, without division, without separation; the distinction of natures being by no means taken away by the union, but rather the property of each nature being preserved, and concurring in one Person and one Subsistence, not parted or divided into two persons, but one and the same Son, and only begotten, God the Word, the Lord Jesus Christ; as the prophets from the beginning [have declared] concerning him, and the Lord Jesus Christ himself has taught us, and the Creed of the holy Fathers has handed down to us.

SOURCE: Philip Schaff, *The Creeds of Christendom*, vol. 2, *The Greek and Latin Creeds* (New York: Harper & Brothers, 1919), 62–63.

17

AUGUSTINE OF HIPPO

AUGUSTINE OF HIPPO (354–430) is regarded as one of the most significant Christian theologians in the Christian tradition. He converted to Christianity in the late 380s and became Bishop of Hippo (North Africa) in 395. He was a prolific writer, combating movements he viewed to be destructive of orthodoxy such as Manichaeism, Pelagianism, and Donatism. Augustinian thought is characterized by a focus on the sovereignty of God, the depravity (original sin) of humanity, and predestination of believers, i.e., monergistic salvation (solely the work of God's irresistible grace without human cooperation). The selections below are from Augustine's autobiographical *Confessions*, a classic of Christian spirituality, and a selection from a sermon on the Trinity.

Youthful Lusts

You are great, O Lord, and greatly to be praised (Ps. 47:2); great is your power, and your wisdom is infinite (Ps. 146:5). Man, a little speck of your creation, desires to praise you; man, that bears about him his mortality, the witness of his sin, the witness that "you resist the proud" (I Pet. 5:5). Yet man, a tiny speck of your creation, still desires to praise you. You awaken in us the delight of your praise, for you have made us for yourself, and our heart is restless until it rests in you . . .

I will now remember my past wickedness and the carnal corruptions of my soul; not because I love them, but that I may love you, O my God. For love of you I will do it, reviewing my most wicked ways in the very bitterness of my memory, so that you may grow sweet to me (your blissful and sure sweetness never fails). You put me back together from the disordered state in which I fell apart, while I turned from you to a multiplicity of other things. As a youth I burned to be full of devilish things, and I dared to be wild with various and dark shadowy loves. My beauty wasted away, and I grew rancid before your eyes, pleasing myself and desiring to please other men's eyes.

And what was it that I delighted in, but to love, and be loved? Yet, I did not keep the measure of love, of mind to mind, friendship's bright boundary. Out of the muddy concupiscence of the flesh and the bubblings of my youth, mists fumed up which clouded and overcast my heart so that I could not discern the clear brightness of love from the fog of lustfulness. Both confusedly boiled in me and, although I was unaware of it, pushed my unstable youthfulness over the precipice of unholy desires and sunk me in a gulf of vice. Your wrath had gathered over me, but I did not know it. I had grown deaf by the clanking of the chain of my mortality, the punishment of the pride of my soul, and I strayed further from you, and you let me. I was tossed about, wasted, dissipated, and I boiled over in fornication, and you, the joy I waited too long to hear, held your peace and kept quiet. I wandered further and further from you . . .

In my sixteenth year, I lived with my parents, leaving school for a while (a season of idleness brought about by the tightening of my parents' fortunes). The briars of unclean desires grew rank over my head, and there was no hand to root them out. When my father saw me at the baths, growing towards manhood and endued with a restless youthfulness, he began anticipating grandchildren, and gladly told my mother. He rejoiced in the tumult of the senses in which the world, intoxicated on the fumes of the invisible wine of its self-will and having turned aside and bowed down to the very basest of things, forgets that you are its Creator and becomes enamored with your creature instead of you. My father had just recently become a catechumen, but in my mother's heart, you had already begun building your temple and the foundation of your holy dwelling. She was startled with a holy fear and trembling, and though I was not yet baptized, she feared I would walk in the crooked ways in which they who "turn their back to you and not their face" (Jer. 2:27).

Woe is me! Dare I say that you held your peace, when in fact I wandered farther from you? Did you then keep silent to me? Were they not your words which my mother, your faithful one, sang in my ears? Nothing sunk into my heart to compel me to heed these words. For she wished, and I remember, in private with great anxiety warned me, "not to commit fornication, and especially never to defile another man's wife." This seemed to me womanish advice, which I would have blushed to obey. It was your advice, but I did not know it. I thought you were silent and that it was her who spoke. But, through her, you were not silent to me, and in her you were despised by me, her son, "the son of your handmaid, your servant" (Ps. 116:6). But I did not know it and ran headlong with such blindness that among my peers I was ashamed of not having more shame when I heard them boast of their scandals. They boasted of their perverse deeds, the more perverse, the more they boasted. There was pleasure, not only in the pleasure of the deed, but in the praise of doing the perverse act. What is worthy of disapproval, but vice? I made myself out worse than I was, so that I might not be criticized. When I had not actually done the deeds my peers did, I said that I had done what I had not so that I might not seem contemptible in their eyes because of my innocence and chastity.

Theft is punished by your Law, O Lord, and by the law written in the hearts of men, which iniquity itself does not destroy. For what thief will allow another thief to steal from him? Not even a rich thief with let someone steal from him because of want. Yet I lusted to steal, and did it, not compelled by hunger or poverty, but through a disgust of doing good and an indulgence of iniquity. For I stole that which I already had enough of and what I already had was better. I did not care about what I stole, but took joy in the theft and sin itself.

There was a pear tree near our vineyard, full of fruit, but it was not tempting because of its taste or appearance. Many of us lewd young men went late one night (having prolonged our street sports as was our custom) to shake and rob that tree. We took huge loads, not so we could eat them, and after tasting the pears, we threw them to the hogs. We did this because we wanted to and because it was prohibited. Behold my heart, O God, behold my heart, which you pitied in the bottom of the bottomless pit. Let my heart tell you what it sought there: that I should be gratuitously evil, having no temptation to wickedness, but wickedness itself. It was foul, and I loved it; I loved to perish, I loved my own faults, not that for which I was at fault, but the fault itself. Foul soul, falling from your heavens to utter destruction, seeking nothing through the shame, only the shame itself! . . .

Introduction to Neoplatonism

I traced in those books [of the Platonists], which said in diverse ways that "the Son was in the form of the Father, and did not think it robbery to be equal with God, for he was of the same substance." But, "He emptied Himself, taking the form of a servant, being made in the likeness of men, and found in fashion as a man, humbled himself, and became obedient unto death, and that the death of the cross. Therefore God exalted him from the dead and gave him a name above every name, that at the name of Jesus every knee should bow, of things in heaven and things in earth, and things under the earth; and that every tongue should confess that the Lord Jesus Christ is in the Glory of God the Father" (Phil. 2:6-11) . . . I believe you wanted me to discover the books of the Platonists before I came to study your scriptures, so that the way in which I was affected by them would be imprinted in my memory. Afterwards, when my spirits were tamed through your books and my wounds touched by your healing fingers, I could discern and distinguish between presumption and confession, between those who saw their goal but did not know how to get to it and those who say the way that leads to dwelling, and not merely beholding, your land of holy bliss.

Conversion

Our lodging had a little garden, which we could use, as with the whole house, because the master of the house, our host, was not living there. The tumult in my heart compelled me to where no man might hinder the hot strife in which I was engaged. While you knew how it would end, I did not, for I was distracted by my health and dying so that I might live. I only knew what an evil thing I was, and not what good thing I would shortly become. I retired into the garden with [my friend] Alypius with me, for his presence did not lessen my privacy. And, how could he forsake me in such a disturbed state? We sat down as far removed as possible from the house. I was troubled in spirit, most vehemently indignant that I had not entered into your will and covenant, O my God, which all my bones cried out to me to enter . . .

I was speaking and weeping in the most bitter contrition of my heart, when I heard from a neighboring house a voice—I do not know if it was a boy or girl—chanting and repeating "*Tolle lege; Tolle lege.*" "Take up and read; Take up and read." Instantly, my demeanor changed, I began to think most intently about whether the children were singing these words in some kind of game, but I could not think of any such game. So checking the torrent of my tears, I arose; interpreting it to be no other than a command from God to open the book, and read the first chapter that I should find . . . Eagerly then I returned to the place where Alypius was sitting; for there I had laid the volume of the Apostle [Paul] when I stood up. I seized it, opened it, and in silence read that section on which my eyes first fell, "Not in rioting and drunkenness, not in sexual immorality and wantonness, not in strife and envying, but put on the Lord Jesus Christ, and make no provision for the flesh in concupiscence" (Rom. 13:13-14). No further would I read, nor did I need to, for instantly, at the end of this sentence, by a light as it were of serenity infused into my heart, all the darkness of doubt vanished away.

The Mystical Vision

The day was approaching in which [Monica, my mother] was to depart this life, a day you knew well, but we did not. It came to pass, by your secret ways of ordering things, that we leaned out of a certain window that looked out into the garden of the house where we now resided, Ostia. Removed from the distraction of the crowds, we were recovering from the fatigue of a long journey. Alone, we were intimately discussing, and "forgetting those things which are behind, and reaching toward those things which are before us" (Phil. 3:13), we were enquiring about the presence of Truth, which you are, and about the kind of eternal life which awaited the saints . . .

Our conversation reached a point where we decided that the very highest delight of our earthly senses, even in the purest material light was, in respect of the sweetness of that earthly life, not only unworthy of comparison to eternal life, but not worth mentioning. We were raising up ourselves towards the "Self-same," passing by degrees all bodily things, even the very heaven where sun, moon, and stars shine upon the earth. We were soaring higher by inward reflection and discourse and admiring your works. We came to our own minds and went beyond them, so as to arrive at that region of never-failing plenty, where "you feed Israel" (Ps. 80:1) forever with the food of truth, and where life is the wisdom by whom all these things are made, both things that have been and what will be . . . And while we were talking and panting after it, we slightly touched it with the whole effort of our heart. We sighed, and left behind "the first fruits of the Spirit" (Rom. 8:23), and returned to vocal expressions of our mouth, where the word spoken has a beginning and an end . . .

Give What You Command

All my hope is nowhere but in your exceedingly great mercy. Give what you command, and command what you will. You command from us self-control; one says "and when I knew that no man could show self-control unless God gives it, this also was a part of wisdom to know whose gift she is." By self-control we are truly bound up and brought back into the One from which we were dissipated into many things. For whoever loves you, loves you too little if he loves anything with you, and not because of you. O Love that burns like a flame that is never put out! O charity, my God! Set me on fire.

You command self-control: give me what you command and command what you will.

Trinity

I ask you, O man, have you memory? If not, how have you retained what I have said? But perhaps you have forgotten already what I said but a little while ago. Yet these very words, "I said"—these two syllables, you could not retain except by memory. For how should you know they were two, if as the second sounded, you had forgotten the first? But why do I dwell longer on this? Why am I so urgent? Why do I so press conviction? For you have memory; it is plain. I am searching then for something else. Do you have understanding? "I have," you will say. For if you didn't have memory, you could not retain what I said; and if you did not have understanding, you could not comprehend what you have retained. You then have this as well as the other. You recalled your understanding unto that which you retain within, and so you see, and by seeing you are fashioned into that state as to be said to know. But I am searching for a third thing. You have memory, by which you retain what is said; and understanding, by which you understand what is retained; but as touching these two, I ask again of you, have you not retained and understood by the will? Undoubtedly, with my will, you will say. So, then you have will. These are the three things which I promised I would bring home to your ears and minds. These three things are in you, which you can number, but cannot separate. These three then, memory, understanding, and will—these three, I say, consider how they are separately exhibited, but their operation is inseparable . . .

The three together have produced each one of these, but yet this one which the three have produced has reference not to the three, but to the one. The three together have produced the word "memory," but this word has reference to the memory alone. The three together have produced the word "understanding," but it has reference to the understanding alone. The three together have produced the word "will," but it has reference to the will alone. So the Trinity concurred in the formation of the Body of Christ, but it belongs to Christ alone. The Trinity concurred in the formation of the Dove from heaven; but it belongs to the Holy Spirit alone. The Trinity formed the Voice from heaven, but this belongs to the Father alone . . .

It is enough, then, that I have shown that there are three things which are exhibited separately, whose operation is yet inseparable. If you have discovered this in yourself; if you have discovered it in man; if you have discovered it in a person walking the earth who has a frail body that weighs down the soul, believe that the Father, Son, and Holy Spirit may be exhibited separately, by certain visible symbols, by certain forms borrowed from the creatures, and still their operations are inseparable. This is enough. I do not say that "memory" is the Father—the "understanding" the Son—and "will" the Spirit; I do not say this. But what do I say? See. I have discovered in you three things, which are exhibited separately, and whose operation is inseparable; and of these three, every single name is produced by the three together; yet this name does not belong to the three, but to one of the three. Believe then in the Trinity, which you cannot see, if in yourself you have heard, seen, and retained it. For what is in your own self you can know. But, what is in Him who made you, whatever that is, how can you know? . . . And even when you will be able, will you be able to know God as He knows Himself? Let then this suffice you, beloved. I have said all I can; I have made good on my promise. As to the rest which must be added, ask the Lord that he might increase your understanding.

SOURCE: Augustine, *Confessions*, trans. Edward B. Pusey, Harvard Classics, vol. 7 (New York: P. F. Collier & Son, 1909), 5, 23, 25–27, 112–13, 121, 141–42, 158–59. Section on Trinity is from "Augustine, Sermon II (Matthew 3:13)," in *A Select Library of Nicene and Post-Nicene Fathers of The Christian Church*, vol. 6, second series, ed. Philip Schaff and Henry Wace (New York: The Christian Literature Co., 1888), 264–66.

18

PELAGIUS

PELAGIUS (354–420) was a Christian ascetic, possibly from Britain, but well known in Rome. He was a moralist who affirmed that God gave humans free will, the ability to do good and fulfill the law. He criticized original sin and denied that depravity was passed down by Adam and Eve. Augustine of Hippo wrote four letters against Pelagianism, and the Council of Carthage (418) declared Pelagius heretical. Today, Pelagius' name is often associated with the idea that a person can initiate reconciliation with God as opposed to responding to God's offer of grace.

Human Nature, Free Will

And so you ought first to measure the good of human nature from its author—God, of course—who, when he made all the works of the world and those within the world, is said to have made them good, exceedingly good. To what degree, do you suppose, did he make man more preeminent, on whose account all of those things are believed to have been created? . . .

For in His willingness to grant His rational creation the gift of voluntary good and the power of free will and by sowing in man the potential for each side, God made him his own in respect to his desires, so that, with a natural capacity for good and evil, he would be capable of both and he would bend his will to one or the other. Nor, indeed, in any other way was he able to have good of his own will except as a creature that was also able to have evil. The creator, in his greatness, wished us capable of both, but to do only one—the good, of course—as He commanded. He gave us the capacity for evil only so that we would accomplish His will of our own accord. But since this is so, the very fact that we are also able to do evil is good. Good, I say, because it makes the side of good better. Indeed, it makes the will itself its own master. Not bound by necessity but freed by its own power to decide. Of course we are permitted to choose, refute, approve, and reject. Nor is there a reason why the rational creation is preferred more to others except that, although everything else has the good merely of its creation, and also of necessity, the rational creature alone also has the good of free will. . . .

Nor indeed is there any other reason for our difficulty in doing good than our long-accustomed practice of vices, which have stained us from our youth. Little by little over many years vice corrupted us, and now afterwards holds us so bound and devoted to it that it seems in a way to have the force of nature. That whole time when we were raised carelessly, that is, when we were instructed in vice, the whole time when we were even eager to be wicked, since, as an inducement to wickedness, innocence was considered foolishness, that whole time now opposes us and comes against us, and our old habit battles our new will, and we wonder why holiness—as if from elsewhere—is conferred upon us, ignorant in our leisure and idleness, who make no habit of doing good, since we have learned evil for so long.

Let this quick discussion of the good of nature suffice . . . it had to be discussed so that we might spread before you a smoother path to complete justice, a path which would be the easier for you to run the less that you saw on it anything harsh or inaccessible. For, as we said, even if certain people should be said to have lived a just and holy life before the law and long before the coming of the Lord our Savior, how much more after the light of His coming ought we (we must believe we are able), who were equipped through the grace of Christ and born again into a better man, we who were atoned for and cleansed by His blood and incited by His example to perfect justice, how much more ought we to be better than they, who lived before the law, better even than those who were under the law, since as the Apostle says: "No longer will sin rule in you. For you are not under the law, but under grace" (Rom. 6:14).

SOURCE: *Excerpts from a letter from Pelagius to Demetrias* (413). Translation from the original Latin by Jeffrey M. Hunt.

19

MAXIMUS THE CONFESSOR

MAXIMUS THE CONFESSOR (580–662) was an Eastern theologian and monk. His support of dyothelitism (the belief that in the person of Christ there are two wills, human and divine) led to his exile and torture. Maximus' tongue was cut out and his writing hand was severed in order to prevent him from propagating his views. He was posthumously vindicated and is considered a saint in both Eastern Orthodoxy and Roman Catholicism. The following selection contains reflections on asceticism—central to monasticism—and the relationship of the body and soul.

Asceticism and Anthropology

"Give us this day our daily bread": for I think this indicates the age up through today, since, if someone were understanding in a clearer sense he would say the passage of prayer in this way: "'our bread,' which from the beginning You prepared for the immortality of nature, 'give us today,' who are mortal in our present life, so that the nourishment of the bread of life and knowledge may conquer the death of sin . . . "

If we are commanded also to ask for ephemeral bread through prayer, bread by which our current life is naturally supported, let us not go past the boundaries of the prayer in thinking greedily of many cycles of years, unaware that we are mortal and, like a shadow, have a fleeting life, but let us ask through prayer for our daily bread without such ruminations on the future and let us show that we, like philosophers, following Christ, consider life preparation for death, as we knowingly anticipate nature and, before death overcomes us, cut the soul off from cares over things of the body. Let us do this that the soul may not be nailed to what is perishable, exchanging the use of its natural desire for physical matter, and that it may not learn the greed that deprives one of an abundance of divine goods. Let us flee, then, as much as possible, love of material things and wash away the practice of it like dust from our mind's eye. And let us be satisfied with that alone which sustains us, but not those things that make our current life delightful. Moreover, as we were taught, let us ask God that we may be able to guard a soul free from slavery and not controlled by a single thing visible to the body, and let us be shown eating for the sake of living, and not exposed as living to eat—the former was established clearly as characteristic of a reasoned nature, the latter of an irrational one—and let us be strict guardians of the prayer, making evident through these matters that we cling fast to only one life in the Holy Spirit, and we make use of the present life to possess it, on which account we are to a degree fond of using this life, as much as not to refuse to support it by bread alone and to guard its physical health as much as possible, not so that we may continue to live, but so that we may live for God. In so doing we make the body by its virtues the messenger of the soul, and by the certainty of its goodness make the soul the herald of God. We limit this bread naturally to one day, not daring to extend the entreaty to a second day because of the giver of the prayer . . .

. . .

And he suggested that the whole world composed of both the visible and invisible is man, according to this image again well imitated. And he further suggested that man, made of soul and body, is the world. For he said intelligible things display the rationality of the soul as also the soul does for intelligible things, and perceptible things display the form of the body just as the body does for perceptible things. And he said that the intelligible is the soul of the perceptible, and the perceptible is the body of the intelligible. Furthermore, just as the soul is in the body, the intelligible is in the perceptible world, and the perceptible assists the intelligible world, as the body does the soul. And from both comes one world, just as one human exists with soul and body through the law of the one binding them, and not with one of these, which are united to each other, rejecting and dismissing the other . . . It shows that they are more each other's than their own in accord with their disposition toward unity, until it seems good to the one binding them to dissolve them for a better and more mystical arrangement at the critical moment of the expected universal end, when the world of visible things, like man, will perish and a new world will rise again from the old, in accord with the presently expected resurrection. Then those like us will be raised with the world as part of the whole, as one small with the great, bearing the power no longer to perish, when the body will become like the soul and the sensible like the intelligible in dignity and glory, as one divine power in its visible and vigorous presence makes itself known through each thing in a suitable way and on its own preserves the unbreakable bond of unity for boundless ages.

Source: Excerpts from *Commentary on the Lord's Prayer* (lines 562–568, 592–628); and *Mystagogy* (7.1–14, 24–38). Translation from the original Greek by Jeffrey M. Hunt.

20

BENEDICT OF NURSIA

St. Benedict (480–547) was the founder of the ascetic community of Monte Cassino in modern-day Italy, and is widely regarded as the father of Western Christian monasticism. His *Rule* offered a very strict guideline for monastic living and quickly became a standard for monasticism in the West. His rule emphasizes obedience and humility, daily hours of prayer, living modestly and without possessions, hard work, and complete obedience to the abbot. Though Benedict never meant his rule to establish a new order, by the late sixth century there were more than a dozen Benedictine monasteries. In 1893 Pope Leo XIII created the Benedictine Confederation, bringing together the formerly autonomous monasteries under the jurisdiction of an Abbot Primate.

Rule of St. Benedict

Prologue

Listen, my son, and turn the ear of your heart to the precepts of your Master. Receive readily, and faithfully carry out the advice of a loving Father, so that by the work of obedience you may return to Him, whom you have left by the sloth of disobedience . . .

First, beg of Him with most earnest prayer to finish the good work begun; that He who now has counted us among His children may never be grieved by our evil deeds. For at all times we must so serve Him with the good things He has given us, that He may not, as an angry Father, disinherit His children, nor as a dread Lord, provoked by our evil deeds, deliver us to everlasting punishment as wicked servants who refuse to follow Him to glory . . .

If we desire to dwell in the shelter of this kingdom, we can reach it only by speeding on the way of good works (by this path alone it is to be attained). But let us, with the prophet, ask our Lord and say to Him: "Lord, who shall dwell in your tabernacle, or who shall rest on your holy hill?" (Ps. 15:1) After this question, Brethren, let us hear our Lord answering and showing us the way that leads to His tabernacle, saying: "He that walks with integrity, and works justice. He that speaks truth in his heart, and does not slander with his tongue. He that has not done evil to his neighbor, and has not received reproach against him" (Ps. 15:2-3). He that rejecting out of his mind the malignant devil with all his suggestions, has brought them all to nothing, and controlling his thoughts when they first arise, has dashed them against the rock, which is Christ. They who, fearing the Lord, are not lifted up by their good observance, but knowing that all that is good in them comes not from themselves but from the Lord, magnify his work in them, and say with the prophet: "Not to us O Lord, not to us, but to your name give glory" (Ps. 115:1) . . .

So questioning the Lord, brethren, we have heard on what conditions we may dwell in His temple, and if we fulfill these we shall be heirs of the kingdom of heaven. Therefore must our hearts and bodies be prepared to fight under the holy obedience of His commands, and we must beg our Lord to supply by the help of His grace what by nature is not possible to us. And if, fleeing from the pains of hell, we will attain to everlasting life, we must, while we have time and we live in this mortal flesh, and may perform all these things by the light of faith, hasten to do now what will profit us for all eternity.

We are therefore now about to institute a school for the service of God, in which we hope nothing harsh nor burdensome will be ordained. But if in some things we proceed with a little severity . . . for the amendment of vices or preserving of love; do not immediately flee because of fear from the way of salvation which is always narrow in the beginning. In living our life, however, and by the growth of faith, when the heart has been enlarged, the path of God's commandments is run with unspeakable loving sweetness, so that never leaving His school, but persevering in the monastery until death in His teaching, we share by our patience in the sufferings of Christ, and so merit to be partakers of His kingdom.

Chapter 33: Whether Monks Ought to Have Anything of Their Own

Above all others let this vice be cut out from the monastery. No one, without permission of the abbot, shall presume to give, or receive, or keep as his own anything whatever; neither book, nor tables, nor pen; nothing at all. For monks are men who can claim no dominion even over their own bodies or wills. All that is necessary, however, they may hope from the Father of the monastery, but they shall keep nothing which the abbot has not given or allowed. Let all things be common to all, as it is written: "Neither did anyone say or think that anything was his own" (Acts 4:32). If anyone shall be found given to this most wicked vice, let him be admonished once or twice, and if he does not amend, let him be subjected to correction.

Chapter 34: Whether All Ought Equally to Receive What Is Needful

It is written: "Distribution was made to everyone, according as he had need" (Acts 4:35). By this we do not mean that there is a personal preference (which God forbid), but a consideration for infirmities. Let him who needs less, give God thanks, and be not distressed, and let him who needs more, be humbled because of his infirmity, and not puffed up because of the mercy that is shown him; so that all the members shall be in peace. Above all things, let not the pest of murmuring, for whatever cause, by any word or sign, be shown. If anyone shall be found guilty in this respect, let him be subjected to most severe discipline.

SOURCE: *The Rule of Saint Benedict*, trans. Abbot Gasquet (London: Chatto & Windus Publishers, 1909), 1–7, 64–66.

21

JOHN OF DAMASCUS

JOHN OF DAMASCUS, also known as John Damascene (ca. 676–749), was raised by an Arab Christian family and received traditional Muslim education until his teen years. He wrote extensively on law, theology, philosophy, spirituality, and music. John's theological writings were more encyclopedic than original, but they heavily influenced the Eastern and Western churches. He is best known for his defense of icons (which were later affirmed at the Second Council of Nicaea, 787; see selection below). Many of his hymns are still used in Eastern Christian monasteries.

Defense of Icons/Images

You see that He forbids image-making on account of idolatry, and that it is impossible to make an image of the immeasurable, uncircumscribed, invisible

God. You have not seen the likeness of Him, the Scripture says, and this was St. Paul's testimony as he stood in the midst of the Areopagus, "Being, therefore, the offspring of God, we must not suppose the divinity to be like gold, or silver, or stone, the engraving of art, and device of man" (Acts 17:29).

These injunctions were given to the Jews on account of their proneness to idolatry . . . Speaking theologically, we have been given the ability to avoid superstitious error, to be with God in the knowledge of the truth, to worship God alone, to enjoy the fullness of His knowledge. We have passed the stage of infancy, and reached the maturity of manhood. We receive our habit of mind from God, and know what may be imaged and what may not. The Scripture says, "You have not seen the likeness of Him." What wisdom is in the law-giver? How [to] depict the invisible? How [to] picture the inconceivable? How [to] give expression to the limitless, the immeasurable, the invisible? How [to] give a form to the immensity? How [to] paint immortality? How [to] depict mystery? It is clear that when you contemplate God, who is a pure spirit, becoming man for your sake, you will be able to clothe Him with the human form. When the Invisible One becomes visible to flesh, you may then draw a likeness of His form. When He who is a pure spirit, without form or limit, immeasurable in the boundlessness of His own nature, existing as God, takes upon Himself the form of a servant in substance and in stature, and a body of flesh, then you may draw His likeness, and show it to anyone willing to contemplate it. Depict His ineffable condescension, His virginal birth, His baptism in the Jordan, His transfiguration on Tabor, His all-powerful sufferings, His death and miracles, the proofs of His Godhead, the deeds which He worked in the flesh through divine power, His saving Cross, His tomb, and resurrection, and ascent into heaven. Give to it all the endurance of engraving and color.

Have no fear or anxiety; veneration is not all of the same kind. Abraham venerated the sons of Emmor, impious men, ignorant of God, when he bought the double cave for a tomb. Jacob venerated his brother Esau and Pharaoh, the Egyptian, bowing over the head of his staff. He venerated, he did not adore [*worship*]. Joshua and Daniel venerated an angel of God ; they did not worship him. Veneration is one thing, and the veneration which is given to those with merit is another. Now, as we are talking of images and worship, let us analyze the exact meaning of each. An image is a likeness of the original with a certain difference, for it is not an exact reproduction of the original . . .

If you bring forward certain practices, they do not condemn our worship of images, but the worship of heathens who make them idols. Because heathens do it foolishly, this is no reason for objecting to our pious practice. If heathen magicians and sorcerers use supplication [*exorcism*], so does the Church with catechumens; the former invoke devils, but the Church calls upon God against devils. Heathens have dedicated images to demons, whom they call gods. Now we have dedicated them to the one Incarnate God, to His servants and friends, who are proof against the diabolical hosts . . .

If we adore the Cross, made of whatever wood it may be, how shall we not adore the image of the Crucified?

SOURCE: *St John Damascene on Holy Images followed by Three Sermons on the Assumption,* trans. Mary H. Allies (London: Thomas Baker, 1898), 8–10, 28–29, 43.

22

XI'AN MONUMENT

THE XI'AN MONUMENT, also known as the Nestorian Stele, is a stone tablet from ca. 781 which provides evidence that a version of Christianity, influenced by the fifth-century archbishop Nestorius, reached China by the seventh century. Various symbols adorn the tablet including a cross. Written in both Chinese and Syriac, the text provides a brief overview of Christian belief followed by a narration of how the religion had come to China. A missionary named Alopen came from Syria in ca. 638 to the Chinese, who translated the Scriptures he had brought and some of whom converted to what was termed the "Illustrious Religion." The poetic portion of the stele ties the different emperors of the reigning Tang Dynasty to Christianity. The tablet's discovery around 1624 has been a source of discussion and study ever since.

A Eulogy to the Illustrious Religion

Preface

Behold the unchangeably true and invisible, who existed through all eternity without origin; the far-seeing perfect intelligence, whose mysterious existence is everlasting; operating on primordial substance he created the universe, being more excellent than all holy intelligences, inasmuch as he is the source of all that is honorable. This is our eternal true lord God, triune and mysterious in substance. He appointed the cross as the means for determining the four cardinal points, he moved the original spirit, and produced the two principles of nature; the somber void was changed, and heaven and earth were opened out; the sun and moon revolved, and day and night commenced; having perfected all inferior objects, he then made the first man; upon him he bestowed an excellent disposition, giving him in charge the government of all created beings; man, acting out the original principles of his nature, was pure and unostentatious; his unsullied and expansive mind was free from the least inordinate desire; until Satan introduced the seeds of falsehood, to deteriorate his purity of principle; the opening thus commenced in his virtue gradually enlarged, and by this crevice in his nature was obscured and rendered vicious; hence three hundred and sixty-five sects followed each other in continuous track, inventing every species of doctrinal complexity; while some pointed to material objects as the source of their faith, others reduced all to vacancy, even to the annihilation of the two primeval principles; some sought to call down blessings by prayers and supplications, while others by an assumption of excellence held themselves up as superior to their fellows; their intellects and thoughts continually wavering, their minds and affections incessantly on the move, they never obtained their vast desires, but being exhausted and distressed they revolved in their own heated atmosphere; till by an accumulation of obscurity they lost their path, and after long groping in darkness they were unable to return. Thereupon, our Trinity being divided in nature, the illustrious and honorable Messiah, veiling his true dignity, appeared in the world as a man; angelic powers promulgated the glad tidings, a virgin gave birth to the Holy One in Syria; a bright star announced the felicitous event, and Persians observing the splendor came to present tribute; the ancient dispensation, as declared by the twenty-four holy men, was then fulfilled, and he laid down great principles for the government of families and kingdoms; he established the new religion of the silent operation of the pure spirit of the Triune; he rendered virtue subservient to direct faith; he fixed the extent of the eight boundaries, thus completing the truth and freeing it from dross; he opened the gate of the three constant principles, introducing life and destroying death; he suspended the bright sun to invade the chambers of darkness, and the falsehoods of the devil were thereupon defeated; he set in motion the vessel of mercy by which to ascend to the bright mansions, whereupon rational beings were then released. Having thus completed the manifestation of his power, in clear day he ascended to his true station. Twenty-seven sacred books have been left, which disseminate intelligence by unfolding the original transforming principles. By the rule for admission, it is the custom to apply the water of baptism; to wash away all superficial show and to cleanse and purify the neophytes.

As a seal, they hold the cross, whose influence is reflected in every direction, uniting all without distinction. As they strike the wood, the fame of their benevolence is diffused abroad; worshiping toward the east, they hasten on the way to life and glory; they preserve the beard to symbolize their outward actions, they shave the crown to indicate the absence of inward affections; they do not keep slaves, but put noble and mean all on an equality; they do not amass wealth, but cast all their property into the common stock; they fast, in order to perfect themselves by self-inspection; they submit to restraints, in order to strengthen themselves by silent watchfulness; seven times a day they have worship and praise for the benefit of the living and the dead; once in seven days they sacrifice, to cleanse the heart and return to purity.

It is difficult to find a name to express the excellence of the true and unchangeable doctrine; but as its meritorious operations are manifestly displayed, by accommodation it is named the Illustrious Religion. Now without holy men, principles cannot become expanded; without principles, holy men cannot become magnified; but with holy men and right principles, united as the two parts of a signet, the world becomes civilized and enlightened.

In the time of the accomplished Emperor Taitsung, the illustrious and magnificent founder of the dynasty, among the enlightened and holy men who arrived was the Most-virtuous Olopun [Alopen], from the country of Syria. Observing the azure clouds, be bore the true sacred books; beholding the direction of the winds, he braved difficulties and dangers. In the year [A.D. 635] he arrived at Chang-an; the Emperor sent his Prime Minister, Duke Fang Hiuen-ling; who, carrying the official staff to the west border, conducted his guest into the interior; the sacred books were translated in the imperial library, the sovereign investigated the subject in his private apartments; when becoming deeply impressed with the rectitude and truth of the religion, he gave special orders for its dissemination. In the seventh month of the year [A.D. 638] the following imperial proclamation was issued:

"Right principles have no invariable name, holy men have no invariable station; instruction is established in accordance with the locality, with the object of benefiting the people at large. The Greatly-virtuous Olopun, of the kingdom of Syria, has brought his sacred books and images from that distant part, and has presented them at our chief capital. Having examined the principles of this religion, we find them to be purely excellent and natural; investigating its originating source, we find it has taken its rise from the establishment of important truths; its ritual is free from perplexing expressions, its principles will survive when the framework is forgot; it is beneficial to all creatures; it is advantageous to mankind. Let it be published throughout the

Empire, and let the proper authority build a Syrian church in the capital in the I-ning May, which shall be governed by twenty-one priests. When the virtue of the Chau dynasty declined, the rider on the azure ox ascended to the west; the principles of the great Tang becoming resplendent, the lllustrious breezes have come to fan the East."

Orders were then issued to the authorities to have a true portrait of the Emperor taken; when it was transferred to the wall of the church, the dazzling splendor of the celestial visage irradiated the Illustrious portals. The sacred traces emitted a felicitous influence, and shed a perpetual splendor over the holy precincts. According to the Illustrated Memoir of the Western Regions, and the historical books of the Han and Wei dynasties, the kingdom of Syria reaches south to the Coral Sea; on the north it joins the Gem Mountains; on the west it extends toward the borders of the immortals and the flowery forests; on the east it lies open to the violent winds and tideless waters. The country produces fire-proof cloth, life-restoring incense, bright moon-pearls, and night-luster gems. Brigands and robbers are unknown, but the people enjoy happiness and peace. None but Illustrious laws prevail; none but the virtuous are raised to sovereign power. The land is broad and ample, and its literary productions are perspicuous and clear.

The Emperor Kautsung respectfully succeeded his ancestor, and was still more beneficent toward the institution of truth. In every province he caused Illustrious churches to be erected, and ratified the honor conferred upon Olopun, making him the great conservator of doctrine for the preservation of the State. While this doctrine pervaded every channel, the State became enriched and tranquility abounded. Every city was full of churches, and the royal family enjoyed luster and happiness. In the year [A.D. 699] the Buddhists, gaining power, raised their voices in the eastern metropolis; in the year [A.D. 713], some low fellows excited ridicule and spread slanders in the western capital. At that time there was the chief priest Lo-han, the Greatly-virtuous Kie-leih, and others of noble estate frorn the golden regions, lofty-minded priests, having abandoned all worldly interests; who unitedly maintained the grand principles and preserved them entire to the end.

The high-principled Emperor Hiuentsung caused the Prince of Ning and others, five princes in all, personally to visit the felicitous edifice; he established the place of worship; he restored the consecrated timbers which had been temporarily thrown down; and reerected the sacred stones which for a time had been desecrated.

In [742] orders were given to the great general Kau Lih-sz', to send the five sacred portraits and have them placed in the church, and a gift of a hundred pieces of silk accompanied these pictures of intelligence. Although the dragon's beard was then remote, their bows and swords were still within reach; while the solar horns sent forth their rays, and celestial visages seemed close at hand.

In [744] the priest Kih-ho, in the kingdom of Syria, looking toward the star [of China], was attracted by its transforming influence, and observing the suri [*i.e., Emperor*], came to pay court to the most honorable. The Emperor commanded the priest Lo-han, the priest Pu-lun, and others, seven in all, together with the Greatly-virtuous Kih-ho, to perform a service of merit in the Hing-king palace. Thereupon the Emperor composed mottoes for the sides of the church, and the tablets were graced with the royal inscriptions; the accumulated gems emitted their effulgence, while their sparkling brightness vied with the ruby clouds; the transcripts of intelligence suspended in the void shot forth their rays as reflected by the sun; the bountiful gifts exceeded the height of the southern hills; the bedewing favors were deep as the eastern sea. Nothing is beyond the range of the right principle, and what is permissible may be identified; nothing is beyond the power of the holy man, and that which is practicable may be related.

The accomplished and enlightened Emperor Suhtsung rebuilt the Illustrious churches in Ling-wu and four other places; great benefits were conferred, and felicity began to increase; great munificence was displayed, and the imperial State became established.

The accomplished and military Emperor Taitsung magnified the sacred succession, and honored the latent principle of nature; always, on the incarnation-day, he bestowed celestial incense, and ordered the performance of a service of merit; he distributed of the imperial viands, in order to shed a glory on the Illustrious Congregation. Heaven is munificent in the dissemination of blessings, whereby the benefits of life are extended; the holy man embodies the original principle of virtue, whence he is able to counteract noxious influences.

Our sacred and sage-like, accomplished and military Emperor Kienchung appointed the eight branches of government, according to which he advanced or degraded the intelligent and dull; he opened up the nine categories, by means of which he renovated the illustrious decrees; his transforming influence pervaded the most abstruse principles, while openness of heart distinguished his devotions. Thus, by correct and enlarged purity of principle, and undeviating consistency in sympathy with others; by extended commiseration rescuing multitudes from misery, while disseminating blessings on all around, the cultivation of our doctrine gained a grand basis, and by gradual advances its influence was diffused. If the winds and rains are seasonable, the world will be at rest; men will be guided by principle, inferior objects will be pure; the living will be at ease, and the dead will rejoice; the thoughts will produce their appropriate response, the affections will be free, and the eyes will be sincere; such is the laudable condition which we of the Illustrious Religion are laboring to attain.

Our great benefactor, the Imperially-conferred-purple-gown priest, I-sz', titular Great Statesman of the Banqueting-house, Associated Secondary Military Commissioner for the Northern Region, and Examination-palace Overseer, was naturally mild and graciously disposed; his mind susceptible of sound doctrine, he was diligent in the performance; from the distant city of Râjagriha, he came to visit China; his principles more lofty than those of the three dynasties, his practice was perfect in every department; at first he applied himself to dulies pertaining to the palace, eventually his name was inscribed on the military roll. When the Duke Koh Tsz'-í, Secondary Minister of State and Prince of Fan-yang, at first conducted the military in the northern region, the Emperor Suhtsung made him [I-sz'] his attendant on his travels; although he was a private chamberlain, he assumed no distinction on the march; he was as claws and teeth to the duke, and in rousing the military he was as ears and eyes; he distributed the wealth conferred upon him, not accumulating treasure for his private use; he made offerings of the jewelry which had been given by imperial favor, he spread out a golden carpet for devotion; now he repaired the old churches, anon he ireased the number of religious establishments; he honored and decorated the various edifices, till they resembled the plumage of the pheasant in its flight; moreover, practising the discipline of the Illustrious Religion, he distributed his riches in deeds of benevolence; every year he assembled those in the sacred office from four churches, and respectfully engaged them for fifty days in purification and preparation; the naked came and were clothed; the sick were attended to and restored; the dead were buried in repose; even among the most pure and self-denying of the Buddhists, such excellence was never heard of; the white-clad members of the lllustrious Congregation, now considering these men, have desired to engrave a broad tablet, in order to set forth a eulogy of their magnanimous deeds.

Ode

The true Lord is without origin,
Profound, invisible, and unchangeable;

With power and capacity to perfect and transform,
He raised up the earth and established the heavens.

Divided in nature, he entered the world,
To save and to help without bounds;
The sun arose, and darkness was dispelled,
All bearing witness to his true original.

The glorious and resplendent, accomplished Emperor,
Whose principles embraced those of preceding monarchs,
Taking advantage of the occasion, suppressed turbulence:
Heaven was spread out and the earth was enlarged.

When the pure, bright Illustrious Religion
Was introduced to our Tang dynasty,
The Scriptures were translated, and churches built,
And the vessel set in motion for the living and the dead:
Every kind of blessing was then obtained,
And all the kingdoms enjoyed a state of peace.

When Kautsung succeeded to his ancestral estate,
He rebuilt the edifices of purity;
Palaces of concord, large and light,
Covered the length and breadth of the land.

The true doctrine was clearly announced,
Overseers of the church were appointed in due form;
The people enjoyed happiness and peace,
While all creatures were exempt from calamity and distress.

When Hiuentsung commenced his sacred career,
He applied himself to the cultivation of truth and rectitude;
His imperial tablets shot forth their effulgence,
And the celestial writings mutually reflected their splendors.

The imperial domain was rich and luxuriant,
While the whole land rendered exalted homage;
Every business was flourishing throughout,
And the people all enjoyed prosperity.

Then came Suhtsung, who commenced anew,
And celestial dignity marked the imperial movements.
Sacred as the moon's unsullied expanse,
While felicity was wafted like nocturnal gales.

Happiness reverted to the imperial household,
The autumnal influences were long removed;
Ebullitions were allayed, and risings suppressed,
And thus our dynasty was firmly built up.

Taitsung the filial and just
Combined in virtue with heaven and earth;
By his liberal bequests the living were satisfied,
And property formed the channel of imparting succor.

By fragrant mementos he rewarded the meritorious,
With benevolence he dispensed his donations;
The solar concave appeared in dignity,
And the lunar retreat was decorated to extreme.

When Kienchung succeeded to the throne,
He began the cultivation of intelligent virtue;
His military vigilance extended to the four seas,
And his accomplished purity influenced all lands.

His light penetrated the secrecies of men,
And to him the diversities of objects were seen as in a mirror;
He shed a vivifying influence through the whole realm of nature,
And all outer nations took him for example.

The true doctrine how expansive!
Its responses are minute;
How difficult to name it!
To elucidate the three in one.

The sovereign has the power to act!
While the ministers record;
We raise this noble monument!
To the praise of great felicity.

This was erected in the second year of Kienchung, of the Tang Dynasty [A.D. 781], on the seventh day of the first month, being Sunday.

Written by Lu Siu-yen, Secretary to Council, formerly Military Superintendent for Taichau; while the Bishop Ning-shu had the charge of the congregations of the Illustrious in the East. . . .

SOURCE: "Inscription of the Nestorian Monument," trans. Alexander Wylie, *The Open Court* 23 (1909): 35–44.

23

POPE URBAN II

Pope Urban II (ca. 1042–1099) initiated the First Crusade at the Council of Clermont (1095) to rescue the Holy Land and Eastern churches from Muslim control. He promised remission of sins for all crusaders. In 1089 he established the modern Roman Curia as a royal court to facilitate administration of the church. The selection below is from his sermon at the Council of Clermont, calling for the crusade.

First Crusade

Although, Oh sons of God, you have promised the Lord more earnestly than before to maintain peace in your midst and faithfully to sustain the rights of the church, yet it is necessary for you, newly fortified by the correction of the Lord, to show the strength of your righteousness in a precious work which is not less your concern than the Lord's. For it behooves you to hasten to carry to your brethren dwelling in the East, the aid so often promised and so urgently needed. For the Turks and the Arabs have attacked them, as many of you know, and have advanced into the territory of Romania as far as that part of the Mediterranean which is called the Arm of St. George; and penetrating farther and farther into the country of those Christians, have already seven times conquered them in battle, have killed and captured many, have destroyed the churches and devastated the kingdom. If you permit them to remain for a time unmolested, they will extend their sway more widely over many faithful servants of the Lord.

Wherefore, I pray and exhort, no not I, but the Lord prays and exhorts you, as heralds of Christ, at all times to urge men of all ranks, peasants and knights, the poor equally with the rich, to hasten to exterminate this vile race from the lands ruled by our brethren, and to bear timely aid to the worshippers of Christ. I speak to those who are present, I shall proclaim it to the absent, but it is Christ who commands. Moreover, if those who set out there lose their lives on the journey, by land or sea, or in fighting against the heathen, their sins shall be remitted in that hour; this I grant through the power of God vested in me.

Oh, what a disgrace if a race so despised, so degenerate, so entirely the slave of the demons, should thus conquer omnipotent God's elect people, rendered illustrious by the name of Christ! Oh, how many reproaches will be heaped upon us by the Lord Himself if we do not aid those who like ourselves glory in the name of Christ! Let those who have formerly been accustomed to contend wickedly in private warfare against the faithful, fight against the infidel and bring to a victorious end the war which ought long since to have been begun. Let those who have until now been robbers now become soldiers. Let those who have formerly contended against their brothers and relatives now fight as they ought against the barbarians. Let those who have formerly been mercenaries at low wages, now gain eternal rewards. Let those who have been exhausting themselves to the detriment both of body and soul, now strive for a two-fold reward. What shall I add? On this side will be the sorrowful and poor, on the other the rich; here the enemies of the Lord, there His friends. Let not the expedition be delayed. But let the warriors arrange their affairs and collect the money necessary for their expenses, and when the winter ends and the spring comes, let them with alacrity start on their journey under the guidance of the Lord.

SOURCE: Dana C. Munro, *Translations and Reprints from the Original Sources of European History. Urban and the Crusaders* (Philadelphia: Department of History of the University of Pennsylvania, 1895), 2–5. This is a fragment from the *Speech at the Council of Clermont* (26 November 1095) according to the version of Fulcher of Chartres (ca. 1059–ca. 1127), a French priest and chronicler of the First Crusade.

24

ANSELM OF CANTERBURY

Anselm (1033–1109), Archbishop of Canterbury, is known as the father of scholasticism. One of the great topics of his era was the relationship between faith and reason. Anselm argued that faith precedes and assists reason: his motto was "faith seeking understanding" (*fides quaerens intellectum*). Anselm is also known for the influential ontological argument for the existence of God (selection below) and for his work on the incarnation and atonement, *Cur Deus Homo* (*Why God Became Man,* 1099). Anselm opposed the ransom theory and proposed the satisfaction theory of the atonement (selection below), which argued that Jesus Christ's obedience in suffering and crucifixion paid the debt that had been created when humanity disobeyed God's commands, thus dishonoring God. The concepts of honor and satisfaction reflect feudal society and the penitential system of the medieval church.

Ontological Argument for the Existence of God

Therefore, O Lord, who grants understanding to faith, grant to me that, so far as you know it to be good for me, I may understand that you are, as we believe; and also that you are what we believe you to be. Truly we believe that you are a being than which none greater can be conceived. Is it possible not to describe such a being? For even "the fool says in his heart, 'There is no God.'" (Ps. 53:1). Yet surely even that fool himself when he hears me speak of a being than which nothing greater can be conceived, understands what he hears, and what he understands is in his understanding, even if he does not understand that it really exists. It is one thing for a thing to be in the understanding, and another to understand that the thing really exists. When a painter considers the work which he is to make, he has it in his understanding; but he does not think that it exists before it is made. But when he has painted his picture, then he both has the picture in his understanding and understands it now exists. Thus even the fool is certain that a being which none greater can be conceived exists, at least in his understanding. Because when he hears this mentioned, he understands it, and whatever is understood exists in the understanding. Surely then a being than which nothing greater can be conceived cannot exist only in the understanding. Since if it exists only in the understanding, it would not be as great as if it existed also in reality. If then that than which none greater can be conceived exists in the understanding only, then that than which none greater can be conceived is something greater than which can be conceived: but this is impossible. Therefore it is certain that a being than which none greater can be conceived exists both in the understanding and also in reality.

Not only does this being than which none greater can be conceived exist, but it exists so truly that it cannot even be conceived not to exist. For it is possible to form the conception of an object whose nonexistence shall be inconceivable; and such an object is of necessity greater than any object which does not have to exist. Therefore if that than which none greater can be conceived can be thought not to exist; it follows that that than which none greater can be conceived is not that than which none greater can be conceived—for there can be conceived a greater than it, namely, an object whose non-existence shall be inconceivable—and this brings us to a contradiction. And thus it is proved that a being than which none greater can be conceived exists so truly that it cannot even be conceived not to exist. This being is you O Lord our God! And so you, O Lord my God, exist so truly that you cannot be conceived not to exist. And this is fitting. For if anyone could conceive a being better than you, then the creature would be ascending above the Creator, and judging the Creator, which is very absurd. Whatever is, except you alone, can be conceived as non-existent. You therefore exist in a truer sense than all else besides you, and are more real than all else beside you; because whatever else exists, exists in a less truer sense than you, and therefore is less real than you. Why then said the fool in his heart, "There is no God," when it is so plain to a rational mind that you are more real than anything else? Why, except that he is a fool indeed?

The Satisfaction Theory of the Atonement

O Christian soul, raised up from a grievous death, soul redeemed and delivered from a miserable slavery by the blood of God, arouse your mind from sleep, think of your resurrection, and remember your redemption and deliverance. Consider where and what is the strength of your salvation, occupy yourself in meditating on it, delight yourself in the contemplation of it; cease being hard to please, force yourself, give your mind to it; taste of the goodness of your Redeemer, kindle within yourself the love of your Savior . . . Where is this strength that is Christ? "He had horns coming out of his hands; and there was the biding of his power" (Hab. 3:4). Horns he had in his hands, because his hands are fastened to the arms of the cross. But what power is there in this great weakness? What loftiness in that great lowliness? What is honorable in that great humiliation? Verily it is therefore a "biding of his power"; it is hidden, because it is in weakness; concealed, because in lowliness; secret, because in humiliation. O hidden power! That a Man, hanging upon the cross should hang on it that eternal death which oppressed mankind, that a man bound to a tree should unbind the world which was bound to death everlasting! O concealed loftiness! That a man condemned with robbers should save men who were condemned with devils, that a man stretched upon the cross should draw all things unto himself! O secret might! That one soul yielded in torment should draw innumerable souls out of hell, that a man should endure the death of the body, and destroy the death of souls! . . .

Shall we say that the devil had any just claim against God or men, on account of which God had to first deal with him on man's behalf, before he could explicitly display his mighty power, so that by unjustly slaying a just man, he might justly lose the power which he had over the unjust? Surely God owed the devil nothing but the punishment of his sins. Man also owed him nothing except to overcome sin in his turn, just as man once allowed himself to be easily overcome by the devil through committing sin, man should overcome the devil in the very straits of death . . . But man only owed this to God, not the devil. For the sin man committed was not against the devil, but against God. Neither did man belong to the devil, but man and the devil alike belonged to God. And in that the devil afflicted men, not out of zeal for righteousness, but out of zeal for wickedness; not by the command of God, but by his permission only; because it was required by the justice, not of the devil, but of God. Therefore, there was nothing in the devil that God had to deal with before revealing his mighty power for the salvation of man.

Was there then any necessity that constrained God to humble himself, and to accomplish a work with such great labor? No, all necessity and impossibility is dependent upon his will. For whatsoever he wills is necessary; and what he does not will, is impossible to be. Only because of God's free will, which is always good, was this done . . . it was the nature of man that required [the death of Christ] in this manner to make satisfaction to God. God had no need to suffer such troublesome things, but man needed to be reconciled to God. God did not need this humiliation, but man needed to be delivered out of the depths of hell. Now the divine nature neither needed humiliation or toil, nor was capable of it. But human nature must suffer all this, that it might be restored to that state for which it was created; yet neither human nature nor anything less than God could be sufficient for the work.

[Man] has received remission from all sins, but this cannot be done unless full satisfaction has been made for them. Now this satisfaction can only be made if the sinner, or someone on his behalf, offers something of his own to God which is not due to God . . . For if sin consists in dishonoring God, and if man ought not to dishonor God, whoever sins should render to God something greater than the honor that He was already due. Human nature by itself had nothing so great to offer, and yet without such satisfaction, it could not be reconciled since God's justice demands satisfaction of all sin. Therefore, the goodness of God came to the aid of his justice, and the Son of God took the nature of man upon him in his own person, so that in that one person there should be a God-man, who should have a sacrifice to offer, exceeding in value not only everything that is not God, but also every debt that sinners ought to pay to God, and so, owing nothing himself, should give this in payment for others, who were not able to pay that which they owed.

For the life of the man who is God is more precious than everything that is not God; and surpasses every debt which sinners owe for the satisfaction of God. For if the putting to death of this man exceeds all sins which can be conceived, (so they do not touch the person of God), it is clear that the goodness of his life is greater than the evil of all sins . . . This man who had not incurred the debt of death, because he had no sin, freely offered his own life for the sake of the Father's honor. [The Son] suffered his life to be taken from him for righteousness' sake, to give an example to all that the righteousness of God should not be abandoned by us even unto that death which they must at some time incur as a debt due from them. Although he had not incurred that death, and could have escaped it without abandoning righteousness, he suffered it freely for righteousness' sake when it was brought to him. Thus, in that man, human nature was freely offered to God and not out of debt, so that it might redeem itself in others who could not do so. In all this the divine nature was not abased, but the human was exalted; the divine was not diminished but the human in mercy sustained.

Human nature in that man suffered nothing through necessity, but through free will alone. Neither was it overcome by any violence. But of its own accord and out of unconstrained goodness, it endured those things which the evil will of others brought upon it for God's honor and to the profit of other men, not through the compulsion of any obligation, but through the appointment of a wisdom that had power to accomplish its purposes. For the Father did not compel that man to die by his commandment. Out of his own free will he performed that which he knew would be pleasing to the Father and profitable to men, for the Father could not compel him to do that which he had no right to exact of him. Neither could this great act of honor which his Son freely offered to him be anything but pleasing to the Father. Thus, in willing freely to do that which he knew would be pleasing to the Father, he rendered unto the Father a free obedience. But because the Father bestowed upon him this good will, though it were free, it is nevertheless rightly said that he received it as the commandment of the Father. In this manner, he was obedient to the Father even unto death; and as the Father gave him commandment, he obeyed, and he drank the cup which his Father had given unto him. This is the perfect and free obedience of human nature: when it freely submits its own free will to God's will, and has then of its own accord carried out in deed that good purpose which God has not exacted but accepted. Thus this man redeems all others by counting that which he has freely given to God towards the debt they owed to God. By this price man is not only once redeemed from his faults but, so often as he returns to God in worthy penitence, he is received . . . As to that which was done on the cross, by his cross has our Christ redeemed us. Therefore those who desire to approach this grace with a worthy affection are saved; but they who despise it, because they pay not the debt which they owe, are condemned.

Source: Anselm of Canterbury, *The Devotions of Saint Anselm*, ed. Clement C. J. Webb (London: Methuen & Co., 1903). Section on the "Ontological Argument" is from *Proslogium*, 12–14. Section on the "Satisfaction Theory" is from *Meditation IV, On Human Redemption*, 105–6, 108–13.

25

PETER ABELARD

PETER ABELARD (1079–1142), a French scholastic, is best known for his moral influence theory of the atonement (selection below). He criticized the ransom theory as a deficient view of God and focused on the forgiving love of God. Abelard was harshly criticized for diminishing the necessity of the crucifixion of Jesus Christ. Abelard also wrote on ethics, emphasizing the importance of intent. He is known for his love affair with Heloise, a student whom he secretly married after conceiving an illegitimate child. Heloise's uncle greatly disapproved of their actions to the extent that he had Abelard castrated, leading both Abelard and Heloise to take monastic orders for refuge.

The Moral Influence Theory of the Atonement

In what respect are we made any more righteous than we were before the death of the Son of God, so that we ought now to be released from punishment? To whom is this blood-price paid for our redemption if not to him in whose power we were? But we have declared that we were in God's power and it was he who handed us over to [the Devil] . . . It certainly does seem cruel and wicked that anyone should demand innocent blood as the price of anything, or that the execution of an innocent person would give him any pleasure—the more so that God should consider the death of his own Son so acceptable as to be reconciled to the whole world by it . . .

It seems to me that we are justified through the blood of Christ and reconciled to God in that, through the disclosure to us of such unique grace—that his Son took our nature upon him, and has persisted in teaching us by word and example even unto death—he has bound us more closely to himself by love. When we are thus enkindled by such a gift of divine grace, there is nothing which true love is afraid to undergo for him. Moreover, we have no doubt that the ancient fathers, who looked forward in faith to this gift, were enkindled with the supreme love of God, just as the men of this time of grace. It is written, "And they that went before and they that followed cried out 'Hosanna to the Son of David'" (Mark 11:9). And after the passion of Christ, everyone becomes still more righteous—i.e., everyone loves the Lord more completely—than ever before; for a gift actually received moves us to greater love than one merely hoped for. So our redemption is that supreme love inspired in us by the passion of Christ. It not only frees us from slavery to sin, but obtains for us the true freedom of the sons of God. So we are obedient in every respect not from fear, but for love of him, who has shown such love towards us that no greater can be found. As he says himself: "Greater love has no man than this, that he lay down his life for his friends" (John 15:13). Of this same love, Our Lord says elsewhere: "I came to cast fire upon the earth and how I wish that it were already kindled" (Luke 12:49). So he testifies that he came to spread the true liberty of love among men. Later on, the Apostle fully acknowledges this, when he says . . . *God shows his love for us in that while yet we were sinners, he died for us* (Rom 5:8) . . . let this statement—compressed though it must be, in view of the brevity of this commentary—suffice as an account of how the manner of our redemption appears to me.

SOURCE: Abelard, *Commentary on the Epistle to the Romans*, in A. D. Galloway, *Basic Readings in Theology* (London: George Allen & Unwin Ltd., 1964), 106–7.

26

BERNARD OF CLAIRVAUX

Bernard of Clairvaux (1090–1153) was known for his exceptional piety. He joined the Cistercian monastic order at Cîteaux and was later sent to found a new monastery at Clairvaux. He wrote a new rule for the Knights Templar at the request of the Council of Troyes (1128). His preaching worked to heal a church schism, inspired the Second Crusade, and rooted out heresy. He is best known for his devotional and spiritual writings. The selection below focuses on the journey toward the mystical love and knowledge of God.

Loving God

You wish me to explain for what reason and in what measure we should love God. I should say that God himself is the motive of our love to him, and that the measure of due love is to be without measure . . .

The witness of natural law

Those who do not know Christ are sufficiently taught by the natural law, and by the gifts they possess of body and soul, to love God for God's own sake . . . Where is the infidel who does not know that from him alone who makes his sun to shine upon the just and unjust, and the rain to fall upon saints and sinners, from him alone he has received all that is necessary for life; light, air, and food? What man refers the excellence peculiar to the human race to any other but to him who says in Genesis, "Let us make man unto Our Own image and likeness"? (Gen. 1:27). Who sees the author of intelligence in any but in him who teaches all men? From what other hand will any think to receive virtue, but from the God of virtue? God then has good reason to be loved for himself, even on the knowledge of the infidel who is ignorant of Christ . . . who is without excuse; for his innate justice and reason cry out from the depth of his soul that he is bound to love him wholly from whom he holds all things. But it is impossible by natural strength or the might of free will to give all to God, instead of keeping back some to our own praise as it is written: "All seek their own" (Phil. 2:21).

The first degree of love: love of self

Love is one of the four natural affections that the entire world knows. It is but natural and right first of all to love the author of nature; and the first and greatest commandment is: "You shall love the Lord your God" (Luke 10:27). But nature is too soft and weak for such a precept; she must begin by loving herself; this is the love which is called carnal, with which man loves himself first and above all; as it is written: "That is not first which is spiritual, but that which is natural." We love first by nature, not by precept: "No man ever hated his own flesh." But if this love should increase too much; if like a river between banks it overflows and floods the lands about, it then becomes voluptuousness, and this dyke is opposed to it: "You shall love thy neighbor as yourself" . . . if any one cannot so love his brethren as to think of their wants, or let us even say of their pleasures, let him deny himself in those very things, in order that he may learn. Let a man think of himself as much as ever he will, if only he take care to think equally of his neighbor. Such, O man, is the curb and just limit imposed upon you by the law of your being and by your conscience, that you be not carried away by your selfishness to your destruction, leaving your nature at the mercy of the enemies of your soul; that is, of your passions . . .

But for love of neighbor to be entirely right, God must have his part in it; it is not possible to love our neighbor as we ought to do, except in God. He that does not love God can love nothing in him. We must therefore begin by loving God, and thus love our neighbor in him. God is the author, as of all other things, so of our love for him—and more—as he created nature, so he sustains it; for she could neither exist nor subsist without him. That we might thoroughly know this, and not attribute anything to ourselves, God, in the depths of his wisdom and love, made us subject to tribulation. Being feeble and needy, we are forced to turn to God, and being saved by him we give glory to his name. These are his words: "Call upon me in the day of trouble; I will deliver you, and you shall glorify me" (Ps. 50:15). In this way man, by nature carnal, with no love but for himself, is brought through self-love to love God, realizing that all his ability, he has from God, and without him he can do nothing.

Second and third degrees of love; love of God for self's sake and love of God for God's sake

Man has some love for God for his own sake, not for God's. It is already something to feel the limits of his own capacity, to know what he cannot do without the help of God, and to keep right with him who sustains his life and strength. But, let a train of disasters occur which causes him to turn to God, if he still gets the aid he wants, his heart must be of brass or marble not at last to be touched by the goodness of his helper, not to begin at length to love him for himself . . . It soon follows that we are brought to love him rightly, far more for the sweetness and beauty that we find in him than for our own self-interest. In the words of the Samaritans to the woman: "We now believe, not because of your witness; for we ourselves have heard him, and know that this is indeed the savior of the world" (John 4:42). In like manner, we come to say to our natural self: It is not because of you that we love the Lord, but we have tasted ourselves, and found how sweet he is . . . "Give praise to the Lord, for he is good" (Ps. 106:1).

The fourth degree of love: to love the self only for God

Happy is he who can rise to the fourth degree of love, and loves himself only for God's sake . . . When shall this flesh and blood, this dust and mire of which I am made, be able to go up there? When shall this soul of mine, entranced with love for God, look on herself as broken shreds, yearn after God, and lose herself in him, for "He who is joined to the Lord is one spirit"? (1 Cor. 6:17) When shall she cry out: "My flesh and my heart have fainted away; Thou art the God of my heart, and the God that is my portion for-ever"? (Ps. 73:26). Holy and happy is he who but once, for but one moment, has felt something like this in his mortal life; for this is no human happiness, it is life eternal to lose oneself, as if one were empty of self, as if one were totally unconscious of self and did not exist.

If some poor mortal attains to this *love* for one moment, returning to this evil time *on earth* seems to delay and embitter his joy of *contemplation*. This body of death drags him down, the cares and anxieties of life pull him back . . . "Unhappy man that I am, who shall deliver me from the body of this death?" (Rom. 7:24) We read in Holy Scripture that God has made all things for himself . . . We ought to offer ourselves entirely to him, studying only his good pleasure, not our own. We shall find happiness, much less in seeking our own advantage, than in the accomplishment of his will in us, according as we daily pray: "Thy will be done on earth as it is in Heaven." O pure and holy love, most sweet and blessed affection, O complete submission of a disinterested soul; most perfect in that there is no thought of self; most sweet and tender in that the soul's whole feeling is divine! To attain to this, is for the soul to be deified; as a small drop of water appears lost if mixed with wine, taking its taste and color; and as, when plunged into a furnace, a bar of iron seems to lose its nature and assume that of fire; or as the air filled with the sun's beams seems rather to become light than to be illuminated. So it is with the natural life of the Saints; they seem to melt and pass away into the will of God. For if anything merely human remained in man, how then should God be all in all? It is not that human nature will be destroyed, but that it will attain another beauty, a higher power and glory. When shall that be? To whom shall it be given to see and know it? When shall I come and appear before the face of God? O God, my Lord, my heart has said to you: "My face has sought you; your face, O Lord, will I seek" (Ps. 27:8).

Will it be given to such as I to see your holy temple? In this life, we must give attention to the body and thus it is impossible, so long as our energies are thus divided, to rest wholly in God and in the contemplation of him, impossible perfectly to obey the precept, "You shall love the Lord your God with all your heart, with all your soul, and with all your strength" (Luke 10:27). We may not hope to possess the fourth degree of love, or rather to be possessed by it, until we have put on a spiritual and immortal body, pure and calm, obedient and subject in all to the spirit, which cannot be our doing, but only the work of the power of God in favor of such as please him. Our soul will easily attain to this perfect love when neither the burden nor the temptations of this body oppress her; then she will spring untrammeled to her joy in the Lord. But are we to doubt that the souls of the holy martyrs before quitting their triumphant bodies tasted, at least in some small measure, of this happiness? This we know for certain, that immense love filled and enraptured their souls, to give them strength to lay down their lives and to endure the torments which they suffered.

SOURCE: Bernard of Clairvaux, *On the Love of God* (London: Burns & Oates, 1884), 3, 10–11, 37–46.

27

FRANCIS OF ASSISI

GIOVANNI FRANCESCO DI BERNARDONE (St. Francis, 1181–1226) founded the Franciscan Order and helped found the Order of St. Clare, a female Franciscan order. Francis modeled mendicant monasticism with his street-preaching and life of voluntary poverty. Francis' conversations with Muslim scholars at the Fourth Lateran Council (1215) permitted Franciscan residency in the Holy Land, even through the Crusades. In his later life, Francis introduced the Christmas nativity scene and tradition says he received the stigmata in 1224. From the legendary stories that describe his speaking with and preaching to animals, he is best known today as the patron saint of animals and creation.

The Song of Brother Sun and of All Creatures

Most High, all powerful, all good, Lord,
Yours be the praise, the glory, the honor, all the blessing.
To you alone, Most High, do they belong,
And no one is worthy to pronounce your Name.
Praise to you, my Lord, for all your creatures,
First of all Brother Sun, who brings us the day and gives us his light.
He is beautiful, radiant with great splendor, and he bears your likeness,
    O Most High.
Praise to you, my Lord, for Sister Moon and the Stars,
Which you have set in the heavens, bright, precious, and beautiful.
Praise to you, my Lord, for Brothers Wind and Air,
For clouds, for all weather, through which you sustain life in all your
    creatures.
Praise to you, my Lord, for Sister Water, who is so useful and humble,
    precious and pure.
Praise to you, my Lord, for Brother Fire, through whom you give light
    to the night,
He is beautiful and pleasant, powerful and strong.
Praise to you, my Lord, for our sister Mother Earth
Who sustains and guides us, and produces different fruits, colored
    flowers, and herbs.
Praise to you, my Lord for those who forgive one another,
Because they love you, and endure sickness and trial.
Blessed are they who shall endure in peace, for you shall crown them,
    O Most High.
Praise to you, Lord, for our Sister Death, from whom no living person
    can escape.
Woe to those who die in mortal sin. Blessed are those she finds in your
    most holy will.
The second death cannot harm them.
Praise and bless my Lord,
Give thanks and serve Him with great humility.

28

CLARE OF ASSISI

CLARE OF ASSISI (1194–1253), the founder of the Poor Clares, was canon-ized in 1255. Her *Rule*, long lost but rediscovered in 1893, reflects the spirit of the religious order founded by Francis of Assisi (1181–1226). The selection below combines autobiographical elements with the central tenet of the mendicant orders, namely the vow of "apostolic poverty."

Apostolic Poverty

When the Most High Heavenly Father vouchsafed to enlighten my heart by his grace to do penance according to the example and doctrine of our most blessed father, Saint Francis, shortly after his own conversion, my sisters and I, of our own free will, bound ourselves to obey him. And when our blessed father had seen that we feared neither want nor toil, nor sorrow nor igno-miny, nor the world's scorn, but rather rejoiced in these things, the bowels of his compassion were moved towards us, and he wrote for us a form of life, which began in this way:

"Because by Divine inspiration you have made yourselves the daughters and handmaids of the Most High Sovereign King our Father who dwelled in heaven, and have espoused yourselves to the Paraclete by electing to live according to the perfection of the Holy Gospel, I will, and I promise in my own name and the names of my successors, ever to have for you the same diligent care and special concern which I have for the brethren."

That promise to the day of his death he most loyally fulfilled, and it was his wish that the brethren should keep it forever. Also to the end that neither we ourselves nor they that should come after us should in any way ever decline from that most holy poverty with which we had begun; not long before he died he sent us another letter, and in this letter he made known to us his last wishes: "I, Brother Francis, least of men, desire to imitate the life and poverty of the Most High Lord Jesus Christ and of His Most Holy Mother. And I counsel and entreat you, my Ladies: do you, too, always live in this most holy life and poverty, and keep watch over yourselves lest by the advice and teaching of any man you ever decline in any way from it."

And as we have been always concerned, myself and my sisters, to observe that holy poverty which we promised to the Lord God and to Blessed Francis, so let the abbesses who shall come after me and their sisters be in like manner solicitous to observe it inviolably to the end; that is to say: they shall neither receive nor hold possessions, nor have any rights of property, or what might be reasonably considered such, in anything whatsoever, either directly themselves or indirectly by means of an interposed person. It is lawful to hold as much land as necessity demanded for the decency and seclusion of the monastery, but such land shall not be cultivated except as a garden for the sisters' own needs.

SOURCE: Ernest Gilliat-Smith, *Saint Clare of Assisi: Her Life and Legislation* (London and Toronto: J. M. Dent & Sons, Ltd., 1914), 280–81.

29

BONAVENTURE

JOHN OF FIDANZA, known as Bonaventure (1221–1274), an Italian scholastic theologian, became Minister General of the Franciscan monastic order. His teachings merged mysticism and Platonism as well as the teachings of Augustine and Aristotle, advocating that knowledge cannot come from reason alone, but from virtue and fellowship with God. Bonaventure produced theological, philosophical, devotional, and exegetical writings. The selections below are hymns of devotion that he wrote.

The Passion of Our Lord

LORD, thy death upon the tree
Brings uplifting thoughts to me,
Calm of mind and holy fire,
Love of God and pure desire.

O to bear in memory
All thy grief and obloquy,
Holy Christ, thy thorny wreath,
Spear and nails and crucial death!

All these blessed wounds of thine,
Witness of thy love divine,
Cruel scourging and distress,
O the mortal bitterness!

Lord, the thought is of such dole,
So intoxicates the soul,
That we bow in tearful prayers;
But what glorious fruit it bears!

Low, before thee, Crucified,
Sink all selfishness and pride;
Loud to thee, dear Christ, we cry;
Join us with thy saints on high.

Honor, praise, and glory bring
Unto Jesus, heavenly King,
Who, all pure and faultless, gave
His sweet life our lives to save.

On the Holy Cross

Wouldn't thou dwell in joy abounding,
All thy life with light surrounding,
Make the cross thy constant care;
On the rood of thy Redeemer
Be thy soul an ardent dreamer,
Bear it with thee everywhere.

Be thou toiling, be thou sleeping,
Be thou smiling, be thou weeping,
Deep in grief or ecstasy;
Be thou coming, be thou going,
Pale with pain, with pleasure glowing,
Let the cross thy comrade be.

Every sin and every sorrow,
Every ill that life can borrow,
In the cross will gain surcease;
In the cross, though sore and grieving,

He that humbly seeks relieving,
Findeth refuge, findeth peace.

'Tis the open door of heaven,
Whence the streaming light was given
To the Saints to conquer shame;
'Tis the world's eternal healing,
Whence the Lord, his mercies dealing,
Works wonders to his name.

Health of souls, salvation's portal,
Guiding light to bliss immortal,
Charm to soothe the hardened heart;
Life of saints in benediction,
Treasure house of all perfection,
Fraught with living joy thou art.

Virtue's glass and manhood's mirror,
Leader guiding souls from error,
Hope of all who hold the faith;
To the bold in Christ a glory,
As the symbol and the story
Of their war on sin and death.

'Tis the tree of holy seeming
Through the blood of Christ, and teeming
With that fruit, the food of might,
Which to struggling souls has given
Strength to climb the hills of Heaven,
Out of darkness into light.

Savior, on the cross extended,
Be my soul with grace amended,
Evermore to mourn thy pain;
Feel the tortures that efface thee,
And with prostrate soul embrace thee,
On the cross where thou art slain.

Source: St. Bonaventure, *In Passione Domini* and *Recordare Sanctae Crucis* (hymns), in Daniel Joseph Donahoe, *Early Christian Hymns: Translations of the Verses of the Most Notable Latin Writers of the Early and Middle Ages* (New York: The Grafton Press, 1908), 179–82.

30

THOMAS OF CELANO

THOMAS OF CELANO (ca. 1200–ca. 1255) became a disciple of St. Francis of Assisi in 1215. He later traveled to Germany to recruit for the Franciscan order, a trip he repeated throughout his life. He wrote the first biography of St. Francis at Pope Gregory IX's request, and he may also be the author of biographical material on St. Clare of Assisi. He died while serving as spiritual director at a convent of Clarissines in Tagliocozzo, where he is buried. Thomas wrote the following hymn which reveals popular piety during medieval Christianity.

The Last Judgment (*Dies Irae*)

Day of ire, that direful day!
Earth in fire shall pass away,
As both saint and Sibyl say.

How the guilty world shall quake,
When the Judge his seat shall take,
Sentence swift and sure to make.

Then the trump with wondrous tone,
Sounding through the graveyards lone,
All shall force before the throne.

Death and nature, wondering, see
How the dead, arising, flee
Swift to hear the dread decree.

Forth the written book is brought,
Bearing every deed and thought,
Whence reward and doom are sought.

So before the Judge full plain
Shall appear each hidden stain;
Unavenged shall nought remain.

What shall be my woeful plaint?
Whither seek a saving saint,
When the just with fear are faint?

King of mighty majesty,
Saving free who saved would be,
Fount of pity, save thou me.

Jesus, think of me, I pray,
Me, who caused thy crucial way,
Lest thou lose me on that day.

Seeking me in wearing pain,
Sorrows sharing, thou wert slain—
Be such labors not in vain.

Righteous and avenging King,
Of my sins remission bring,
Ere the day of reckoning.

Bowed in grief upon the sod,
Flushed with guilt, I feel the rod—
Spare thy supplicant, O God.

Who from sin didst Mary free,
And the thief upon the tree,
Thou hast given hope to me.

Without worth are prayers of mine;
Turn to me thy face divine,
Lest in endless fire I pine.

Give me grace, O God, to stand
With the sheep on thy right hand,
Guarded from the cursed band.

When the wicked in defeat,
Fast in flames thy judgment meet,
Call me home with blessings sweet.

Humbled down to earth in prayer,
With a contrite heart, I dare
Beg, O Father, for thy care.

Day of weeping, day of sighs,
When from ruin shall arise
Guilty man, with soul laid bare,

Spare him, Lord, in mercy spare!
Gentle Jesus, with the blest
Grant the faithful endless rest.

Source: Daniel Joseph Donahoe, *Early Christian Hymns: Translations of the Verses of the Most Notable Latin Writers of the Early and Middle Ages* (New York: The Grafton Press, 1908), 173–75.

31

THOMAS AQUINAS

Thomas Aquinas (1225–1274), a Dominican monk, has been called the most influential Christian theologian of the medieval period. His *Summa Theologica* (or *Theologiae*) (1265–1274), the most extensive theological writing of his time, is his best-known work. Aquinas was a great systematizer of the faith, and later Catholic doctrine reflected his teachings. He believed that God was revealed through reason (natural revelation) and faith (special revelation). Proofs for the existence of God (selection below) could be found in the natural order. Today, there is still significant interest in the writings of Aquinas on natural law. A second reading below is a hymn composed by Aquinas for the Mass of Corpus Christi, ca. 1264.

Proofs for the Existence of God

On The Existence of God

Article II. Whether the existence of God is demonstrable.

Let us proceed to the second point. It is objected that the existence of God is not demonstrable: that God's existence is an article of faith, and that articles of faith are not demonstrable, because the office of demonstration is to prove, but faith pertains (only) to things that are not to be proven, as is evident from the Epistle to the Hebrews, chapter 11. Hence, that God's existence is not demonstrable.

Again, that the subject matter of demonstration is that something exists, but in the case of God we cannot know what exists, but only what does not, as Damascus says (John of Damascus, *Of the Orthodox Faith*, I, 4). Hence, that we cannot demonstrate God's existence.

Again, that if God's existence is to be proved it must be from what He causes, and that what He effects is not sufficient for His supposed nature, since He is infinite, but the effects finite, and the finite is not proportional to the infinite. Since, therefore, a cause cannot be proved through an effect not proportional to itself, it is said that God's existence cannot be proved.

But against this argument the apostle says, "The unseen things of God are visible through His manifest works" (Rom. 1:20). But this would not be so unless it was possible to demonstrate God's existence through His works. What ought to be understood concerning anything, is first of all, whether it exists.

Conclusion. It is possible to demonstrate God's existence, although not *a priori* (by pure reason), yet *a posteriori* from some work of His more surely known to us.

In answer I must say that the proof is double. One is through the nature of a cause and is called *propter quid*: this is through the nature of preceding events simply. The other is through the nature of the effect, and is called *quia*, and is through the nature of preceding things as respects us.

Since the effect is better known to us than the cause, we proceed from the effect to the knowledge of the cause. From any effect whatsoever it can be proved that a corresponding cause exists, if only the effects of it are sufficiently known to us, for since effects depend on causes, the effect being given, it is necessary that a preceding cause exists. Thus, that God exists, although this is not itself known to us, is provable through effects that are known to us.

To the first objection above, I reply, therefore, that God's existence, and those other things of this nature that can be known through natural reason concerning God, as is said in Romans 1, are not articles of faith, but preambles to these articles. So faith presupposes natural knowledge, so grace nature, and perfection a perfectible thing. Nothing prevents a thing that is in itself demonstrable and knowable, from being accepted as an article of faith by someone that does not accept the proof of it.

To the second objection, I reply that, since the cause is proven from the effect, one must use the effect in the place of a definition of the cause in demonstrating that the cause exists; and that this applies especially in the case of God, because for proving that anything exists, it is necessary to accept in this method what the name signifies, not however that anything exists, because the question "what it is" is secondary to the question "whether it exists at all." The characteristics of God are drawn from His works . . . by proving that God exists through His works, we are able by this very method to see what the name God signifies.

To the third objection, I reply that although a perfect knowledge of the cause cannot be had from inadequate effects, yet that from any effect manifest to us it can be shown that a cause does exist, as has been said. And thus from the works of God His existence can be proved, although we cannot in this way know Him perfectly in accordance with His own essence.

Article III. Whether God exists.

Let us proceed to the third article. It is objected that God does not exist, because if one of two contradictory things is infinite, the other will be totally destroyed; that it is implied in the name God that there is a certain infinite goodness: if then God existed, no evil would be found. But evil is found in the world; therefore it is objected that God does not exist.

Again, that what can be accomplished through fewer principles will not be accomplished through more. It is objected that all things that appear on the earth can be accounted for through other principles, without supposing that God exists, since what is natural can be traced to a natural principle, and what proceeds from a proposition can be traced to the human reason or will. Therefore that there is no necessity to suppose that God exists. But as against this note what is said of the person of God, "I am that I am" (Exod. 3:14).

Conclusion. There must be found in the nature of things one first immovable Being, a primary cause, necessarily existing, not created; existing the most widely, good, even the best possible; the first ruler through the intellect, and the ultimate end of all things, which is God.

I answer that it can be proved in five ways that God exists. The first and plainest is the method that proceeds from the point of view of motion. It is certain and in accord with experience, that things on earth undergo change. Now everything that is moved is moved by something; nothing is changed except it is changed to something which it is in potentiality. Moreover, anything moves in accordance with something actually existing; change itself, is nothing else than to bring forth something from potentiality into actuality.

Now nothing can be brought from potentiality to actual existence except through something actually existing: thus heat in action, as fire, makes firewood, which is hot in potentiality, to be hot actually, and through this process, changes itself. The same thing cannot at the same time be actually and potentially the same thing, but only in regard to different things. What is actually hot cannot be at the same time potentially hot, but it is possible for it at the same time to be potentially cold. It is impossible, then, that anything should be both mover and the thing moved, in regard to the same thing and in the same way, or that it should move itself. Everything, therefore, is moved by something else. If, then, that by which it is moved, is also moved, this must be moved by something still different, and this, again, by something else. But this process cannot go on to infinity because there would not be any first mover, nor, because of this fact, anything else in motion, as the succeeding things would not move except because of what is moved by the first mover, just as a stick is not moved except through what is moved from the hand. Therefore it is necessary to go back to some first mover, which is itself moved by nothing, and this all men know as God.

The second proof is from the nature of the efficient cause. We find in our experience that there is a chain of causes: nor is it found possible for anything to be the efficient cause of itself, since it would have to exist before itself, which is impossible. Nor in the case of efficient causes can the chain go back indefinitely, because in all chains of efficient causes, the first is the cause of the middle, and these of the last, whether they be one or many. If the cause is removed, the effect is removed. Hence if there is not a first cause, there will not be a last, nor a middle. But if the chain were to go back infinitely, there would be no first cause, and thus no ultimate effect, nor middle causes, which is admittedly false. Hence we must presuppose some first efficient cause, which all call God.

The third proof is taken from the natures of the merely possible and necessary. We find that certain things either may or may not exist, since they are found to come into being and be destroyed, and in consequence potentially, either existent or non-existent. But it is impossible for all things that are of this character to exist eternally, because what may not exist, at length will not. If, then, all things were merely possible (mere accidents), eventually nothing among things would exist. If this is true, even now there would be nothing, because what does not exist, does not take its beginning except through something that does exist. If then nothing existed, it would be impossible for anything to begin, and there would now be nothing existing, which is admittedly false. Hence not all things are mere accidents, but there must be one necessarily existing being. Now every necessary thing either has a cause of its necessary existence, or has not. In the case of necessary things that have a cause for their necessary existence, the chain of causes cannot go back infinitely, just as not in the case of efficient causes, as proved. Hence there must be presupposed something necessarily existing through its own nature, not having a cause elsewhere but being itself the cause of the necessary existence of other things—which all call God.

The fourth proof arises from the degrees that are found in things. For there is found a greater and a less degree of goodness, truth, nobility, and the like. But more or less are terms spoken of various things as they approach in diverse ways toward something that is the greatest, just as in the case of hotter (more hot) which approaches nearer the greatest heat. There exists therefore something that is the truest, and best, and most noble, and in consequence, the greatest being. For what are the greatest truths are the greatest beings . . . What moreover is the greatest in its way, in another way is the cause of all things of its own kind (or genus); thus fire, which is the greatest heat, is the cause of all heat . . . Therefore there exists something that is the cause of the existence of all things and of the goodness and of every perfection whatsoever—and this we call God.

The fifth proof arises from the ordering of things for we see that some things which lack reason such as natural bodies are operated in accordance with a plan. It appears from this that they are operated always or the more frequently in this same way the closer they follow what is the Highest; thus it is clear that they do not arrive at the result by chance but because of a purpose. The things, moreover, that do not have intelligence do not tend toward a result unless directed by someone knowing and intelligent; just as an arrow is sent by an archer. Therefore there is something intelligent by which all natural things are arranged in accordance with a plan—and this we call God.

In response to the first objection, then, I reply what Augustine says; that since God is entirely good, He would permit evil to exist in His works only if He were so good and omnipotent that He might bring forth good even from the evil. It therefore pertains to the infinite goodness of God that he permits evil to exist and from this brings forth good.

My reply to the second objection is that since nature is ordered in accordance with some defined purpose by the direction of some superior agent, those things that spring from nature must be dependent upon God, just as upon a first cause. Likewise what springs from a proposition must be traceable to some higher cause which is not the human reason or will, because this is changeable and defective and everything changeable and liable to non-existence is dependent upon some unchangeable first principle that is necessarily self-existent as has been shown.

Sequence for Corpus Christi (*Lauda Sion*)

Sing aloud, O Zion, praising
Christ, thy Royal Shepherd, raising
Hymns of love and songs of joy;
Let the music sound forever,
Never ceasing, tiring never,
All thy powers of praise employ.

Lo, the theme of all thanksgiving,
Vivifying bread and living,
On the holy altar shown!
Yea, the selfsame bread of heaven,
At the sacred supper given
To the twelve by Christ the Son.

Sing aloud in song sonorous,
Sing his praise in swelling chorus,
Sing in love and sweet accord;
Men of every race and nation
Hold the feast of Christ's creation,
Founded by his holy word.

Lo, the King upon his table
Lays a pasch more new and stable,
Ending every ancient rite;
Older laws give place to newer,
Shadows fly, and worship truer
Cometh with the wondrous light.

And today, as Christ ordaineth,
To his memory still remaineth
Joy, descending from above,
Still remain for our salvation
Bread and wine in consecration,
Making earth a home of love.

To the faithful Jesus giveth,
In his love, this truth that liveth,
To his blood is changed the wine;
Bread unto his body turneth;
Man by living faith discerneth
All the mystery divine.

Here, two different species under,
Hides in signs awaking wonder,
Christ's best gift, most excellent,
From his flesh and blood he giveth
Food and drink; in each he liveth
Whole within the sacrament.

Never by partaking groweth
Less the gift which he bestoweth,
Comes to all the sweet reward;
Whether single or in union,
Few or thousands at Communion,
Every soul receives the Lord.

And the good and bad receive him,
They who doubt and who believe him;
But with what a different end!
To the worthy soul, salvation;
To the impenitent, damnation,
Death to foe and life to friend.

Though the sacrament ye sever
Into fragments, fear ye never,
In each part remaineth ever
What the whole contained before;
In the sign alone obtaineth
Change; but as the Lord ordaineth,
He, the Signified, remaineth
Whole and perfect evermore.

Lo, the bread of angels, bearing
Strength to souls in sorrow wearing,

With the sons of mercy sharing,
Not the unregenerate;
Food prefigured and foretold in
Sacred signs and symbols olden,
Bringing unto man the golden
Hour of glory consecrate.

Gentle Jesus, Shepherd tender,
Bread of life, in mercy render
Peace, and blessed hope engender;
Savior be our sure defender,
Make us worthy of thy love;
Thou all-knowing and all-heeding
Save thy flock with care and feeding;
Let us follow in thy leading,
Hear us in our earnest pleading,
Guide us to the fold above.

SOURCE: The first selection is from Thomas Aquinas, "The Five Ways," *Summa Theologiae* I. Q.1, Art. 2–3, in Oliver Joseph Thatcher, *The Library of Original Sources: Early Medieval Age* (New York: University Research Extension, 1907), 359–63. *Lauda Sion* is from Daniel Joseph Donahoe, *Early Christian Hymns: Translations of the Verses of the Most Notable Latin Writers of the Early and Middle Ages* (New York: The Grafton Press, 1908), 191–94.

32

POPE BONIFACE VIII

POPE BONIFACE VIII (ca. 1235–1303) was pope at the turn of the thirteenth century (1294–1303). In addition to frequent sparring with the poet Dante, Boniface made groundbreaking claims of papal authority. In the context of disagreements with King Philip IV of France, Boniface issued the papal bull, *Unam Sanctam* (1302), in which he stipulated that every human authority, including that of the state, was obligated to submit to the papacy and the church. In 1311 Boniface was posthumously tried for heresy and immorality but is still venerated.

Papal Authority: *Unam Sanctam*

That there is one holy Catholic and apostolic Church we are impelled by our faith to believe and to hold—this we do firmly believe and openly confess— and outside of this there is neither salvation nor remission of sins, as the bridegroom proclaims in *Canticles*, "My dove, my undefiled is but one; she is the only one of her mother, she is the choice one to her that bore her" (Song. 6:9). The Church represents one mystic body, and of this body Christ is the head; of Christ, indeed, God is the head. In it is one Lord, and one faith, and one baptism. In the time of the flood there was one ark of Noah, prefiguring the one Church, finished in one cubit, having one Noah as steersman and commander. Outside of this all things upon the face of the earth were, as we read, destroyed. This Church we venerate and this alone . . . It is that seamless coat of the Lord, which was not rent but fell by lot. Therefore, in this one and only Church there is one body and one head—not two heads as if it were a monster—namely, Christ and Christ's vicar, Peter and Peter's successor; for the Lord said to Peter himself, "Feed my sheep" (John 21:7). "My sheep," he said, using a general term and not designating these or those sheep, so that we must believe that all the sheep were committed to him. If, then, the Greeks, or others, shall say that they were not entrusted to Peter and his successors, they, must unavoidably admit that they are not of Christ's sheep, as the Lord says in John, "there is one fold, and one shepherd" (John 10:16).

In this Church and in its power are two swords, a spiritual and a temporal, and this we are taught by the words of the Gospel; for when the apostles said, "Behold, here are two swords" (Luke 22:38) (in the Church, namely, since the apostles were speaking), the Lord did not reply that it was too many, but enough. And surely he who claims that the temporal sword is not in the power of Peter has but ill understood the word of our Lord when he said, "Put up again your sword into his place" (Matt. 26:52). Both the spiritual and the material swords, therefore, are in the power of the Church, the latter to be used for the Church, the former by the Church, the one by the priest, the other by the hand of kings and soldiers, but by the will and tolerance of the priest.

It is fitting, moreover, that one sword should be under the other, and the temporal authority subject to the spiritual power. For when the apostle said, "there is no power but of God: the powers that be are ordained of God" (Rom. 13:1), they would not be ordained unless one sword were under the other, and one, as inferior, was brought back by the other to the highest place. For, according to St. Dionysius, the law of divinity is to lead the lowest through the intermediate to the highest. Therefore, according to the law of the universe, things are not reduced to order directly and upon the same footing, but the lowest through the intermediate, and the inferior through the superior. It behooves us, therefore, the more freely to confess that the spiritual power excels in dignity and nobility any form of earthly power, as spiritual interests exceed the temporal in importance . . .

Therefore, the truth bearing witness, it is for the spiritual power to establish the earthly power and judge it, if it be not good. Thus, in the case of the Church and the power of the Church, the prophecy of Jeremiah is fulfilled: "See, I have this day set you over the nations and over the kingdoms" (Jer. 1:10), etc. Therefore, if the earthly power shall err, it shall be judged by the spiritual power; if the lesser spiritual power err, it shall be judged by the higher. But if the supreme power err, it can be judged by God alone and not by man, the apostles bearing witness, saying, the spiritual man judges all things, but he himself is judged by no one. Thus this power, although given to man and exercised by man, is not human, but rather a divine power, given by the divine lips to Peter, and founded on a rock for him and his successors in him [Christ] whom he confessed, the Lord saying to Peter himself, "Whatsoever you shall bind" (Matt. 16:19), etc.

Whoever, therefore, shall resist this power, ordained by God, resists the ordination of God, unless there should be two beginnings [*i.e., principles*], as the Manichean imagines. But this we judge to be false and heretical, since, by the testimony of Moses, not in the beginnings but in the beginning, God created the heaven and the earth. We, moreover, proclaim, declare, and pronounce that it is altogether necessary to salvation for every human being to be subject to the Roman pontiff.

SOURCE: James Harvey Robinson, *Readings in European History* (Boston: Ginn & Co., 1904), 1:346–48.

33

MARSILIUS OF PADUA

MARSILIUS OF PADUA (ca. 1275–ca. 1342) was an important fourteenth-century politician and Italian scholar. In his *Defensor pacis* (1324), he challenged the church's assertions about papal power, its relation to the state, and even the foundation of its claim to authority, apostolic succession. He argued for the independence of the Holy Roman Empire from the papacy, said the state derived its authority from the people and thus was the unifier of the society rather than the church. Ecclesiastical matters should be decided by a general council of priests and laity. Marsilius has been described as a forerunner of modern democracy and the Protestant Reformation. During his era, his ideas were deemed heretical and he sought refuge with the Holy Roman Emperor.

Church and State

The power of making the laws should belong to the whole body of citizens, for there is no lawgiver among men superior to the people themselves. The argument that there are an infinite number of fools in the world may be met by pointing out that "foolish" is a relative term, and that the people know their own needs best and will not legislate against their own interests. Any particular class of people is, however, likely to be self-seeking, as is shown by the decrees of the popes and the clergy, where the self-interest of the law-maker is only too apparent.

The actual administration must, nevertheless, be in the hands of a single person or group of persons. Perhaps a king is the best head for the state, but the monarch should be elected and not hold his office hereditarily, and should be deposed if he exceeds his powers.

. . . We have found that civil discord and dissension in the various kingdoms and communities is due, above all, to a cause which, unless it be obviated, will continue to be a source of future calamity—namely, the claims, aspirations, and enterprises of the Roman bishop and of his band of ecclesiastics, bent upon gaining secular power and superfluous worldly possessions. The bishop of Rome is accustomed to support his claim to supreme authority over others by the assertion that the plenitude of power was delegated to him by Christ through the person of St. Peter . . . But in reality no princely authority, nor any coercive jurisdiction in this world—to say nothing of supreme authority—belongs to him or to any other bishop, priest, or clerk, whether jointly or severally . . .

Now, in order that this plague which has scattered the seeds of discord and strife in kingdoms and communities, nor has ceased to provoke dissension, may be more speedily checked and prevented from further increase, we add . . . a collection of the clear and inevitable deductions from the statements and demonstrations given above. If these conclusions be duly attended to and acted upon this plague and its sophistical source will be easily abolished, now and hereafter, from the various kingdoms and other states.

[Selected Conclusions]

It is necessary to accept as true and essential to salvation only the holy and canonical Scriptures, together with their clear implications as interpreted by a general council of the faithful. This is assuredly true and may be assumed . . .

Doubtful points in the Christian belief are to be determined by a general council—in no case by a single person, whoever he may be . . .

No one, according to the gospel, may be forced to observe the divine law by a temporal penalty or any punishment of this world . . .

The human lawgiver can only be the whole body of citizens or a majority of them . . .

No one may be compelled by temporal penalties to obey the decretals or ordinances of the bishops of Rome, or of any other bishop, unless the decrees are issued with the sanction of the human lawgiver [namely, the people] . . .

No bishop or priest, as such, has any coercive authority or jurisdiction over any clerk or layman, even over a heretic . . .

No bishop or priest, or assembly of bishops or priests, may excommunicate any person, or interdict the performance of divine services, except with the authority of the lawgiver [namely, the people].

All bishops have equal authority immediately from Christ, nor, according to divine law, can it be shown that any one of them is superior to, or subordinate to, another, either in divine or temporal matters.

With the consent of the human legislator, other bishops may, together or separately, excommunicate the Roman bishop and exercise other forms of authority over him . . .

The determination of the number of churches and of priests, deacons, and other officials necessary to administer them, belongs to the rulers who shall conform to the laws of the faithful people . . .

The temporal possessions of the Church, except such as are necessary for the support of the priests and other ministers of the gospel and for the maintenance of divine services and the relief of the helpless poor, may properly, and according to divine law, be devoted, in whole or in part, by the human law, to public needs and the public defense.

SOURCE: James Harvey Robinson, *Readings in European History* (Boston: Ginn & Co. 1904), 1:491–97.

34

COUNCIL OF CONSTANCE

A SERIES OF MEETINGS of Western church leaders from 1414–1418, known collectively as the Council of Constance, produced the two famous declarations *Haec Sancta* (1415) and *Frequens* (1417). The council, promoted by Holy Roman Emperor Sigismund, was primarily intended to decide who was the rightful pope. At the time, three men simultaneously claimed the title, a situation referred to as the Great Schism (not to be confused with the East-West Schism). An early meeting issued *Haec Sancta Synodus* (This Holy Synod) which declared that a general council's judgments were final, overruling even the pope. This prioritization of councils over the papacy is known as conciliarism. *Frequens*, issued in a separate session, specified how frequently general church councils should be held. The selections from the declarations below highlight these themes. Neither statement is considered binding on the Roman Catholic Church today.

Decrees on Conciliarism

Session 5 (6 April 1415, Haec Sancta*)*

In the name of the Holy and indivisible Trinity; of the Father, Son, and Holy Ghost. Amen. This holy synod of Constance, forming a general council for the extirpation of the present schism and the union and reformation, in head and members, of the Church of God, legitimately assembled in the Holy Ghost, to the praise of Omnipotent God, in order that it may the more easily, safely, effectively and freely bring about the union and reformation of the church of God, hereby determines, decrees, ordains, and declares what follows: It first declares that this same council, legitimately assembled in the Holy Ghost, forming a general council and representing the Catholic Church militant, has its power immediately from Christ, and every one, whatever his state or position, even if it be the Papal dignity itself, is bound to obey it in all those things which pertain to the faith and the healing of the said schism, and to the general reformation of the Church of God, in head and members. It further declares that any one, whatever his condition, station or rank, even if it be the Papal, who shall contumaciously refuse to obey the mandates, decrees, ordinances, or instructions which have been, or shall be issued by this holy council, or by any other general council, legitimately summoned, which concern, or in any way relate to the above mentioned objects, shall, unless he repudiate his conduct, be subject to condign penance and be suitably punished, having recourse, if necessary, to the other resources of the law. . . .

Session 39 (9 October 1417, Frequens)

A frequent celebration of general councils is an especial means for cultivating the field of the Lord and effecting the destruction of briars, thorns, and thistles, to wit, heresies, errors, and schism, and of bringing forth a most abundant harvest. The neglect to summon councils fosters and develops all these evils, as may be plainly seen from a recollection of the past and a consideration of existing conditions. Therefore, by a perpetual edict, we sanction, decree, establish, and ordain that general councils shall be celebrated in the following manner, so that the next one shall follow the close of this present council at the end of five years. The second shall follow the close of that, at the end of seven years, and councils shall thereafter be celebrated every ten years in such places as the Pope shall be required to designate and assign, with the consent and approbation of the council, one month before the close of the council in question, or which, in his absence, the council itself shall designate. Thus, with a certain continuity, a council will always be either in session, or be expected at the expiration of a definite time. This term may, however, be shortened on account of emergencies, by the Supreme Pontiff, with the counsel of his brothers, the cardinals of the Holy Roman Church, but it may not be hereafter lengthened. The place, moreover, designated for the future council may not be altered without evident necessity. If, however, some complication shall arise, in view of which such a change shall seem necessary, as, for example, a state of siege, a war, a pest, or other obstacles, it shall be permissible for the Supreme Pontiff, with the consent and subscription of his said brethren or two-thirds of them [*duarum partium*] to select another appropriate place near one determined upon, which must be within the same country, unless such obstacles, or similar ones, shall exist throughout the whole nation. In that case, the council may be summoned to some appropriate neighboring place, within the bounds of another nation. To this the prelates, and others, who are wont to be summoned to a council, must betake themselves, as if that place had been designated from the first. Such change of place, or shortening of the period, the Supreme Pontiff is required legitimately and solemnly to publish and announce one year before the expiration of the term fixed, that the said persons may be able to come together for the celebration of the council within the term specified. . . .

SOURCE: *Readings in European History: A Collection of Extracts from the Sources Chosen for the Purpose of Illustrating the Progression of Culture in Western Europe since the German Invasions*, vol. 1: *From the Breaking Up of the Roman Empire to the Protestant Revolt*, ed. and trans. James H. Robinson (Boston: Ginn & Co., 1904), 511–13.

35

DESIDERIUS ERASMUS

DESIDERIUS ERASMUS OF ROTTERDAM (1466–1536), a Dutch humanist and theologian, was the leading Renaissance scholar of his day. His groundbreaking printed edition of the Greek New Testament (1515–1516) was an expression of the humanist stress on original languages. Erasmus worked to reform Catholicism from within, particularly concerning clerical abuses and doctrine. While he initially saw some positive signs in Martin Luther's reform, Erasmus was unwilling to leave the church. Erasmus and Luther engaged in a harsh debate over the role of human free will, with Erasmus affirming human cooperation with God in the process of salvation. In the selection below, Erasmus reveals his reforming spirit, speaking against society's ready acceptance of war.

Attitudes toward War

It is both an elegant proverb, and among all others, by the writings of many excellent authors, often and solemnly used, *Dulce bellum inexpertis*, that is to say, "War is sweet to them that know it not." There are some things among mortal men's businesses, in which there is great danger and pain, a man cannot perceive until he makes a proof . . . It seems a pleasant thing to be in love with a young damsel; but they have not yet perceived how much grief and bitterness is in such love . . .

Aristotle, in his book of Rhetoric, shows the cause why youth is bolder, and old age more fearful: for young men's lack of experience is cause of great boldness, but the experience of much grief engenders fear and doubting. If there is anything in the world that should be taken in hand with fear and doubting, yea, that ought to be fled by all manner of means, to be withstood with prayer, and to be clearly avoided, truly it is war; for nothing is either more wicked, or more wretched, or destroys more . . . or does more hurt, or is more horrible, and speaking briefly, nothing affects a man worse (I will not say a Christian man) than war. And yet it is a wonder to speak of, how nowadays in every place, how lightly, how for every trifling matter, how outrageously and barbarously it was done, not only of heathen people, but also of Christian men; not only of secular men, but also of priests and bishops; not only of young men and of them that have no experience, but also of old men and of those that so often have had experience; not only of the common and movable vulgar people, but most specially of the princes, whose duty had been, by wisdom and reason, to set in a good order and to pacify the light and hasty actions of the foolish multitude. Neither is there a lack of lawyers nor divines which are ready with their firebrands to kindle such abominable things, and they encourage others that were cold, and they secretly provoke those to it that were weary of it. And by these means it is come to pass that war is a thing now so well accepted, that men wonder at him that is not pleased with it. It is so much approved that it is counted a wicked thing (and I had almost said heresy) to reprove it, although it is the most mischievous and the most wretched. But how more justly should this be wondered at, what evil spirit, what pestilence, what mischief, and what madness put first in man's mind a thing so beyond disgusting measure, that this most pleasant and reasonable creature man, which nature has brought forth to peace and benevolence, which one alone she has brought forth to the help and aid of all others, should with so wild willfulness, with so mad rages, run headlong one to destroy another? . . .

If one would consider the behavior and shape of man's body, shall he not immediately perceive that nature, or rather God, has shaped this creature, not to war, but to friendship, not to destruction, but to health, not to wrong, but to kindness and benevolence? . . . Besides all this, nature has endowed man with knowledge of liberal sciences and a fervent desire of knowledge . . . For I dare boldly say, that neither affinity nor family bind the minds of men together with straighter and surer bands of friendship, than does the fellowship of them that is learned in good letters and honest studies . . . Moreover, God has ordained man in this world, as it were the very image of himself, to the intent, that he, as it were a god on earth, should provide for the wealth of all creatures . . . So man is, when all things fail, the last refuge to all manner of creatures. He is to them all the very assured altar and sanctuary.

I have here painted out to you the image of man as well as I can. On the other side (it is like you) against the figure of man, let us portray the fashion and shape of war.

Now, then, imagine in your mind, that you behold two hosts of barbarous people, who look fierce and cruel, with a horrible voice; the terrible and fearful rustling and glistering of their harness and weapons; the unlovely murmur of so huge a multitude; the eyes sternly menacing; the bloody blasts and terrible sounds of trumpets and clarions; the thundering of the guns, no less fearful than thunder, but much more hurtful; the frenzied cry and clamor, the furious and mad running together, the outrageous slaughter, the cruel chances of them that flee and of those that are stricken down and slain, the heaps of slaughters, the fields overflowed with blood, the rivers dyed red with man's blood. And it happens many times, that the brother fights with the brother, one kinsman with another, friend against friend; and in that common furious desire often times one thrusts his weapon quite through the body of another that never gave him so much as a foul word. Truly, this tragedy contains so many mischiefs, that it would abhor any man's heart to speak of it. I will not speak of the less severe hurts, as the treading down and destroying of the corn all about, the burning of towns and villages, the driving away of cattle, the ravishing of maidens, the old men taken in captivity, the robbing of churches, and all things confounded and full of thefts, pillages, and violence. Neither will I speak now of those things which are accustomed to follow the most happy and most just war of all . . .

But we run headlong to destroy others, even from that heavenly sacrifice of the altar, whereby is represented that perfect and ineffable knitting together of all Christian men. And of so wicked a thing, we make Christ both author and witness. Where is the kingdom of the devil, if it be not in war? Why do we draw Christ into war, with whom a brothel-house agrees more than war? Saint Paul disdains that there should be any discord so great among Christian men that they should need any judge to discuss the matter between them. What if he should come and behold us now through all the world, warring for every light and trifling cause, striving more cruelly than any heathen people, and more cruelly than any barbarous people? Yea, and you shall see it done by the authority and exhortations of those that represent Christ, the prince of peace . . .

There is one special precept, which Christ called his, that is, charity [*love*]. And what thing is so repugnant to charity as war? Christ saluted his disciples with the blessed fortune of peace. To his disciples he gave nothing except peace . . . In those holy prayers, he specially prayed the Father of heaven, that in like manner as he was one with the Father, so all his, that is to say, Christian men, should be one with him. Lo, here you may perceive a thing more than peace, more than amity, more than concord.

SOURCE: Erasmus of Rotterdam, *Erasmus Against War* [*Dulce bellum inexpertis*, 1515], ed. J. W. Mackail (Boston: The Merrymount Press, 1907), 3–11, 24–25, 34.

36

MARTIN LUTHER

MARTIN LUTHER (1483–1546), a German Augustinian monk, sparked the Protestant Reformation on October 31, 1517 with the publication of the "95 Theses." As a reformer, Luther affirmed "sola Scriptura," the primary authority of Scripture instead of church tradition and papal authority. Other key theological ideas included justification by faith—salvation by faith in the grace of Jesus Christ and not by works—and the priesthood of all believers. Luther translated the Bible into German, which facilitated making Scripture more accessible to the laity, and he married Katharine von Bora in 1525, setting an example of clerical marriage. His extensive writings—exegetical works, hymns, theological treatises, catechisms—widely influenced the spread of Protestantism across Europe. The selections below highlight Luther's contention that the Bible taught justification by faith alone as well as his attack on Rome's claim to be the sole interpreter of Scripture. The "95 Theses" reveal Luther's call for church reform, especially against the practice of penance through the sale of indulgences. The section on "sin boldly" is often cited in discussions of the ethics of borderline situations where all alternatives appear to be sinful and thus believers do the lesser of two evils.

---

95 Theses

1. Our Lord and Master Jesus Christ, in saying "Repent ye," etc., intended that the whole life of believers should be penitence.
2. This word cannot be understood of sacramental penance, that is, of the confession and satisfaction which are performed under the ministry of priests.

3. It does not, however, refer solely to inward penitence; nay such inward penitence is naught, unless it outwardly produces various mortifications of the flesh.

5. The Pope has neither the will nor the power to remit any penalties, except those which he has imposed by his own authority, or by that of the canons.

6. The Pope has no power to remit any guilt, except by declaring and warranting it to have been remitted by God . . .

20. Therefore the Pope, when he speaks of the full remission of all penalties, does not mean simply of all, but only of those imposed by himself.

21. Thus those preachers of indulgences are in error who say that, by the indulgences of the Pope, a man is freed and saved from all punishment.

27. They preach man, who say that the soul flies out of purgatory as soon as the money thrown into the chest rattles.

28. It is certain that, when the money rattles in the chest, avarice and gain may be increased, but the intercession of the Church depends on the will of God alone.

31. Rare as is a true penitent, so rare is one who truly buys indulgences— that is to say, most rare.

32. Those who believe that, through letters of pardon, they are made sure of their own salvation, will be eternally damned along with their teachers.

33. We must especially beware of those who say that these pardons from the Pope are that inestimable gift of God by which man is reconciled to God.

35. They preach no Christian doctrine, who teach that contrition is not necessary for those who buy souls out of purgatory or buy confessional licenses.

36. Every Christian who feels true compunction has of right full remission of pain and guilt, even without letters of pardon.

40. True contrition seeks and loves punishment; while the ampleness of pardons relaxes it, and causes men to hate it, or at least gives occasion for them to do so.

43. Christians should be taught that he who gives to a poor man, or lends to a needy man, does better than if he bought pardons.

44. Because, by a work of charity, charity increases and the man becomes better; while, by means of pardons, he does not become better, but only freer from punishment.

45. Christians should be taught that he who sees any one in need, but passes him by and instead gives money for pardons, is not purchasing for himself the indulgences of the Pope, but the anger of God.

50. Christians should be taught that, if the Pope were acquainted with the exactions of the preachers of pardons, he would prefer that the Basilica of St. Peter should be burnt to ashes, than that it should be built up with the skin, flesh, and bones of his sheep.

54. Wrong is done to the word of God when, in the same sermon, an equal or longer time is spent on pardons than on it.

62. The true treasure of the Church is the Holy Gospel of the glory and grace of God.

82. Why does not the Pope empty purgatory for the sake of most holy charity and of the supreme necessity of souls—this being the most just of all reasons—if he redeems an infinite number of souls for the sake of that most fatal thing, money, to be spent on building a basilica—this being a very slight reason?

86. Again: why does not the Pope, whose riches are at this day more ample than those of the wealthiest of the wealthy, build the one Basilica of St. Peter with his own money, rather than with that of poor believers?

87. Again: what does the Pope remit or impart to those who, through perfect contrition, have a right to full remission and participation?

94. Christians should be exhorted to strive to follow Christ their Head through pains, deaths, and hells

95. And thus trust to enter heaven through many tribulations, rather than in the security of peace.

Three Roman Walls

The Romanists have, with great cleverness, drawn three walls round themselves, with which they have until now protected themselves, so that no one could reform them, whereby all Christendom has fallen terribly.

Firstly, if pressed by the temporal power, they have affirmed and maintained that the temporal power has no jurisdiction over them, but, on the contrary, that the spiritual power is above the temporal.

Secondly, if one tried to admonish them with the Scriptures, they objected that no one may interpret the Scriptures but the Pope.

Thirdly, if they are threatened with a council, they pretend that no one may call a council but the Pope.

Thus they have secretly stolen our three rods, so that they may be unpunished, and entrenched themselves behind these three walls, to act with all the wickedness and malice, which we now witness. And whenever they have been compelled to call a council, they have made it of no avail by binding the princes beforehand with an oath to leave them as they were, and to give moreover to the Pope full power over the procedure of the council, so that it is all one whether we have many councils or no councils, in addition to which they deceive us with false pretenses and tricks. So grievously do they tremble for their skin before a true, free council; and thus they have overawed kings and princes, that these believe they would be offending God, if they were not to obey them in all such knavish, deceitful tricks . . .

The First Wall

Let, us, in the first place, attack the first wall.

It has been devised that the Pope, bishops, priests, and monks are called the *spiritual estate*, princes, lords, artificers, and peasants are the *temporal estate*. This is an artful lie and hypocritical device, but let no one fear it because all Christians are truly of the spiritual estate, and there is no difference among them, except for office. As St. Paul says (1 Cor. 12) we are all one body, though each member does his own work, to serve others. This is because we have one baptism, one Gospel, one faith, and we are all Christians; for baptism, Gospel, and faith, these alone make spiritual and Christian people.

As for the anointing by a pope or a bishop, tonsure, ordination, consecration, and clothes differing from those of lay people—all this may make a hypocrite or an anointed puppet, but never a Christian or a spiritual man. Thus we are all consecrated as priests by baptism, as St. Peter says: "You are a royal priesthood, a holy nation" (I Pet. 2:9); and in the book of Revelation: "and has made us to our God (by your blood) kings and priests" (Rev. 5:10) . . . In cases of necessity every man can baptize and absolve, which would not be possible if we were not all priests . . .

We, see then, that just as those that we call spiritual, or priests, bishops, or popes, do not differ from other Christians in any other or higher degree but in that they are to be concerned with the word of God and the sacraments—that being their work and office—in the same way the temporal authorities hold the sword and the rod in their hands to punish the wicked and to protect the good. A cobbler, a smith, a peasant, every man, has the office and function of his calling, and yet all alike are consecrated priests and bishops, and every man should by his office or function be useful and beneficial to the rest, so that various kinds of work may all be untied for the furtherance of body and soul, just as the members of the body all serve one another.

The Second Wall

The second wall is even more tottering and weak: that they alone pretend to be considered masters of the Scriptures; although they learn nothing of them all their life. They assume authority, and juggle before us with impudent words, saying that the Pope cannot err in matters of faith, whether he be evil or good, even though they cannot prove it by a single letter. That is why the canon law contains so many heretical and unchristian, nay unnatural, laws . . . But not to fight them with our own words, we will quote the Scriptures. St. Paul says, "If anything be revealed to another who is sitting down let the first hold his peace" (1 Cor. 14:30). What would be the use of this commandment, if we were to believe him alone that teaches or has the highest seat? Christ Himself says, "And they shall be all taught of God" (John 6:45). Thus it may come to pass that the Pope and his followers are wicked and not true Christians, and not being taught by God, have no true understanding, whereas a common man may have true understanding. Why should we then not follow him? Has not the Pope often erred? Who could help Christianity, in case the Pope errs, if we do not rather believe another who has the Scriptures for him?

Therefore it is a wickedly devised fable—and they cannot quote a single letter to confirm it—that it is for the Pope alone to interpret the Scriptures or to confirm the interpretation of them. They have assumed the authority of their own selves. And though they say that this authority was given to St. Peter when the keys were given to him, it is plain enough that the keys were not given to St. Peter alone, but to the whole community. Besides, the keys were not ordained for doctrine or authority, but for sin, to bind or loose; and what they claim besides this from the keys is mere invention. But what Christ said to St. Peter: "I have prayed for you that your faith fail not" (Luke 22:32), cannot be said of the Pope, inasmuch as the greater part of the Popes have been without faith, as they are themselves forced to acknowledge; nor did

Christ pray for Peter alone, but for all the Apostles and all Christians, as He says, "Neither pray I for these alone, but for them also which shall believe on Me through their word" (John 17:20). Is not this plain enough?

Only consider the matter. They must acknowledge that there are pious Christians among us that have the true faith, spirit, understanding, word, and mind of Christ. Why then should we reject their word and understanding, and follow a pope who has neither understanding nor spirit? Surely this would be to deny our whole faith and the Christian Church. Moreover, if the article of our faith is right, "I believe in the holy Christian Church," the Pope cannot alone be right; else we must say, "I believe in the Pope of Rome," and reduce the Christian Church to one man, which is a devilish and damnable heresy. Besides that, we are all priests, as I have said, and have all one faith, one Gospel, one Sacrament; how then should we not have the power of discerning and judging what is right or wrong in matters of faith? What becomes of St. Paul's words, "But he that is spiritual judges all things, yet he himself is judged of no man" (1 Cor. 2:15), and also, "we having the same spirit of faith"? (1 Cor. 4:13). Why then should we not perceive as well as an unbelieving pope what agrees or disagrees with our faith?

By these and many other texts we should gain courage and freedom, and should not let the spirit of liberty (as St. Paul has it) be frightened away by the inventions of the popes; we should boldly judge what they do and what they leave undone by our own believing understanding of the Scriptures, and force them to follow the better understanding, and not their own. Did not Abraham in old days have to obey his Sarah, who was in stricter bondage to him than we are to any one on earth? Thus, too, Balaam's ass was wiser than the prophet. If God spoke by an ass against a prophet, why should He not speak by a pious man against the Pope? Besides, St. Paul withstood St. Peter as being in error (Gal. 2). Therefore it behooves every Christian to aid the faith by understanding and defending it and by condemning all errors.

Justification by Faith, not Works

A Christian man is the most free lord of all, and subject to none; a Christian man is the most dutiful servant of all, and subject to everyone.

Although these statements appear contradictory, yet, when they are found to agree together, they will make excellently for my purpose. They are both the statements of Paul himself, who says, "Though I be free from all men, yet have I made myself servant unto all" (1 Cor. 9:19), and "Owe no man anything, but to love one another" (Rom. 13:8). Now love is by its own nature dutiful and obedient to the beloved object. Thus even Christ, though Lord of all things, was yet made of a woman; made under the law; at once free and a servant; at once in the form of God and in the form of a servant.

Let us examine the subject on a deeper and less simple principle. Man is composed of a twofold nature, spirit and body. As regards the spiritual nature, which they name the soul, he is called the spiritual, inward, new man; as regards the bodily nature, which they name the flesh, he is called the fleshly, outward, old man. The Apostle speaks of this: "Though our outward man perish, yet the inward man is renewed day by day" (1 Cor. 4:16). The result of this diversity is that in the Scriptures opposing statements are made concerning the same man, the fact being that in the same man these two men are opposed to one another; the flesh lusting against the spirit, and the Spirit against the flesh (Gal. 5:17).

We first approach the subject of the inward man, that we may see by what means a man becomes justified, free, and a true Christian; that is, a spiritual, new, and inward man. It is certain that absolutely none among outward things, under whatever name they may be reckoned, has any influence in producing Christian righteousness or liberty, nor, on the other hand, unrighteousness or slavery . . .

And to cast everything aside, even speculation, meditations, and whatever things can be performed by the exertions of the soul itself, are of no profit. One thing, and one alone, is necessary for life, justification, and Christian liberty; and that is the most holy word of God, the Gospel of Christ, as He says, "I am the resurrection and the life; he that believes in Me shall not die eternally" (John 11:25), and also, "If the Son shall make you free, you shall be free indeed" (John 8:36) and "Man shall not live by bread alone, but by every word that proceeds out of the mouth of God" (Matt. 4:4) . . .

But you will ask, What is this word, and by what means is it to be used, since there are so many words of God? I answer, The Apostle Paul (Rom. 1) explains what it is, namely the Gospel of God, concerning His Son, incarnate, suffering, risen, and glorified, through the Spirit, the Sanctifier. To preach Christ is to feed the soul, to justify it, to set it free, and to save it, if it believes the preaching. For faith alone and the efficacious use of the word of God bring salvation. "If you shall confess with thy mouth the Lord Jesus, and shall believe in your heart that God has raised Him from the dead, you shall be saved" (Rom. 10:9) . . . and "The just shall live by faith" (Rom. 1:17). For the word of God cannot be received and honored by any works, but by faith alone. Thus it is clear that as the soul needs the word alone for life and justification, so it is justified by faith alone, and not by any works.

. . . For this would be to halt between two opinions, to worship Baal, and to kiss the hand of him, which is a very great iniquity, as Job says. Therefore, when you begin to believe, you learn at the same time that all that is in you is utterly guilty, sinful, and damnable, according to that saying, "All have sinned, and come short of the glory of God" (Rom. 3:23), and also: "There is none righteous, no, not one; they are all gone out of the way; they are together become unprofitable: there is none that do good, no, not one" (Rom. 3:10-12). When you have learned this, you will know that Christ is necessary for you, since He has suffered and risen again for you, that, believing on Him, you might by this faith become another man, all your sins being remitted, and you being justified by the merits of another, namely of Christ alone . . .

And now let us turn to the other part: to the outward man. Here we shall give an answer to all those who, taking offense at the word of faith and at what I have asserted, say, "If faith does everything, and by itself suffices for justification, why then are good works commanded? Are we then to take our ease and do no works, content with faith?" Not so, impious men, I reply; not so. That would indeed really be the case, if we were thoroughly and completely inner and spiritual persons; but that will not happen until the last day, when the dead shall be raised. As long as we live in the flesh, we are but beginning and making advances in that which shall be completed in a future life. On this account the Apostle calls that which we have in this life the first fruits of the Spirit (Rom. 8:23). In the future we shall have the tenths, and the fullness of the Spirit. To this part belongs the fact I have stated before: that the Christian is the servant of all and subject to all. For in that part in which he is free he does no works, but in that in which he is a servant he does all works . . .

These works, however, must not be done with any notion that by them a man can be justified before God—for faith, which alone is righteousness before God, will not bear with this false notion—but solely with this purpose: that the body may be brought into subjection, and be purified from its evil lusts, so that our eyes may be turned only to purging away those lusts. For when the soul has been cleansed by faith and made to love God, it would have all things to be cleansed in like manner, and especially its own body, so that all things might unite with it in the love and praise of God. Thus it comes that, from the requirement of his own body, a man cannot take his ease, but is compelled on its account to do many good works, that he may bring it into subjection. Yet these works are not the means of his justification before God; he does them out of disinterested love to the service of God;

looking to no other end than to do what is well-pleasing to Him whom he desires to obey most dutifully in all things . . .

True, then, are these two sayings: "Good works do not make a good man, but a good man does good works"; "Bad works do not make a bad man, but a bad man does bad works." Thus it is always necessary that the substance or person should be good before any good works can be done, and that good works should follow and proceed from a good person. As Christ says, "A good tree cannot bring forth evil fruit, neither can a corrupt tree bring forth good fruit" (Matt. 7:18). Now it is clear that the fruit does not bear the tree, nor does the tree grow on the fruit; but, on the contrary, the trees bear the fruit, and the fruit grows on the trees.

Sin Boldly

If you are a preacher of grace, preach not a fictitious grace, but a true grace. If it is a true grace, let it deal with true, not fictitious sin. God does not save fictitious sinners. Be a sinner and sin boldly, but still more boldly believe and rejoice in Christ, who is conqueror of sin, of death, and of the world. Sin is a necessity so long as we are in our present state. This life is not the habitation of righteousness, but we, says Peter, look for new heavens and a new earth in which righteousness dwells (2 Pet. 3:13). It is enough that we have known, through the riches of glory, the Lamb of God, who takes away the sin of the world. Sin will not separate us from Him, although we commit fornication or murder a thousand times in one day. Do you think that it is a small price that has been paid, a small redemption that has been made, for our sins by so great and such a Lamb? Pray boldly, for you are the boldest of sinners.

SOURCE: Martin Luther, *Ninety-Five Theses*, ed. Charles W. Eliot, *The Harvard Classics*, vol. 36 (New York: P. F. Collier & Son, 1910), 265–72. In the same Eliot edition, *To the German Nobility*, 274–86, and *Concerning Christian Liberty*, 353–97. Section on "Sin Boldly" found in "Letter, Martin Luther to Philip Melanchthon, August 1, 1521," Peter Bayne, *Martin Luther, His Life and Work*, vol. 2 (London: Cassell and Co., 1887), 156–57.

37

ANNE ASKEW

Aᴺᴺᴇ Aꜱᴋᴇᴡ (1521–1546), an English Protestant martyr, was the only woman known to be tortured at the Tower of London before being burned at the stake. She abandoned her husband and son in order to distribute Protestant literature. She was arrested for possessing banned books, but escaped and continued to preach. At her second arrest, she was tortured to attempt to force her to share names of other Protestant preachers in England, but she outlasted her torturers. King Henry VIII ordered Askew to be burned at the stake, to which she was carried in a chair because she had been so severely tortured at the Tower.

Prelude to Martyrdom

To satisfy your expectation, good people, this was my first examination in the year of our Lord 1545, and in the month of March, first Christopher Dare examined me at Saddlers Hall, being one of the jury, and asked if I did not believe that the sacrament hanging over the altar was the very body of Christ really. Then I demanded this question of him, why was St. Steven stoned to death? And he said he could not tell. Then I answered that I would not address his vain question any more . . . Secondly he said that there was a woman who testified that I would read that God was not in temples made with hands. Then I showed him what Steven and Paul had said in the seventh and the twelfth chapters of the Apostles' Acts. Then he asked me, how I took those sentences? I answered that I would not throw pearls among swine, for acorns were good enough . . . Thirdly he asked me the reason why I said that I had rather read five lines in the Bible, than to hear five masses in the temple. I confessed that I said no less. I was not criticizing the Epistle or the Gospel but reading the Bible greatly edified me but the masses did not. As St. Paul witnessed in 1 Corinthians 14 [v. 8], "If the trumpet gives an uncertain sound, who will prepare himself to the battle?" . . . Fourthly he accused me that I should say, if an ill [*i.e., wicked*] priest ministered, it was the devil and not God. My answer was that I never spoke such thing. What I said was, whoever ministered to me, his ill [*wicked*] condition could not hurt my faith. But in spirit I received, nevertheless, the body and blood of Christ . . . Fifthly he asked me, what I said concerning confession. I answered him, as St. James says, that every man ought to acknowledge his faults to another and to pray for the other . . . Seventhly he asked me, if I had the spirit of God in me? I answered if I had it not, I was but a reprobate or caste away . . . Eighthly he asked me, if I did not think that private masses helped departed souls. And I said, it was great idolatry to believe in them more than in the death which Christ died for us . . . Besides this my lord Mayor made an accusation against me which was never spoken of me, but of them. And that was whether a mouse eating the host, received God or not? I never asked this question but indeed they asked it of me. I gave them no answer, but smiled . . . Then the bishop's chancellor rebuked me, and said that I was much to blame for uttering the scriptures. For St. Paul (he said) forbade women to speak or to talk of the word of God. I answered him that I knew Paul's meaning as well as he, which is 1 Corinthians 14 [v. 34], that a woman ought not to speak in the congregation by the way of teaching. And then I asked him, how many women he had seen go into the pulpit and preach. He said he never saw one. Then I said, he ought to find no fault in poor women unless they had offended the law.

SOURCE: Anne Askew, *The first examination[n] of Anne Askew lately martyred in Smithfield, by the Romish popes upholders, with the elucidation of John Bale* ([London: Printed by Nicholas Hill?], 1546 [1547?]).

38

ACT OF SUPREMACY

THE ACT OF SUPREMACY (1534) is a legislative act of the English parliament which recognized King Henry VIII as the supreme head of the Church of England. Before the act, the English church, like most European churches at the time, recognized the Roman pope as its leader. The act broke the English church away from Rome, starting the English Reformation. Henry pressured parliament to pass the act in large part to circumvent the pope, who refused to annul Henry's marriage to Catherine of Aragon. The king needed a male heir to succeed him but with Catherine he had only had a daughter, Mary. After the act, he no longer needed the pope's approval. Later, Queen Mary repealed her father's act, but her sister, Elizabeth I, issued a second act of supremacy which is still in effect today.

The King as Head of the Church

Albeit the King's Majesty justly and rightfully is and ought to be the Supreme Head of the Church of England, and so is recognized by the clergy of this realm in their Convocations; yet nevertheless for corroboration and confirmation thereof, and for increase of virtue in Christ's religion within this realm of England, and to repress and extirp all errors, heresies, and other enormities and abuses heretofore used in the same: Be it enacted by authority of this present Parliament that the King our Sovereign Lord, his heirs and successors kings of this realm, shall be taken, accepted, and reputed the only Supreme Head in earth of the Church of England called *Anglicana Ecclesia*, and shall have and enjoy annexed and united to the imperial Crown of this realm as well the title and style thereof, as all honors, dignities, preeminences, jurisdictions, privileges, authorities, immunities, profits, and commodities to the said dignity of the Supreme Head of the same Church belonging and appertaining: And that our said Sovereign Lord, his heirs and successors kings of this realm, shall have full power and authority from time to time to visit, repress, redress, reform, order, correct, restrain, and amend all such errors, heresies, abuses, offenses, contempts, and enormities, whatsoever they be, which by any manner spiritual authority or jurisdiction ought or may lawfully be reformed, repressed, ordered, redressed, corrected, restrained, or amended, most to the pleasure of Almighty God, the increase of virtue in Christ's religion, and for the conservation of the peace, unity, and tranquility of this realm; any usage, custom, foreign laws, foreign authority, prescription, or any other thing or things to the contrary hereof notwithstanding.

SOURCE: J. R. Tanner, ed., *Tudor Constitutional Documents A.D. 1485–1603, with an historical commentary* (Cambridge: Cambridge University Press, 1922), 46.

39

JOHN CALVIN

JOHN CALVIN (1509–1564) is considered one of the most significant figures of the Protestant Reformation. The "Reformed tradition" is tied to his teachings. In 1536 he published the *Institutes of the Christian Religion*, one of the most influential systematic expositions of Protestantism. He revised and enlarged the *Institutes* until the work appeared in its final form in 1559. Rejecting both transubstantiation, the Roman Catholic position, and consubstantiation, the Lutheran position, Calvin offered a less metaphysical "spiritual presence" understanding of the Lord's Supper, in which the Spirit participated in communion with the believer to strengthen him. Calvin is also known for his views on the sovereignty of God, double predestination, and infant baptism as a sign of God's covenant with the elect. His teachings and establishment of the "Holy Commonwealth" in Geneva greatly influenced English Protestantism, especially seen in the development of Puritan theology and Presbyterian polity.

God's Providence

As the minds of men are prone to vain subtleties, there is the greatest danger that those who know not the right use of this doctrine will embarrass themselves with intricate perplexities. It will therefore be necessary to touch in a brief manner on the end and design of the Scripture doctrine of the divine ordination of all things. And here let it be remarked, in the first place, that the providence of God is to be considered in regard to the future and the past; secondly, that it governs all things in such a manner as to operate sometimes by the intervention of means, sometimes without means, and sometimes in opposition to all means; lastly, that it tends to show the care of God for the whole human race, and especially his vigilance in the government of the church, which he favors with more particular attention. It must also be observed, that although the fatherly favor and beneficence of God, or the severity of his justice is frequently conspicuous in the whole course of his providence, yet sometimes the causes of events are concealed, so that a suspicion intrudes itself, that the revolutions of human affairs are conducted by the blind impulse of fortune; or the flesh solicits us to murmur, as though God amused himself with tossing men about like tennis-balls . . . So it must be concluded, that while the turbulent state of the world deprives us of our judgment, God, by the pure light of his own righteousness and wisdom, regulates all those commotions in the most exact order, and directs them to their proper end. And certainly the madness of many in this respect is monstrous, who dare to criticize the works of God, to scrutinize his secret counsels, and even to pass a rash sentence on things unknown, with greater freedom than on the actions of mortal men. For what is more preposterous than to observe such modesty towards our equals, as rather to suspend our judgment than to incur the imputation of boldness, but impudently to insult the mysterious judgments of God, which we ought to hold in admiration and reverence?

None, therefore, will attain just and profitable views of the providence of God, but the one who considers that he has to deal with his Maker and the Creator of the world, and submits himself to fear and reverence with all humility. Thus it happens that so many worthless characters in the present day virulently oppose this doctrine, because they will admit nothing to be lawful for God but what agrees with the dictates of their own reason. They shamelessly revile us, because, not content with the precepts of the law which comprehend the will of God, we say that the world is governed also by his secret counsels; as though what we assert were only an invention of our own brain, and the Holy Spirit did not everywhere plainly announce the same, and repeat it in innumerable forms of expression. But as they are restrained by some degree of shame from daring to discharge their blasphemies against heaven, in order to indulge their extravagance with greater freedom, they pretend that they are contending with us. But unless they admit that whatever comes to pass in the world is governed by the incomprehensible counsel of God, let them answer, to what purpose is it said in the Scripture that his "judgments are a great deep"? (Ps. 36:6) For since Moses proclaims, that the will of God is not to be sought far off, in the clouds or in the deep, (Deut. 30:12-14; Rom. 10:6-7) because it is familiarly explained in the law, it follows that there is another secret will, which is compared to a profound abyss; concerning which Paul also says, "O the depth of the riches both of the wisdom and knowledge of God; how unsearchable are his judgments, and his ways past finding out! For who has known the mind of the Lord, or who has been his counselor?" (Rom. 11:33-34) It is true, that the law and the Gospel contain mysteries which far transcend our capacities; but since God illuminates the minds of his people with the spirit of understanding, to apprehend these mysteries which he has condescended to reveal in his Word, there we have now no abyss, but a way in which we may safely walk, and a lamp for the direction of our feet, the light of life, and the school of certain and evident truth. But his admirable method of governing the world is justly called a "great deep," because, while it is concealed from our view, it ought to be the object of our profound adoration.

Scripture

Though the light which presents itself to all eyes, both in heaven and in earth, is more than sufficient to deprive the ingratitude of men of every excuse, since God, in order to involve all mankind in the same guilt, sets before them all, without exception, an exhibition of his majesty, delineated in creatures—yet we need another and better assistance, properly to direct us to the Creator of the world. Therefore he has not unnecessarily added the light of his Word, to make himself known unto salvation, and has honored with this privilege those whom he intended to unite in a closer and intimate connection with himself. For, seeing the minds of all men to be agitated with unstable dispositions, when he had chosen the Jews as his peculiar flock, he enclosed them as in a fold so that they might not wander after the vanities of other nations. And it is not without cause that he preserves us in the pure knowledge of himself by the same means; for, otherwise, they who seem to stand firm, would soon fall. For, as persons who are old, or whose eyes are by any means become dim, if you show them the most beautiful book, though they perceive something written, can scarcely read two words together, yet, by the assistance of spectacles, will begin to read distinctly—so the Scripture, collecting in our minds the otherwise confused notions of deity, dispels the darkness, and gives us a clear view of the true God.

God's Predestination

We shall never be clearly convinced as we ought to be, that our salvation flows from the fountain of God's free mercy until we are acquainted with his eternal election, which illustrates the grace of God by this contrast, that he does not indiscriminately adopt all to the hope of salvation, but gives to some what he refuses to others. Ignorance of this principle detracts from the Divine glory and diminishes real humility. But according to Paul, what is so necessary to be known, never can be known, unless God, without any regard to works, chooses those whom he has decreed. "At this present time also, there is a remnant according to the election of grace. And if by grace, then it is no more of works; otherwise, grace is no more grace. But if it be of works, then it is no more grace; otherwise; work is no more work" (Rom. 11:5-6) . . . In ascribing the salvation of the remnant of the people to the election of grace, Paul clearly testifies, that it is then only known that God saves whom he will of his mere good pleasure and does not dispense a reward to which there can be any claim. They who shut the gates to prevent anyone from presuming to approach and taste this doctrine, do no less injury to man than to God; for nothing else will be sufficient to produce in us suitable humility, or to impress us with a due sense of our great obligations to God. Nor is there any other basis for solid confidence, even according to the authority of Christ, who, in order to deliver us from all fear and render us invincible amidst so many dangers, snares, and deadly conflicts, promises to preserve in safety all whom the Father has committed to his care. . . . First, then, let them remember that when they inquire into predestination, they penetrate the inmost recesses of divine wisdom, where the careless and confident intruder will obtain no satisfaction to his curiosity, but will enter a labyrinth from which he will find no way to depart. For it is unreasonable that man should scrutinize with impunity those things which the Lord has determined to be hidden in himself; and investigate, even from eternity, that sublimity of wisdom which God would have us to adore and not comprehend, to promote our admiration of his glory . . .

No pious person dares to absolutely deny predestination, by which God adopts some to the hope of life, and adjudges others to eternal death. Those who make foreknowledge its cause wrap it up in trivial objections. We maintain that both belong to God; but it is preposterous to represent one as dependent on the other. When we attribute foreknowledge to God, we mean that all things have ever been, and perpetually remain, before his eyes, so that to his knowledge nothing is future or past, but all things are present; and present in such a manner, that he does not merely conceive of them from ideas formed in his mind, as things remembered by us appear present to our minds, but really beholds and sees them as if actually placed before him.

And this foreknowledge extends to the whole world, and to all the creatures. Predestination we call the eternal decree of God, by which he has determined in himself, what he would have to become of every individual person. For they are not all created with a similar destiny; but eternal life is foreordained for some, and eternal damnation for others. Every man, therefore, being created for one or the other of these ends, we say, is predestinated either to life or to death. This God has not only testified in particular persons, but has given a specimen of it in the whole posterity of Abraham, which should evidently show the future condition of every nation to depend upon his decision. "When the Most High divided the nations, when he separated the sons of Adam, the Lord's portion was his people; Jacob was the lot of his inheritance" (Deut. 32:8-9). The separation is before the eyes of all: in the person of Abraham, as in the dry trunk of a tree, one people is peculiarly chosen, while others are rejected. No reason for this appears, except that Moses, to deprive their posterity of all occasion of glorying, teaches them that their exaltation is wholly from God's gratuitous love. He assigns this reason for their deliverance, that "he loved their fathers, and chose their seed after them" (Deut. 4:37). More fully in another chapter: "The Lord did not set his love upon you, nor choose you, because you were more in number than any people; but because the Lord loved you" (Deut. 7:7-8). . . . For the gifts given to them by God all attest to gratuitous love, not only from a consciousness that these were not obtained by any merit of theirs, but from a conviction that the holy patriarch himself was not endued with such excellence as to acquire the privilege of so great an honor for himself and his posterity.

Baptism

As God, when he adopts the posterity of Abraham to be his people, commands them to be circumcised, so Moses pronounces it to be necessary to circumcise the heart, thereby declaring the true signification of that carnal circumcision. Then, that no one might attempt this in his own strength, he teaches that it is the work of Divine grace. All these things are so often inculcated by the prophets, that there is no need to collect here the numerous testimonies which everywhere present themselves. We have ascertained, therefore, that a spiritual promise, the very same which is given to us in baptism, was given to the fathers in circumcision; which represented to them remission of sins and the mortification of the flesh. Moreover, as we have shown that Christ, in whom both these things are achieved, is the foundation of baptism, the same must be evident of circumcision. For he was promised to Abraham, and in him the blessing of all nations; and the sign of circumcision was added in confirmation of this grace.

There is now no difficulty in discovering what similarity or what difference there is between these two signs. The promise, in which we have stated the virtue of the signs to consist, is the same in both, including the paternal favor of God, remission of sins, and eternal life. In the next place, the thing signified also is one and the same, namely, regeneration. The foundation, on which the accomplishment of these things rests, is the same in both. Thus there is no difference in the internal mystery, by which all the force and peculiar nature of sacraments must be determined. All the difference lies in the external ceremony, which is the smallest portion of it; whereas the principal part depends on the promise and the thing signified.

Eucharist

Our souls are fed by the flesh and blood of Christ just as our bodily life is preserved and sustained by bread and wine. For otherwise the analogy of the sign would not be fitting, if our souls did not find their food in Christ; which cannot be the case unless Christ truly becomes one with us, and refreshes us by the eating of his flesh and the drinking of his blood. Though it appears incredible for the flesh of Christ, from such an immense distance, to reach us, so as to become our food, we should remember how much the secret power of the Holy Spirit transcends all our senses, and what folly it is to apply any measure of ours to his immensity. Let our faith receive, therefore, what our understanding is not able to comprehend, that the Spirit really unites things which are separated by great distance.

Now, that holy partaking of his flesh and blood, by which Christ communicates his life to us, just as if he actually penetrated every part of our frame, in the sacred supper he also testifies and seals; and that not by the exhibition of a vain or ineffectual sign, but by the exertion of the energy of his Spirit, by which he accomplishes that which he promises. And the thing signified he exhibits and offers to all who come to that spiritual banquet; though it is advantageously enjoyed by believers alone, who receive such great goodness with true faith and gratitude of mind. For which reason the apostle said, "The cup of blessing which we bless, is it not the communion of the blood of Christ? The bread which we break, is it not the communion of the body of Christ?" (1 Cor. 10:16) Nor is there any cause to object, that it is a figurative expression, by which the name of the thing signified is given to the sign. I grant that the breaking of the bread is symbolical, and not the substance itself: yet, this being admitted, from the display of the symbol we may justly infer the display of the substance; for, unless any one would call God a deceiver, he can never presume to affirm that he sets before us an empty sign. Therefore, if, by the breaking of the bread, the Lord truly represents the participation of his body, it ought not to be doubted that he truly presents and communicates it. And it must always be a rule with believers, whenever they see the signs instituted by the Lord, to assure and persuade themselves that they are also accompanied with the truth of the thing signified. For to what end would the Lord deliver into our hands the symbol of his body, except to assure us of a real participation of it? If it be true that the visible sign is given to us to seal the donation of the invisible substance, we ought to have a confident assurance that in receiving the symbol of his body, we at the same time truly receive the body itself . . .

Now, if anyone should ask me the manner in which this takes place, I will not be ashamed to acknowledge that it is a mystery too sublime for me to be able to express, or even to comprehend, and to be still more explicit, I rather experience it than understand it . . .

Civil Government

Civil government is designed, as long as we live in this world, to cherish and support the external worship of God, to preserve the pure doctrine of religion, to defend the constitution of the Church, to regulate our lives in a manner requisite for the society of men, to form our manners to civil justice, to promote our concord with each other, and to establish general peace and tranquility; all which I confess to be superfluous if the kingdom of God, as it now exists in us, extinguishes the present life. But if it is the will of God, that while we are aspiring towards our true country we are pilgrims on the earth, and if such aids are necessary to our pilgrimage, they who take them from man deprive him of his human nature . . .

It is equally as necessary to mankind as bread, water, sun, and air; indeed, its place of honor is far more excellent. For it not only tends to secure the accommodations arising from all these things, that men may breathe, eat, drink and be sustained in life, though it surely contains all these things as it causes them to live together, this is not its only function. It also ensures that idolatry, sacrileges against the name of God, blasphemies against his truth, and other offenses against religion, may not openly appear and be disseminated among the people; that the public tranquility may not be disturbed; that every person may enjoy his property without harm; that men may transact their business together without fraud or injustice; that integrity and modesty may be cultivated among them; in short that there may be a public form of religion among Christians, and that humanity may be maintained among men . . .

The Lord has not only testified that the function of magistrates has his approval and acceptance, but has eminently commended it to us, by dignifying it with the most honorable titles . . .

Source: John Calvin, *Institutes of the Christian Religion*, trans. John Allen, 6th ed., 2 vols. (Philadelphia: Presbyterian Board of Publication, 1857). "God's Providence" is from 1:194–97 (*Institutes* I.xvii.1-2). "Scripture" is from 1:71 (*Institutes* I.vi.1). "God's Predestination" is from 2:140–42 (*Institutes* III.xxi.1) and 2:144–46 (*Institutes* III.xxi.5). "Baptism" is from 2:496 (*Institutes* IV.xvi.3-4). "Eucharist" is from 2:533–35, 562 (*Institutes* IV.xvii.10-11, 32). "Civil Government" is from 2:634–37 (*Institutes* IV.xx.2-4).

40

WESTMINSTER CONFESSION

DRAFTED IN 1646, through five years of meetings of the Westminster Assembly, the Westminster Confession defined orthodox theology for the Church of England in the mid-seventeenth century. It adopted Presbyterian theology and polity, moving away from the episcopal polity of Anglicanism. The Confession helped to solidify Puritan/Calvinist understandings of theology. Selections below address the priority of Scripture, the role of covenant in Calvinist thought, and infant baptism as the sign of the covenant.

Scripture

6. The whole counsel of God, concerning all things necessary for his own glory, man's salvation, faith, and life, is either expressly set down in Scripture, or by good and necessary consequence may be deduced from Scripture: unto which nothing at any time is to be added, whether by new revelations of the Spirit, or traditions of men. Nevertheless we acknowledge the inward illumination of the Spirit of God to be necessary for the saving understanding of such things as are revealed in the Word; and that there are some circumstances concerning the worship of God, and government of the Church, common to human actions and societies, which are to be ordered by the light of nature and Christian prudence, according to the general rules of the Word, which are always to be observed.

7. All things in Scripture are not alike plain in themselves, nor alike clear unto all; yet those things which are necessary to be known, believed, and observed, for salvation, are so clearly propounded and opened in some place of Scripture or other, that not only the learned, but the unlearned, in a due use of the ordinary means, may attain unto a sufficient understanding of them.

9. The infallible rule of interpretation of Scripture, is the Scripture itself; and therefore, when there is a question about the true and full sense of any scripture (which is not manifold, but one), it may be searched and known by other places that speak more clearly.

Covenant

1. The distance between God and the creature is so great, that although reasonable creatures do owe obedience unto him as their Creator, yet they could never have any fruition of him, as their blessedness and reward, but by some voluntary condescension on God's part, which he hath been pleased to express by way of covenant.

2. The first covenant made with man was a covenant of works, wherein life was promised to Adam, and in him to his posterity, upon condition of perfect and personal obedience.

3. Man, by his Fall, having made himself incapable of life by that covenant, the Lord was pleased to make a second, commonly called the covenant of grace: wherein he freely offered unto sinners life and salvation by Jesus Christ, requiring of them faith in him, that they may be saved, and promising to give unto all those that are ordained unto life, his Holy Spirit, to make them willing and able to believe.

4. This covenant of grace is frequently set forth in the Scripture by the name of a testament, in reference to the death of Jesus Christ, the testator, and to the everlasting inheritance, with all things belonging to it, therein bequeathed.

5. This covenant was differently administered in the time of the law, and in the time of the gospel: under the law it was administered by promises, prophecies, sacrifices, circumcision, the paschal lamb, and other types and ordinances delivered to the people of the Jews, all foresignifying Christ to come, which were for that time sufficient and efficacious, through the operation of the Spirit, to instruct and build up the elect in faith in the promised Messiah, by whom they had full remission of sins, and eternal salvation; and is called the Old Testament.

6. Under the gospel, when Christ the substance was exhibited, the ordinances in which this covenant is dispensed, are the preaching of the Word, and the administration of the sacraments of Baptism and the Lord's Supper; which, though fewer in number, and administered with more simplicity and less outward glory, yet in them it is held forth in more fullness, evidence, and spiritual efficacy, to all nations, both Jews and Gentiles; and is called the New Testament. There are not, therefore, two covenants of grace differing in substance, but one and the same under various dispensations.

Baptism

1. Baptism is a sacrament of the New Testament, ordained by Jesus Christ, not only for the solemn admission of the party baptized into the visible Church, but also to be unto him a sign and seal of the covenant of grace, of his ingrafting into Christ, of regeneration, of remission of sins, and of his giving up unto God, through Jesus Christ, to walk in newness of life: which sacrament is, by Christ's own appointment, to be continued in his church until the end of the world.

2. The outward element to be used in this sacrament is water, wherewith the party is to be baptized in the name of the Father, and of the Son, and of the Holy Ghost, by a minister of the gospel, lawfully called thereunto.

3. Dipping of the person into the water is not necessary, but baptism is rightly administered by pouring or sprinkling water upon the person.

4. Not only those that do actually profess faith in and obedience unto Christ, but also the infants of one or both believing parents are to be baptized.

5. Although it be a great sin to contemn or neglect this ordinance, yet grace and salvation are not so inseparably annexed unto it as that no person can be regenerated or saved without it, or that all that are baptized are undoubtedly regenerated.

6. The efficacy of Baptism is not tied to that moment of time wherein it is administered; yet, notwithstanding, by the right use of this ordinance the grace promised is not only offered, but really exhibited and conferred by the Holy Ghost, to such (whether of age or infants) as that grace belongeth unto, according to the counsel of God's own will, in his appointed time.

7. The sacrament of Baptism is but once to be administered to any person.

Source: *The Book of Confessions* (PCUSA) (Louisville, Ky.: Office of the General Assembly, 2002), 123, 128–29, 154–55. Reprinted with permission of the Office of the General Assembly, PC (USA).

41

MENNO SIMONS

AFTER EXTENSIVE STUDY OF SCRIPTURE, MENNO SIMONS (1496–1561) left the Roman Catholic Church in the 1520s, rejecting transubstantiation and infant baptism. He affirmed believer's baptism, separation from the world, and repudiation of violence. His followers, known as Mennonites, became a driving force in the Radical Reformation and are still a thriving Believers' Church today. The selection below includes Menno's focus on believer's baptism, the Lord's Supper as a memorial, pacifism, and the necessity of keeping the church pure through church discipline, also known as the ban.

Baptism

Here we have the Lord's command concerning baptism, when and how, after the ordinance of God, it shall be administered and received; namely, that the gospel must first be preached, and then those baptized who believe in it, as Christ says "Go ye into all the world, and preach the gospel to every creature; he that believes and is baptized shall be saved, but he that believes not, shall be damned" (Mark 16:15). Thus has the Lord commanded and ordered; therefore, let no other be taught or practiced forever. The word of God abides forever. Young children are without understanding and cannot be taught, therefore, baptism cannot be administered to them without perverting the ordinance of the Lord; misusing his exalted name, and doing violence to his holy word. In the New Testament there are no ordinances enjoined upon infants, for it treats, both in doctrines and sacraments, with those who have ears to hear, and hearts to understand (Matt. 13:16). Even as Christ commanded, so the holy apostles also taught and practiced, as may be plainly perceived in many parts of the New Testament. Thus Peter said "Repent, and be baptized every one of you in the name of Jesus Christ for the remission of sins, and you shall receive the gift of the Holy Spirit" (Acts 2:38). Again, Philip said to the eunuch, "If you believe with all your heart, you may" (Acts 8:37). Here, faith did not follow baptism, but baptism followed faith (Mark 16:16) . . .

Since we have not a single command in the Scriptures that infants are to be baptized, or that the apostles practiced it, we modestly confess, with a good conscience, that infant baptism is but human invention; a selfish notion;

a perversion of the ordinance of Christ; a manifest abomination, standing in the holy place, where it ought properly not to be (Matt. 24:15) . . .

What need then to urge this upon us by tyranny and punishment? . . . We humbly seek to walk according to the divine ordinances, word and will, for which we, poor miserable men, are shamefully reviled, banished, robbed and slain by everyone in many countries, like innocent sheep but let the Lord be eternally praised . . .

It is our determination, in this matter as in all other matters of conscience, in view of the wrath of almighty God, that we will not be influenced by lords and princes, nor by doctors and teachers of schools, nor by the influence of the fathers, and long established customs, for in this matter, neither emperors, nor kings, nor doctors, nor licentiates, nor councils, nor proscriptions against the word of God, will avail. We dare not be bound to any person, power, wisdom or times, but we must be governed alone, by the expressed and positive commands of Christ . . .

Observe, all of you who persecute the word of the Lord and his people, this is our instruction, doctrine and belief concerning baptism, according to the instruction of the words of Christ, namely, we must first hear the word of God, believe it, and then upon our faith be baptized; we are not seditious or contentious; we do not approve of polygamy; neither do we seek nor wait for any kingdom upon earth.

O no! no! to God be eternal praise; we well know what the word of the Lord teaches us and testifies to, on this subject. The word of the Lord commands us that we, with a sincere heart, desire to die to sin, to bury our sins with Christ, and with him to rise to a new life, even as baptism is a figure of it.

Lord's Supper

It is to be observed that there is no greater evidence of love, than that one suffers death for another, as Christ says, "Greater love has no man than this, that a man lay down his life for his friends" (John 15:13). Since this holy sign is only a memorial of the Lord's death, and since death is the greatest evidence of love, as said, we are therefore reminded, when we are at the Lord's table, to eat his bread and to drink his cup, that we not only earnestly show forth and remember his death, but also all the glorious fruits of divine love, manifested towards us in Christ . . .

When Christ instituted and celebrated the Holy Supper with his beloved disciples, he said, with desire I have desired to eat this Passover with you before I suffer . . . But now my hour is at hand; this night I shall be betrayed.

All that the prophet said of me has come to an end. But since I can serve you no longer with my doctrine and life, I will, at least, serve you with my painful sufferings, body, blood, cross, and death.

And this is the reason why I called you to this Supper, so that I might institute a memorial for you in the use of bread and wine, that you might occasionally come together after my death and commemorate the gracious favors of my fervent love so abundantly manifested toward you.

Pacifism

I tell you the truth in Christ; notice the rightly baptized disciples of Christ, who are baptized inwardly with spirit and fire, and externally with water, who are baptized according to the word of God; know of no weapons other than patience, hope, quiet, and God's word. Paul says, "The weapons of our warfare are not carnal, but mighty through God to the pulling down of strongholds; casting down imaginations, and every high thing that exalts itself against the knowledge of God, and brings into captivity every thought to the obedience of Christ" (1 Cor. 10:4-5). Our weapons are not weapons with which cities and countries are desolated; walls and gates broken down and human blood shed in torrents like water, but they are weapons with which the spiritual kingdom of the devil is destroyed, and the ungodly passions are annihilated, and the flinty hearts are broken, that have never been sprinkled with the heavenly dew of the holy word. We have and know no other weapons besides, the Lord knows, even if we should be torn into a thousand pieces, and as many false witnesses were to rise against us, as there are spears of grass in the fields, and grains of sand upon the sea shore.

Again, Christ is our fortress; patience our defense; the word of God our sword; and our victory is a candid, firm unfeigned faith in Jesus Christ. We let those take spears and swords, who, alas, regard human blood and swine's blood alike. He that is wise let him judge what I mean.

Ban

And thus it is in the Christian dispensation: for his church is a congregation of saints, or an assembly of the righteous . . . From which, according to the doctrine of the holy apostles, it is evident that the obstinate disturber or sectary who causes, contrary to the doctrine of godliness, offence and discord, and those who do not abide in the doctrine of Christ, who lead an offensive life, or the over-curious, inquisitive, and lazy, who live at the expense of others, shall not be suffered in the holy house, camp, city, temple, church, and body of Christ, which is the church; but that we, with one accord, should exclude and shun them, according to Scripture, to our salvation, and their reformation . . .

Since then it is evident that God is love, and will be forever, who in the beginning manifested the glorious fruit of love towards his children, he now likewise does this by exclusion or separation, although it is terrible and severe, and notwithstanding that it has such a terrible consequence with the stubborn and unconverted sinner . . .

Since the Scripture admonishes and commands, that we shall not associate with such, or eat with them, or greet them, nor receive them into our houses, etc., and yet if somebody should say, I will associate with them, I will eat with them, I will greet them in the Lord and receive them into my house—he would plainly prove that he did not fear the commandment and admonition of the Lord, but that he despised it, rejected the Holy Spirit and that he trusted, honored and followed his own opinion rather than the word of God . . .

Question 3: Should husband and wife shun each other on account of the ban—as also parents and children? Answer: First, that the rule of the ban is a general rule, and excepts none; neither husband nor wife, nor parent nor child. For God's judgment judges all flesh with the same judgment and knows no respect of persons . . . Separation must be made by the church; and therefore the husband must consent and vote with the church, in the separation of his wife; and the wife in the separation of her husband. If the pious spouse must give his consent, then it is also becoming that he also shun her, with the church; for what use is there in the ban when the shunning and avoiding are not connected with it (1 Cor. 5:3).

SOURCE: Menno Simons, "Doctrine (1539)," *The Complete Works of Menno Simons, First Part* (Elkhart, Ind.: John F. Funk & Brother, 1871), 24, 25, 29, 31, 42, 44, 81, 246, 276, 277. The selections on baptism, Lord's Supper, and pacifism are found in "Foundation of Christian Doctrine." The selections on the "ban" come from "Excommunication (1558)" and "Some Questions and Answers on Church Discipline (1550)."

42

COUNCIL OF TRENT

THE COUNCIL OF TRENT (1545–1547, 1551–1552, 1559–1563) was the response of the Roman Catholic Church to calls for reform within the church and to the challenges of the Protestant Reformation(s). The Council met several times over an eighteen-year period and published the *Decrees and Canons of the Council of Trent*. Decrees were doctrinal in nature; canons targeted Protestants (or other heretics) with a series of anathemas (curses). Scholars refer to this era in the history of the Roman Catholic Church as the Catholic Reformation or the Counter-Reformation. In the selections below, the council reaffirms the use of the Latin Vulgate as the only acceptable translation of Scripture, the indispensable role of the church as interpreter of Scripture, and the proper understanding of the doctrine of original sin. The decisions at Trent held sway until Vatican II in the twentieth century.

Decree Concerning the Canonical Scriptures

Session IV (8 April 1546)

The sacred and holy, ecumenical and general Synod of Trent, lawfully assembled in the Holy Ghost, the same three legates of the Apostolic See presiding therein—keeping this always in view, that, errors being removed, the purity itself of the Gospel be preserved in the Church; which [Gospel], before promised through the prophets in the holy Scriptures, our Lord Jesus Christ, the Son of God, first promulgated with his own mouth, and then commanded to be preached by his apostles to every creature, as the fountain both of every saving truth, and discipline of morals; and perceiving that this truth and discipline are contained in the written books, and the unwritten traditions which, received by the apostles from the mouth of Christ himself, or from the apostles themselves, the Holy Ghost dictating, have come down even to us, transmitted as it were from hand to hand; [the synod] following the examples of the orthodox fathers, receives and venerates with equal affection of piety and reverence all the books both of the Old and of the New Testament—seeing that one God is the author of both, also the said traditions, as well those appertaining to faith and morals, as having been dictated, either by Christ's own word of mouth, or by the Holy Ghost, and preserved by a continuous succession in the Catholic Church. And it has thought it good that a catalogue of the sacred books be inserted in this decree, lest doubt arise in any one's mind as to which are the books that are received by this synod. They are as set down here below: of the Old Testament: the five books of Moses: Genesis, Exodus, Leviticus, Numbers, Deuteronomy; Joshua, Judges, Ruth, four books of Kings, two of Chronicles, the first book of Esdras [Ezra], and the second which is entitled Nehemiah; Tobit, Judith, Esther, Job, the Davidical Psalter, [containing] a hundred and fifty psalms; the Proverbs, Ecclesiastes, the Canticle of Canticles, Wisdom, Ecclesiasticus, Isaiah, Jeremiah, with Baruch; Daniel; the twelve minor prophets: Hosea, Joel, Amos, Obadiah, Jonah, Micah, Nahum, Habakkuk, Zephaniah, Haggai, Zachariah, Malachi; two books of the Maccabees, the first and the second. Of the New Testament: the four Gospels, according to Matthew, Mark, Luke, and John; the Acts of the Apostles written by Luke the Evangelist; fourteen epistles of Paul the apostle, [one] to the Romans, two to the Corinthians, [one] to the Galatians, to the Ephesians, to the Philippians, to the Colossians, two to the Thessalonians, two to Timothy, [one] to Titus, to Philemon, to the Hebrews; two of Peter the apostle, three of John the apostle, one of the apostle James, one of Jude the apostle, and the Apocalypse of John the Apostle. But if any one does not receive all of these books in their entirety as sacred and canonical, as they have been read in the Catholic Church, and as they are contained in the old Latin vulgate edition; and knowingly and deliberately despise the traditions mentioned; let him be anathema. Let all, therefore, understand in what order and in what manner, this synod, after having laid the foundation of the confession of faith, will proceed, and what testimonies and defenses it will mainly use in confirming dogmas, and in restoring morals in the Church.

Decree Concerning the Edition and the Use of the Sacred Books

Moreover, the same sacred and holy synod, considering that no little utility may accrue to the Church of God, if, out of all the Latin editions now in circulation of the sacred books, it be known which is to be held as authentic, ordains and declares, that the old and vulgate edition, which, by the long usage of so many ages, has been approved in the Church, be, in public lectures, disputations, preachings, and expositions, held as authentic; and that no one is to dare, or presume to reject it under any pretext whatsoever.

Furthermore, in order to restrain petulant spirits, it decrees, that no one, relying on his own skill, shall, in matters of faith and morals pertaining to the edification of Christian doctrine, wresting the sacred Scripture to his own senses, dare to interpret the sacred Scripture contrary to that sense which holy mother Church, whose it is to judge the true sense and interpretation of the holy Scriptures, has held and does hold; or even contrary to the unanimous consent of the Fathers; even though suchlike interpretations were never [intended] to be at any time published. They who shall contravene shall be made known by their ordinaries, and be punished with the penalties by law established . . .

Decree Concerning Original Sin

Session V (17 June 1546)

That our Catholic *faith, without which it is impossible to please God,* may, errors being cleared away, continue in its own perfect and undefiled integrity, and that the Christian people may not *be carried about with every wind of doctrine;* whereas that old serpent, the perpetual enemy of the human race, among the very many evils by which the Church of God is in these our times disturbed, has also stirred up not only new, but even old dissensions touching original sin, and its remedy; the sacred and holy, ecumenical and general Synod of Trent, lawfully assembled in the Holy Ghost, the three same legates of the Apostolic See presiding therein—wishing now to come to the recalling of the erring, and the confirming of the wavering, following the testimonies of the sacred Scriptures, and of the holy fathers, and of the most approved councils, and the judgment and consent of the Church itself, ordains, confesses, and declares these things touching original sin:

1. If any one does not confess that the first man, Adam, when he had transgressed the commandment of God in Paradise, immediately lost the holiness and justice in which he had been constituted; and that he incurred, through the offence of such prevarication, the wrath and indignation of God, and consequently death, which God had previously threatened to him, and, together with death, captivity under the power of him who had the empire of death, that is to say, the devil, and that the entire Adam, through that offence of prevarication, was changed in body and soul for the worse; let him be anathema.

2. If anyone asserts, that the prevarication of Adam injured himself alone, and not his posterity; and that he lost for himself alone, and not for us also, the holiness and justice received of God; or that

he, defiled by the sin of disobedience, has only transferred death and pains of the body, into the whole human race, but not sin also, which is the death of the soul, let him be anathema; inasmuch as he contradicts the apostle, who says: *By one man sin entered into the world, and by sin death, and so death passed upon all men, in whom all have sinned.*

3. If anyone asserts that this sin of Adam, which in its origin is one, being transferred into all by propagation, not by imitation, is in each one as his own [sin], is taken away either by the powers of human nature, or by any other remedy than the merit of the *one mediator, our Lord Jesus Christ, who has reconciled us to God in his own blood, made unto us righteousness, sanctification, and redemption*; or, if he denies that the same merit of Jesus Christ is applied, both to adults and to infants, by the sacrament of baptism rightly administered in the form of the Church; let him be anathema: *For there is no other name under heaven given to men, whereby we must be saved.* Whence that voice: *Behold the Lamb of God, behold him who takes away the sins of the world*; and that other—*As many of you as have been baptized have put on Christ.*

4. If any one denies that infants, newly born from their mother's wombs, born from baptized parents, are to be baptized; or says that they are baptized for the remission of sins, but that they draw nothing of original sin from Adam, which needs to be expiated by the water of regeneration for obtaining everlasting life—thus it follows, as a consequence, that in them the form of baptism, for the remission of sins, is understood to be not true, but false—let him be anathema. For that which the apostle has said, *By one man sin entered into the world, and by sin death, and so death passed upon all men in whom all have sinned,* is not to be understood otherwise than as the Catholic Church spread everywhere has always understood it. For, by reason of this rule of faith, from a tradition of the apostles, even infants, who could not as yet in themselves commit any sin, are for this cause truly baptized for the remission of sins, that in them that which they have contracted by generation, may be cleansed away by regeneration. *For, unless a man be born again of water and the Holy Ghost, he cannot enter into the kingdom of God.*

5. If any one denies that by the grace of our Lord Jesus Christ, which is conferred in baptism, the guilt of original sin is remitted; or even asserts that all that which has the true and proper nature of sin is

not taken away, but says that it is only erased, or not imputed—let him be anathema. For, in those who are born again, God hates nothing, because, *There is no condemnation to those who are truly buried together with Christ by baptism into death; who walk not according to the flesh*, but, *putting off the old man, and putting on the new one, who is created according to God*, are made innocent, immaculate, pure, harmless, and beloved of God, *heirs indeed of God, but joint heirs with Christ*; so that there is nothing whatever to retard them from entrance into heaven. But this holy synod confesses and is sensible, that in the baptized there remains concupiscence, or an incentive [to sin]; which, since it is left for us to strive against, cannot injure those who do not consent, but resist manfully by the grace of Jesus Christ; yea, he who shall have *striven lawfully shall be crowned*. This concupiscence, which the apostle sometimes calls sin, the holy synod declares that the Catholic Church has never understood to be called sin, as being truly and properly sin in those born again, but because it is of sin, and inclines to sin. And if anyone is of a contrary opinion, let him be anathema.

This same holy synod does nevertheless declare that it is not in its intention to include in this decree, where original sin is treated, the blessed and immaculate Virgin Mary, the mother of God; but that the constitutions of Pope Sixtus IV, of happy memory, are to be observed, under the pains contained in the constitutions, which it renews.

Source: Selection is from *Canons and Decrees of the Council of Trent*, trans. Theodore Alois Buckley (London: George Routledge & Co., 1851), 17–19, 21–24.

43

IGNACIO OF LOYOLA

Ignacio of Loyola (1491–1556), or Iñigo de Loyola, was the founder of the Society of Jesus, and his work was pivotal to the Catholic Reformation/Counter-Reformation. He began writing his *Spiritual Exercises*, which reflect his military training, while in a retreat at Manresa, a town near Barcelona, Spain. He finalized his work while in Rome between 1539 and 1541 and was canonized by the Roman Catholic Church in 1622.

Spiritual Exercises

To have True Sentiment which we ought to have in the Church Militant, Let the following Rules be observed:

First Rule. The first: All private judgment laid aside, we ought to have our mind ready and prompt to obey, in all things, the true Spouse of Christ our Lord, which is our holy Mother the Church Hierarchical.

Second Rule. The second: To praise confession to a priest, and the reception of the most Holy Sacrament of the Altar once in the year, and much more each month, and much better from week to week, with the required and due conditions.

Third Rule. The third: To praise the hearing of mass often, likewise hymns, psalms, and long prayers, in the church and out of it; likewise the hours set at the time fixed for each divine office and for all prayer and all canonical hours.

Fourth Rule. The fourth: To give much praise to religious orders, virginity, continence, and marriage, but not as much as the others.

Fifth Rule. The fifth: To praise vows of religion, obedience, poverty, chastity and of other works of perfection and devotion. It is to be noted that these vows are about things which relate to evangelical perfection. Thus a vow ought not to be made in the things which withdraw from this perfection, such as becoming a merchant or getting married, etc.

Sixth Rule. To praise relics of the saints, giving veneration to them and praying to the saints; and to praise stations, pilgrimages, indulgences, pardons, *cruzadas* [*crusade indulgences*], and candles lighted in the churches.

Seventh Rule. To praise rules about fasts and abstinence, like Lent, ember days, vigils, Friday and Saturday; likewise praise penances, not only interior, but also exterior.

Eighth Rule. To praise the ornaments and the buildings of churches; likewise images, and to venerate them according to what they represent.

Ninth Rule. Finally, to praise all precepts of the Church, being ready to defend them and never criticize them.

Tenth Rule. We ought to be more prompt to find good and praise in the guidelines and recommendations of our superiors as well as their behavior. Because, although some are not or have not been good, to speak against them, whether preaching in public or talking with the common people, would give rise to fault-finding and scandal rather than good; and so the people would be incensed against their superiors, whether temporal or spiritual. Although it is harmful to speak evil to the common people about superiors in their absence, it can be beneficial to speak of the evil ways of the superiors to those who can remedy the conduct.

Eleventh Rule. To praise positive and scholastic learning. It is a trait of the positive doctors like St. Jerome, St. Augustine, and St. Gregory, etc., to move the heart to love and serve God our Lord in everything. It is a trait for the scholastics like St. Thomas, St. Bonaventure, and the Master of the Sentences, etc., to define or explain for our times the things necessary for eternal salvation and to combat and explain clearly all errors and fallacies. The scholastic doctors, being more recent, understand Sacred Scripture and the positive and holy doctors, and being enlightened and clarified by divine virtue, receive help from the councils, canons and constitutions of our holy Mother the Church.

Twelfth Rule. We ought to be on our guard in making comparison between the living and the blessed who are dead. Errors often come from this; that is to say, when we say, this one knows more than St. Augustine; he is like or greater than St. Francis; he is another St. Paul in goodness, holiness, etc.

Thirteenth Rule. To be right in everything, we ought always to hold that the white which I see is black, if the Hierarchical Church so decides it, believing that between Christ our Lord, the bridegroom, and the Church, his bride, there is the same Spirit which governs and directs us for the salvation of our souls. Our holy Mother the Church is directed and governed by the same Spirit and our Lord who gave the Ten Commandments.

Fourteenth Rule. Although there is much truth in the assertion that no one can save himself without being predestined and without having faith and grace; we must be very cautious in the manner of speaking and communicating with others about all these things.

Fifteenth Rule. We ought not to speak frequently about predestination. If this is done, let him speak so that the common people may not fall into any error, as sometimes happens, when it is said, "Whether I have to be saved or condemned is already determined, and no other thing can happen if I do good or evil." In this case, they grow lazy and become negligent in the works which lead to the salvation and spiritual profit of their souls.

Sixteenth Rule. In the same way, we must be on our guard that by talking too much and with too much insistence of faith, without any distinction and explanation, occasion not be given to the people to be lazy and slothful in works, whether before or after faith is formed in charity.

Seventeenth Rule. Likewise, we ought not to speak so much with insistence on grace that the belief in free will be poisoned. So one can speak of faith and grace as much as is possible with the divine help for the greater praise of his divine majesty, but not in such way nor in such manners, especially in our dangerous times, that works and free will receive any harm, or be regarded as nothing.

Eighteenth Rule. Although generously serving God our Lord out of pure love is to be esteemed above all, we ought to give much praise to the fear of his divine majesty, because not only filial fear but servile fear is pious and holy. When the man cannot succeed in using anything else, servile fear frequently helps one to get out of mortal sin. Then he can easily move to filial fear, which is fully acceptable and pleasing to God our Lord, since it is one with the divine love.

SOURCE: Ignatius of Loyola, *The Spiritual Exercises of St. Ignatius of Loyola*, trans. Elder Mullen, S.J. (New York: P. J. Kennedy & Sons, 1914), 189–94.

44

TERESA OF AVILA

TERESA OF AVILA (1515–1582) was the reformer of the Discalced Carmelites, who founded convents and helped reform monastic life in Spain. She was canonized in 1622 by the Roman Catholic Church, and named a Doctor of the Church in 1970. Her work *The Interior Castle* (1577) is considered a classic of Christian spirituality, and explores the mystical ascent of the soul to God through mental prayer. The selection below uses an allegorical story to explain the mystical ascent of the soul.

Prayer of Recollection

The effects of this prayer are many, some of which I will now mention. And first, there is another kind of prayer, which commences most always before this, whereof I will say but little, having spoken of it elsewhere.

It is the Prayer of Recollection, which also seems to me to be supernatural; for it does not require being in the dark, nor to shut the eyes, nor does it consist in any exterior thing. It often happens that, without our wishing it, our eyes close, and we desire solitude; and, without any contrivance, a building seems to be erected for the prayer mentioned above. For the senses and external things seem to lose their hold, so that the soul may recover hers—which was lost. They say the soul enters within herself, and sometimes that she ascends above herself. By these expressions I shall not be able to explain anything; for I have this unhappiness in thinking you will understand me best according to the way I can express myself: perhaps no one except myself will understand.

Let *us* imagine that the senses and faculties, which I called the guards of the castle—(and this is the comparison I made use of, whereby to explain my meaning) have gone out, and associated with strangers, who wish evil to this castle for some days and years. Afterwards, perceiving themselves lost, and sensible of their ruin, they endeavor to return, and approach the castle, though not resolved to enter it (for habit is a hard master); yet they are no longer traitors, for they remain around the environs.

The Great King, who is within the castle, perceiving their good inclination, in His mercy is willing to pardon them; and like a good shepherd (acts towards his sheep), He makes them know His voice by so sweet a whistle, that they themselves can scarcely hear it. This He does that they may not wander and be lost, but return to their mansion. This whistle of the Shepherd has such power, that they immediately abandon all those external things which deceived them, and hasten into the castle.

I think I never explained myself in the way I have now; for in order to seek God in our interior, where He is found with more benefit than in creatures (St. Augustine tells us he found Him there, after having sought him in several places), it is a great help if God should bestow this favor upon us. Think not that this is acquired by means of the understanding, laboring to consider God within itself. This is good, and an excellent method of meditation, for it is founded on this truth, viz, that God is within us. But this is not what I mean; because every one may do this by the assistance of our Lord. What I speak of is of a different nature; for sometimes these persons, before they begin to think of God, have already got into the castle; by what way I know not, nor how they heard the whistle of their Shepherd: it was not by means of their ears, since nothing is heard, but a sweet recollection in the interior is clearly perceived, as those who go along this way will find. I know not how to express my meaning better.

SOURCE: St. Teresa of Avila, *The Interior Castle; or, The Mansions*, trans. Rev. John Dalton (London: Paternoster Row, 1852), 54–55.

45

RACOVIAN CATECHISM

WIDELY REGARDED AS THE CONFESSIONAL STATEMENT of Socinianism, the Racovian Catechism is attributed to Valentin Schmalz and Johannes Völkel, who drafted the document based on notes from lectures and works by Fausto Paolo Sozzini (1539–1604). Fausto refined the anti-Trinitarian thought of his uncle Lelio Francesco Maria Sozzini (1525–1562) into a systematic form of Christian Unitarianism. Socinians believed that Jesus Christ is divine by office and not by nature. Written in Latin, the catechism was first published in the city of Racow in 1605.

Nature of Christ

[Q:] As you have stated that there are some things relating to the will of God, which were first revealed by Jesus Christ, and also asserted, at the commencement, that the way of salvation consisted in the knowledge of him, I now wish you to specify what those particulars are, concerning Jesus Christ, which I ought to know?

[A:] Certainly: You must be informed, then, that there are some things relating to the person or nature of Jesus Christ, and some to his office, with which you ought to be acquainted.

[Q:] What are the things relating to his person which I ought to know?

[A:] This one particular alone, that by nature he was truly a man; a mortal man while he lived on earth, but now immortal. That he was a real man the Scriptures testify in several places: Thus, 1 Timothy 2:5, "There is one God, and one mediator between God and men, the MAN Christ Jesus." 1 Corinthians 15:21-22, "Since by MAN came death, by MAN came also the resurrection of the dead. For as in ADAM all die, even so in CHRIST shall all be made alive." Romans 5:5, "If through the offence of one, many be dead, much more the grace of God, and the gift by grace, which is by one MAN, Jesus Christ, has abounded unto many." John 8:40, "But now you seek to kill me, A MAN that has told you the truth." See also Hebrews 5:1, etc. Such, besides, was the person whom God promised of old by the prophets; and such also does the Creed called the Apostles', which all Christians, in common with ourselves, embrace, declare him to be.

[Q:] Was, then, the Lord Jesus a mere or common man?

[A:] By no means: because, first, though by nature he was a man, he was nevertheless, at the same time, and even from his earliest origin, the only begotten Son of God. For being conceived of the Holy Spirit, and born of a virgin, without the intervention of any human being, he had properly no father besides God: though considered in another light, simply according to the flesh, without respect to the Holy Spirit, of which he was conceived, and with which he was anointed, he had David for his father, and was therefore his son. Concerning his supernatural conception, the angel thus speaks to Mary, Luke 1:35, "The Holy Ghost shall come upon you, and the power of the Highest shall overshadow you; therefore also that holy thing which shall be born of you shall be called the Son of God." Secondly, because, as Christ testifies of himself, he was sanctified and sent into the world by the Father; that is, being in a most remarkable manner separated from all other men, and, besides being distinguished by the perfect holiness of his life, endued with divine wisdom and power, was sent by the Father, with supreme authority, on an embassy to mankind. Thirdly, because, as the apostle Paul testifies, both in the Acts of the Apostles, and in his Epistle to the Romans, he was raised from the dead by God, and thus as it were begotten a second time; particularly as by this event he became like God immortal. Fourthly, because by his dominion and supreme authority over all things, he is made to resemble, or, indeed, to equal God: on which account, "a king anointed by God," and "Son of God," are used in several passages of Scripture as phrases of the same import. And the sacred author of the Epistle to the Hebrews (1:5) shows from the words of the Psalmist (Ps. 2:7), "You are my Son, this day have I begotten you," that Christ was glorified by God, in order that he might be made a priest, that is, the chief director of our religion and salvation, in which office are comprised his supreme authority and dominion. He was, however, not merely the only begotten Son of God, but also a God, on account of the divine power and authority which he displayed even while he was yet mortal: much more may he be so denominated now that he has received all power in heaven and earth, and that all things, God himself alone excepted, have been put under his feet. But of this you shall hear in its proper place.

[Q:] But do you not acknowledge in Christ a divine, as well as a human nature or substance?

[A:] If by the terms divine nature or substance I am to understand the very essence of God, I do not acknowledge such a divine nature in Christ; for this were repugnant both to right reason and to the Holy Scriptures. But if, on the other hand, you intend by a divine nature the Holy Spirit which dwelt in Christ, united, by an indissoluble bond, to his human nature, and displayed in him the wonderful effects of its extraordinary presence; or if you understand the words in the sense in which Peter employs them (2 Pet. 1:4), when he asserts that "we are partakers of a divine nature," that is, endued by the favor of God with divinity, or divine properties, I certainly do so far acknowledge such a nature in Christ as to believe that next after God it belonged to no one in a higher degree.

Source: "Section IV. Of the Knowledge of Christ, Chapter I. Of the Person of Christ," of the *Racovian Catechism*, in *The Racovian catechism, with notes and illustrations, translated from the Latin: to which is prefixed a sketch of the history of Unitarianism in Poland and the adjacent countries*, trans. Thomas Rees (London: Longman, Hurst, Rees, Orme, & Brown, 1818), 51–56.

46

THOMAS HELWYS

Tʜᴏᴍᴀs Hᴇʟᴡʏs (ca. 1570–1616) was an English Puritan Separatist. In 1609 he established with John Smyth what is considered the first Baptist church in the city of Amsterdam. Soon after, Helwys and about ten others returned to England and established the first Baptist church in England at Spitalsfield (near London). The Helwys congregation had several practices that characterized much of the later Baptist movement: believer's church rooted in voluntary faith and believer's baptism, local church independence, and congregational polity. In the *Mistery of Iniquity* (1612), Helwys was the first English writer to call for religious liberty for all people.

Religious Liberty

It is spiritual obedience that the Lord requires, and the king's sword cannot smite the spirits of men. And if our lord the king shall force and compel men to worship and eat the Lord's Supper against their consciences, so shall he make his poor subjects to worship and eat unworthily, whereby he shall compel them to sin against God, and increase their own judgments.

Oh, let not our lord the king suffer such evil to be done by his power . . . we bow ourselves to the earth before our lord the king in greatest humbleness, beseeching the king to judge righteous judgment herein, whether there be so unjust a thing and of so great cruel tyranny under the sun as to force men's consciences in their religion to God, seeing that if they err, they must pay the price of their transgressions with the loss of their souls. Oh, let the king judge, is it not most equal [*fair*] that men should choose their religion themselves, seeing they only must stand themselves before the judgment seat of God to answer for themselves, when it shall be no excuse for them to say we were commanded or compelled to be of this religion by the king or by them that had authority from him? . . .

But these lord bishops cannot in any wise endure ones that do faithfully seek for reformation, because such are only adversaries to their kingdom. We still pray our lord the king that we may be free from suspect, for having any thoughts of provoking evil against them of the Romish religion, in regard of their profession, if they are true and faithful subjects to the kings. For we do freely profess that our lord the king has no more power over their consciences than over ours, and that is none at all. For our lord the king is but an earthly king, and he has no authority as a king but in earthly causes. And if the king's people be obedient and true subjects, obeying all human laws made by the king, our lord the king can require no more. For men's religion to God is between God and themselves. The king shall not answer for it. Neither may the king be judge between God and man. Let them be heretics, Turks, Jews, or whatsoever, it appertains not to the earthly power to punish them in the least measure. This is made evident to our lord the king by the Scriptures. When Paul was brought before Gallio, deputy of Achaia, and accused by the Jews for persuading men to worship God contrary to the law, Gallio said to the Jews, "If it were a matter or wrong or evil deed, O you Jews, I would according to right maintain you. And he drove them from the judgment hall" (Acts 18:12, 17) showing them that matters of wrong and evil deeds, which were between man and man appertained only to the judgment seat, and not questions of religion.

SOURCE: Thomas Helwys, *A Short Declaration of the Mystery of Iniquity (1611/1612)*, ed. Richard Groves (Macon, Ga.: Mercer University Press, 1998), 37, 53. Used by permission.

ॐ

47

JOHN WINTHROP

J OHN WINTHROP (1588–1649) was the first governor of the Massachusetts
Bay colony. En route to America (1630), he delivered the sermon, "Model
of Christian Charity," which set forth Winthrop's Puritan vision of the colony as God's "city on a hill." Winthrop's vision remains a key understanding
to this day in the debates over the early Christian character of the nation. His
leadership was also influential to the development of the Puritan concept of
"Holy Commonwealth" that tolerated no dissent. The diary selection below
references the dissent of Roger Williams, religious liberty pioneer, who was
later banished from the colony and subsequently founded Rhode Island.

Model of Christian Charity

. . . It is by a mutual consent through a special overruling providence, and a
more than ordinary approbation of the churches of Christ to seek out a place
of cohabitation and consortship under a due form of government both civil
and ecclesiastical. In such cases as this the care of the public must oversway
all private respects, by which not only conscience, but mere civil policy does
bind us . . .

. . . We are entered into covenant with him for this work, we have taken
out a commission, the Lord has given us leave to draw our own articles, we
have professed to enterprise these actions upon these and these ends, we
have besought of him favor and blessing: Now if the Lord shall please to
hear us, and bring us in peace to the place we desire, then hath he ratified
this covenant and sealed our commission, (and) will expect a strict performance of the articles contained in it, but if we shall neglect the observation of
these articles which are the ends we have propounded, and dissembling with
our God, shall fall to embrace this present world and prosecute our carnal
intentions, seeking great things for ourselves and our posterity, the Lord will
surely break out in wrath against us be revenged of such a perjured people
and make us know the price of the breach of such a covenant.

Now the only way to avoid this shipwreck and to provide for our posterity is to follow the counsel of Micah, to do justly, to love mercy, to walk humbly with our God, for this end, we must be knit together in this work as one

man, we must entertain each other in brotherly affection, we must be willing to abridge our selves of our superfluities, for the supply of other's necessities, we must uphold a familiar commerce together in all meekness, gentleness, patience, and liberality, we must delight in each other, make others conditions our own, rejoice together, mourn together, labor, and suffer together, always having before our eyes our commission and community in the work, our community as members of the same body, so shall we keep the unity of the spirit in the bond of peace, the Lord will be our God and delight to dwell among us, as his own people and will command a blessing upon us in all our ways, so that we shall see much more of his wisdom, power, goodness, and truth then formerly we have been acquainted with. We shall find that the God of Israel is among us, when ten of us shall be able to resist a thousand of our enemies, when he shall make us a praise and glory, that men shall say of succeeding plantations: the Lord make it like that of New England: for we must consider that we shall be as a city upon a hill, the eyes of all people are upon us; so that if we shall deal falsely with our God in this work we have undertaken and so cause him to withdraw his present help from us, we shall be made a story and a by-word through the world, we shall open the mouths of enemies to speak evil of the ways of God and all professors for God's sake; we shall shame the faces of many of God's worthy servants, and cause their prayers to be turned into curses upon us till we be consumed out of the good land whether we are going: and to shut up this discourse with that exhortation of Moses that faithful servant of the Lord in his last farewell to Israel (Deut. 30). Beloved there is now set before us life, and good, death and evil in that we are commanded this day to love the Lord our God, and to love one another to walk in his ways and to keep his commandments and his ordinance, and his laws, and the articles of our covenant with him that we may live and be multiplied, and that the Lord our God maybe bless us in the land whether we go to possess it: But if our hearts shall turn away so that we will not obey, but shall be seduced and worship other God's our pleasures, and profits, and serve them; it is propounded unto us this day, we shall surely perish out of the good land whether we pass over this vast sea to possess it.

Diary Entry: Roger Williams

July 8, 1635: At the general court, Mr. Williams of Salem was summoned, and did appear. It was laid to his charge, that, being under question before the magistracy and churches for diverse dangerous opinions, viz. 1, that the magistrate ought not to punish the breach of the first table, otherwise than in such cases as did disturb the civil peace; 2, that he ought not to tender an oath to an unregenerate man; 3, that a man ought not to pray with such, though wife, child, etc.; 4, that a man ought not to give thanks after the sacrament nor after food, etc.; and that the other churches were about to write to the church of Salem to admonish him of these errors; notwithstanding the church had since called him to [the] office of teacher. Much debate was about these things. The said opinions were adjudged by all, magistrates and ministers, (who were desired to be present) to be erroneous, and very dangerous, and the calling of him to office, at that time, was judged a great contempt of authority. So, in fine, time was given to him and the church of Salem to consider these things till the next general court, and then either to give satisfaction to the court, or else to expect the sentence; it being professedly declared by the ministers (at the request of the court to give their advice) that he who should obstinately maintain such opinions, (whereby a church might run into heresy, apostasy, or tyranny, and yet the civil magistrate could not intermeddle) were to be removed, and that the other churches ought to request the magistrates so to do.

Source: Reprinted courtesy of the Massachusetts Historical Society. John Winthrop, "A Modell of Christian Charity," in *Winthrop Papers*, ed. Stewart Mitchell (Boston: Massachusetts Historical Society, 1931), 2:294–95. John Winthrop, *Winthrop's Journal: "History of New England," 1630–1649*, vol. 1 (New York: Charles Scribner's Sons, 1908), 154.

48

ROGER WILLIAMS

ROGER WILLIAMS (ca. 1603–1683) was an English religious leader who came to America in 1631 and later founded the colony which eventually became Rhode Island. Advocating strict separation from the Church of England, Williams and his wife sailed to the Massachusetts Bay Colony, where his shifting religious views—including criticizing the workings of the Holy Commonwealth's union of church and state—got him into trouble. The leaders in Massachusetts eventually banished him from the colony altogether. He and those loyal to him founded Providence Plantation, a colony which Williams ensured allowed for "soul liberty"/"liberty of conscience," or freedom of religion for all persons. At Providence, during a short tenure as a Baptist, Williams also helped establish the first Baptist church in

America at Providence (1639). His most important book on religious liberty was the *Bloudy Tenent of Persecution, for Cause of Conscience* (1644), a portion of which comprises the first selection below. The second selection below is from a famous letter Williams wrote to the colony while he was its president. It exemplifies the liberty of conscience Williams valued so highly.

Religious Liberty

First, that the blood of so many hundred thousand souls of Protestants and papists, spilled in the wars of present and former ages for their respective consciences, is not required nor accepted by Jesus Christ the Prince of Peace.

Secondly, pregnant Scriptures and arguments are throughout the work proposed against the doctrine of persecution for cause of conscience.

Thirdly, satisfactory answers are given to Scriptures and objections produced by Mr. Calvin, Beza, Mr. Cotton, and the ministers of the New English churches, and others former and later, tending to prove the doctrine of persecution for cause of conscience.

Fourthly, the doctrine of persecution for cause of conscience is proved guilty of all the blood of the souls crying for vengeance under the altar.

Fifthly, all civil states, with their officers of justice, in their respective constitutions and administrations, are proved essentially civil, and therefore not judges, governors, or defenders of the spiritual, or Christian, state and worship.

Sixthly, it is the will and command of God that, since the coming of his Son the Lord Jesus, a permission of the most paganish, Jewish, Turkish, or anti-Christian consciences and worships be granted to all men in all nations and countries, and they are only to be fought against with that sword which is only, in soul matters, able to conquer, that is, the sword of God's Spirit, the word of God.

Seventhly, the state of the land of Israel, the kings and people thereof, in peace and war, is proved figurative and ceremonial, and no pattern nor precedent for any kingdom or civil state in the world to follow.

Eighthly, God requires not a uniformity of religion to be enacted and enforced in any civil state; which enforced uniformity, sooner or later, is the greatest occasion of civil war, ravishing of conscience, persecution of Christ Jesus in his servants, and of the hypocrisy and destruction of millions of souls.

Ninthly, in holding an enforced uniformity of religion in a civil state, we must necessarily disclaim our desires and hopes of the Jews' conversion to Christ.

Tenthly, an enforced uniformity of religion throughout a nation or civil state confounds the civil and religious, denies the principles of Christianity and civility, and that Jesus Christ is come in the flesh.

Eleventhly, the permission of other consciences and worships than a state professes only can, according to God, procure a firm and lasting peace; good assurance being taken, according to the wisdom of the civil state, for uniformity of civil obedience from all sorts.

Twelfthly, lastly, true civility and Christianity may both flourish in a state or kingdom, notwithstanding the permission of divers and contrary consciences, either of Jew or Gentile.

. . . The unknowing zeal of Constantine and other emperors did more hurt to Christ Jesus' crown and kingdom than the raging fury of the most bloody Neros. In the persecutions of the latter, Christians were sweet and fragrant, like spice pounded and beaten in mortars. But these good emperors, persecuting some erroneous persons, Arius, etc., and advancing the professors of some truths of Christ—for there was no small number of truths lost in those times—and maintaining their religion by the material sword—I say, by this means Christianity was eclipsed, and the professors of it fell asleep (Song. 5:[2]). Babel, or confusion, was ushered in, and by degrees the gardens of the churches of saints were turned into the wilderness of whole nations, until the whole world became Christian, or Christendom (Rev. 12, 13).

Doubtless those holy men, emperors and bishops, intended and aimed right to exalt Christ; but not attending to the command of Christ Jesus, to permit the tares to grow in the field of the world, they made the garden of the church and field of the world to be all one; and might not only sometimes, in their zealous mistakes, persecute good wheat instead of tares, but also pluck up thousands of those precious stalks by commotions and combustions about religion . . .

Letter to the Town of Providence, January 1654/5

That ever I should speak or write a tittle, that tends to such an infinite liberty of conscience, is a mistake, and which I have ever disclaimed and abhorred. To prevent such mistakes, I shall at present only propose this case: There goes many a ship to sea, with many hundred souls in one ship, whose weal and woe is common, and is a true picture of a commonwealth, or a human combination or society. It hath fallen out of sometimes, that both papists and protestants, Jews and Turks, may be embarked in one ship; upon which supposal I affirm, that all the liberty of conscience, that ever I pleaded for, turns upon these two hinges—that none of the papists, protestants, Jews, or Turks, be forced to come to the ship's prayers or worship, nor compelled from their own particular prayers or worship, if they practice any. I further add, that I never denied, that notwithstanding this liberty, the commander of this ship ought to command the ship's course, yea, and also command that justice, peace, and sobriety, be kept and practiced, both among the seamen and all passengers to pay their freight; if any refuse to help, in person or purse, towards the common charges or defense; if any shall mutiny and rise up against their commanders and officers; if any should preach or write that there ought to be no commanders or officers, because all are equal in Christ, therefore no matters nor officers, no laws nor orders, nor corrections nor punishments; I say, I never denied, but in such cases, whatever is pretended, the commander or commanders may judge, resist, compel, and punish such transgressors, according to their deserts and merits. This if seriously and honestly minded, may, if so please the Father of lights, let some light to such as willingly shut not their eyes.

I remain studious of your common peace and liberty.

Source: Roger Williams, *The Bloudy Tenent of Persecution, for Cause of Conscience*, ed. Richard Groves (Macon, Ga.: Mercer University Press, 2001), 3, 4, 112. Used by permission. "Letter to the Town of Providence" is taken from *Letters of Roger Williams, 1632–1682*, ed. John Bartlett (Providence, 1874), 278–79.

49

ROBERT BARCLAY

THE QUAKERS, OR SOCIETY OF FRIENDS, were founded by George Fox in England in the mid-seventeenth century (1647). Robert Barclay (1648–1690) of Scotland became one of the chief apologists for the movement. His *An Apology For The True Christian Divinity* (1676) was his most important writing. The Quakers were considered more radical than most religious dissenters, prioritizing the "inner light" of Christ and the authority of Spirit-led revelation over Scripture. Worship was spiritual, and thus external rituals like baptism and the Lord's Supper were internalized rather than actually performed. Quakers were often persecuted for their views and pleaded for freedom of conscience.

Immediate Revelation

Seeing no man knows the Father, but the Son, and he, to whom the Son reveals him, and seeing the revelation of the Son is in and by the Spirit; therefore the testimony of the Spirit is that alone, by which the true knowledge of God has been, is and can be only revealed, who, as by the moving of his own Spirit, converted the chaos of this world, into that wonderful order, wherein it was in the beginning, and created man, a living soul to rule and govern it, so by the revelation of the same Spirit, he has manifested himself all along to the sons of men, both patriarchs, prophets and apostles, which revelations of God by the Spirit, whether by outward voices and appearances, dreams, or inward objective manifestations in the heart, were of old the formal object of their faith, and remains yet so to be, since the object of the saints faith is the same in all ages.

Scriptures

From these revelations of the Spirit of God to the saints, have proceeded the Scriptures of Truth . . . Because they are only a declaration of the fountain, and not the fountain itself, therefore they are not to be esteemed the principal ground of all truth and knowledge, nor yet the adequate primary rule of faith and manners. Nevertheless, as that which gives a true and faithful testimony of the first foundation, they are and may be esteemed a secondary rule, subordinate to the Spirit, from which they have all their excellency and certainty; for as by the inward testimony of the Spirit we do alone truly know them, so they testify that the Spirit is that guide, by which the saints are led into all truth. Therefore according to the Scriptures the Spirit is the first and principal leader. And seeing we do therefore receive and believe the Scriptures, because they proceeded from the Spirit, therefore also the Spirit is more originally and principally the rule.

Salvation, Inner Light

God out of his infinite love, who delights not in the death of a sinner but that all should live and be saved, has so loved the world, that he has given his only Son a Light, that whosoever believes in him should be saved, who enlightens every man, that comes into the world, and makes manifest all things that are reprovable, and teaches all temperance, righteousness, and godliness; and this Light enlightens the hearts of all in a day in order to salvation, if not resisted; nor is it less universal than the seed of sin, being the purchase of his death, who tasted death for every man; for as in Adam all die, even so in Christ all shall be made alive.

Baptism

As there is one Lord, and one faith, so there is one baptism, which is not the putting away the filth of the flesh, but the answer of a good conscience before God, by the resurrection of Jesus Christ, and this baptism is a pure and spiritual thing, that is to say, the baptism of the Spirit and fire, by which we are buried with him, that being washed and purged from our sins, we may walk in newness of life, of which the baptism of John was a figure, which was commanded for a time, and not to continue forever; as to the baptism of infants it is a mere human tradition, for which neither precept nor practice is to be found in all the Scripture.

Lord's Supper

The communion of the body and blood of Christ is inward and spiritual, which is the participation of his flesh and blood, by which the inward man is daily nourished in the hearts of those in whom Christ dwells, of which things the breaking of bread by Christ with his disciples was a figure, which they even used in the Church for a time, who had received the substance, for the cause of the weak: even as abstaining from things strangled, and from blood, the washing one another's feet, and the anointing of the sick with oil, all which are commanded with no less authority and solemnity than the former; yet seeing they are but the shadows of better things, they cease in such as have obtained the substance.

Conscience

Since God has assumed to himself the power and dominion of the conscience, who alone can rightly instruct and govern it, therefore it is not lawful for any whatsoever, by virtue of any authority or principality they bear in the government of this world, to force the consciences of others; and therefore all killing, banishing, fining, imprisoning, and other such things, which men are afflicted with for the alone exercise of their conscience or difference in worship, or opinion, proceeds from the Spirit of Cain, the murderer, and is contrary to the Truth, providing always that no man under the pretense of conscience, prejudice his neighbor in his life or estate; or do anything destructive to, or inconsistent with human society, in which case the law is for the transgressor, and justice is to be administered upon all without respect of persons.

SOURCE: Robert Barclay, *An Apology For The True Christian Divinity Being an Explanation and Vindication of the Principles and Doctrines of the People Called Quakers* (1676), 9th ed. (Philadelphia, 1775), 3–13.

50

JOHN WESLEY

JOHN WESLEY (1703–1791), along with his brother Charles, is considered the founder of the Methodist movement. As a leader of the "evangelical revival" in England that paralleled the First Great Awakening in America, Wesley focused on the need for personal piety and discipleship communities and advocated Christian responses to social issues like slavery and the prison system. The selections below highlight some of Wesley's and subsequent Methodism's distinctives: the need for "conversion"; an ecumenical "catholic" spirit; Arminian theology; and the movement's most unique theological contribution, Christian Perfection, in which Wesley asserted that Christians could attain a state of perfect love (i.e., a believer has purity of motives and never intentionally sins). This emphasis was popularized as a "second blessing" of sanctification in later (Wesleyan) Holiness traditions.

Aldersgate Experience

. . . The next day he [Peter Bohler] came again with three others, all of whom testified of their own personal experience that a true living faith in Christ is inseparable from a sense of pardon for all past and freedom from all present sins. They added with one mouth that this faith was the gift, the free gift of God; and that he would surely bestow it upon every soul who earnestly and perseveringly sought it. I was now thoroughly convinced and, by the grace of God, I resolved to seek it until the end, (1) by absolutely renouncing all dependence, in whole or in part, upon *my own* works or righteousness; on which I had really grounded my hope of salvation, though I knew it not, from my youth up; (2) by adding to the constant use of all the other means of grace, continual prayer for this very thing, justifying, saving faith, a full reliance on the blood of Christ shed for *me*, a trust in Him, and *my* Christ, as *my* sole justification, sanctification, and redemption.

I continued thus to seek it, (though with strange indifference, dullness, and coldness, and usually frequent relapses into sin) . . .

In the evening [May 24, 1738], I went very unwillingly to a society in Aldersgate Street, where one was reading Luther's preface to the Epistle to the Romans. About a quarter before nine, while he was describing the change which God works in the heart through faith in Christ, I felt my heart strangely warmed. I felt I did trust in Christ, Christ alone, for salvation; and an assurance was given me, that he had taken away *my* sins, even *mine*, and saved *me* from the law of sin and death.

I began to pray with all my might for those who had in a more especial manner despitefully used me and persecuted me. I then testified openly to all there what I now first felt in my heart. But it was not long before the enemy suggested, "This cannot be faith; for where is thy joy?" Then was I taught, that peace and victory over sin are essential to faith in the Captain of our salvation; but, that as to the transports of joy that usually attend the beginning of it, especially in those who have mourned deeply, God sometimes gives, sometimes withholds them, according to the counsels of his own will.

After my return home, I was much buffeted with temptations; but cried out, and they fled away. They returned again and again. I as often lifted up my eyes, "and he sent me help from his holy place" (Ps. 20:2). And herein I found the difference between this and my former state chiefly consisted. I was striving, yea, fighting with all my might under the law, as well as under grace; but then I was sometimes, if not often, conquered: now, I was always conqueror.

Catholic Spirit

"And when he departed, he lighted on Jehonadab the son of Rechab coming to meet him, and he saluted him, and said to him, Is your heart right, as my heart is with thy heart? And Jehonadab answered: It is. If it be, give me your hand" (2 Kgs. 10:15).

The very first thing we may observe in these words, is, that here is no inquiry concerning Jehonadab's opinions. And yet it is certain, he held some which were very uncommon, indeed quite peculiar to himself . . .

It is very possible, that many good men now also may entertain peculiar opinions: and some of them may be as singular herein as even Jehonadab was. And it is certain, so long as *we know* but *in part*, that all men will not see all things alike. It is an unavoidable consequence of the present weakness and shortness of human understanding, that several men will be of several minds in religion as well as in common life. So it has been from the beginning of the world, and so it will be till the restitution of all things . . .

Every wise man, therefore, will allow others the same liberty of thinking which he desires they should allow him: and will no more insist on their embracing his opinions, than he would have them to insist on his embracing theirs. He bears with those who differ from him, and only asks him with whom he desires to unite in love that single question, "Is your heart right, as my heart is with your heart?"

We may, secondly, observe that here is no inquiry made concerning Jehonadab's mode of worship: although it is highly probable there was, in this respect also, a very wide difference between them. For we may well believe Jehonadab, as well as all his posterity, worshiped God at Jerusalem: whereas Jehu did not; he had more regard to state-policy than religion. And therefore although he slew the worshippers of Baal, and destroyed Baal out of Israel, yet from the convenient sin of Jeroboam, the worship of the "golden calves," he "departed not" (2 Kgs. 10:29).

But even among men of an upright heart, men who desire to have a conscience void of offence, it must needs be, that, as long as there are various opinions, there will be various ways of worshiping God: seeing a variety of opinion necessarily implies a variety of practice. And as in all ages, men have differed in nothing more than in their opinions concerning the Supreme Being, so in nothing have they more differed from each other, than in the manner of worshiping him . . .

And how shall we choose, among so much variety? No man can choose for, or prescribe to another. But everyone must follow the dictates of his own conscience, in simplicity and godly sincerity. He must be fully persuaded in his own mind and then act according to the best light he has. Nor has any creature power, to constrain another to walk by his own rule. God has given no right to any of the children of men, thus to lord it over the conscience of his brethren. But every man must judge for himself, as every man must give an account of himself to God . . .

But while he is steadily fixed in his religious principles, in what he believes to be the truth as it is in Jesus; while he firmly adheres to that worship of God, which he judges to be most acceptable in his sight; and while he is united by the tenderest and closest ties to one particular congregation: his heart is enlarged toward all mankind, those he knows and those he does not: he embraces with strong and cordial affection neighbors and strangers, friends and enemies. This is catholic or universal love. And he that has this is of a catholic spirit. For love alone gives the title to this character. Catholic love is a catholic spirit.

Christian Perfection

In the first place I shall endeavor to show, in what sense Christians are not perfect. And both from experience and Scripture it appears, first that they are not perfect in knowledge. They are not so perfect in this life, as to be free from ignorance . . . Nor secondly, from mistake which indeed is almost an unavoidable consequence of it, seeing those who know but in part, are ever liable to err . . . In things not essential to salvation, they do err, and that frequently . . . Even the children of God are not agreed, as to the interpretation of Holy Scripture. Nor is their difference of opinion any proof that they are not the children of God on either side. But it is proof, that we are no more to expect any living man, to be infallible than to be omniscient.

We may thirdly add, nor from infirmities . . . So, one man tells us, "every man has his infirmity, and mine is drunkenness." Another has the infirmity of uncleanness; another of taking God's holy name in vain . . . It is plain, that all you who thus speak, with your infirmities, if you don't repent, you shall go quickly to Hell. But I mean, not only those which are properly termed bodily infirmities, but all those inward or outward imperfections, which are not of a moral nature. Such are weakness or slowness of understanding, dullness or confusedness of apprehension, incoherency of thought, irregular quickness or heaviness of imagination . . . Nor can we expect to be freed from temptation . . . The Son of God himself, in the days of his flesh, was tempted even to the end of his life . . .

Christian perfection therefore does not imply . . . an exemption either from ignorance or mistake, or infirmities or temptations. Indeed it is only another term for holiness . . . (but) there is no perfection of degrees, as it is termed, none of which does not admit a continual increase. So that how much any man has attained, or in how high a degree he is perfect, he has still need to grow in grace, and daily to advance in the knowledge and love of God his Savior . . .

Every one of these can say with St. Paul, "I am crucified with Christ. Nevertheless I live. Yet not I, but Christ lives in me" (Gal. 2:20). Words that manifestly describe a deliverance from inward, as well as outward sin. This is expressed negatively, "I live not." My evil nature, the body of sin is destroyed. And positively, "Christ lives in me" and therefore all that is holy, and just, and good. Indeed, both of these, "Christ lives in me" and "I live not" are inseparably connected. For what communion has light with darkness, or Christ with Satan?

He therefore who lives in true believers, has purified their hearts by faith. Insomuch that every one that has Christ in him, the hope of glory, purifies himself even as he is pure (I John 3:3). He is purified from pride, for Christ was lowly of heart. He is pure from self-will, or desire; for Christ desired only to do the will of his Father, and to finish his work. And he is pure from anger, in the common sense of the word; for Christ was meek and gentle, patient and long-suffering . . .

"Herein is our love made perfect, that we may have boldness in the day of judgment, because as he is, so are we in this world" . . . (here) he flatly affirms, that not only at, or after death, but in this world, they are as their Master (I John 4:17).

Arminianism

To say, "This man is an Arminian," has the same effect on many hearers, as to say, "This is a mad dog." It puts them into a fright at once. They run away from him with all speed and diligence; and will hardly stop, unless it be to throw a stone at the dreadful and mischievous animal . . .

The errors charged upon these (usually termed Arminians) by their opponents, are five: (1) That they deny original sin; (2) That they deny justification by faith; (3) That they deny absolute predestination; (4) That they deny the grace of God to be irresistible; and (5) That they affirm, a believer may fall from grace.

With regard to the first two of these charges, they plead, not guilty. They are entirely false. No man that ever lived, not John Calvin himself, ever asserted either original sin, or justification by faith, in more strong, more clear and express terms than Arminius has done . . .

But there is an undeniable difference between the Calvinists and Arminians, with regard to the three other questions. Here they divide; the former believe absolute, the latter only conditional, predestination. The Calvinists hold (1) God has absolutely decreed, from all eternity, to save such and such persons, and no others; and that Christ died for these, and none else. The Arminians hold, God has decreed, from all eternity, touching all that have the written word, "He that believes shall be saved; He that believes not, shall be condemned." And in order to this, "Christ died for all, all that were dead in trespasses and sins," (1 Cor. 5:14) that is, for every child of Adam, since "in Adam all died" (1 Cor. 15:22).

The Calvinists hold, secondly, that the saving grace of God is absolutely irresistible; that no man is any more able to resist it, than to resist the stroke of lightning. The Arminans hold, that although there may be some moments wherein the grace of God acts irresistibly, yet, in general, any man may resist and that to his eternal ruin, the grace whereby it was the will of God he should have been eternally saved.

The Calvinists hold, thirdly, that a true believer in Christ cannot possibly fall from grace. The Arminians hold, that a true believer may "make shipwreck of faith and a good conscience" (1 Tim. 1:19); that he may fall, not only foully, but finally, so as to perish forever.

SOURCE: "Aldersgate Experience" selection is from Nehemiah Curnock, ed., *The Journal of the Rev. John Wesley, A.M.*, standard ed., vol. 1 (London: Robert Culley, 1909), 472–77. John Wesley, *Catholick Spirit. A Sermon on 2 Kings, X.15* (London: printed by H. Cock, 1755), 3, 6, 8–10, 25. John Wesley, *Christian Perfection: A Sermon* (London: Printed by W. Strahan, 1746), 7, 9–12, 14–15, 38–40. Arminianism selection from "What is an Arminian?" in John Wesley, *The Works of the Rev. John Wesley, A.M.*, vol. 10, *Letters, Essays, Dialogs and Addresses* (London: Wesleyan-Methodist Book-Room, 1872), 358–60.

51

CHARLES WESLEY

CHARLES WESLEY (1707–1788), along with his brother John, cofounded the Methodist movement within the Church of England. Charles was an avid hymnodist, and many of his hymns are still sung today, including "Christ the Lord Is Risen Today," "Hark! the Herald Angels Sing," and "Love Divine, All Loves Excelling." The hymn below expresses the Wesleyan understanding of sanctification and perfect love, a blessing through which a believer never intentionally sins.

Love Divine

Love divine, all love excelling, Joy of Heav'n, to earth come down!
Fix in us Thy humble dwelling; All Thy faithful mercies crown.
Jesus, Thou art all compassion, Pure, unbounded love Thou art;
Visit us with Thy salvation; Enter ev'ry trembling heart.

Breathe, O breathe Thy loving Spirit, Into ev'ry troubled breast!
Let us all in Thee inherit, Let us find that second rest.
Take away our bent to sinning; Alpha and Omega be;
End of faith, as its beginning, Set our hearts at liberty.

Come, Almighty to deliver, Let us all Thy life receive;
Suddenly return, and never, Never-more Thy temples leave;
Thee we would be always blessing, Serve Thee as Thy hosts above,
Pray, and praise Thee without ceasing, Glory in Thy perfect love.

Finish then Thy new creation; Pure and spotless let us be;
Let us see Thy great salvation, Perfectly restored in Thee;
Changed from glory into glory, Till in Heav'n we take our place,
Till we cast our crowns before Thee, Lost in wonder, love, and praise.

Source: Charles Wesley, "Love Divine," *The Popular Hymnal: Old Standard Hymns and Popular Gospel Songs for Use in All Departments of Church, Sunday School and Young People's Work*, ed. Robert H. Coleman (Dallas: Robert Coleman, 1918), 132.

52

JONATHAN EDWARDS

Jonathan Edwards (1703–1758) was a Congregationalist minister in Northampton, Massachusetts, and considered by some to be one of America's greatest theologians. His preaching and writing were integral to the "First Great Awakening," often referred to as the first major revival in American Christianity. Edward's Calvinistic understanding of conversion is apparent in *A Faithful Narrative of the Surprising Work of God* (1737) (excerpt below). His account of revival became a model for subsequent revival activity. Edwards' most influential sermon was *Sinners in the Hands of an Angry God* (1741) (excerpt below), which has been caricatured into high-volume "hellfire and brimstone" evangelistic preaching.

First Great Awakening

Just after my grandfather's death, it seemed to be a time of extraordinary dullness in religion: licentiousness for some years greatly prevailed among the youth of the town; they were many of them very much addicted to night-walking, and frequenting the tavern, and lewd practices, wherein some by their examples exceedingly corrupted others. It was their manner very frequently to get together, in conventions of both sexes, for mirth and jollity, which they called frolics, and they would often spend the greater part of the night in them . . .

And then it was, in the latter part of December [1734], that the Spirit of God began extraordinarily to set in and wonderfully to work among us . . . A great and earnest concern about the great things of religion, and the eternal world, became universal in all parts of the town, and among persons of all degrees, and all ages; the noise among the dry bones waxed louder and louder. All other talk but about spiritual and eternal things was soon thrown by . . . .

Persons are first awakened with a sense of their miserable condition by nature, the danger they are in of perishing eternally . . . Some are more suddenly seized with convictions . . . Their consciences are suddenly smitten as if their hearts were pierced through with a dart. Others have awakenings that come upon them more gradually; they begin at first to be something more thoughtful and considerate, so as to come to a conclusion in their minds that it is their best and wisest way to delay no longer . . .

Conversion is a great and glorious work of God's power, at once changing the heart, and infusing life into the dead soul; though that grace that is then implanted does more gradually display itself in some than in others. But as to fixing on the precise time when they put forth the very first act of grace, there is a great deal of difference in different persons; in some it seems to be very discernible when the very time of this was; but others are more at a loss . . . In some, converting light is like a glorious brightness suddenly shining in upon a person, and all around him. They are in a remarkable manner brought out of darkness into marvelous light. In many others it has been like the dawning of the day, when at first but a little light appears, and it may be presently hid with a cloud, and then it appears again, and shines a little brighter . . .

Hellfire and Brimstone

There is the dreadful Pit of the glowing Flames of the Wrath of God; there is Hell's wide gaping Mouth open; and you have nothing to stand upon, nor any Thing to take hold of: There is nothing between you and Hell but the Air; 'tis only the Power and mere Pleasure of God that holds you up.

You probably are not sensible of this; you find you are kept out of Hell, but don't see the Hand of God in it, but look at other Things, as the good State of your bodily Constitution, your Care of your own Life, and the Means you use for your own Preservation. But indeed these Things are nothing; if God should withdraw his Hand, they would avail no more to keep you from falling, than the thin Air to hold up a Person that is suspended in it.

Your Wickedness makes you as it were heavy as Lead, and to tend downwards with great Weight and Pressure towards Hell; and, if God should let you go, you would immediately sink, and swiftly descend and plunge into the bottomless Gulf; and your healthy Constitution, and your own Care and Prudence, and best Contrivance, and all your Righteousness, would have no more Influence to uphold you and keep you out of Hell, than a Spider's Web would have to stop a falling Rock. Were it not that so is the sovereign Pleasure of God, the Earth would not bear you one Moment; for you are a Burden to it; the Creation groans with you; the Creature is made subject to the Bondage of your Corruption, not willingly; the Sun doesn't willingly shine upon you, to give you Light to serve Sin and Satan; the Earth doesn't willingly yield her Increase to satisfy your Lusts, nor is it willingly a Stage for your Wickedness to be acted upon; the Air doesn't willingly serve you for Breath to maintain the Flame of Life in your Vitals, while you spend your Life in the Service of God's enemies. God's Creatures are good, and were made for Men to serve God with, and don't willingly submit to any other Purpose, and groan when they are abused to Purposes so directly contrary to the Nature and End. And the World would spew you out, were it not for the sovereign Hand of him who hath subjected it in Hope. There are the black Clouds of God's Wrath now hanging directly over your Heads, full of the dreadful Storm, and big with Thunder; and, were it not for the restraining Hand of God, it would immediately burst forth upon you. The sovereign Pleasure of God for the present stays his rough Wind; otherwise it would come with Fury, and your Destruction would come like a Whirlwind, and you would be like the Chaff of the Summer Threshing-floor.

SOURCE: Selection on First Great Awakening from Jonathan Edwards, *Edwards on Revivals Containing A Faithful Narrative of the Surprising Work of God in the Conversion of Many Hundred Souls in Northampton, Massachusetts, A.D. 1735* (New York: Dunning & Spalding, 1832), 33–38, 47–49, 69–70. "Hellfire and Brimstone" is from *Sinners in the Hands of an Angry God. A sermon preached at Enfield, July 8th 1741 at a time of great awaknings* [sic]; . . . by Jonathan Edwards . . . (Edinburgh: Boston, printed: Edinburgh, reprinted by T. Lumisden and J. Robertson, and sold at their Printing-house, 1745).

53

IMMANUEL KANT

IMMANUEL KANT (1724–1804) was a German philosopher who was a seminal thinker in the development of modern philosophy and the age of the Enlightenment. He primarily wrote about epistemology, reason, and ethics. His influential books included *Critique of Pure Reason* (1781) and *Critique of Practical Reason* (1788). In the latter, he developed his moral philosophy of the categorical imperative, the ethical theory that absolute moral commands are rooted in universal duty.

Ethics

ETHIC, in so far as founded on the Idea of Humanity as a free Agent, binding himself, by virtue of that very Freedom, to an unconditionate Law of Reason, is by itself complete and entire; so that mankind neither requires the idea of any Superior Person to enable him to investigate his duty, nor does he need any incentive or spring to its execution other than the law itself. At least it must be his own fault if there exist any such want or need; a defect, however, quite without remedy from any foreign sources; since, whatsoever is not originated by himself from his own freedom, cannot supply or make up the want of his own morality.

A System of Ethics, therefore, needs no Religion, neither *objectively* to aid man's WILL, nor *subjectively*, as respects his ability, to aid his POWER; but stands, by force of pure practical reason, self-sufficient and independent: for, since its decrees have ethical virtue to oblige by the bare form of that universal legality wherewith all maxims must coincide, such formal fitness for law universal, being the supreme and unconditionate condition of the intent of all actions whatsoever, it results that Ethic needs no material determinator of choice, i.e. requires no ulterior end, either to recognize what is duty, or to excite toward its execution, but, on the contrary, can and ought, in a question regarding duty, to abstract from all ends whatsoever. To take an instance, suppose I wish to know, if I SHOULD (or can) speak truth in the witness-box, or re-deliver a deposit entrusted to my care, then I require to make no inquiry concerning any end or purpose which my evidence or re-delivery may accomplish; for he who in such a case should cast about for some ulterior motive, would show by doing so that he is a villain . . . Thus, for morality no end is required, only the law, which is the formal condition of the use of freedom; but ETHIC gives birth to an end: nor can reason remain indifferent to the question, WHAT IS TO BE THE RESULT OF ALL HER RIGHT ACTING? toward which final result as a goal (even supposing that goal beyond our reach) she might direct all her actions, as toward a common center . . .

ETHIC issues then inevitably in RELIGION, by extending itself to the idea of an Omnipotent Moral Lawgiver, in whose will, *that* is the end of the creation, which at the same time can and ought to be likewise mankind's chief end.

. . . When, therefore, it is said, "Mankind is by Nature Good," or "He is by Nature Evil," those positions merely mean "he contains within him an *unsearchable* last ground of adopting good or of adopting bad maxims;" which ground, unfathomable even by his own reason, pervades and tinges so universally the species, as to serve for an exponent whereby to indicate the character of the whole race . . . for the man himself is at all times the sole author of his character.

. . . It behooves him to become a good man; and he can only be deemed *morally good*, in regard of whatever, as done by himself, can be imputed to his account.

Against this proposal of self-amelioration, Reason, now naturally disinclined to the irksomeness of any moral task, seeks refuge by screening itself under the allegation of mankind's natural imbecility, and there shielding itself by all sorts of impure religious ideas (amongst which is to be reckoned the ascribing to God greatest-happiness-principles as the condition of his Law). Again, all religions may be divided into those of MERE WORSHIP and THE RELIGION OF A MORAL LIFE. Agreeably to the former, mankind either flatters himself that God will provide for his everlasting welfare, quite apart from his becoming a morally better man (by remitting his sins): or, should this last appear to him incredible, that God may perhaps straightway make him better, and that too independently of his own exertions, provided he only earnestly beseech it by instant prayers and supplications; whereby since, in the eye of an all-seeing person, PRAYING can be nothing else than tantamount to WISHING, nothing need at all be done; for indeed if a wish could accomplish such a transformation, then would everyone be good. But the principles of MORAL RELIGION (which, amid all public ones that have hitherto appeared, THE CHRISTIAN RELIGION alone is), this is the unalterable decree, "*that everyone must do as much as in him lies in order to render himself a better man*, and only then, *when he has not buried his connate talent, nor tied it up in a napkin (Luke 19:12-20) i.e. when he has unfolded the germs latent in his aboriginal susceptibilities for good, may he hope, that what lies beyond his power may be supplied by a higher cooperation."*

SOURCE: Immanuel Kant, *Religion Within the Boundary of Pure Reason*, trans. J. W. Semple (Edinburgh: Thomas Clark, 1838), 1–4, 20–21, 61–62.

54

FRIEDRICH SCHLEIERMACHER

FRIEDRICH SCHLEIERMACHER (1768–1834) was a German Protestant theologian who has been called the "father of liberal theology." Important writings included *On Religion: Speeches to Its Cultured Despisers* (1799) and *The Christian Faith* (1821 and revised 1830). Schleiermacher argued that personal religious experience, and not reason, was the authoritative basis of religious truth. His Christology was one example of the liberal effort to redefine doctrinal tenets in an attempt to make them more palatable to the modern mind. Christ was described as a human who functioned as divine for others; he was fully God-conscious but not divine in substance as Nicene orthodoxy had stated. The following texts are examples of Schleiermacher's emphases on religion, the relationship between religion and the individual's feelings, and God-consciousness.

On Religion

From time immemorial faith has not been everyone's affair, for at all times only a few have understood something of religion while millions have variously played with its trappings with which it has willingly let itself be draped out of condescension.

Especially now, the life of cultivated persons is removed from everything that would in the least way resemble religion. I know that you worship the deity in holy silence just as little as you visit the forsaken temples, that in your tasteful dwellings there are no other household gods than the maxims of the sages and the songs of the poets, and that humanity and fatherland, art and science (for you imagine yourselves capable of all of this) have taken possession of your minds so completely that no room is left over for the eternal and holy being that for you lies beyond the world, and that you have no feelings for and with it. You have succeeded in making your earthly lives so rich and many-sided that you no longer need the eternal, and after having created a universe for yourselves, you are spared from thinking of that which created you. You are agreed, I know, that nothing new and nothing convincing can be said anymore about this matter, which has been sufficiently belabored in all directions by philosophers and prophets and, if only I might not add, by scoffers and priests. Least of all—something that can escape no one—are you inclined to listen to something on this subject from the last mentioned, who have long since made themselves unworthy of your trust, as the kind of people who best like to dwell only in the dilapidated ruins of the sanctuary and who cannot live even there without disfiguring and damaging it still more. All this I know and am nevertheless convinced to speak by an inner and irresistible necessity that divinely rules me, and cannot retract my invitation that you especially should listen to me.

The power that is religion's due, which it merits anew in every moment, satisfies it; and for religion, which considers everything holy, what maintains the same rank with it in human nature is even holier. But it is actually supposed to serve as those wish; it is to have a purpose, and is to render itself useful. What denigration! And should its defenders greedily procure this for religion? Yet those who thus proceed from utility, for whom, in the end, even ethical life and law are there for the sake of another advantage, might themselves better founder in this eternal cycle of general utility in which they allow everything good to perish and of which no person who even wishes to be something for himself understands a sound work. Better that than to set themselves up as defenders of religion whose cause they are truly the most inept to lead. A lovely fame for heavenly religion, if it were now able to provide so passably for the earthly affairs of humanity! Much honor to this free and carefree one, if it were only somewhat more vigilant and active than the conscience! Religion does not descend to you from heaven for such purpose. What is loved and esteemed only for an advantage that lies outside may well be needed, but it is not in itself necessary; it can always remain a pious wish that never comes into existence, and a reasonable person places no extraordinary value on it, but merely the value that is appropriate to the other thing. And this would be little enough in the case of religion. I, at least, would bid for it stingily, for I must only confess that I do not believe that the unjust actions it hinders and the ethical deeds it is supposed to have produced are so serious. If that should be the only thing that can command respect for it, I want to have nothing to do with its cause. To recommend it merely as an aside is too insignificant. An imagined praise that disappears when one observes it more closely cannot assist something that deals in higher claims. What I assert and what I should like to establish for religion include the following: It springs necessarily and by itself from the interior of every better soul, it has its own province in the mind in which it reigns sovereign, and it is worthy of moving the noblest and the most excellent by means of its innermost power and by having its innermost essence known by them. Now it is up to you to decide whether it is worth your while to listen to me before you become still more entrenched in your contempt.

Feeling of Dependence

Let us now think of the feeling of dependence and the feeling of freedom as *one*, in the sense that not only the subject but the corresponding Other is the same for both. Then the total self-consciousness made up of both together is one of *Reciprocity* between the subject and the corresponding Other. Now let us suppose the totality of all moments of feeling, of both kinds, as one whole: then the corresponding Other is also to be supposed as a totality or as one, and then that term "reciprocity" is the right one for our self-consciousness in general, inasmuch as it expresses our connection with everything which either appeals to our receptivity or is subjected to our activity. And this is true not only when we particularize this Other and ascribe to each of its elements a different degree of relation to the twofold consciousness within us, but also when we think of the total "outside" as one, and moreover (since it contains other receptivities and activities to which we have a relation) as one together and ourselves, that is, as a *World*. Accordingly our self-consciousness, as our consciousness of our existence in the world or of our coexistence with the world, is a series in which the feeling of freedom and the feeling of dependence are divided . . . But the self-consciousness which accompanies all our activity, and therefore, since that is never zero, accompanies our whole existence, and negatives absolute freedom, is itself precisely a consciousness of absolute dependence.

Christology

The Redeemer, then, is like all men in virtue of the identity of human nature, but distinguished from them all by the constant potency of His God-consciousness, which was a veritable existence of God in Him . . .

But in admitting that what is peculiar in the Redeemer's kind of activity belongs to a general aspect of human nature, we by no means wish to reduce this activity, and the personal dignity by which it is conditioned, to the same measure as that of others. The simple fact that faith in Christ postulates a relation on His part to the whole race, while everything analogous is valid only for definite individual times and places, is sufficient to prove this. For no one has yet succeeded, in any sphere of science or art, and no one will ever succeed, in establishing himself as head, universally animating and sufficient for the whole human race.

For this peculiar dignity of Christ, however, in the sense in which we have already referred back the ideality of His person to this spiritual function of the God-consciousness implanted in the self-consciousness, the terms of our proposition alone are adequate; for to ascribe to Christ an absolutely powerful God-consciousness, and to attribute to Him an existence of God in Him, are exactly the same thing. The expression, "the existence of God in anyone" can only express the relation of the omnipresence of God to this one . . . But so far as the rational self-consciousness is concerned, it is certain that the God-consciousness which (along with the self-consciousness) belongs to human nature originally, before the Redeemer and apart from all connexion with Him, cannot fittingly be called an existence of God in us, not only because it was not a pure God-consciousness (either in polytheism or even in Jewish monotheism, which was everywhere tinctured with materialistic conceptions, whether cruder or finer), but also because such as it was, it did not assert itself as activity, but in these religions was always dominated by the sensuous self-consciousness. If, then, it was able neither to portray God purely and with real adequacy in thought, nor yet to exhibit itself as pure activity, it cannot be represented as an existence of God in us . . . We posit the God-consciousness in His self-consciousness as continually and exclusively determining every moment, and consequently also this perfect indwelling of the Supreme Being as His peculiar being and His inmost self. Indeed, working backwards we must now say, if it is only through Him that the human God-consciousness becomes an existence of God in human nature, and only through the rational nature that the totality of finite powers can become an existence of God in the world, that in truth He alone mediates all existence of God in the world and all revelation of God through the world, in so far as He bears within Himself the whole new creation which contains and develops the potency of the God-consciousness . . .

The origin of every human life may be regarded in a twofold manner, as issuing from the narrow circle of descent and society to which it immediately belongs, and as a fact of human nature in general. The more definitely the weaknesses of that narrow circle repeat themselves in an individual, the more valid becomes the first point of view. The more the individual by the kind and degree of his gifts transcends that circle, and the more he exhibits what is new within it, the more we are thrown back upon the other explanation. This means that the beginning of Jesus' life cannot in any way be explained by the first factor, but only and exclusively by the second; so that from the beginning He must have been free from every influence from earlier generations which disseminated sin and disturbed the inner God-consciousness, and He can only be understood as an original act of human nature, i.e. as an act of human nature as not affected by sin. The beginning of His life was also a new implanting of the God-consciousness which creates receptivity in human nature; hence this content and that manner or origin are in such a close relation that they mutually condition and explain each other. That new implanting came to be through the beginning of His life, and therefore that beginning must have transcended every detrimental influence of His immediate circle; and because it was such an original and sin-free act of nature, a filling of His nature with God-consciousness became possible as its result. So that upon this relation too the fullest light is thrown if we regard the beginning of the life of Jesus as the completed creation of human nature. The appearance of the first man constituted at the same time the physical life of the human race; the appearance of the Second Adam constituted for this nature a new spiritual life, which communicates and develops itself by spiritual fecundation . . . If the impartation of the Spirit to human nature which was made in the first Adam was insufficient, in that the spirit remained sunk in sensuousness and barely glanced forth clearly at moments as a presentiment of something better, and if the work of creation has only been completed through the second and equally original impartation to the Second Adam, yet both events go back to one undivided eternal divine decree and form, even in a higher sense, only one and the same natural system, though one unattainable by us.

SOURCE: The selection "On Religion" is from Friedrich Schleiermacher, *On Religion*, ed. and trans. Richard Crouter (Cambridge: Cambridge University Press, 1996), 3–4, 17. Reprinted with the permission of Cambridge University Press. The selections "Christology" and "Feeling of Dependence" are from Friedrich Schleiermacher, *The Christian Faith* (New York: T&T Clark, 1999), 14–16, 385–89. By kind permission of T&T Clark, an imprint of Bloomsbury Publishing, Plc.

55

SØREN KIERKEGAARD

SØREN KIERKEGAARD (1813–1855), known as the father of existential-ism, contributed to the fields of philosophy, theology, literature, and psychology. His writings (often pseudonymous) emphasize personal choice, Christian ethics, and relationship with God. Kierkegaard often attacked the institutional church and its control by the state as damaging to the individual nature of faith. In the selection below, Kierkegaard addresses the paradoxical nature of faith and the ethical demands it places upon one's life.

Paradox of Faith

The paradox [of faith] can also be expressed by saying that there is an absolute duty toward God; for in this relationship of duty the individual as an indi-vidual stands related absolutely to the absolute. So when in this connection it is said that it is a duty to love God . . . if this duty is absolute, the ethical is reduced to a position of relativity. From this, however, it does not follow that the ethical is to be abolished, but it acquires an entirely different expression, the paradoxical expression—that for example, love to God may cause the knight of faith to give his love to his neighbor the opposite expression to that which, ethically speaking is required by duty . . .

In the story of Abraham we find such a paradox. His relation to Isaac, ethically expressed, is this, that the father should love the son. This ethical relation is reduced to a relative position in contrast with the absolute relation to God. To the question, "Why?" Abraham has no answer except that it is a trial, a temptation {*Fristelse*}—terms which, as was remarked above, express the unity of the two points of view: that it is for God's sake and for his own sake. In common usage these two ways of regarding the matter are mutually exclusive. Thus when we see a man do something which does not comport with the universal, we say that he scarcely can be doing it for God's sake, and by that we imply that he does it for his own sake . . .

Faith is this paradox, and the individual absolutely cannot make himself intelligible to anybody. People imagine maybe that the individual can make himself intelligible to another individual in the same case. Such a notion would be unthinkable if in our time people did not in so many ways seek to creep slyly into greatness. The one knight of faith can render no aid to the other. Either the individual becomes a knight of faith by assuming the burden of the paradox, or he never becomes one . . .

He who believes that it is easy enough to be the individual can always be sure that he is not a knight of faith, for vagabonds and roving geniuses are not men of faith. The knight of faith knows, on the other hand, that it is glorious to belong to the universal. He knows that it is beautiful and salutary to be the individual who translates himself into the universal, who edits as it were a pure and elegant edition of himself, as free from errors as possible and which everyone can read . . . But he knows also that higher than this there winds a solitary path, narrow and steep; he knows that it is terrible to be born outside the universal, to walk without meeting a single traveler. He knows very well where he is and how he is related to men. Humanly speaking, he is crazy and cannot make himself intelligible to anyone . . .

SOURCE: Excerpts from *Fear and Trembling* are republished with permission of Princeton University Press, from Søren Kierkegaard, *Fear and Trembling: A Dialectical Lyric*, translated with introduction and notes by Walter Lowrie (Princeton, N.J.: Princeton University Press, 1941), 105–7, 114–15; permission conveyed through Copyright Clearance Center, Inc.

56

LUDWIG FEUERBACH

LUDWIG FEUERBACH (1804–1872) was a German philosopher and an atheist. Many of his writings, especially *The Essence of Christianity* (1841), attacked Christianity. Feuerbach provided an anthropological approach to the study of religion. He believed that religion and perceptions of God were only projections of human thoughts, aspirations, and feelings (excerpt below).

Religion as Projection

Religion is the childlike condition of humanity; but the child sees his nature-man-out of himself; in childhood a man is an object to himself, under the form of another man. Hence the historical progress of religion consists in this: that what by an earlier religion was regarded as objective, is now recognized as subjective; that is, what was formerly contemplated and worshipped as God is now perceived to be something *human* . . . And it is our task to show that the antithesis of divine and human is altogether illusory, that it is nothing else than the antithesis between the human nature in general, and the human individual: that, consequently, the object and contents of the Christian religion are altogether human.

Religion, at least the Christian, is the relation of man to himself, or more, correctly to his own nature (i.e., his subjective nature); but a relation to it, viewed as nature apart from his own. The divine being is nothing else than the human being, or, rather the human nature purified, freed from the limits of the individual man . . .

You believe in love as a divine attribute because you yourself love; you believe that God is a wise, benevolent being because you know nothing better in yourself than benevolence and wisdom; and you believe that God exists, and therefore he is a subject—whatever exists is a subject, whether it be defined as substance, person, essence, or otherwise—because you yourself exists, are yourself a subject. You know no higher human good than to love, than to be good and wise; and even so you know no higher happiness than to exist, to be a subject; for the consciousness of all reality, of all bliss, is for you bound up in the consciousness of being a subject, of existing. God is an existence, a subject to you, for the same reason that he is to you a wise, a blessed, a personal being. The distinction between the divine predicates and the divine subject is only this, that to you the subject, the existence, does not appear an anthropomorphism, because the conception of it is necessarily involved in your own existence as a subject, where as the predicates do appear anthropomorphisms, because their necessity—the necessity that God should be conscious, wise, good, & etc.—is not an immediate necessity, identical with the being of man, but is evolved by his self-consciousness, by the activity of his thought . . .

Thus, in religion man denies his reason; of himself he knows nothing of God, his thoughts are only worldly, earthly; he can only believe what God reveals to him. But on this account the thoughts of God are human, earthly thoughts: like man, He has plans in His mind, he accommodates himself to circumstances and grades of intelligence, like a tutor with his pupils; he calculates closely the effect of his gifts and revelations; he observes man in all his doings; he knows all things; even the most earthly, the commonest, the most trivial. In brief, man in relation to God denies his own knowledge, his own thoughts, that he may place them in God. Man gives up his personality; but in return, God, the Almighty, infinite, unlimited being, is a person; he denies human dignity, the human *ego;* but in return God is to him a selfish, egoistical being, who in all things seeks only Himself, his own honor, his own ends; he represents God as simply seeking the satisfaction of his own selfishness, while yet He frowns on that of every other being; his God is the very luxury of egoism . . .

Man—this is the mystery of religion—projects his being into objectivity, and then again makes himself an object to this projected image of himself thus converted into a subject he thinks of himself, is an object to himself, but as the object of an object, of another being than himself. Thus here. Man is an object to God. That man is good or evil is not indifferent to God; no! He has a lively, profound interest in man's being good; he wills that man should be good, happy for without goodness there is no happiness. Thus the religious man virtually retracts the nothingness of human activity, by making his dispositions and actions an object to God, by making man the end of God—for that which is an object to the mind is an end in action; by making the divine activity a means of human salvation. God acts, that man may be good and happy. Thus man, while he is apparently humiliated to the lowest degree, is in truth exalted to the highest. Thus, in and through God, man has in view himself alone. It is true that man places the aim of his action in God, but God has no other aim of action than the moral and eternal salvation of man: thus man has in fact no other aim than himself. The divine activity is not distinct from the human.

SOURCE: Ludwig Feuerbach, *The Essence of Christianity*, trans. Marian Evans (London: John Chapman, 1854), 13–14, 18, 26–27, 29–30.

57

PETER CARTWRIGHT

PETER CARTWRIGHT (1785–1872) was a Methodist revivalist who is especially known for his participation in the Second Great Awakening on the American frontier. Cartwright was not formally trained in ministry and relied on extemporaneous anecdotal sermons, both traits of antebellum frontier religion. The selection below is from Cartwright's autobiography and chronicles the physical manifestations believed to be the Spirit's work in the revival meetings.

The Great Revival: The Jerks

In this revival, usually termed in the West the Cumberland revival, many joined the different Churches, especially the Methodist and Cumberland Presbyterians. The Baptists also came in for a share of the converts, but not to any great extent. Infidelity quailed before the mighty power of God, which was displayed among the people. Universalism was almost driven from the land. The Predestinarians of almost all sorts put forth a mighty effort to stop the work of God.

Just in the midst of our controversies on the subject of the powerful exercises among the people under preaching, a new exercise broke out among us, called the *jerks*, which was overwhelming in its effects upon the bodies and minds of the people. No matter whether they were saints or sinners, they would be taken under a warm song or sermon, and seized with a convulsive jerking all over, which they could not by any possibility avoid, and the more they resisted the more they jerked. If they would not strive against and pray in good earnest, the jerking would usually abate. I have seen more than five hundred persons jerking at one time in my large congregations. Most persons taken with the jerks, to obtain relief, as they said, would rise up and dance. Some would run, but could not get away. Some would resist; on such the jerks were generally very severe.

To see those proud young gentlemen and young ladies, dressed in their silks, jewelry, and prunella, from top to toe, take the *jerks*, would often excite my risibilities. The first jerk or so, you would see their fine bonnets, caps, and combs fly; and so sudden would be their jerking of the head that their long loose hair would crack almost as loud as a wagoner's whip.

. . . While I am on this subject I will relate a very serious circumstance which I knew to take place with a man who had the jerks at a camp-meeting, on what was called the Ridge, in William Magee's congregation. There was a great work of religion in the encampment. The jerks were very prevalent. There was a company of drunken rowdies who came to interrupt the meeting. These rowdies were headed by a very large drinking man. They came with their bottles of whiskey in their pockets. This large man cursed the jerks, and all religion. Shortly afterward he took the jerks, and he started to run, but he jerked so powerfully he could not get away. He halted among some saplings, and, although he was violently agitated, he took out his bottle of whiskey, and swore he would drink the damned jerks to death; but he jerked at such a rate he could not get the bottle to his mouth, though he tried hard. At length he fetched a sudden jerk, and the bottle struck a sapling and was broken to pieces, and spilled his whiskey on the ground. There was a great crowd gathered round him, and when he lost his whiskey he became very much enraged, and cursed and swore very profanely, his jerks still increasing. At length he fetched a very violent jerk, snapped his neck, fell, and soon expired, with his mouth full of cursing and bitterness.

I always looked upon the jerks as a judgment sent from God, first, to bring sinners to repentance; and, secondly, to show professors that God could work with or without means, and that he could work over and above means, and do whatsoever seemeth him good, to the glory of his grace and the salvation of the world.

There is no doubt in my mind that, with weakminded, ignorant, and superstitious persons, there was a great deal of sympathetic feeling with many that claimed to be under the influence of this jerking exercise; and yet, with many, it was perfectly involuntary. It was, on all occasions, my practice to recommend fervent prayer as a remedy, and it almost universally proved an effectual antidote.

SOURCE: Peter Cartwright, *Autobiography of Peter Cartwright*, ed. W. P. Strickland (New York: Hunt & Eaton, 1856), 48–51.

58

CHARLES G. FINNEY

CHARLES G. FINNEY (1792–1875), often called the "father of modern revivalism," was one of the key figures of the Second Great Awakening of the early nineteenth century. His revival methods—"new measures" like the anxious bench and protracted meetings—revealed a move away from the Calvinistic "surprising work of God" gradual conversion experiences of the First Great Awakening to more free will-friendly instantaneous conversion events. Finney was also involved in social reform. The selection below emphasizes revival methodology that came to characterize most American evangelism in the nineteenth and twentieth centuries.

Revivalism

Lectures on Revivals

It is altogether improbable that religion will ever make progress among *heathen* nations except through the influence of revivals. The attempt is now making to do it by education, and other cautious and gradual improvements. But so long as the laws of mind remain what they are, it cannot be done in this way. There must be excitement sufficient to wake up the dormant moral powers, and roll back the tide of degradation and sin. And precisely so far as our own land approximates to heathenism, it is impossible for God or man to promote religion in such a state of things but by powerful excitements. This is evident from the fact that this has always been the way in which God has done it. God does not create these excitements, and choose this method to promote religion for nothing, or without reason. Where mankind are so reluctant to obey God, they will not act until they are excited. For instance, how many there are who know that they ought to be religious, but they are afraid if they become pious they shall be laughed at by their companions. Many are wedded to idols, others are procrastinating repentance, until they are settled in life, or until they have secured some favorite worldly interest. Such persons never will give up their false shame, or relinquish their ambitious schemes, till they are so excited that they cannot contain themselves any longer . . .

A Revival of Religion Is Not a Miracle

A miracle has been generally defined to be, a Divine interference, setting aside or suspending the laws of nature. It is not a miracle, in this sense. All the laws of matter and mind remain in force. They are neither suspended nor set aside in a revival . . .

It is not a miracle, or dependent on a miracle, in any sense. It is a purely philosophical result of the right use of the constituted means—as much so as any other effect produced by the application of means. There may be a miracle among its antecedent causes, or there may not. The apostles employed miracles, simply as a means by which they arrested attention to their message, and established its Divine authority. But the miracle was not the revival. The miracle was one thing; the revival that followed it was quite another thing. The revivals in the apostles' days were connected with miracles, but they were not miracles.

I said that a revival is the result of the *right* use of the appropriate means. The means which God has enjoined for the production of a revival, doubtless have a natural tendency to produce a revival. Otherwise God would not have enjoined them. But means will not produce a revival, we all know, without the blessing of God. No more will grain, when it is sowed, produce a crop without the blessing of God. It is impossible for us to say that there is not as direct an influence or agency from God, to produce a crop of grain, as there is to produce a revival. What are the laws of nature, according to which, it is supposed, that grain yields a crop? They are nothing but the constituted manner of the operations of God. In the Bible, the word of God is compared to grain, and preaching is compared to sowing seed, and the results to the springing up and growth of the crop. And the result is just as philosophical in the one case, as in the other, and is as naturally connected with the cause . . .

I wish this idea to be impressed on all your minds, for there has long been an idea prevalent that promoting religion has something very peculiar in it, not to be judged of by the ordinary rules of cause and effect; in short, that there is no connection of the means with the result, and no tendency in the means to produce the effect, No doctrine is more dangerous than this to the prosperity of the church, and nothing more absurd.

Suppose a man were to go and preach this doctrine among farmers, about their sowing grain. Let him tell them that God is a sovereign, and will give them a crop only when it pleases him, and that for them to plow and plant and labor as if they expected to raise a crop is very wrong, and taking the work out of the hands of God, that it interferes with his sovereignty, and is going on in their own strength; and that there is no connection between the means and the result on which they can depend. And now, suppose the farmers should believe such doctrine. Why, they would starve the world to death.

Just such results will follow from the church's being persuaded that promoting religion is somehow so mysteriously a subject of Divine sovereignty, that there is no natural connection between the means and the end. What *are* the results? Why, generation after generation have gone down to hell. No doubt more than five thousand millions have gone down to hell, while the church has been dreaming, and waiting for God to save them without the use of means. It has been the devil's most successful means of destroying souls. The connection is as clear in religion as it is when the farmer sows his grain . . .

I Am to Show What a Revival Is

. . . It presupposes that the church is sunk down in a backslidden state, and a revival consists in the return of the church from her backslidings, and in the conversion of sinners.

A revival always includes conviction of sin on the part of the church. Backslidden professors cannot wake up and begin right away in the service of God, without deep searchings of heart. The fountains of sin need to be broken up. In a true revival, Christians are always brought under such convictions; they see their sins in such a light, that often they find it impossible to maintain a hope of their acceptance with God. It does not always go to that extent; but there are always, in a genuine revival, deep and convictions of sin, and often cases of abandoning all hope.

Backslidden Christians will be brought to repentance. A revival is nothing else than a new beginning of obedience to God. Just as in the case of a converted sinner, the first step is a deep repentance, a breaking down of heart, a getting down into the dust before God, with deep humility, and forsaking of sin . . . When the churches are thus awakened and reformed, the reformation and salvation of sinners will follow, going through the same stages of conviction, repentance, and reformation.

SOURCE: Charles G. Finney, *Lectures on Revivals of Religion* (New York: Fleming H. Revell Co., 1868), 11–15.

59

RICHARD FURMAN

RICHARD FURMAN (1755–1825) was one of the most influential Baptists in antebellum America. As a Baptist pastor in Charleston, South Carolina, Furman was a leader in promoting missions and education and served as the first president of the Triennial Convention, the first national organization of Baptists (1814). Furman also wrote one of the most well-known Southern defenses of slavery—excerpted below—on behalf of South Carolina Baptists upon the occasion of the aborted slave revolt of Denmark Vesey in 1822.

A Defense of Slavery

. . . The right of holding slaves is clearly established by the Holy Scriptures, both by precept and example. In the Old Testament, the Israelites were directed to purchase their bond-men and bond-maids of the heathen nations; except they were of the Canaanites, for these were to be destroyed. And it is declared, that the persons purchased were to be their "bond-men forever," and an "inheritance for them and their children." They were not to go out free in the year of jubilee, as the Hebrews, who had been purchased, were: the line being clearly drawn between them. In example, they are presented to our view as existing in the families of the Hebrews as servants, or slaves, born in the house, or bought with money: so that the children born of slaves are here considered slaves as well as their parents. And to this well known state of things, as to its reason and order, as well as to special privileges, St. Paul appears to refer, when he says, "But I was free born" (Acts 22:28).

In the New Testament, the Gospel History, or representation of facts, presents us a view correspondent with that, which is furnished by other authentic ancient histories of the state of the world at the commencement of Christianity. The powerful Romans had succeeded, in empire, the polished Greeks; and under both empires, the countries they possessed and governed were full of slaves. Many of these with their masters, were converted to the Christian Faith, and received, together with them into the Christian Church, while it was yet under the ministry of the inspired Apostles. In things purely spiritual, they appear to have enjoyed equal privileges; but their relationship, as masters and slaves, was not dissolved . . .

Had the holding of slaves been a moral evil, it cannot be supposed, that the inspired Apostles, who feared not the faces of men, and were ready to lay down their lives in the cause of their God, would have tolerated it, for a moment, in the Christian Church. If they had done so on a principle of accommodation, in cases where the masters remained heathen, to avoid offences and civil commotion; yet, surely, where both master and servant were Christian, as in the case before us, they would have enforced the law of Christ, and required, that the master should liberate his slave in the first instance. But, instead of this, they let the relationship remain untouched, as being lawful and right, and insist on the relative duties.

In proving this subject justifiable by Scriptural authority, its morality is also proved; for the Divine Law never sanctions immoral actions.

The Christian golden rule, of doing to others, as we would they should do to us, has been urged as an unanswerable argument against holding slaves. But surely this rule is never to be urged against that order of things, which the Divine government has established; nor do our desires become a standard to us, under this rule, unless they have a due regard to justice, propriety, and the general good.

A father may very naturally desire, that his son should be obedient to his orders. Is he, therefore, to obey the orders of his son? A man might be pleased to be exonerated from his debts by the generosity of his creditors; or that his rich neighbor should equally divide his property with him; and in certain circumstances might desire these to be done. Would the mere existence of this desire, oblige him to exonerate *his* debtors, and to make such a division of his property? Consistency and generosity, indeed, might require it of him, if he were in circumstances which would justify the act of generosity;

but, otherwise, either action might be considered as the effect of folly and extravagance . . .

That Christian nations have not done all they might, or should have done, on a principle of Christian benevolence, for the civilization and conversion of the Africans; that much cruelty has been practiced in the slave trade, as the benevolent Wilberforce, and others have shown; that much tyranny has been exercised by individuals, as masters over their slaves, and that the religious interests of the latter have been too much neglected by many cannot, will not be denied. But the fullest proof of these facts, will not also prove, that the holding men in subjection, as slaves, is a moral evil, and inconsistent with Christianity. Magistrates, husbands, and fathers, have proved tyrants. This does not prove, that magistracy, the husband's right to govern, and parental authority, are unlawful and wicked. The individual who abuses his authority, and acts with cruelty, must answer for it at the Divine tribunal; and civil authority should interpose to prevent or punish it; but neither civil nor ecclesiastical authority can consistently interfere with the possession and legitimate exercise of a right given by the Divine Law . . .

Should, however, a time arrive, when the Africans in our country might be found qualified to enjoy freedom; and, when they might obtain it in a manner consistent with the interest and peace of the community at large, the Convention would be happy in seeing them free. And so they would, in seeing the state of the poor, the ignorant, and the oppressed of every description, and of every country meliorated; so that the reputed free might be free indeed, and happy. But there seems to be just reason to conclude that a considerable part of the human race, whether they bear openly the character of slaves or are reputed freemen, will continue in such circumstances, with mere shades of variation, while the world continues . . . Slavery, when tempered with humanity and justice, is a state of tolerable happiness; equal, if not superior, to that which many poor enjoy in countries reputed free.

SOURCE: Richard Furman, "Exposition of the Views of the Baptists Relative To The Coloured Population Of The United States In A Communication To The Governor of South Carolina" (dated December 24, 1822), in James Rogers, *Richard Furman: Life and Legacy* (Macon, Ga.: Mercer University Press, 1985), 274–86. Used by permission.

60

CIVIL WAR RELIGION

J OHN WILLIAM JONES (1836–1909) was a Baptist minister and chaplain in the Confederate military. His book *Christ in the Camp* described religion, especially revivalism in the Southern armies of General Robert E. Lee. Jones is considered one of the chief exponents of the "Lost Cause," i.e., the Southern way of life (a separate regional cultural identity, Christian faith, Southern honor, segregated races—the war was not an indictment against slavery) in the late nineteenth century. In the selection below from Jones' work, Robert Ryland (1805–1899), the first president of Richmond College (1832–1866), writes his son about participation in the Civil War. The selection highlights the Southern perspective that the war was a holy, just, defensive conflict and emphasizes the evangelistic tenor of evangelical religion.

War as Holy Cause

A Letter to a Son in Camp, July 17, 1861

My Dear Son:

It may have seemed strange to you that a professing Christian father so freely gave you, a Christian son, to enlist in the volunteer service. My reason was that I regard this as a *purely defensive war*. Not only did the Southern Confederacy propose to adjust the pending difficulties by peaceful and equitable negotiations, but Virginia used again and again the most earnest and noble efforts to prevent a resort to the sword. These overtures having been proudly spurned, and our beloved South having been threatened with invasions and subjugation, it seemed to me that nothing was left us but stern resistance or abject submission to unconstitutional power. A brave and generous people could not for a moment hesitate between such alternatives. A war in defense of our homes and firesides—of our wives and children—of all that makes life worth possessing is the result. While I most deeply deplore the necessity for the sacrifice, I could not but rejoice that I had a son to offer to the service of the country, and if I had a dozen *I would most freely give them all*. As you are now cheerfully enduring the hardships of the camp, I know you will listen to a father's suggestions touching the duties of your new mode of life . . .

The rules of war require prompt and unquestioning obedience. You may sometimes think the command arbitrary and the officer supercilious, but it is yours to obey. An undisciplined army is a curse to its friends and a derision to its foes. Give your whole influence, therefore, to the maintenance of lawful authority and strict order. Let your superiors feel that whatever they entrust to you will be faithfully done. Composed of such soldiers, and led by skillful and brave commanders, our army, by the blessing of God, will never be defeated. It is, moreover, engaged in a holy cause, and must triumph.

Try to maintain your Christian profession among your comrades. I need not caution you against strong drink as useless and hurtful, nor against profanity, so common among soldiers. Both these practices you abhor. Aim to take at once a decided stand for God. If practicable, have prayers regularly in your tent, or unite with your fellow-disciples in prayer-meetings in the camp. Should preaching be accessible, always be a hearer. Let the world know that you are a Christian. Read a chapter in the New Testament which your mother gave you, every morning and evening when you can, and engage in secret prayer to God for his Holy Spirit to guide and sustain you. I would rather hear of your death than of the shipwreck of your faith and good conscience . . .

Should it be your lot to enter into an engagement with the enemy, lift up your heart in secret ejaculations to the ever-present and good Being, that He will protect you from sudden death; or, if you fall, that He will receive your departing spirit, cleansed in the blood of Jesus, into His kingdom. It is better to trust in the Lord than to put confidence in princes. Commit your eternal interests, therefore, to the keeping of the Almighty Savior. You should not, even in the hour of deadly conflict, cherish personal rage against the enemy, any more than an officer of the law hates the victim of the law. How often does a victorious army tenderly care for the dead and wounded of the vanquished. War is a tremendous scourge which Providence sometimes uses to chastise proud and wicked nations. Both parties must suffer, even though one may get the advantage. There is no occasion, then, for adding to the intrinsic evils of the system the odious feature of animosity to individuals. In the ranks of the foe are thousands of plain men who do not understand the principles for which we are struggling. They are deceived by artful demagogues into a posture of hostility to those whom, knowing, they would love. It is against such men that you may perhaps be arrayed, and the laws of war do not forbid you to pity them, even in the act of destroying them. It is more important that *we* should exhibit a proper temper in this unfortunate context, because many professed Christians and ministers of the Gospel at the North are breathing out, in their very prayers and sermons, threatenings and slaughter against us! Oh! How painful that a gray-headed pastor should publicly exclaim, "*I would hang them as soon as I would shoot a mad dog.*"

Providence has placed you in the midst of thoughtless and unpardoned men. What a beautiful thing it would be if you could win some of them to the Savior! Will you not try? You will have many opportunities of speaking a word in season. The sick, you may comfort; the wavering, you may confirm; the backslidden, you may reclaim; the weary and heavy laden, you may point to Jesus for rest to the soul. It is not presumptuous for a young man, kindly and meekly, to commend the Gospel to his brother soldiers. The hardest of them will not repel a gentle approach, made in private. And many of them would doubtless be glad to have the subject introduced to them. They desire to hear of Jesus, but they lack courage to inquire of his people. An unusually large proportion of pious men have entered the army, and I trust they will give a new complexion to military life. Let them search out each other, and establish a fraternity among all the worshipers of God. To interchange religious views and administer brotherly counsel will be mutually edifying. "He that watereth shall be watered also himself."

And now, as a soldier has but little leisure, I will not occupy you longer. Be assured that every morning and evening we remember you, at the family altar to our Father in Heaven. We pray for a "speedy, just and honorable peace," and for the safe return of all the volunteers to their loved homes. All the children speak often of "brother," and hear your letters read with intense interest. That God Almighty may be your shield and your exceeding great reward is the constant prayer of your loving father.

Ro. Ryland

Source: Rev. J. W. M. Jones, *Christ in the Camp; or Religion in Lee's Army* (Waco, Tex.: James E. Yeager Publisher, 1887), 28–31.

61

FREDERICK DOUGLASS

FREDERICK DOUGLASS (1818–1895) was an escaped slave who became a well-known social reformer and international statesman. He argued for the equality of all people, whether African Americans, Native Americans, immigrants, or women. He is best known as an abolitionist in the battle against slavery in the United States. The selection below, from his autobiography that helped the abolitionist cause, highlights the inconsistencies Douglass finds in the religion of American Christians who are "in union with slaveholders."

Slavery and Christianity

I FIND, on reading over the foregoing Narrative that I have, in several instances, spoken in such a tone and manner, respecting religion, as may possibly lead those unacquainted with my religious views to suppose me an opponent of all religion. To remove the liability to such misapprehension, I deem it proper to append the following brief explanation. What I have said respecting and against religion, I mean strictly to apply to the *slaveholding religion* of this land, and with no reference whatever to Christianity proper; for, between the Christianity of this land, and the Christianity of Christ, I recognize the widest possible difference—so wide, that to receive the one as good, pure, and holy, is of necessity to reject the other as bad, corrupt, and wicked. To be the friend of the one, is of necessity to be the enemy of the other. I love the pure, peaceable, and impartial Christianity of Christ: I therefore hate the corrupt, slaveholding, women-whipping, cradle-plundering, partial and hypocritical Christianity of this land. Indeed, I can see no reason, but the most deceitful one, for calling the religion of this land Christianity. I look upon it as the climax of all misnomers, the boldest of all frauds, and the grossest of all libels. Never was there a clearer case of "stealing the livery of the court of heaven to serve the devil in." I am filled with unutterable loathing when I contemplate the religious pomp and show, together with the horrible inconsistencies, which every where surround me. We have men-stealers for ministers, women-whippers for missionaries, and cradle-plunderers for church members. The man who wields the blood-clotted cowskin during the week fills the pulpit on Sunday, and claims to be a minister of the meek and lowly Jesus. The man who robs me of my earnings at the end of each week meets me as a class-leader on Sunday morning, to show me the way of life, and the path of salvation. He who sells my sister, for purposes of prostitution, stands forth as the pious advocate of purity. He who proclaims it a religious duty to read the Bible denies me the right of learning to read the name of the God who made me. He who is the religious advocate of marriage robs whole millions of its sacred influence, and leaves them to the ravages of wholesale pollution. The warm defender of the sacredness of the family relation is the same that scatters whole families—sundering husbands and wives, parents and children, sisters and brothers—leaving the hut vacant, and the hearth desolate. We see the thief preaching against theft, and the adulterer against adultery. We have men sold to build churches, women sold to support the gospel, and babes sold to purchase Bibles for the *poor heathen! all for the glory of God and the good of souls!* The slave auctioneer's bell and the church-going bell chime in with each other, and the bitter cries of the heart-broken slave are drowned in the religious shouts of his pious master. Revivals of religion and revivals in the slave-trade go hand in hand together. The slave prison and the church stand near each other. The clanking of fetters and the rattling of chains in the prison, and the pious psalm and solemn prayer in the church, may be heard at the same time. The dealers in the bodies and souls of men erect their stand in the presence of the pulpit, and they mutually help each other. The dealer gives his blood-stained gold to support the pulpit, and the pulpit, in return, covers his infernal business with the garb of Christianity. Here we have religion and robbery the allies of each other—devils dressed in angels' robes, and hell presenting the semblance of paradise . . .

The Christianity of America is a Christianity, of whose votaries it may be as truly said, as it was of the ancient scribes and Pharisees . . . They strain at a gnat, and swallow a camel. Could anything be more true of our churches? They would be shocked at the proposition of fellowshiping a sheep-stealer; and at the same time they hug to their communion a *manstealer,* and brand me with being an infidel, if I find fault with them for it. They attend with Pharisaical strictness to the outward forms of religion, and at the same time neglect the weightier matters of the law, judgment, mercy, and faith. They are always ready to sacrifice, but seldom to show mercy. They are they who are represented as professing to love God whom they have not seen, whilst they hate their brother whom they have seen. They love the heathen on the other side of the globe. They can pray for him, pay money to have the Bible put into his hand, and missionaries to instruct him; while they despise and totally neglect the heathen at their own doors.

Such is, very briefly, my view of the religion of this land; and to avoid any misunderstanding, growing out of the use of general terms, I mean, by the religion of this land, that which is revealed in the words, deeds, and actions, of those bodies, north and south, calling themselves Christian churches, and yet in union with slaveholders.

SOURCE: Frederick Douglass, *Narrative of the Life of Frederick Douglass, an American Slave* (Boston: Published at the Anti-Slavery Office, 1845), 108–12.

62

PETER RANDOLPH

PETER RANDOLPH (ca. 1825–1897) was an emancipated slave (1840s) who began preaching at the age of ten. He was a Baptist, serving as a missionary and pastor. His work included freeing and protecting fugitive slaves. His autobiography *From Slave Cabin to the Pulpit* (1893) revealed cooperation with white Christians and an emphasis on becoming respectable; however, the selection below remembers in vivid images the cruelty of slavery, a topic Randolph did not want forgotten.

The True Nature of Slavery

Slaves on the Auction-Block. The auctioneer is crying the slave to the highest bidder. "Gentlemen, here is a very fine boy for sale. He is worth twelve hundred dollars. His name is Emanuel. He belongs to Deacon William Harrison, who wants to sell him because his overseer don't like him. How much, gentlemen—how much for this boy? He's a fine, hearty nigger. Bid up, bid up, gentlemen; he must be sold." Some come up to look at him, pull open his mouth to examine his teeth, and see if they are good. Poor fellow! he is handled and examined like any piece of merchandise; but he must bear it. Neither tongue nor hand, nor any other member, is his own—why should he attempt to use another's property?

Again the bidder goes on: "I will give one thousand dollars for that boy." The auctioneer says, "Sir, he is worth twelve hundred at the lowest. Bid up, gentlemen, bid up; going, going—are you all done?—once, twice, three times—all done? GONE!"

See the slave-holder, who has just bought the image of God, come to his victim, and take possession of him. Poor Emanuel must go away from his wife, never to see her again. All the ties of love are severed; the declaration of the Almighty, which said, "What God hath joined together, let not man put asunder," is unheeded, and he must leave all to follow his *Christian* master, a member of the Episcopal Church—a partaker, from time to time, of the Lord's Sacrament. Such men mock religion and insult God. Oh, that God would rend the heavens and appear unto these heartless men!

Next comes Jenny and her five children. Her husband was sold and gone. The oldest of her children is a girl seventeen years old—her name, Lucy.

Auctioneer—"Here, gentlemen, is a fine girl for sale: how much for her? Gentlemen, she will be a fortune for anyone who buys her who wants to raise niggers. Bid up, gentlemen, bid up! Fine girl; very hearty; good health; only seventeen years old; she's worth fifteen hundred dollars to anyone who wants to raise niggers. Here's her mother; she's had nine children; the rest of them are sold. How much, gentlemen—how much? Bid up! bid up!"

Poor Lucy is sold away from all the loved ones, and goes to receive the worst of insults from her cruel task-master. Her poor mother stands by heartbroken, with tears streaming down her face. Oh! is there a heart, not all brutish, that can witness such a scene without falling to the earth with shame, that the rights of his fellow-creatures are so basely trampled upon? The seller or buyer of a human being, for purposes of slavery, is not human, and has no right to the name . . .

The next of the children was Mary. She was put upon the block and sold. Then the mother became so affected that she seemed like one crazy. So the old rough slave-holder went to the mother, and began to lay the lash upon her; but it mattered not to her—her little Mary was gone, and now her turn had come. Oh, mothers who sit in your comfortable homes, surrounded by your happy children, think of the poor slave mother, robbed so cruelly of her all, by a fate worse than death! Oh, think of her, pray for her, toil for her, ever; teach your blooming daughters to think with compassion of their far-off colored sisters, and train them up anti-slavery women! . . .

Here Jesus Christ was sold to the highest bidder; sold in Jenny to keep her honest, to bring gold to the slave-holder. Jenny was sold away from all her little children, never to see them again . . . So she commends them to the care of the God of the widow and the fatherless, by bathing her bosom in tears, and giving them the last affectionate embrace, with the advice to meet her in heaven. Oh, the tears of the poor slave that are in bottles, to be poured out upon his blood-stained nation, as soon as the cup of wrath of the almighty

Avenger is full, when he shall say, "I have heard the groanings of my people, and 1 will deliver them from the oppressor!"

Slave-holders carry the price of blood upon their backs and in their pockets; the very bread they eat is the price of blood; the houses they live in are bought with blood; all the education they have is paid for by the blood and sorrow of the poor slaves . . .

The sin of holding slaves is not only against one nation, but against the whole world, because we are here to do one another good, in treating each other well; and this is to be done by having right ideas of God and his religion. But this privilege is denied to three millions and a half of the people of this, our own "free" land. The slave-holders say we have not a true knowledge of religion; but the great Teacher said, when he came on his mission, "The Spirit of the Lord is upon me, because he hath anointed me to preach the Gospel to the poor. He hath sent me to heal the broken-hearted; to preach deliverance to the captive, and recovering of sight to the blind; to set at liberty them that are bruised, and to preach the acceptable year of the Lord" (Luke 4:18-19). This ought to be the work of the ministers and the churches. Anything short of this is not the true religion of Jesus.

This is the great commandment of the New Testament—"Love the Lord your God with all your heart, and your neighbor as yourself" (Luke 10:27). "Do unto others as you would that they should do to you" (Matt. 7:12) is the golden rule for all men to follow. By this rule shall all men be judged . . .

In view of these things, I earnestly beg my readers to renew their interest in the anti-slavery cause, never turning a deaf ear to the pleadings of the poor slave, or to those who speak, however feebly, for him. The anti-slavery cause is the cause of HUMANITY, the cause of RELIGION, the cause of God!

SOURCE: Peter Randolph, *From Slave Cabin to the Pulpit. The Autobiography of Rev. Peter Randolph: The Southern Question Illustrated and Sketches of Slave Life* (Boston: James H. Earle, Publisher, 1893), 184–90.

63

FIRST VATICAN COUNCIL

VATICAN I (1869–1870) was the twentieth ecumenical church council in Roman Catholicism. The council was convened by Pope Pius IX (r. 1846–1878) and dealt with the threat of modernism. The council is known for affirming as dogma the doctrine of papal infallibility (the pope is infallible in matters of faith and morals when speaking *ex cathedra*—out of the chair—as pastor of the universal church). All but two of the 435 bishops in attendance voted to affirm the decree.

Papal Infallibility

Moreover that the supreme power of teaching is also included in the Apostolic Primacy, which the Roman Pontiff, as successor of Peter, Prince of the Apostles, enjoys over the whole Church, this Holy See has always held, the perpetual practice of the Church attests, and ecumenical councils themselves have declared, especially those in which the East with the West met in the union of faith and charity. For the Fathers of the Fourth Council of Constantinople, following in the footsteps of their predecessors, gave forth this solemn profession: The first condition of salvation is to keep the rule of the true faith. And because the sentence of our Lord Jesus Christ cannot be passed by, who said: Thou art Peter, and upon this Rock I will build my Church, these things which have been said are approved by events, because in the Apostolic See the Catholic Religion and her holy solemn doctrine have always been kept immaculate. Desiring, therefore, not to be in the least degree separated from the faith and doctrine of that See, we hope that we may deserve to be in the one communion, which the Apostolic See preaches, in which is the entire and true solidity of the Christian religion. And, with the approval of the Second Council of Lyons, the Greeks professed that the Holy Roman Church enjoys supreme and full Primacy and preeminence over the whole Catholic Church, which it truly and humbly acknowledges that it has received with the plenitude of power from our Lord Himself in the person of blessed Peter, Prince or Head of the Apostles, whose successor the Roman Pontiff is; and as the Apostolic See is bound before all others to defend the truth of faith, so also if any questions regarding faith shall arise, they must be defined by its judgment. Finally, the Council of Florence defined: That the Roman Pontiff is the true Vicar of Christ, and the head of the whole Church, and the Father and Teacher of all Christians; and that to him in blessed Peter was delivered by our Lord Jesus Christ the full power of feeding, ruling, and governing the whole Church.

To satisfy this pastoral duty our predecessors ever made unwearied efforts that the salutary doctrine of Christ might be propagated among all the nations of the earth, and with equal care watched that it might be preserved sincere and pure where it had been received. Therefore the bishops of the whole world, now singly, now assembled in synod, following the long-established custom of churches, and the form of the ancient rule, sent word to this Apostolic See of those dangers which sprang up in matters of faith, that there especially the losses of faith might be repaired where faith cannot feel any defect. And the Roman Pontiffs, according to the exigencies of times and circumstances, sometimes assembling ecumenical councils, or asking for the mind of the Church scattered throughout the world, sometimes by particular synods, sometimes using other helps which divine providence supplied, defined as to be held those things which with the help of God they had recognized as conformable with the Sacred Scriptures and Apostolic Traditions. For the Holy Spirit was not promised to the successors of Peter that under His revelation they might make known new doctrine, but that under His assistance they might scrupulously keep and faithfully expound the revelation or deposit of faith delivered through the Apostles. And, indeed, all the venerable Fathers have embraced, and the holy orthodox doctors have venerated and followed, their Apostolic doctrine; knowing most fully that this See of holy Peter remains ever free from all blemish of error, according to the divine promise of the Lord our Savior made to the Prince of His disciples: "I have prayed for thee that thy faith fail not, and thou, at length converted, confirm thy brethren" (Luke 22:32).

This gift, then, of truth and never-failing faith was conferred by Heaven upon Peter and his successors in this chair, that they might perform their high office for the salvation of all; that the whole flock of Christ, kept away by them from the poisonous food of error, might be nourished with the pasture of heavenly doctrine; that the occasion of schism being removed, the whole Church might be kept one, and, resting on its foundation, might stand firm against the gates of hell.

But since, in this very age, in which the salutary efficacy of the Apostolic office is even most of all required, not a few are found who take away from its authority, We judge it altogether necessary solemnly to assert the prerogative which the only begotten Son of God vouchsafed to join with the supreme pastoral office.

Therefore We, faithfully adhering to the tradition received from the beginning of the Christian faith, for the glory of God our Savior, the exaltation of the Roman Catholic Religion, and the salvation of Christian people, with the approbation of the Sacred Council, teach and define that it is a dogma divinely revealed: that the Roman Pontiff, when he speaks *ex cathedra*, that is, when in discharge of the office of Pastor and Doctor of all Christians, by virtue of his supreme Apostolic authority he defines a doctrine regarding faith or morals to be held by the Universal Church, by the divine assistance promised to him in Blessed Peter, enjoys that infallibility with which the divine Redeemer wished that His Church be provided for defining doctrine regarding faith or morals; and that therefore such definitions of the Roman Pontiff are irreformable of themselves, and not from the consent of the Church.

But if anyone—which may God avert!—presume to contradict this Our definition: let him be anathema.

Source: John Francis Maguire, *Pius the Ninth* (London: Longmans, Green, & Co., 1878), 396–99. *Pastor Aeternus*, chap. 4, "Concerning the Infallible Teaching of the Roman Pontiff."

64

CHARLES HODGE

CHARLES HODGE (1797–1878) was a theologian who taught at Princeton Theological Seminary. Along with Benjamin Warfield and Archibald Alexander, Hodge is known as one of the nineteenth-century "Princeton theologians" who articulated a strong Reformed/Calvinist theology and constructed the influential technical view of biblical inspiration called "inerrancy" which suggested that the Bible was without error in its original manuscripts. The doctrine of inerrancy, seen below, became a key component of the conservative response to the threat of theological modernism.

Infallibility of Scripture

The infallibility and divine authority of the Scriptures are due to the fact that they are the word of God; and they are the word of God because they were given by the inspiration of the Holy Ghost . . . The sacred writers were the organs of God, so that what they taught, God taught. It is to be remembered, however, that when God uses any of his creatures as his instruments, He uses them according to their nature. He uses angels as angels, men as men, the elements as elements. Men are intelligent voluntary agents; and as such were made the organs of God. The sacred writers were not made unconscious or irrational. The spirits of the prophets were subject to the prophets (1 Cor. 14:32). They were not like calculating machines which grind out logarithms with infallible correctness. The ancients, indeed, were accustomed to say, as some theologians have also said, that the sacred writers were as pens in the hand of the Spirit; or as harps, from which He drew what sounds He pleased. These representations were, however, intended simply to illustrate one point, namely, that the words uttered or recorded by inspired men were the words of God. The Church has never held what has been stigmatized as the mechanical theory of inspiration. The sacred writers were not machines. Their self-consciousness was not suspended; nor were their intellectual powers superseded. Holy men spoke as they were moved by the Holy Ghost. It was men, not machines; not unconscious instruments, but living, thinking, willing minds, whom the Spirit used as his organs. Moreover, as inspiration did not involve the suspension or suppression of the human faculties, so neither did it interfere with the free exercise of the distinctive mental characteristics of the individual. If a Hebrew was inspired, he spoke Hebrew; if a Greek, he spoke Greek; if an educated man, he spoke as a man of culture; if uneducated, he spoke as such a man is wont to speak. If his mind was logical, he reasoned, as Paul did; if emotional and contemplative, he wrote as John wrote. All this is involved in the fact that God uses his instruments according to their nature. The sacred writers impressed their peculiarities on their several productions as plainly as though they were the subjects of no extraordinary influence. This is one of the phenomena of the Bible patent to the most cursory reader. It lies in the very nature of inspiration that God spoke in the language of men; that He uses men as his organs, each according to his peculiar gifts and endowments . . .

Plenary Inspiration

The view presented . . . is known as the doctrine of plenary inspiration. Plenary is opposed to partial. The Church doctrine denies that inspiration is confined to parts of the Bible; and affirms that it applies to all the books of the sacred canon. It denies that the sacred writers were merely partially inspired; it asserts that they were fully inspired as to all that they teach, whether of doctrine or fact. This of course does not imply that the sacred writers were infallible except for the special purpose for which they were employed. They were not imbued with plenary knowledge. As to all matters of science, philosophy, and history, they stood on the same level with their contemporaries. They were infallible only as teachers, and when acting as the spokesmen of God. Their inspiration no more made them astronomers than it made them agriculturists. Isaiah was infallible in his predictions, although he shared with his countrymen the views then prevalent as to the mechanism of the universe. Paul could not err in anything he taught, although he could not recollect how many persons he had baptized in Corinth. The sacred writers also, doubtless, differed as to insight into the truths which they taught. The Apostle Peter intimates that the prophets searched diligently into the meaning of their own predictions. When David said God had put "all things" under the feet of man, he probably little thought that "all things" meant the whole universe (Heb. 4:8). And Moses, when he recorded the promise that childless Abraham was to be the father "of many nations," little thought that it meant the whole world (Rom. 4:13). Nor does the Scriptural doctrine on this subject imply that the sacred writers were free from errors in conduct. Their infallibility did not arise from their holiness, nor did inspiration render them holy. Balaam was inspired, and Saul was among the prophets. David committed many crimes, although inspired to write psalms. Peter erred in conduct at Antioch; but this does not prove that he erred in teaching. The influence which preserved him from mistakes in teaching was not designed to preserve him from mistakes in conduct.

SOURCE: Charles Hodge, *Systematic Theology*, vol. 1 (New York: Charles Scribner & Sons, 1895), 153, 156–57, 165–66.

65

CHARLES A. BRIGGS

CHARLES A. BRIGGS (1841–1913) was a Presbyterian minister and professor at Union Theological Seminary in New York. In the 1880s he became a staunch advocate of higher biblical criticism and increasingly opposed the traditional Calvinist/Reformed "Princeton theology." In 1891, upon his selection as chair of biblical studies at the seminary, Briggs delivered an inaugural address, "The Authority of Holy Scripture" (excerpt below), which repudiated long-held views about the Bible and the doctrine of biblical inerrancy. The address led to a heresy trial and Briggs' suspension from the Presbyterian ministry. Briggs' story was a key element of the fundamentalist-modernist conflict in American Christianity.

The Bible and Modernism

The Bible is the book of God, the greatest treasure of the Church. Its ministry are messengers to preach the Word of God, and to invite men to His presence and government. It is pharisaic to obstruct their way by any fences or stumbling-blocks . . .

(1) *Superstition.*—The first barrier that obstructs the way to the Bible is *superstition*. We are accustomed to attach superstition to the Roman Catholic Mariolatry, Hagiolatry, and the use of images and pictures and other external things in worship. But superstition is no less superstition if it takes the form of *Bibliolatry*. It may be all the worse if it concentrates itself on this one thing. But the Bible has no magical virtue in it, and there is no halo enclosing it. It will not stop a bullet any better than a mass-book. It will not keep off evil spirits any better than a cross. It will not guard a home from fire half so well as holy water. If you desire to know when and how you should take a journey, you will find a safer guide in an almanac or a daily newspaper . . . [*Briggs' footnote*: My argument is against those Protestants who exhibit the same superstition toward the Bible as some Roman Catholics show in the ceremonies of their religion].

(2) *Verbal Inspiration.*—The second barrier, keeping men from the Bible, is the dogma of *verbal inspiration*. The Bible in use in our churches and homes is an English Bible. Upon the English Bible our religious life is founded. But the English Bible is a translation from Hebrew, Aramaic, and Greek originals. It is claimed for these originals by modern dogmaticians that they are verbally inspired. No such claim is found in the Bible itself, or in any of the creeds of Christendom . . . The text of the Bible, in which these languages have been handed down, has shared the fortunes of other texts of other literature.

We find there are errors of transmission. There is nothing divine in the text—in its letters, words, or clauses. There are those who hold that thought and language are as inseparable as body and soul. But language is rather the dress of thought. A master of many languages readily clothes the same thought in half a dozen different languages. The same thought in the Bible itself is dressed in different literary styles . . .

(3) *Authenticity.*—The third barrier is the *authenticity of the Scriptures.* The only authenticity we are concerned about in seeking for the divine authority of the Scriptures is *divine authenticity* and yet many theologians have insisted that we must prove that the Scriptures were written by or under the superintendence of prophets and apostles . . . It is just here that the Higher Criticism has proved such a terror in our times. Traditionalists are crying out

that it is destroying the Bible, because it is exposing their fallacies and follies. It may be regarded as the certain result of the science of the Higher Criticism that Moses did not write the Pentateuch or Job . . . written by authors whose names or connection with their writings are lost in oblivion. If this is destroying the Bible, the Bible is destroyed already. But who tells us that these traditional names were the authors of the Bible? The Bible itself? The creeds of the Church? Any reliable historical testimony? None of these! Pure, conjectural tradition! Nothing more! . . .

(4) *Inerrancy.*—The fourth barrier set up by theologians to keep men away from the Bible is the dogma of the inerrancy of Scripture. This barrier confronts Historical Criticism. It is not a pleasant task to point out errors in the sacred Scriptures. Nevertheless Historical Criticism finds them, and we must meet the issue whether they destroy the authority of the Bible or not. It has been taught in recent years, and is still taught by some theologians, that one proved error destroys the authority of Scripture. I shall venture to affirm that, so far as I can see, there are errors in the Scriptures that no one has been able to explain away; and the theory that they were not in the original text is sheer assumption, upon which no mind can rest with certainty. If such errors destroy the authority of the Bible, it is already destroyed for historians. Men cannot shut their eyes to truth and fact. But on what authority do these theologians drive men from the Bible by this theory of inerrancy? The Bible itself nowhere makes this claim. The creeds of the Church nowhere sanction it. It is a ghost of modern evangelicalism to frighten children . . . If we should abandon the whole field of providential superintendence so far as inspiration and divine authority are concerned and limit divine inspiration and authority to the essential contents of the Bible, to its religion, faith, and morals, we would still have ample room to seek divine authority where alone it is essential, or even important, in the teaching that guides our devotions, our thinking, and our conduct . . .

(5) *Violation of the Laws of Nature.*—The fifth obstruction to the Bible has been thrown up in front of modern science. It is the claim that the *miracles* disturb, or violate, the laws of nature and the harmony of the universe; and so the miracles of the Bible have become to men of science sufficient evidence that the Bible is no more than other sacred books of other religions. But the theories of miracles that have been taught in the Christian Church are human inventions for which the Scriptures and the Church have no responsibility whatever.

The miracle of the Bible . . . the tests that they [Moses and Jesus] gave to discriminate the true from the false were not their marvelous character, their violation of the laws of nature, their suspension of the uniformity of law . . . nothing of the kind; but the simple test whether they set forth the holy character and the gracious teaching of God and His Messiah.

SOURCE: Charles Augustus Briggs, *The Authority of Holy Scripture: An Inaugural Address* (New York: Charles Scribner's Sons, 1891), 29–37.

66

ELIZABETH CADY STANTON

E LIZABETH CADY STANTON (1815–1902) was a leader of nineteenth-century American feminism. She was an advocate for abolitionism, temperance, and women's rights (such as women's suffrage and equality in marriage). Stanton was a leading participant in the first women's rights convention in America at Seneca Falls, New York, in 1848. The selection below is from Stanton's *The Woman's Bible* (1895), a biblical commentary written by Stanton and other women, which was extremely controversial in its day.

The Woman's Bible

Genesis Chapter I: Here is the sacred historian's first account of the advent of woman; a simultaneous creation of both sexes, in the image of God. It is evident from the language that there was consultation in the Godhead, and that the masculine and feminine elements were equally represented. Scott in his commentaries says, "this consultation of the Gods is the origin of the doctrine of the Trinity." But instead of three male personages, as generally represented, a Heavenly Father, Mother, and Son would seem more rational.

The first step in the elevation of woman to her true position, as an equal factor in human progress, is the cultivation of the religious sentiment in regard to her dignity and equality, the recognition by the rising generation of an ideal Heavenly Mother, to whom their prayers should be addressed, as well as to a Father.

If language has any meaning, we have in these texts a plain declaration of the existence of the feminine element in the Godhead, equal in power and glory with the masculine. The Heavenly Mother and Father! "God created man in his *own image, male and female*" (Gen. 1:27). Thus Scripture, as well as science and philosophy, declares the eternity and equality of sex—the philosophical fact, without which there could have been no perpetuation of creation, no growth or development in the animal, vegetable, or mineral kingdoms, no awakening nor progressing in the world of thought. The masculine and feminine elements, exactly equal and balancing each other, are as essential to the maintenance of the equilibrium of the universe as positive and negative electricity, the centripetal and centrifugal forces, the laws of attraction which bind together all we know of this planet whereon we dwell and of the system in which we revolve.

In the great work of creation the crowning glory was realized, when man and woman were evolved on the sixth day, the masculine and feminine forces in the image of God, that must have existed eternally, in all forms of matter and mind. All the persons in the Godhead are represented in the Elohim the divine plurality taking counsel in regard to this last and highest form of life . . . All those theories based on the assumption that man was prior in the creation, have no foundation in Scripture.

As to woman's subjection, on which both the canon and the civil law delight to dwell, it is important to note that equal dominion is given to woman over every living thing, but not one word is said giving man dominion over woman.

Genesis Chapter II: As the account of the creation in the first chapter is in harmony with science, common sense, and the experience of mankind in natural laws, the inquiry naturally arises, why should there be two contradictory accounts in the same book, of the same event? It is fair to infer that the second version, which is found in some form in the different religions of all nations, is a mere allegory, symbolizing some mysterious conception of a highly imaginative editor.

The first account dignifies woman as an important factor in the creation, equal in power and glory with man. The second makes her a mere afterthought. The world in good running order without her. The only reason for her advent being the solitude of man.

. . . It is on this allegory that all the enemies of women rest their battering rams, to prove her inferiority. Accepting the view that man was prior in the creation, some Scriptural writers say that as the woman was of the man, therefore, her position should be one of subjection. Grant it, then as the historical fact is reversed in our day, and the man is now of the woman, shall his place be one of subjection? . . . Paul, in speaking of equality as the very soul and essence of Christianity, said, "There is neither Jew nor Greek, there is neither bond nor free, there is neither male nor female; for you are all one in Christ Jesus" (Gal. 3:28). With this recognition of the feminine element in the Godhead in the Old Testament and this declaration of the equality of the sexes in the New, we may well wonder at the contemptible status woman occupies in the Christian Church of today.

Genesis Chapter III: As out of this allegory grows the doctrines of original sin, the fall of man, and woman the author of all our woes, and the curses on the serpent, the woman, and the man; the Darwinian theory of the gradual growth of the race from a lower to a higher type of animal life, is more hopeful and encouraging. However, as our chief interest is in woman's part in the drama, we are equally pleased with her attitude, whether as a myth in an allegory, or as the heroine of an historical occurrence.

In this prolonged interview, the unprejudiced reader must be impressed with the courage, the dignity, and the lofty ambition of the woman. The tempter evidently had a profound knowledge of human nature, and saw at a glance the high character of the person he met by chance in his walks in the garden. He did not try to tempt her from the path of duty by brilliant jewels, rich dresses, worldly luxuries, or pleasures, but with the promise of knowledge, with the wisdom of the Gods. Like Socrates or Plato, his powers of conversation and asking puzzling questions, were no doubt marvelous, and he roused in the woman that intense thirst for knowledge, that the simple pleasures of picking flowers and talking with Adam did not satisfy. Compared with Adam she appears to great advantage through the entire drama.

SOURCE: Elizabeth Cady Stanton, *The Woman's Bible: Part I, Comments on Genesis, Exodus, Leviticus, Numbers and Deuteronomy* (New York: European Publishing Co., 1895), 14–15, 20–21, 24–25.

67

RUSSELL H. CONWELL

RUSSELL H. CONWELL (1843–1925) was the founder of Temple University. He became pastor of The Baptist Temple, Philadelphia, in 1882, and by 1893 the church was the largest Protestant congregation in America with over 3,000 members. The church was an institutional church (today's "megachurch") with a gymnasium and two hospitals. Institutional churches were an alternative to meeting social needs which differed from the developing "social gospel" that argued for change (and redemption) of social structures. In his day, Conwell was best known for his speech "Acres of Diamonds" which he delivered over 6,000 times. His message was similar to the "Gospel of Wealth" associated with philanthropist Andrew Carnegie. Conwell preached a gospel of prosperity which asserted that everyone could be rich (thus the poor usually had themselves to blame) and should use their money to help others. Acres of diamonds—opportunities—were in everyone's backyard.

Gospel of Prosperity

I say you ought to be rich; you have no right to be poor. To live in Philadelphia and not be rich is a misfortune, and it is doubly a misfortune, because you could have been rich just as well as be poor. Philadelphia furnishes so many opportunities. You ought to be rich. But persons with certain religious prejudice will ask, "How can you spend your time advising the rising generation to give their time to getting money—dollars and cents—the commercial spirit?"

Yet I must say that you ought to spend time getting rich. You and I know there are some things more valuable than money; of course, we do. Ah, yes! By a heart made unspeakably sad by a grave on which the autumn leaves now fall, I know there are some things higher and grander and sublimer than money. Well does the man know, who has suffered, that there are some things sweeter and holier and more sacred than gold. Nevertheless, the man of common sense also knows that there is not any one of those things that is not greatly enhanced by the use of money. Money is power. Love is the grandest thing on God's earth, but fortunate the lover who has plenty of money. Money is power; money has powers; and for man to say, "I do not want money," is to say, "I do not wish to do any good to my fellowmen." It is absurd thus to talk. It is absurd to disconnect them. This is a wonderfully great life, and you ought to spend your time getting money, because of the power there is in money. And yet this religious prejudice is so great that some people think it is a great honor to be one of God's poor. I am looking in the faces of people who think just that way. I heard a man once say in a prayer-meeting that he was thankful that he was one of God's poor, and then I silently wondered what his wife would say to that speech, as she took in washing to support the man while he sat and smoked on the veranda. I don't want to see any more of that kind of God's poor. Now, when a man could have been rich just as well, and he is now weak because he is poor, he has done some great wrong; he has been untruthful to himself; he has been unkind to his fellowmen. We ought to get rich if we can by honorable and Christian methods, and these are the only methods that sweep us quickly toward the goal of riches.

I remember, not many years ago a young theological student who came into my office and said to me that he thought it was his duty to come in and "labor with me." I asked him what had happened, and he said: "I feel it is my duty to come in and speak to you, sir, and say that the Holy Scriptures declare that money is the root of all evil." I asked him where he found that saying, and he said he found it in the Bible. I asked him whether he had made a new Bible, and he said, no, he had not gotten a new Bible, that it was in the old Bible. "Well," I said, "if it is in my Bible, I never saw it. Will you please get the text-book and let me see it?" He left the room and soon came stalking in with his Bible open, with all the bigoted pride of the narrow sectarian, who founds his creed on some misinterpretation of Scripture, and he puts the Bible down on the table before me and fairly squealed into my ear, "There it is. You can read it for yourself." I said to him, "Young man, you will learn, when you get a little older, that you cannot trust another denomination to read the Bible for you." I said, "Now, you belong to another denomination. Please read it to me, and remember that you are taught in a school where emphasis is exegesis." So he took the Bible and read it: "The *love* of money is the root of all evil" (1 Tim. 6:10). Then he had it right. The Great Book has come back into the esteem and love of the people, and into the respect of the greatest minds of earth, and now you can quote it and rest your life and your death on it without more fear. So, when he quoted right from the Scriptures he quoted the truth. "The love of money is the root of all evil." Oh, that is it. It is the worship of the means instead of the end, though you cannot reach the end without the means. When a man makes an idol of the money instead of the purposes for which it may be used, when he squeezes the dollar until the eagle squeals, then it is made the root of all evil. Think, if you only had the money, what you could do for your wife, your child, and for your home and your city. Think how soon you could endow the Temple College yonder if you only had the money and the disposition to give it; and yet, my friend, people say you and I should not spend the time getting rich.

SOURCE: Russell H. Conwell, "Acres of Diamonds," in Agnes Rush Burr, *Russell H. Conwell and His Work* (Philadelphia: The John C. Winston Co., 1917), 414–16.

68

WALTER RAUSCHENBUSCH

W ALTER RAUSCHENBUSCH (1861–1918) was an American Baptist whose pastorate in Hell's Kitchen (1886–1897) in the city of New York awakened him to social problems and their relationship to the Christian faith. As a church history professor at Rochester Seminary (1897–1918), he wrote several books (especially *Christianity and the Social Crisis*, 1907; *Christianizing the Social Order*, 1912, and *A Theology of the Social Gospel*, 1917) that moved him to the forefront of the Social Gospel movement. Christian faith did not abandon the need for individual conversion, but the essence of Jesus' teaching—the Kingdom of God—meant that the gospel was social, i.e., social structures sinned (seen in the profit motive of capitalism) and needed social salvation.

Social Gospel

The chief purpose of the Christian Church in the past has been the salvation of individuals. But the most pressing task of the present is not individualistic. Our business is to make over an antiquated and immoral economic system
. . .

The Christian Church in the past has taught us to do our work with our eyes fixed on another world and a life to come. But the business before us is concerned with refashioning this present world, making this earth clean and sweet and habitable.

Here is the problem for all religious minds: we need a great faith to serve as a spiritual basis for the tremendous social task before us, and the working creed of our religion, in the form in which it has come down to us, has none . . . It has manifestly furnished no sufficient religious motives to bring the unregenerate portions of our social order under the control of the Christian law. Its hymns, its ritual, its prayers, its books of devotion, are so devoid of social thought that the most thrilling passions of our generation lie in us half stifled for lack of religious utterance. The whole scheme of religion which tradition has handed down to us was not devised for such ends as we now have in hand and is inadequate for them. We need a new foundation for Christian thought . . .

Twenty-five years ago the social wealth of the Bible was almost undiscovered to most of us. We used to plow it six inches deep for crops and never dreamed that mines of anthracite were hidden down below. Even Jesus talked like an individualist in those days and seemed to repudiate the social interest when we interrogated him. He said his kingdom was not of this world; the things of God had nothing to do with the things of Caesar; the poor we would always have with us; and his ministers must not be judges and dividers when Labor argued with Capital about the division of the inheritance. Today he has resumed the spiritual leadership of social Christianity, of which he was the founder . . .

With true Christian instinct men have turned to the Christian law of love as the key to the situation. If we all loved our neighbor, we should "treat him right," pay him a living wage, give sixteen ounces to the pound, and not charge so much for beef. But this appeal assumes that we are still living in the simple personal relations of the good old times, and that every man can do the right thing when he wants to do it. But suppose a business man would be glad indeed to pay his young women the $12 a week which they need for a decent living, but all his competitors are paying from $7 down to $5. Shall he love himself into bankruptcy? In a time of industrial depression shall he employ men whom he does not need? And if he does, will his five loaves feed the five thousand unemployed that break his heart with their hungry eyes? If a man owns a hundred shares of stock in a great corporation, how can his love influence its wage scale with that puny stick? The old advice of love breaks down before the hugeness of modern relations. We might as well try to start a stranded ocean liner with the oar which poled our old dory from the mud banks many a time. It is indeed love that we want, but it is socialized love. Blessed be the love that holds the cup of water to thirsty lips. We can never do without the plain affection of man to man. But what we most need today is not the love that will break its back drawing water for a growing factory town from a well that was meant to supply a village, but a love so large and intelligent that it will persuade an ignorant people to build a system of waterworks up in the hills, and that will get after the thoughtless farmers who contaminate the brooks with typhoid bacilli, and after the lumber concern that is denuding the watershed of its forests. We want a new avatar of love.

The Church has also put a new stress on the doctrine of stewardship, hoping to cure the hard selfishness of our commercial life by quickening the sense of responsibility in men of wealth . . . The doctrine is not yet based on modern democratic feeling and on economic knowledge about the sources of modern wealth. It calls for no fundamental change in economic distribution, but simply encourages faithful disbursement of funds. That is not enough for our modern needs . . .

The Church has also revived the thought of following Jesus in daily conduct, living over again the life of Christ, and doing in all things as he would do in our place. That has been an exceedingly influential thought in Christian history. In the life of Saint Francis and his brotherhood, in the radical sects, and in single radiant lives it has produced social forces of immense power. In our own time the books of Mr. Charles M. Sheldon have set it forth with winning spirit, and we have seen thousands of young people trying for a week to live as Jesus would. But it is so high a law that only consecrated individuals can follow it permanently and intelligently, and even they may submit to it only in the high tide of their spiritual life. To most men the demand to live as Jesus would, is mainly useful to bring home the fact that it is hard to live a Christlike life in a mammonistic society. It convicts our social order of sin, but it does not reconstruct it.

These are all truly religious ideas, drawn from the teaching of Jesus himself, and very effective in sweetening and ennobling our personal relations. But they set up no ideal of human society, demand no transformation of social institutions, create no collective enthusiasms, and furnish no doctrinal basis for a public morality. They have not grown antiquated, and never will. But every step in the evolution of modern society makes them less adequate for its religious needs.

SOURCE: Walter Rauschenbusch, *Christianizing the Social Order* (New York: The Macmillan Co., 1919; rpt. Waco, Tex.: Baylor University Press, 2010), 41–46.

69

CHARLES SHELDON

CHARLES SHELDON (1857–1946) was an advocate of the Social Gospel movement in the United States in the late nineteenth century. His novel *In His Steps* (1897) helped spread the movement's ideas about social justice at the popular level. It was a "best seller" and was published in over a dozen languages. Sheldon introduced the principle "what would Jesus do" that would become a popular slogan in evangelicalism one hundred years later.

Imitating Jesus: *In His Steps*

The sermon had come to a close. Mr. Maxwell had just turned the half of the big Bible over upon his manuscript and was about to sit down as the quartet prepared to arise to sing the closing selection, "All for *Jesus,* all for Jesus, All my being's ransomed powers," when the entire congregation was startled by the sound of a man's voice. It came from the rear of the church, from one of the seats under the gallery. The next moment the figure of a man came out of the shadow there and walked down the middle aisle. Before the startled congregation fairly realized what was going on the man had reached the open space in front of the pulpit and had turned about facing the people.

"I've been wondering since I came in here"—they were the words he used under the gallery, and he repeated them—"if it would be just the thing to say a word at the close of the service. I'm not drunk and I'm not crazy, and I am perfectly harmless, but if I die, as there is every likelihood I shall in a few days, I want the satisfaction of thinking that I said my say in a place like this, and before this sort of a crowd." . . . "I'm not an ordinary tramp, though I don't know of any teaching of Jesus that makes one kind of a tramp less worth saving than another. Do you?" . . .

"I lost my job ten months ago. I am a printer by trade. The new linotype machines are beautiful specimens of invention, but I know six men who have killed themselves inside of the year just on account of those machines. Of course I don't blame the newspapers for getting the machines. Meanwhile, what can a man do? I know I never learned but the one trade, and that's all I can do. I've tramped all over the country trying to find something. There are a good many others like me. I'm not complaining, am I? Just stating facts. But I was wondering as I sat there under the gallery, if what you call following Jesus is the same thing as what He taught. What did He mean when He said: 'Follow me!'" The minister said, "here the man turned about and looked up at the pulpit, that it is necessary for the disciple of Jesus to follow His steps, and he said the steps are 'obedience, faith, love and imitation.' But I did not hear him tell you just what he meant that to mean, especially the last step. What do you Christians mean by following the steps of Jesus?"

"I've tramped through this city for three days trying to find a job; and in all that time I've not had a word of sympathy or comfort except from your minister here, who said he was sorry for me and hoped I would find a job somewhere. I suppose it is because you get so imposed on by the professional tramp that you have lost your interest in any other sort. I'm not blaming anybody, am I? Just stating facts. Of course, I understand you can't all go out of your way to hunt up jobs for other people like me. I'm not asking you to; but what I feel puzzled about is, what is meant by following Jesus. What do you mean when you sing 'I'll go with Him, with Him all the way?' Do you mean that you are suffering and denying yourselves and trying to save lost, suffering humanity just as I understand Jesus did? What *do* you mean by it? I see the ragged edge of things a good deal. I understand there are more than five hundred men in this city in my case. Most of them have families. My wife died four months ago. I'm glad she is out of trouble. My little girl is staying with a printer's family until I find a job. Somehow I get puzzled when I see so many Christians living in luxury and singing 'Jesus, I my cross have taken, all to leave and follow Thee,' and remember how my wife died in a tenement in New York city, gasping for air and asking God to take the little girl too. Of course I don't expect you people can prevent every one from dying of starvation, lack of proper nourishment and tenement air, but what *does* following Jesus mean? I understand that Christian people own a good many of the tenements. A member of a church was the owner of the one where my wife died, and I have wondered if following Jesus all the way was true in his case. I heard some people singing at a church prayer meeting the other night, 'All for Jesus, all for Jesus, All my being's ransomed powers, All my thoughts, and all my doings, All my days, and all my hours,' and I kept wondering as I sat on the steps outside just what they meant by it. It seems to me there's an awful lot of trouble in the world that somehow wouldn't exist if all the people who sing such songs went and lived them out. I suppose I don't understand. But what would Jesus do? Is that what you mean by following His steps? It seems to me sometimes as if the people in the big churches had good clothes and nice houses to live in, and money to spend for luxuries, and could go away on summer vacations and all that, while the people outside the churches, thousands of them, I mean, die in tenements, and walk the streets for jobs, and never have a piano or a picture in the house, and grow up in misery and drunkenness and sin."

The man suddenly gave a queer lurch over in the direction of the communion table and laid one grimy hand on it . . . He had fainted away. (Ed: He died three days later in the home of the minister).

Source: Charles M. Sheldon, *In His Steps: "What Would Jesus Do?"* (New York: Grosset & Dunlap, 1917), 11–16.

$$\sim\!\!\Omega\!\!\sim$$

70

WILLIAM J. SEYMOUR

WILLIAM J. SEYMOUR (1870–1922) was an itinerant Holiness evangelist who accepted Pentecostal beliefs—particularly speaking in tongues as the initial evidence of the baptism of the Holy Spirit—under the tutelage of Pentecostal pioneer Charles Parham. The Azusa Street (Los Angeles) revival, from which Pentecostalism spread, erupted under Seymour's preaching on April 9, 1906. The leadership of Seymour, an African American, reveals the interracial character of the birth of the movement. In the following selection, Seymour gives his understanding of the atonement in the first issue of *The Apostolic Faith*, the journal that helped spread the revival.

Atonement and Pentecostal Faith

Children of God, partakers of the precious atonement, let us study and see what there is in it for us.

First. Through the atonement we receive forgiveness of sins.

Second. We receive sanctification through the blood of Jesus. "Wherefore Jesus also that he might sanctify the people with his own blood, suffered without the gate." Sanctified from all original sin, we become sons of God. "For both he that sanctifies and they who are sanctified are all of one: for which cause he is not ashamed to call them brethren" (Heb. 2:11). (It seems that Jesus would be ashamed to call them brethren, if they were not sanctified.) Then you will not be ashamed to tell men and demons that you are sanctified, and are living a pure and holy life free from sin, a life that gives you power over the world, the flesh, and the devil. The devil does not like that kind of testimony. Through this precious atonement, we have freedom from all sin, though we are living in this old world, we are permitted to sit in heavenly places in Christ Jesus.

Third. Healing of our bodies. Sickness and disease are destroyed through the precious atonement of Jesus. O how we ought to honor the stripes of Jesus, for "with his stripes we are healed" (Isa. 53:5). How we ought to honor that precious body which the Father sanctified and sent into the world, not simply set apart, but really sanctified, soul, body and spirit, free from sickness, disease and everything of the devil. A body that knew no sin and disease was given for these imperfect bodies of ours. Not only is the atonement for the sanctification of our souls, but for the sanctification of our bodies from inherited disease. It matters not what has been in the blood. Every drop of blood we received from our mother is impure. Sickness is born in a child just as original sin is born in the child. He was manifested to destroy the works of the devil. Every sickness is of the devil.

Man in the garden of Eden was pure and happy and knew no sickness till that unholy visitor came into the garden, then his whole system was poisoned and it has been flowing in the blood of all the human family down the ages till God spoke to his people and said, "I am the Lord that healeth thee" (Exod. 15:26). The children of Israel practiced divine healing. David, after being healed of rheumatism (perhaps contracted in the caves where he hid himself from his pursuers), testified saying, "Bless the Lord, O my soul, and all that is within me bless his holy name, who forgiveth all thine iniquities, who healeth all thy diseases" (Ps. 103:1-3). David knew what it was to be healed. Healing continued with God's people till Solomon's heart was turned away by strange wives, and he brought in the black arts and mediums, and they went whoring after familiar spirits. God had been their healer, but after they lost the Spirit, they turned to the arm of flesh to find something to heal their diseases.

Thank God, we have a living Christ among us to heal our diseases. He will heal every case. The prophet had said, "With his stripes we are healed," and it was fulfilled when Jesus came. Also "He hath borne our griefs" (which means sickness, as translators tell us). Now if Jesus bore our sicknesses, why should we bear them? So we get full salvation through the atonement of Jesus.

Fourth. And we get the baptism with the Holy Ghost and fire upon the sanctified life. We get Christ enthroned and crowned in our hearts. Let us lift up Christ to the world in all His fulness, not only in healing and salvation from all sin, but in His power to speak all the languages of the world. We need the triune God to enable us do this.

We that are the messengers of this precious atonement ought to preach all of it, justification, sanctification, healing, the baptism with the Holy Ghost, and signs following. "How shall we escape if we neglect so great salvation?" (Heb. 2:3) God is now confirming His word by granting signs and wonders to follow the preaching of the full gospel in Los Angeles.

SOURCE: W. J. Seymour, "The Precious Atonement," *The Apostolic Faith* 1, no. 1 (September 1906): 2.

71

AIMEE SEMPLE McPHERSON

AIMEE SEMPLE McPHERSON (1890–1944) was the founder of the Pente-costal denomination, the International Church of the Foursquare Gos-pel, still with headquarters in Los Angeles, California. McPherson, the most famous representative of the role of women preachers in early Pentecostalism, was a media celebrity and even attracted Hollywood celebrities to her ser-vices. McPherson's personal life was filled with controversy and rumors of a faked kidnapping. The following selection discusses the cornerstone belief of Pentecostalism: baptism of the Holy Spirit evidenced by speaking in tongues.

Baptism of the Holy Spirit

The curtains of the clouds which angelic hands had swept together when, the redemptive work of Jesus on earth completed, His ascending form disap-peared from view, had again been parted, and the Holy Spirit, of whom Jesus had said—"He will abide with you forever" (John 14:16)—had been sent forth from the presence of the Father. No sooner were they filled with the Holy Spirit than they began to speak with other tongues as the Spirit gave them utterance.

And they were all filled with the Spirit.

What was the immediate result and the outward evidence of that fill-ing?—They began to speak with other tongues.

Is there any record of anyone ever having spoken in other tongues (lan-guages which they had never learned and were unknown to themselves; see 1 Cor. 14:2), previous to the day of Pentecost and the opening of the dispensa-tion of the Holy Spirit? NO.

The devout Jews who were gathered into Jerusalem at this time, for the religious feasts and ceremonies, came running together in multitudes, and, upon hearing the languages of the countries in which they had been born, spoken by these simple, unlearned Galileans, they were amazed, astonished, and in doubt.

At what were the people astonished? At what did they marvel? At the rushing mighty wind? No.

The tongues of fire? No; they are not again mentioned, and it is doubtful whether those who came together after the one hundred and twenty had been filled even saw them.

What then? They were amazed and marveled at the supernatural power that rested upon these men and women, causing them to reel and stagger, Acts 2:13, as though drunken with wine, and to speak with tongues unknown to themselves.

The spectators who looked upon the out-pouring of the Holy Ghost on the day of Pentecost were divided into two classes just as they are today.

One class were the mockers, who said in derision, "These men are full of new wine. Come on, let's have nothing to do with these people. They are fanatics. This is all excitement. 'Tis ridiculous to create so much noise and excitement over religion; the whole city is in an uproar; nothing but wildfire. They ought to be arrested," etc.

The other class were the thinkers—the thoughtful, intelligent men and women, who said:

"Wait a moment. There must surely be something behind all this. The ring in these people's voices—the shout in their souls—the joy and love, worship and adoration reflected in their faces—there must be some specific reason for it. They are certainly not reeling and staggering about like that for nothing. They must surely realize that the people who look on will make fun of them and think they have lost their senses.

If they are not doing it for money nor for popularity, then why are they doing it? They are certainly not all fools. If there were only one or two we might think they were, but here are about one hundred and twenty; surely they cannot all be mad. I am going to investigate this matter and see what there is behind it all.

Tell us, Oh tell us, some of you good, happy people in there—stop your shouting and your rejoicing for a little space, and answer—WHAT MEANETH THIS?"

Then Peter, standing up—"Peter, what are you rising up for? Are you frightened, Peter? Are you going to run away and seek to escape from this big, excited, questioning multitude as you did from the little girl that night you denied the Lord?"

"Run away? Oh no! I will never run away any more now. I have been baptized with the Holy Ghost and fire. He has endued me with power from on high. He has taken fear away and put a holy boldness within my heart and words within my mouth" . . .

Oh, tell me, Peter and Paul, tell me John and James, and all you who received this mighty incoming of the Holy Ghost with its attendant power and glory, may we, in this twentieth century, receive this like precious gift, or did the Holy Spirit empty Himself of all His power in the apostolic days? Did you consume all of these supernatural wondrous blessings, or did you leave enough to spare for us today?

"Yes, indeed," they answer in unison. "Heaven has not gone bankrupt. Heaven's storehouse still is full. The Holy Spirit has never lost His power, the promise is unto them that are afar off, even as many as the Lord our God shall call. Did not our Lord say: 'When He is come, He will abide with you forever'?"

"Doubt no longer, but with open heart ask ye of the Lord rain in the time of the latter rain. Remember the words of Joel the prophet: 'It shall come to pass in the LAST days,' saith God, 'I will pour out My Spirit upon all flesh' (Joel 2:28). Remember, too, that when the high priest went in to the Holy of Holies the bells rang, and when the high priest came out the bells rang again."

"When Jesus ascended up on high the bells rang and the people spoke with tongues and magnified God. Now this same Jesus, our high priest, is coming forth again for His waiting church, and on earth the bells are ringing, the latter rain is falling, and again those who have received the oldtime power speak with other tongues."

SOURCE: Aimee McPherson, *This Is That: Personal Experiences, Sermons, and Writings* (Los Angeles: The Bridal Call Publishing House, 1919), 418–24.

72

ADAM CLAYTON POWELL SR.

ADAM CLAYTON POWELL SR. (1865–1953) was a prominent African American pastor and advocate for racial equality in the United States. He is best known as pastor of Abyssinian Baptist Church in New York City, which grew to be one of the country's largest and most influential African American churches under his leadership. In his ministry, Powell sought to improve both African Americans' Christian faith and, through social programs, their material lives. Powell's national reputation led to his appointment to the first board of directors of the National Association for the

Advancement of Colored People (NAACP). In the excerpt below, from a 1919 sermon entitled "The Colored Man's Contribution to Christianity," Powell advocates appealing to God and spiritual revival as an answer to the plight of African Americans.

An Appeal to Non-violent Resistance

Ethiopia shall soon stretch out her hands unto God.

—Psalm 68:31 (KJV)

. . .

In the extended hands of the prophecy we have a picture of utter helplessness. This picture most fittingly represents the condition of the twelve million colored people in America at the present hour. Reaching after God is our one hope. The colored people, like Peter, are walking on a rough sea.

. . .

"Father, I stretch my hands to Thee,
No other help I know;
If Thou withdraw Thyself from me,
Ah, whither shall I go?"

As a race we have sung this hymn for fifty years but we have never put it into practice. In fact, in our distress we have stretched our hands to everybody and everything but God. Our leaders told us to get education and property and other people would respect us and treat us as men and American citizens. Following their leadership, we reached after property and education. Our bitterest enemies, including Congressman Byrne, publicly acknowledge that no group of people has ever made greater intellectual and material progress. Instead of hatred and injustice diminishing in proportion to our progress, their rapid increase threatens the very foundations of our democratic government. I am second to no one in my desire to see my race accumulate property and acquire an education, but the most stupid observer of the signs of the times is forced to admit that the solution of the race problem does not lie along the lines of advance.

Another group of leaders is saying now with fiery vehemence, "The only way for the colored man to save himself is to arm and defend himself." I have absolutely no apology to make to any man for the vigorous and successful way colored people defended themselves against the mobs in Washington, Chicago and other places, and I do not advise them not to resort to similar defense under similar circumstances. The fact remains, however, that colored people can never save themselves by physical force. Such a course can only end in the extinction of the race in this country. There are about twelve million colored people in the United States and ninety million whites. Suppose the same number should be killed on both sides in the slaughter. There would be seventy-eight million white people left doing business after the colored people were all annihilated.

Every department of the government, including the machinery of destruction, is in the hands of white men, except a few razors and pistols. The men who are advising colored people to arm and fight are either fools or they are deliberately preparing the race to commit suicide. Nowhere in the world is the colored man prepared to fight the white man. Even if we were prepared to fight, this method would not assure us racial permanency. This is not the method proclaimed by the text. It is not taught anywhere in the Bible or even in experience, that a race will be blessed and made a blessing by carrying carnal weapons in its hands, but by stretching its *hands* to God.

No group has been so sorely disappointed in the after effects of the war as the colored race in America. We bought liberty bonds and stamps for bread and we have been given stones from the rioters in return. We sacrificed and died on battlefields for an egg and on our return home we are whipped to death with scorpions in the hands of the mob. But all these horrible experiences will be richly rewarded if we will learn that the only thing that can save any race or individual is to repent of sin and to seek the kingdom of God and his righteousness. If the weapons of persecution in the hands of white men will but force us to stretch out our hands unto God, we will yet live to see the day when we shall rejoice in these awful tribulations. Had I a stentorian voice touched with Pentecostal fire, I would burn the words Paul uttered on Mars Hill into the heart of every member of my race, "And hath made of one blood all nations of men, for to dwell on all the face of the earth and hath determined the times before appointed, and the bounds of their habitation. That they should seek the Lord if haply they might feel after him, and find him, though he be not far from every one of us."

The thought to be stressed here is not "of one blood all nations," but "feeling after God and finding Him." The race which feels after God always finds Him a very present help in the time of trouble. If my race would seriously read the book of Esther and translate its teachings into action, a marvelous deliverance would come and come quickly. A conspiracy was formed to put to death every Jew living in the one hundred and twenty-seven provinces of the Medo-Persian Empire during the twelfth month of the year. The conspiracy was not only sanctioned by the government, but a huge sum of money was appropriated from the national treasury to meet the expense of the slaughter. Mordecai apprised Queen Esther of the impending doom and the following proclamation was issued by her: "Go, gather together all the Jews that are present in Shushan, and fast ye for me, and neither eat nor drink for three days or nights: I also and my maidens will fast likewise; and so will I go in unto the king, which is not according to the law; and if I perish, I perish."

. . .

The colored people of America are in a similar situation. The present policy of the white Hamans is to either reduce them to the status of a plantation mule or completely annihilate them with the gun, rope and torch. This policy has the silent sanction of the United States government. While this country is lifting its hands in holy horror and shedding crocodile tears over the oppressed peoples of Europe and Asia, colored men and boys are dragged through the streets in open daylight, shot, hanged and burned, and mothers are ripped open and their unborn children murdered, without even so much as creating a ripple in the Department of Justice. The only remedy left is for Ethiopia to stretch forth her helpless hands to God. The God who delivered the Jews in the Medo-Persian Empire two thousand five hundred years ago is not dead. "Behold, the Lord's hand is not shortened that it cannot save, neither His ear heavy that it cannot hear." He is the same yesterday, today and forever to those who feel after Him with both hands.

Why should not the colored people of America begin the fulfillment of the prophecy of the text and hasten on the day when Ethiopia shall everywhere stretch forth her hands to God? If I were the Pope of my people I would issue a proclamation calling every colored man, woman and child to prayer and fasting on a certain day. The proclamation would not only forbid them to eat or drink or enter any place of amusement on that day, but to abstain from all work and to keep off the street corners. Every colored man and woman away from work and from the streets, shut up in their homes, laying insults, indignities, injustices and all the unspeakable outrages heaped upon their race before God, would be the most powerful and effective protest that ever went to Heaven from any continent. It is just as certain that God cannot tell a lie. In spite of all the appeals and protests made to the government, the situation for us is growing more serious and tense. Everything else under the sun has been tried; let the race now try God. When the Supreme Court of the United States declared that no black man had a single right that any white man was bound to respect and the master was fulfilling his boast by calling the roll of his runaway slaves at the foot of Bunker Hill, some white people asked a good old Christian woman what her people thought of the

Dred Scott decision. She replied, "We are going to take an appeal." "Appeal to what?" asked her interrogators. "Don't you know there is no appeal from the Supreme Court of the United States?" "But," said she, "honeys, we are going to appeal to the Supreme Court of Glory." On their humble knees they did appeal to Almighty God.

Up from the blue grass hills of Kentucky, up from the cane-brakes of Louisiana, up from the rice swamps of Mississippi, up from the orange groves of Florida, up from the cotton fields of Georgia and Alabama, up from the turpentine hills of North and South Carolina, up from the tobacco patches of Virginia, up from the corn fields of Maryland, up from the coal fields of Ohio and Pennsylvania, up from sand-enshrouded New Jersey, up from the busy marts of New York, up from the rock-ribbed hills of New England, went the agonizing appeal to the Lord God which caused the Supreme Court of Glory to reverse the decision of the Supreme Court of the United States and it was declared in the midst of the awful roar of cannon and the terrible flow of blood that the black man had some rights which the white man was bound to respect.

Let us try this appeal again. We have appealed to legislators and they will not hear us; we have appealed to governors and they will not hear us; we have appealed to every session of Congress for twenty-five years and they will not hear us; and we have appealed to all of the Presidents, Democrats and Republicans, and they will not hear us; we have appealed to members of the League of Nations and they will not hear us; we have appealed to the white pulpits and churches and they will not hear us. I ask you now, I beseech you, I beg you, I implore you, my people everywhere, to carry our protest to the Supreme Court of Glory and with outstretched hands let us make our appeal at the Great White Throne of God, and we will be heard, for the Judge of all the earth has not only promised to do right, but He has said, "Call upon me in the day of trouble and I will deliver thee." If the race heeds this call, it will not only save itself as surely as the God of the Bible lives, but it will become a savior of other races and will add a lasting contribution to the Christian religion.

SOURCE: Adam Clayton Powell, Sr., "The Colored Man's Contribution to Christianity and When It Will Be Made, 1919" (sermon delivered at Abyssinian Baptist Church and in other settings, housed in Schomburg Center for Research in Black Culture, New York).

73

HELEN BARRETT MONTGOMERY

H ELEN BARRETT MONTGOMERY (1861–1934), a social reformer and women's activist, was licensed to preach in 1892. She was elected president of the Northern Baptist Convention in 1921, the first woman chosen to lead a mainline Protestant denomination in America. Montgomery was known for her missions leadership and support of women's roles (selection below). Notably, Montgomery was the first woman to publish a translation of the New Testament into English, "The New Testament in Modern English."

Christianity and Women

We live in a country where the discussion of "Woman's Rights" is ever *to* the front. We are to study lands where they are just beginning to recognize woman's wrongs—lands where the slogan "Ladies First" is consistently and persistently "Ladies Last" . . . If women fully recognized the emancipatory nature of the pure religion of Jesus, the force of the religious missionary arguments would be tremendously strengthened . . .

In the Bible are enunciated the principles which will finally lead to *the complete emancipation of women.*—The legislation of the Old Testament, while partial and preparatory, and in that sense imperfect, is marked by a consideration for the rights of the weak and dependent, of women, children, the poor, the slave, that sets it apart from all other ancient literature. The very account of the creation, "In the image of God created he him, male and female created he them" (Gen 1:27) is strange to primitive thought. As someone has said of the beautiful garden story, "Eve was taken neither from man's head, to be his divinity, nor from his feet, to be his slave, but from his side, to be his companion and helper."

The gradual development of the doctrine of the individual in the teachings of the prophets laid the foundation for a democracy that should at last abolish the caste of sex. The democracy of the New Testament got its seal and inspiration in the teachings and practice of Jesus. He took up the old teaching of the prophets, obscured by the prejudice of centuries, brushed aside the dishonoring conventions which the rabbis had built up, and associated with women in the plane of a beautiful, free, human relationship. He sat wearied by the well conversing with a woman to the scandalizing of his disciples, who thought this quite beneath him as a holy man and rabbi. To women he reared the lovely memorial of his praise, and at the faith of women he marveled. Women followed him and ministered to him. He alone among religious teachers had a word of hope for the harlot, and to a woman he gave the first resurrection commission.

It is not strange if his disciples could not rise at once to the height of his example and his teaching. Paul labors hard to assure us that he is speaking quite on his own responsibility and is not at all inspired, though he thinks he understands the mind of Christ, when he writes those directions to the Corinthian church which have been a stumbling-block to so many. All these specific directions of his are to be read first in the light of conditions then existing in Greek society . . . where the only women free to speak and associate with the men were women of loose character. Hence Paul's urgency that the cause be not imperiled by insisting on a liberty which was turning the unaccustomed heads of the women . . . But when it comes to principles, Paul, unencumbered by the need of practical adjustment that so bothers the best philosophers, lays down the Magna Charta of womanhood in a Christianity in which there is neither male nor female, bond nor free, but in which all are one in Christ Jesus. He sees clearly that the duty of subordination and service is laid on all alike in Christ's great democracy and only those who love most are most honored.

It does not yet appear what we shall be, but is already manifest that the spirit of Jesus as revealed to us in the word of his truth is already making a new world; not a man's world, hard, cruel, bitter toward the weak, nor a woman's world, weak, sentimental, tasteless, but a world of humanity in which for the first time the full orb of all the qualities that serve to mark the human shall have free course and be glorified.

It may be asked why, then, if the Christian Scriptures contain these teachings concerning women, there is so long delayed and imperfectly realized an expression of the same in social and political institutions. The answers are many: (1) The Bible is only in possession of a fraction of the people, and that only within the last two or three centuries. For ages the Book was either prohibited to the people by the hierarchy, or rendered inaccessible by its cost, or made of none effect by the illiteracy and sodden ignorance of the masses. (2) The Bible doctrines in regard to women are the last word in democracy, and the first word is just getting itself uttered. Step by step democracy must fight its way against the self-interest, the pride, the passion, and the prejudices of mankind. (3) A steady progress upward can be seen in Christian countries; laws are ameliorated, violence is curbed, child labor is limited, women do come to their rights in exact proportion as Christian ideals become dominant in a nation. (4) The influence of these principles can already be seen to begin to penetrate non-Christian lands in proportion as they come in contact with the religion, the institutions, the literature of Christian lands.

If, as we have seen, the ethnic faiths have no clear gospel for the emancipation of woman and child; if outside of Christian countries they still labor under the most cruel disabilities of both law and custom; if in our own land it is the spirit of the Gospel of Christ which most powerfully wars against intemperance, lust, and greed—woman's hereditary foes—the duty of Christian women to put within the reach of their sisters in other lands this good tidings of great joy is plain. The great Emancipator of the mother and child must be made known in every dark corner of the earth. In the title of our chapter is cleverly summed up by a recent writer on India, the difference between that land and our own—"Ladies First," "Ladies Last," there stand two warring theories of life. In the one insolent strength triumphs over weakness, greed takes what it can get, the wise oppress the ignorant. Helpless because she bears the child in her bosom, woman is pushed to the wall. In the other the very spirit of the Christ is incarnate. Shoulders are strong not to shove, but to bear burdens, wise men are to learn of the child-like, the masters are to be chief servants of all.

SOURCE: Helen Barrett Montgomery, *Western Women in Eastern Lands* (New York: Macmillan, 1910), 45, 66–75.

74

EDGAR Y. MULLINS

Edgar Young Mullins (1860–1928) is considered the most influential Southern Baptist theologian and denominational leader of the first half of the twentieth century. He was president of The Southern Baptist Theological Seminary (1899–1928) and a leader in the Baptist World Alliance. *The Axioms of Religion* (1908), his most enduring book, said that soul competency, the right of each person to a direct relationship with God, was the "historical significance of Baptists." The selection below reveals Mullins' understanding of Baptist principles.

The Axioms of Religion

What then is the distinguishing Baptist principle? Is it separation of Church and State? Or is it the doctrine of soul freedom, the right of private judgment in religious matters and in the interpretation of the Scriptures? Assuredly these are distinctive Baptist principles, which have been held by no religious denomination so consistently. And yet they are scarcely an adequate statement by themselves . . .

The sufficient statement of the historical significance of the Baptists is this: The competency of the soul in religion. Of this means a competency under God, not a competency in the sense of human self-sufficiency. There is no reference here to the question of sin and human ability in the moral and theological sense, nor in the sense of independence of the Scriptures . . . On many vital matters of doctrine, such as the atonement, the person of Christ, and others Baptists are in substantial agreement with the evangelical world in general. This conception of the competency of the soul under God in religion . . . is of course a New Testament principle and carries at its heart the very essence of that conception of man's relations to God which we find in the teaching of Christ.

Observe then that the idea of the competency of the soul in religion excludes at once all human interference, such as episcopacy and infant baptism, and every form of religion by proxy. Religion is a personal matter between the soul and God. The principle is at the same time inclusive of all the particulars which were named above and more. It must include the doctrine of separation of Church and State because State churches stand on the assumption that civil government is necessary as a factor in man's life in order to a fulfillment of his religious destiny; that man without the aid of the State is incompetent in religion. Justification by faith is also included because this doctrine is simply one detail in the soul's general religious heritage from Christ. Justification asserts man's competency to deal directly with God in the initial act of the Christian life. Regeneration is also implied in the principle of the soul's competency because it is the blessing which follows close upon the heels of justification or occurs at the same time with it, as a result of the soul's direct dealing with God. The necessity for a regenerated church membership follows of necessity from the doctrine of the regenerated individual life. The doctrine of the soul's competency, however, goes further than individualism in that it embraces capacity for action in social relations as well as on the part of the individual. The church is a group of individuals sustaining to each other important relations, and organized for a great end and mission. The idea of the soul's competency embraces the social as well as the individual aspect of religion.

Let it be noted further that the steps we have already traced lead directly to democracy in church life and the priesthood of all believers. The competency of the regenerated individual implies that at bottom his competency is derived from the indwelling Christ. Man's capacity for self-government in religion is nothing more than the authority of Christ exerted in and through the inner life of believers, with the understanding always, of course, that he regulates that inner life in accordance with his revealed word. There is no conceivable justification, therefore, for lodging ecclesiastical authority in the hands of an infallible pope or a bench of bishops. Democracy in church government is an inevitable corollary of the general doctrine of the soul's competency in religion. The independence and autonomy of the local church, therefore, is not merely an inference from a verse of Scripture here and there. It inheres in the whole philosophy of Christianity. Democracy in church government is simply Christ himself animating his own body through his Spirit. The decisions of the local congregation on ecclesiastical matters are the "consensus of the competent."

The priesthood of all believers, again, is but the expression of the soul's competency on the Godward, as democracy is its expression on the ecclesiastical side of its religious life. No human priest may claim to be mediator between the soul and God because no possible reason can be assigned for any competency on his part not common to all believers . . .

I will put my plea in the form of six brief propositions, and I will predict . . . that you will recognize that these axioms of Christianity grow out of the mother principle for which Baptists have stood through the ages, as set forth, viz., the competency of the soul in religion under God. These six simple propositions are as six branches from that one trunk of New Testament teaching.

The Axioms of Religions

The theological axiom: The holy and loving God has a right to be sovereign.

The religious axiom: All souls have an equal right to direct access to God.

The ecclesiastical axiom: All believers have a right to equal privileges in the church.

The moral axiom: To be responsible man must be free.

The religio-civic axiom: A free Church in a free State.

The social axiom: Love your neighbor as yourself.

Now my claim is that these are axioms; they are to those who accept Christianity at all self-evident. Indeed, they will not be denied so far as they are general principles by any evangelical Christian or intelligent unbeliever. They are the very alphabet of the Christian religion. Understand me. They do not exhaust the specific beliefs as to the Scriptures, Christ, the church, the ordinances. They are not an exhaustive creed. They are rather the great New Testament assumptions, which are the very basis of our Baptist faith. What we wish the world to see is that our conception of the church and of Christianity rests upon an impregnable foundation.

Source: E. Y. Mullins, *The Axioms of Religion*, ed. C. Douglas Weaver (Macon, Ga.: Mercer University Press, 2010), 62–66, 75–76. Used by permission.

75

WILLIAM B. RILEY

WILLIAM BELL RILEY (1861–1947), pastor of First Baptist Church, Minneapolis, Minnesota, was one of the leading fundamentalists during the fundamentalist-modernist controversy in the 1920s that wreaked havoc in the Northern Baptist Convention. He founded the interdenominational World Christian Fundamentals Association (1919) and strongly opposed the increasing influence of Darwinian evolution in American life. The selection below is representative of the literal interpretation of the Bible characteristic of fundamentalism in its attack against liberal modernism.

The Menace of Modernism

Again this recognized leader [Charles Edward Jefferson] among the modern thinkers makes the interpretation of the Bible *a matter of mental and personal convenience.* When he comes upon a statement in Scripture that seems to be in conflict with science, such as Joshua's command of the sun to stand still, he calls it "poetry." When he comes upon a prophecy in Daniel in which he does not believe he says: "Daniel was mistaken." When he comes to the book of Job he declares it "fiction." The book of Jonah goes into the same category. The creation of Eve "is a myth." When he comes to the question of authorship, is it of God or man, he says, "It is of man." In answer to the question, "Is it right to say that God wrote the Bible" he says, "No, He did not write it. Every page of the Bible is written by man. The lights and shadows of his moods, the depression and rapture of his spirit play over its pages. Its contents came up out of the cavernous depths of the human heart. The light that lights every man that comes into the world came up out of the heart."

These were nominal Disciples . . . We do not desire to be harsh, nor uncharitable; but we must declare our deepest conviction, namely, that the greatest enemy of any Church of Jesus Christ is the man who remains in her, assumes to be one of her teachers, calmly wears her good name, and yet denies the deity of Him who brought her into being, and disputes the authority of the Book upon which she has rested her every contention. I regard myself as declaring a most patent truth when I say that "modernism"—so called—is just such an enemy. By lip and pen, it has alike rejected Jesus (whom John describes) and repudiated the Bible.

It is a matter of more than passing interest, also, to trace the parallelism between the opponents of John's description and the present-day opponents of Jesus.

They Denied His Physical Manifestations. The language in which John indicted them is this: "They confess not that Jesus Christ is coming in the flesh." The King James version, as you recall, has it, "is come in the flesh." If that translation were correct, it might refer to the first appearance of Jesus. If the text of the 1911 version is correct, "who confess not that Jesus is coming in the flesh," then the second coming is in the mind of the sacred writer. But in either event, that which these false teachers opposed was the physical manifestation of God in Christ Jesus. Truly they have their successors. "God manifest in the flesh" is a miracle of such transcendent import as to be utterly rejected by our advocates of evolution! They almost universally resort to the statements that Jesus, while being God's best representative, was yet born of Mary and begotten by Joseph. The Virgin birth, is doubtless one of those "New Testament concepts" which, says one of their number, "the modern world, under the domination of science, finds it impossible to understand, much less to believe." Concerning the second appearance of Jesus in personal, visible form, known as Messianism, we are blithely told by the same writer that "it is a survival of Judaism and its influence and implications must be removed before we can see the essential elements of the gospel." Of course the resurrection of Jesus is another physical manifestation, which, while not expressly mentioned in the text, is involved in the question; and, it is now well nigh the common custom among "new theologians" to hold that New Testament contention to ridicule. In fact, we are plainly asked the question, "If a man believes in a risen Christ without believing in the events of the first Easter Day, or in the objective character of the appearances of Jesus to Paul and the other apostles" should "he be excluded from preaching the gospel of salvation?" and answered, "assuredly not!", and are told that "he, too, can bring and must bring his conviction of the continued life of Jesus to bear upon men and women."

But this raises the logical and inevitable question, "What Jesus is he preaching, and whence does he bring either his Master or his message?" Manifestly it cannot be the Jesus of the Bible, for He was "flesh and blood" before His crucifixion, and "flesh and bones" after His resurrection, physical and visible in His ascension, and destined to be visible and personal in His glorious second appearance! . . .

Any Jesus, not begotten by the Holy Ghost, born of Mary, crucified on Calvary, raised the third day, ascended to the right hand of God, and destined to descend to the earth and take His throne and reign from sea to sea, is as much the figment of a distempered imagination as are the dreams resulting from an overdose of meat; and any message based upon it has no more claims upon intelligent, thinking men than do the unintelligible, incoherent babblings of a Mary Baker Eddy. What would you think of a man who said he believed in George Washington, but not the George Washington who was born in 1732 in Westmoreland County, Virginia, who was the first President of the United States, who led in the Revolution, and whose opinions gave rise and final form to the very constitution of the country itself; he believed rather, in a Washington who never had a visible, physical existence, but whose ideas and spirit dominated the colonies in the Puritan days, and still lives. Candidly, one finds it difficult to be patient with men who name themselves "Rationalists," while dispensing with reason, and call themselves "thinkers," while giving proof that they are incapable of clearly stating premises or reaching logical conclusions.

SOURCE: Excerpt is from a sermon on 2 John 1:7-11. William B. Riley, *The Menace of Modernism* (New York: Christian Alliance Publishing Co., 1917), 19, 34–39.

76

RUDOLF BULTMANN

R UDOLF BULTMANN (1884–1976) was a German theologian and New Testament scholar. He is known for his attempt to demythologize the New Testament in order to make Jesus' teaching accessible for modern readers formed by scientific principles. His ideas on demythologization were highly controversial but influential in the field of biblical criticism during the twentieth century. The reading below captures his challenges to a literal pre-critical reading of Scripture.

Demythologization

The Mythical View of the World and the Mythical Event of Redemption

The cosmology of the New Testament is essentially mythical in character. The world is viewed as a three-storied structure, with the earth in the centre, the heaven above, and the underworld beneath. Heaven is the abode of God and of celestial beings—the angels. The underworld is hell, the place of torment. Even the earth is more than the scene of natural, everyday events of the trivial round and common task. It is the scene of the supernatural activity of God and his angels on the one hand, and of Satan and his daemons on the other. These supernatural forces intervene in the course of nature and in all that men think and will and do. Miracles are by no means rare. Man is not in control of his own life. Evil spirits may take possession of him. Satan may inspire him with evil thoughts. Alternatively, God may inspire his thought and guide his purposes. He may grant him heavenly visions. He may allow him to hear his word of succor or demand. He may give him the supernatural power of his Spirit. History does not follow a smooth unbroken course; it is set in motion and controlled by these supernatural powers. This aeon is held in bondage by Satan, sin, and death (for "powers" is precisely what they are), and hastens towards its end. That end will come very soon, and will take the form of a cosmic catastrophe. It will be inaugurated by the "woes" of the last time. Then the Judge will come from heaven, the dead will rise, the last judgment will take place, and men will enter into eternal salvation or damnation.

The Mythological View of the World Obsolete

All this is the language of mythology, and the origin of the various themes can be easily traced in the contemporary mythology of Jewish Apocalyptic and in the redemption myths of Gnosticism. To this extent *the kerygma is incredible to modern man, for he is convinced that the mythical view of the world is obsolete.* We are therefore bound to ask whether, when we preach the Gospel today, we expect our converts to accept not only the Gospel message, but also the mythical view of the world in which it is set. If not, does the New Testament embody a truth which is quite independent of its mythical setting? If it does, theology must undertake the task of stripping the *kerygma* from its mythical framework, of "demythologizing" it.

Can Christian preaching expect modern man *to accept the mythical view of the world as true?* To do so would be both senseless and impossible. It would be senseless, because there is nothing specifically Christian in the mythical view of the world as such. It is simply the cosmology of a pre-scientific age. Again, it would be impossible, because no man can adopt a view of the world by his own volition—it is already determined for him by his place in history . . .

Man's knowledge and mastery of the world have advanced to such an extent through science and technology that it is no longer possible for anyone seriously to hold the New Testament view of the world—in fact, there is hardly anyone who does. What meaning, for instance, can we attach to such phrases in the creed as "descended into hell" or "ascended into heaven"? We no longer believe in the three-storied universe which the creeds take for granted. The only honest way of reciting the creeds is to strip the mythological framework from the truth they enshrine—that is, assuming that, they contain any truth at all, which is just the question that theology has to ask. No one who is old enough to think for himself supposes that God lives in a local heaven. There is no longer any heaven in the traditional sense of the word. The same applies to hell in the sense of a mythical underworld beneath our feet. And if this is so, we can no longer accept the story of Christ's descent into hell or his Ascension into heaven as literally true. We can no longer look for the return of the Son of Man on the clouds of heaven or hope that the faithful will meet him in the air (1 Thess. 4:15ff.).

Now that the forces and the laws of nature have been discovered, we can no longer believe in *spirits, whether good or evil.* We know that the stars are physical bodies whose motions are controlled by the laws of the universe, and not daemonic beings which enslave mankind to their service. Any influence they may have over human life must be explicable in terms of the ordinary laws of nature; it cannot in any way be attributed to their malevolence. Sickness and the cure of disease are likewise attributable to natural causation; they are not the result of daemonic activity or of evil spells. The *miracles of the New Testament* have ceased to be miraculous, and to defend their historicity by recourse to nervous disorders or hypnotic effects only serves to underline the fact . . . It is impossible to use electric light and the wireless and to avail ourselves of modern medical and surgical discoveries, and at the same time to believe in the New Testament world of daemons and spirits. We may think we can manage it in our own lives, but to expect others to do so is to make the Christian faith unintelligible and unacceptable to the modern world . . .

The Nature of Myth

The real purpose of myth is not to present an objective picture of the world as it is, but to express man's understanding of himself in the world in which he lives. Myth should be interpreted not cosmologically, but anthropologically, or better still, existentially. Myth speaks of the power or the powers which man supposes he experiences as the ground and limit of his world and of his own activity and suffering. He describes these powers in terms derived from the visible world, with its tangible objects and forces, and from human life, with its feelings, motives, and potentialities. He may, for instance, explain the origin of the world by speaking of a world egg or a world tree. Similarly he may account for the present state and order of the world by speaking of a primeval war between the gods. He speaks of the other world in terms of this world, and of the gods in terms derived from human life . . .

Myth is an expression of man's conviction that the origin and purpose of the world in which he lives are to be sought not within it but beyond it—that is, beyond the realm of known and tangible reality—and that this realm is perpetually dominated and menaced by those mysterious powers which are its source and limit. Myth is also an expression of man's awareness that he is not lord of his own being. It expresses his sense of dependence not only within the visible world, but more especially on those forces which hold sway beyond the confines of the known. Finally, myth expresses man's belief that in this state of dependence he can be delivered from the forces within the visible world . . .

Hence the importance of the New Testament mythology lies not in its imagery but in the understanding of existence which it enshrines. The real question is whether this understanding of existence is true. Faith claims that it is, and faith ought not to be tied down to the imagery of New Testament mythology.

Source: Rudolf Bultmann, *Kerygma and Myth: A Theological Debate*, ed. Hans Werner Bartsch (London: SPCK, 1953), 1–5, 10–11. Used by permission from SPCK.

77

PAUL TILLICH

Paul Tillich (1886–1965) was a Lutheran theologian who taught in Germany before being dismissed from his teaching position for opposing the Third Reich. At the urging of Reinhold Niebuhr, Tillich joined the faculty at Union Theological Seminary, New York (1933–1955) and later taught at Harvard University (1955–1962) and the University of Chicago (1962–1965). Tillich authored several works, including a three-volume *Systematic Theology*. He is known for his "method of correlation," hoping to correlate existential questions and revelation. One particular focus was Tillich's grappling with "ultimate concern" (selection below) and faith.

Faith as Ultimate Concern

Ultimate concern is the abstract translation of the great commandment: "The Lord, our God, the Lord is one; and you shall love the Lord your God with all your heart, and with all your soul and with all your mind, and with all your strength" (Mark 12:29). The religious concern is ultimate; it excludes all other concerns from ultimate significance; it makes them preliminary. The ultimate concern is unconditional, independent of any conditions of character, desire, or circumstance. The unconditional concern is total: no part of ourselves or of our world is excluded from it; there is no "place" to flee from it (Ps. 139). The total concern is infinite: no moment of relaxation and rest is possible in the face of a religious concern which is ultimate, unconditional, total, and infinite.

The word "concern" points to the "existential" character of religious experience. We cannot speak adequately of the "object of religion" without simultaneously removing its character as an object. That which is ultimate gives itself only to the attitude of ultimate concern. It is the correlate of an unconditional concern but not a "highest thing" . . . For this reason we have avoided terms like "*the* ultimate," "*the* unconditioned," "*the* universal," "*the* infinite" and have spoken of ultimate, unconditional, total, infinite concern. Of course, in every concern there is *something* about which one is concerned; but this something should not appear as a separated object which could be known and handled without concern. This, then, is the first formal criterion of theology: *The object of theology is what concerns us ultimately. Only those propositions are theological which deal with their object in so far as it can become a matter of ultimate concern for us* . . .

What is the content of our ultimate concern? What *does* concern us unconditionally? The answer obviously, cannot be a special object, not even God, for the first criterion of theology must remain formal and general. If more is to be said about the nature of our ultimate concern, it must be derived from an analysis of the concept "ultimate concern." *Our ultimate concern is that which determines our being or not-being. Only those statements are theological which deal with their object in so far as it can become a matter of being or not-being for us.* This is the second formal criterion of theology.

Nothing can be of ultimate concern for us which does not have the power of threatening and saving our being. The term "being" in this context does not designate existence in time and space. Existence is continuously threatened and saved by things and events which have no ultimate concern for us. But the term "being" means the whole of human reality, the structure, the meaning, and the aim of existence. All this is threatened; it can be lost or saved. Man is ultimately concerned about his being and meaning. "To be or not to be" in this sense is a matter of ultimate, unconditional, total, and infinite concern.

Source: Paul Tillich, *Systematic Theology*, vol. 1 (Chicago: University of Chicago Press, 1951), 11–14. © 1951 by The University of Chicago. All rights reserved. Used by permission.

78

KARL BARTH

Karl Barth (1886–1968) was a Swiss pastor, professor, and one of the most important theologians of the twentieth century. His *Church Dogmatics* (fourteen volumes) remains his most influential work. Barth responded to what he considered a human-centered theology in liberal Protestantism with an emphasis upon God's revelation in Jesus Christ, the Word made flesh. Barth was a part of the larger Reformed tradition that focused on the sovereignty of God and election. However, he resituated the doctrine of election, moving the discussion from the election of individuals to God's election of grace in Jesus Christ. Included in the selections below is the *Barmen Declaration*, Barth's indictment of German Nazism made by the dissenting Confessing Church.

The Barmen Theological Declaration

[. . .] In view of the errors of the "German Christians" and of the present Reich Church Administration, which are ravaging the Church and at the same time also shattering the unity of the German Evangelical Church, we confess the following evangelical truths:

1. "I am the Way and the Truth and the Life; no one comes to the Father except through me." (John 14:6)

   "Truly, truly I say to you, he who does not enter the sheepfold through the door but climbs in somewhere else, he is a thief and a robber. I am the Door; if anyone enters through me, he will be saved." (John 10:1, 9)

   Jesus Christ, as he is attested to us in Holy Scripture, is the one Word of God which we have to hear, and which we have to trust and obey in life and in death.

   We reject the false doctrine that the Church could and should recognize as a source of its proclamation, beyond and besides this one Word of God, yet other events, powers, historic figures, and truths as God's revelation.

2. "Jesus Christ has been made wisdom and righteousness and sanctification and redemption for us by God." (1 Cor. 1:30)

   As Jesus Christ is God's comforting pronouncement of the forgiveness of all our sins, so, and with equal seriousness, he is also God's vigorous announcement of his claim upon our whole life. Through him there comes to us joyful liberation from the godless ties of this world for free, grateful service to his creatures.

   We reject the false doctrine that there could be areas of our life in which we would belong not to Jesus Christ but to other lords, areas in which we would not need justification and sanctification through him.

3. "Let us, however, speak the truth in love, and in every respect grow into him who is the head, into Christ, from whom the whole body is joined together." (Eph. 4:15-16)

The Christian Church is the community of brethren in which, in Word and sacrament, through the Holy Spirit, Jesus Christ acts in the present as Lord. With both its faith and its obedience, with both its message and its order, it has to testify in the midst of the sinful world, as the Church of pardoned sinners, that it belongs to him alone and lives and may live by his comfort and under his direction alone, in expectation of his appearing.

We reject the false doctrine that the Church could have permission to hand over the form of its message and of its order to whatever it itself might wish or to the vicissitudes of the prevailing ideological and political convictions of the day.

4. "You know that the rulers of the Gentiles exercise authority over them and those in high position lord it over them. So shall it not be among you; but if anyone would have authority among you, let him be your servant." (Matt. 20:25-26)

The various offices in the Church do not provide a basis for some to exercise authority over others but for the ministry with which the whole community has been entrusted and charged to be carried out.

We reject the false doctrine that, apart from this ministry, the Church could, and could have permission to, give itself or allow itself to be given special leaders [*Führer*] vested with ruling authority.

5. "Fear God, honor the King!" (1 Pet. 2:17)

Scripture tells us that by divine appointment the State, in this still unredeemed world in which also the Church is situated, has the task of maintaining justice and peace, so far as human discernment and human ability make this possible, by means of the threat and use of force. The Church acknowledges with gratitude and reverence toward God the benefit of this, his appointment. It draws attention to God's Kingdom [*Reich*], God's commandment and justice, and with these the responsibility of those who rule and those who are ruled. It trusts and obeys the power of the Word, by which God upholds all things.

We reject the false doctrine that beyond its special commission the State should and could become the sole and total order of human life and so fulfil the vocation of the Church as well.

We reject the false doctrine that beyond its special commission the Church should and could take on the nature, tasks and dignity which belong to the State and thus become itself an organ of the State.

6. "See, I am with you always, to the end of the age." (Matt. 28:20) "God's Word is not fettered." (2 Tim. 2:9)

The Church's commission, which is the foundation of its freedom, consists in this: in Christ's stead, and so in the service of his own Word and work, to deliver to all people, through preaching and sacrament, the message of the free grace of God.

We reject the false doctrine that with human vainglory the Church could place the Word and work of the Lord in the service of self-chosen desires, purposes and plans. [. . .]

Election

In its simplest and most comprehensive form the dogma of predestination consists, then, in the assertion that the divine predestination is the election of Jesus Christ. But the concept of election has a double reference—to the elector and to the elected. And so, too, the name of Jesus Christ has within itself the double reference; the One called by this name is both very God and very man. Thus the simplest form of the dogma may be derived at once into the two assertions that Jesus Christ is the electing God, and that He is also the elected man.

In so far as He is the electing God, we must obviously—and above all—ascribe to Him the active determination of electing. It is not that He does not also elect as man, i.e., elect God in faith. But this election can only follow His prior election, and that means that it follows the divine electing which is the basic and proper determination of His existence.

In so far as He is man, the passive determination of election is also and necessarily proper to Him. It is true, of course, that even as God He is elected: the Elected of His Father. But because as the Son of the Father He has no need of any special election, we must add at once He is the Son of God elected in His oneness with man, and in fulfillment of God's covenant with man. Primarily, then, electing is the divine determination of the existence of Jesus Christ, and election (being elected) the human . . .

Jesus Christ, then, is not merely one of the elect but *the* elect of God. From the very beginning (from eternity itself), as elected man He does not stand alongside the rest of the elect, but before and above them as the One who is originally and properly the Elect. From the very beginning (from eternity itself), there are no other elect together with or apart from Him, but, as Eph. 1:4 tells us, only " in" Him. "In Him" does not simply mean with Him, together with Him, in His company. Nor does it mean only through Him, by means of that which He as elected man can be and do for them. "In Him" means in His person, in His will, in His own divine choice, in the basic decision of God which He fulfills over against every man. What singles Him out from the rest of the elect, and yet also, and for the first time, unites Him with them, is the fact that as elected man He is also the electing God, electing them in His own humanity. In that He (as God) wills Himself (as man), He also wills them. And so they are elect "in Him," in and with His own election. And so, too, His election must be distinguished from theirs. It must not be distinguished from theirs merely as the example and type, the revelation and reflection of their election. All this can, of course, be said quite truly of the election of Jesus Christ. But it must be said further that His election is the original and all-inclusive election; the election which is absolutely unique, but which in this very uniqueness is universally meaningful and efficacious, because it is the election of Him who Himself elects . . .

We have to remove completely from our minds the thought of the foreordination of a rigid and balanced system of election and reprobation. Above all, we have to expunge completely the idolatrous concept of a *decretum absolutum*. In place of these we have to introduce the knowledge of the elect man Jesus Christ as the true object of the divine predestination.

Atonement

In the sense of the Apostolic witness of the Crucifixion of Jesus Christ is the concrete deed and action of God Himself. God changes Himself, God Himself comes most near, God thinks it not robbery to be divine, that is, He does not hold on to the booty like a robber, but God parts with Himself. Such is the glory of His Godhead, that He can be "selfless," that he can actually forgive Himself something. He remains genuinely true to Himself, but just through not having to limit Himself to His Godhead. It is the depth of the Godhead, the greatness of His glory which is revealed in the very fact that it can also completely hide itself in its sheer opposite, in the profoundest rejection and the greatest misery of the creature. What takes place in the Crucifixion of Christ is that God's Son takes to Himself that which must come to the creature existing in revolt, which wants to deliver itself from its creatureliness and itself be the Creator. He puts Himself into this creature's need and does not abandon it to itself. Moreover, He does not only help it from without and greet it only from afar off; He makes the misery of His creature His own. To what end? So that His creature may go out freely, so that the burden which it has laid upon itself may be born, borne away. The creature itself must have gone to pieces, but God does not want that; He wants it to be saved. So great is the ruin of the creature that less than the self-surrender of God would not suffice for its rescue. But so great is God, that it is His will to render up Himself. Reconciliation means God taking man's place . . .

God Himself, in Jesus Christ His Son, at once true God and true man, takes the place of the condemned man. God's judgment is executed, God's law takes its course, but in such a way that what man had to suffer is suffered by the One, who as God's Son stands for us before God, by taking upon Himself what belongs to us. In Him God makes Himself liable, at the point at which we are accursed and guilty and lost. He it is in His Son, who in the person of this crucified man bears on Golgotha all that ought to be laid on us. And in this way He makes an end of the curse. It is not God's will that man should perish; it is not God's will that man should pay what he was bound to pay; in other words, God extirpates the sin. And God does this, not in spite of His righteousness but it is God's very righteousness that He, the holy One, steps in for us the unholy, that He wills to save and does save us. Righteousness in the Old Testament sense is not the righteousness of the judge who makes the debtor pay, but the action of a judge who in the accused recognizes the wretch whom he wishes to help by putting him to rights. This is what righteousness means. Righteousness means to setting right. And that is what God does.

SOURCE: "The Barmen Theological Declaration: A New Translation," by Douglas S. Bax, *Journal of Theology for Southern Africa* 47 (1984): 78–81. Reprinted by permission of the publisher. Section on "election" is from Karl Barth, *Church Dogmatics,* Vol. II/2, *The Doctrine of God,* ed. G. W. Bromiley and T. F. Torrance (Edinburgh: T&T Clark, 1957), 103, 116–17, 143. By kind permission of Continuum International Publishing Group. Section on "atonement" is from (i) *Dogmatics in Outline* by Karl Barth ©SCM Press, 1959 and is reproduced by permission of Hymns Ancient & Modern Ltd. See pp. 116–19.

79

REINHOLD NIEBUHR

REINHOLD NIEBUHR (1892–1971) was an American theologian and ethicist who taught at Union Theological Seminary, New York, for thirty-two years. Niebuhr's theology, often associated with neoorthodoxy or neoliberalism, is called "Christian Realism." He focused on social issues and the dialectic of the ethics of love and justice. Niebuhr, in reaction to liberalism, reemphasized the sinfulness of humanity. He affirmed but redefined original sin; sin was inevitable but not necessary. His teaching on sin as self-pride (selection below) was an influential element in his key work, *The Nature and Destiny of Man* (2 vols., 1941–1943).

Sin of Pride

Moral pride is revealed in all "self-righteous" judgments in which the other is condemned because he fails to conform to the highly arbitrary standards of the self. Since the self judges itself by its own standards it finds itself good. It judges others by its own standards and finds them evil, when their standards fail to conform to its own. This is the secret of the relationship between cruelty and self-righteousness. When the self mistakes its standards for God's standards it is naturally inclined to attribute the very essence of evil to non-conformists . . . Moral pride is the pretension of the finite man that his highly conditioned virtue is the final righteousness and that his very relative moral standards are absolute. Moral pride thus makes virtue the very vehicle of sin, a fact which explains why the New Testament is so critical of the righteous in comparison with "publicans and sinners" . . .

The sin of moral pride, when it has conceived, brings forth spiritual pride. The ultimate sin is the religious sin of making the self-deification implied in moral pride explicit. This is done when our partial standards and relative attainments are explicitly related to the unconditioned good, and claim divine sanction. For this reason religion is not simply as is generally supposed an inherently virtuous human quest for God. It is merely a final battleground between God and man's self-esteem. In that battle even the most pious practices may be instruments of human pride. The same man may in one moment regard Christ as his judge and in the next moment seek to prove that the figure, the standards and the righteousness of Christ bear a greater similarity to his own righteousness than to that of his enemy. The worst form of class domination is religious class domination in which, as for instance in the Indian caste system, a dominant priestly class not only subjects subordinate classes to social disabilities but finally excludes them from participation in any universe of meaning. The worst form of intolerance is religious intolerance, in which the particular interest of the contestants hide behind religious absolutes. The worst form of self-assertion is religious self-assertion in which under the guise of contrition before God, He is claimed as the exclusive ally of our contingent self . . .

Christianity rightly regards itself as a religion, not so much of man's search for God, in the process of which he may make himself God; but as a religion of revelation in which a holy and loving God is revealed to man as the source and end of all finite existence against whom the self-will of man is shattered and his pride abased. But as soon as the Christian assumes that he is, by virtue of possessing this revelation, more righteous because more contrite, than other men, he increases the sin of self-righteousness and makes the forms of a religion of contrition the tool of his pride . . .

Our analysis of man's sin of pride and self-love has consistently assumed than an element of deceit is involved in this self-glorification. This dishonesty must be regarded as a concomitant, and not as the basis, of self-love. Man loves himself inordinately. Since his determinate existence does not deserve the devotion lavished upon it, it is obviously necessary to practice some deception in order to justify such excessive devotion. While such deception is constantly directed against competing wills, seeking to secure their acceptance and validation of the self's too generous opinion of itself, its primary purpose is to deceive, not others, but the self. The self must at any rate deceive itself first. Its deception of others is partly an effort to convince itself against itself. The fact that this necessity exists is an important indication of the vestige of truth which abides with the self in all its confusion and which it must placate before it can act. The dishonesty of man is thus an interesting refutation of the doctrine of man's total depravity.

SOURCE: Reinhold Niebuhr, *The Nature and Destiny of Man* (New York: Charles Scribner & Sons, 1941), 199–203. Reprinted with the permission of the estate of Reinhold Niebuhr.

80

DIETRICH BONHOEFFER

DIETRICH BONHOEFFER (1906–1945) was a German theologian whose thought was greatly influenced by Adolf von Harnack and Karl Barth. Bonhoeffer introduced a new theology of Christian community based on sharing the sufferings of Christ by enacting justice. Bonhoeffer publicly warned the German people against Hitler's Nazism and wrote the 1933 Bethel Confession against German Christianity because of its toleration of Hitler. Bonhoeffer was arrested in 1944 after Nazis discovered documents implicating him in an assassination attempt of Hitler. After over a year of imprisonment in a military prison and concentration camp, Bonhoeffer was executed on April 4, 1945.

The Cost of Discipleship

CHEAP GRACE is the mortal enemy of our church. Our struggle today is for costly grace.

Cheap grace means grace as bargain-basement goods, cut-rate forgiveness, cut-rate comfort, cut-rate sacrament; grace as the church's inexhaustible pantry, from which it is doled out by careless hands without hesitation or limit. It is grace without a price, without costs. It is said that the essence of grace is that the bill for it is paid in advance for all time. Everything can be had for free, courtesy of that paid bill. The price paid is infinitely great and, therefore, the possibilities of taking advantage of and wasting grace are also infinitely great. What would grace be, if it were not cheap grace?

Cheap grace means grace as doctrine, as principle, as system. It means forgiveness of sins as a general truth; it means God's love as merely a Christian conception of God. Those who affirm it have already had their sins forgiven. The church that teaches this doctrine of grace thereby confers such grace upon itself. The world finds in this church a cheap cover-up for its sins, for which it shows no remorse and from which it has even less desire to be set free. Cheap grace is, thus, denial of God's living word, denial of the incarnation of the word of God.

Cheap grace means justification of sin but not of the sinner. Because grace alone does everything, everything can stay in its old ways. "Our action is in vain." The world remains world and we remain sinners "even in the best of lives." Thus, the Christian should live the same way the world does. In all things the Christians should go along with the world and not venture (like sixteenth-century enthusiasts) to live a different life under grace from that under sin! The Christian better not rage against grace or defile that glorious cheap grace by proclaiming anew a servitude to the letter of the Bible in an attempt to live an obedient life under the commandments of Jesus Christ! The world is justified by grace, therefore—because this grace is so serious! because this irreplaceable grace should not be opposed—the Christian should live just like the rest of the world! Of course, a Christian would like to do something exceptional! Undoubtedly, it must be the most difficult renunciation not to do so and to live like the world. But the Christian has to do it, has to practice such self-denial so that there is no difference between Christian life and worldly life. The Christian has to let grace truly be grace enough so that the world does not lose faith in this cheap grace. In being worldly, however, in this necessary renunciation required for the sake of the world—no, for the sake of grace!—the Christian can be comforted and secure in possession of that grace which takes care of everything by itself. So the Christian need not follow Christ, since the Christian is comforted by grace. That is cheap grace as justification of sin, but not justification of the contrite sinner who turns away from sin and repents. It is not forgiveness of sin which separates those who sinned from sin. Cheap grace is that grace which we bestow on ourselves.

Cheap grace is preaching forgiveness without repentance; it is baptism without the discipline of community; it is the Lord's Supper without confession of sin; it is absolution without personal confession. Cheap grace is grace without discipleship, grace without the cross, grace without the living, incarnate Jesus Christ.

Costly grace is the hidden treasure in the field; for the sake of which people go and sell with joy everything they have. It is the costly pearl, for whose price the merchant sells all that he has; it is Christ's sovereignty, for the sake of which you tear out an eye if it causes you to stumble. It is the call of Jesus Christ which causes a disciple to leave his nets and follow him . . .

It is costly because it calls to discipleship; it is grace, because it calls us to follow Jesus Christ. It is costly, because it costs people their lives; it is grace, because it thereby makes them live. It is costly, because it condemns sin; it is grace, because it justifies the sinner. Above all, grace is costly, because it was costly to God, because it costs God the life of God's Son—"you were bought with a price"—and because nothing can be cheap to us which is costly to

God. Above all, it is grace because the life of God's Son was not too costly for God to give in order to make us live. God did, indeed, give him up for us. Costly grace is the incarnation of God.

Life Together

So between the death of Christ and the Last Day it is only by a gracious anticipation of the last things that Christians are privileged to live in visible fellowship with other Christians. It is by the grace of God that a congregation is permitted to gather visibly in this world to share God's Word and sacrament. Not all Christians receive this blessing. The imprisoned, the sick, the scattered lonely, the proclaimers of the Gospel in heathen lands stand alone. They know that visible fellowship is a blessing. They remember, as the Psalmist did, how they went "with the multitude . . . to the house of God, with the voice of joy and praise, with a multitude that kept holyday" (Ps. 42:4) . . .

The physical presence of other Christians is a source of incomparable joy and strength to the believer. Longingly, the imprisoned apostle Paul calls his "dearly beloved son in the faith," Timothy, to come to him in prison in the last days of his life; he would see him again and have him near. Paul has not forgotten the tears Timothy shed when last they parted (2 Tim. 1:4). Remembering the congregation in Thessalonica, Paul prays "night and day . . . exceedingly that we might see your face" (1 Thess. 3:10). The aged John knows that his joy will not be full until he can come to his own people and speak face to face instead of writing with ink (2 John 12).

The believer feels no shame, as though he were still living too much in the flesh, when he yearns for the physical presence of other Christians. Man was created a body, the Son of God appeared on earth in the body, he was raised in the body, in the sacrament the believer receives the Lord Christ in the body, and the resurrection of the dead will bring about the perfected fellowship of God's spiritual-physical creatures. The believer therefore lauds the Creator, the Redeemer, God, Father, Son and Holy Spirit, for the bodily presence of a brother. The prisoner, the sick person, the Christian in exile sees in the companionship of a fellow Christian a physical sign of the gracious presence of the triune God. Visitor and visited in loneliness recognize in each other the Christ who is present in the body; they receive and meet each other as one meets the Lord, in reverence, humility, and joy. They receive each other's benedictions as the benediction of the Lord Jesus Christ. But if there is so much blessing and joy even in a single encounter of brother with brother, how inexhaustible are the riches that open up for those who by God's will are privileged to live in the daily fellowship of life with other Christians!

It is true, of course, that what is an unspeakable gift of God for the lonely individual is easily disregarded and trodden under foot by those who have the gift every day. It is easily forgotten that the fellowship of Christian brethren is a gift of grace, a gift of the Kingdom of God that any day may be taken from us, that the time that still separates us from utter loneliness may be brief indeed. Therefore, let him who until now has had the privilege of living a common Christian life with other Christians praise God's grace from the bottom of his heart. Let him thank God on his knees and declare: It is grace, nothing but grace, that we are allowed to live in community with Christian brethren . . .

Christianity means community through Jesus Christ and in Jesus Christ. No Christian community is more or less than this. Whether it be a brief, single encounter or the daily fellowship of years, Christian community is only this. We belong to one another only through and in Jesus Christ.

SOURCE: From *The Cost of Discipleship* by Dietrich Bonhoeffer, translated from the German by R. H. Fuller, with revisions by Irmgard Booth. Copyright © 1959 by SCM Press Ltd. SCM Translation 1948, 1959 © SCM Press. Used by permission of Hymns Ancient and Modern Ltd. Reprinted with the permission of Scribner, a division of Simon & Schuster, Inc. All rights reserved. Excerpts from pp. 18–21 (639 words) from *Life Together* by Dietrich Bonhoeffer and translated by John Doberstein. English translation copyright © 1954 by Harper & Brothers, copyright renewed 1982 by Helen S. Doberstein. Reprinted by permission of HarperCollins Publishers.

81

DOROTHY DAY

DOROTHY DAY (1897–1980), a native of New York, was the cofounder of the Catholic Worker Movement. After converting to Roman Catholicism from agnosticism, Day worked to restructure society through *The Catholic Worker* newspaper, communal farms, and hospitality houses. The selection below written during World War II—representative of her social teachings—combines elements of her experiences living among the poor with pacifism, the fight against poverty, and equality between different races and socioeconomic groups.

Catholic Worker Movement

"But we are at war," people say. "This is no time to talk of peace. It is demoralizing to the armed forces to protest, not to cheer them on in their fight for Christianity, for democracy, for civilization. Now that it is under way, it is too late to do anything about it." One reader writes to protest against our "frail" voices "blatantly" crying out against war. (The word blatant comes from bleat, and we are indeed poor sheep crying out to the Good Shepherd to save us from these horrors.) Another Catholic newspaper says it sympathizes with our sentimentality. This is a charge always leveled against pacifists. We are supposed to be afraid of the suffering, of the hardships of war.

But let those who talk of softness, of sentimentality, come to live with us in cold, unheated houses in the slums. Let them come to live with the criminal, the unbalanced, the drunken, the degraded, the pervert. (It is not the decent poor, it is not the decent sinner who was the recipient of Christ's love.) Let them live with rats, with vermin, bedbugs, roaches, lice (I could describe the several kinds of body lice).

Let their flesh be mortified by cold, by dirt, by vermin; let their eyes be mortified by the sight of bodily excretions, diseased limbs, eyes, noses, mouths.

Let their noses be mortified by the smells of sewage, decay and rotten flesh. Yes, and the smell of the sweat, blood and tears spoken of so blithely by Mr. [Winston] Churchill, and so widely and bravely quoted by comfortable people.

Let their ears be mortified by harsh and screaming voices, by the constant coming and going of people living herded together with no privacy. (There is no privacy in tenements just as there is none in concentration camps.)

Let their taste be mortified by the constant eating of insufficient food cooked in huge quantities for hundreds of people, the coarser foods, the cheaper foods, so that there will be enough to go around; and the smell of such cooking is often foul.

Then when they have lived with these comrades, with these sights and sounds, let our critics talk of sentimentality.

"Love in practice is a harsh and dreadful thing compared to love in dreams." [*The Brothers Karamazov*, Dostoevsky]

Our Catholic Worker groups are perhaps too hardened to the sufferings in the class war, living as they do in refugee camps, the refugees being as they are victims of the class war we live in always. We live in the midst of this war now these many years. It is a war not recognized by the majority of our comfortable people. They are pacifists themselves when it comes to the class war. They even pretend it is not there.

Many friends have counseled us to treat this world war in the same way. "Don't write about it. Don't mention it. Don't jeopardize the great work you are doing among the poor, among the workers. Just write about constructive things like Houses of Hospitality and Farming Communes." "Keep silence with a bleeding heart," one reader, a man, pro-war and therefore not a sentimentalist, writes us.

But we cannot keep silent. We have not kept silence in the face of the monstrous injustice of the class war, or the race war that goes on side by side with this world war (which the Communist used to call the imperialist war.)

Read the letters in this issue of the paper, the letter from the machine shop worker as to the deadening, degrading hours of labor. Read the quotation from the missioner's letter from China. Remember the unarmed steel strikers, the coal miners, shot down on picket lines. Read the letter from our correspondent in Seattle who told of the treatment accorded agricultural workers in the North West. Are these workers supposed to revolt? These are Pearl Harbor incidents! Are they supposed to turn to arms in the class conflict to defend their lives, their homes, their wives and children?

Last month a Negro in Missouri was shot and dragged by a mob through the streets behind a car. His wounded body was then soaked in kerosene. The mob of white Americans then set fire to it, and when the poor anguished victim had died, the body was left lying in the street until a city garbage cart trucked it away. Are the Negroes supposed to "Remember Pearl Harbor" and take to arms to avenge this cruel wrong? No, the Negroes, the workers in general, are expected to be "pacifist" in the face of this aggression.

Perhaps we are called sentimental because we speak of love. We say we love our president, our country. We say that we love our enemies, too. "Hell," Bernanos said, "is not to love any more."

"Greater love hath no man than this," Christ said, "that he should lay down his life for his friend" (John 15:13).

"Love is the measure by which we shall be judged," St. John of the Cross said.

"Love is the fulfilling of the law," St. John, the beloved disciple said.

Read the last discourse of Jesus to his disciples. Read the letters of St. John in the New Testament. And how can we express this love—by bombers, by blockades? . . .

Love is a breaking of bread . . . Love is not the starving of whole populations. Love is not the bombardment of open cities. Love is not killing, it is
the laying down of one's life for one's friend.

SOURCE: Dorothy Day, "Why Do the Members of Christ Tear One Another?" *The Catholic
Worker* (February 1942): 1, 4, 7. Dorothy Day Library at http://www.catholicworker.org/
dorothyday/.

82

SECOND VATICAN COUNCIL

VATICAN II (1962–1965) was the twenty-first and most recent ecumenical church council in Roman Catholicism. The council was called
by Pope John XXIII—who emphasized *aggiornamento*, the updating and
renewal of the church—and concluded under Pope Paul VI. The council has
been hailed as one of the most momentous events in Catholic history. While
traditional doctrines, like papal infallibility, were affirmed, many Catholic
practices were revised: mass could be in the vernacular, communion could
be in both kinds, and non-Catholic Christians were acknowledged as "separated brethren" rather than outside the faith. In the selection below, the focus
on ecumenism, especially regarding adherents of other world religions, is
highlighted.

Nonchristian Religions

1. In our time, when day by day mankind is being drawn closer together,
and the ties between different peoples are becoming stronger, the Church
examines more closely her relationship to non-Christian religions. In her task
of promoting unity and love among men, indeed among nations, she considers above all in this declaration what men have in common and what draws
them to fellowship.

One is the community of all peoples, one their origin, for God made the
whole human race to live over the face of the earth (cf. Acts 17:26). One also is
their final goal, God. His providence, His manifestations of goodness, His saving design extend to all men (cf. Wis. 8:1; Acts 14:17; Rom. 2:6-7; 1 Tim. 2:4),
until that time when the elect will be united in the Holy City, the city ablaze
with the glory of God, where the nations will walk in His light (cf. Rev. 21:23f.).

Men expect from the various religions answers to the unsolved riddles of the human condition, which today, even as in former times, deeply stir the hearts of men: What is man? What is the meaning, the aim of our life? What is moral good, what is sin? Whence suffering and what purpose does it serve? Which is the road to true happiness? What are death, judgment and retribution after death? What, finally, is that ultimate inexpressible mystery which encompasses our existence: whence do we come, and where are we going?

2. From ancient times down to the present, there is found among various peoples a certain perception of that hidden power which hovers over the course of things and over the events of human history; at times some indeed have come to the recognition of a Supreme Being, or even of a Father. This perception and recognition penetrates their lives with a profound religious sense.

Religions, however, that are bound up with an advanced culture have struggled to answer the same questions by means of more refined concepts and a more developed language. Thus in Hinduism, men contemplate the divine mystery and express it through an inexhaustible abundance of myths and through searching philosophical inquiry. They seek freedom from the anguish of our human condition either through ascetical practices or profound meditation or a flight to God with love and trust. Again, Buddhism, in its various forms, realizes the radical insufficiency of this changeable world; it teaches a way by which men, in a devout and confident spirit, may be able either to acquire the state of perfect liberation, or attain, by their own efforts or through higher help, supreme illumination. Likewise, other religions found everywhere try to counter the restlessness of the human heart, each in its own manner, by proposing "ways," comprising teachings, rules of life, and sacred rites. The Catholic Church rejects nothing that is true and holy in these religions. She regards with sincere reverence those ways of conduct and of life, those precepts and teachings which, though differing in many aspects from the ones she holds and sets forth, nonetheless often reflect a ray of that Truth which enlightens all men. Indeed, she proclaims, and ever must proclaim Christ "the way, the truth, and the life" (John 14:6), in whom men may find the fullness of religious life, in whom God has reconciled all things to Himself (cf. 2 Cor. 5:18-19).

The Church, therefore, exhorts her sons, that through dialogue and collaboration with the followers of other religions, carried out with prudence and love and in witness to the Christian faith and life, they recognize, preserve and promote the good things, spiritual and moral, as well as the sociocultural values found among these men.

3. The Church regards with esteem also the Moslems. They adore the one God, living and subsisting in Himself; merciful and all-powerful, the Creator of heaven and earth (cf. St. Gregory VII, letter XXI to Anzir [Nacir], King of Mauritania [Pl. 148, col. 450f.]), who has spoken to men; they take pains to submit wholeheartedly to even His inscrutable decrees, just as Abraham, with whom the faith of Islam takes pleasure in linking itself, submitted to God. Though they do not acknowledge Jesus as God, they revere Him as a prophet. They also honor Mary, His virgin Mother; at times they even call on her with devotion. In addition, they await the day of judgment when God will render their deserts to all those who have been raised up from the dead. Finally, they value the moral life and worship God especially through prayer, almsgiving and fasting.

Since in the course of centuries not a few quarrels and hostilities have arisen between Christians and Moslems, this sacred synod urges all to forget the past and to work sincerely for mutual understanding and to preserve as well as to promote together for the benefit of all mankind social justice and moral welfare, as well as peace and freedom.

4. As the sacred synod searches into the mystery of the Church, it remembers the bond that spiritually ties the people of the New Covenant to Abraham's stock.

Thus the Church of Christ acknowledges that, according to God's saving design, the beginnings of her faith and her election are found already among the Patriarchs, Moses and the prophets. She professes that all who believe in Christ—Abraham's sons according to faith (cf. Gal. 3:7.)—are included in the same Patriarch's call, and likewise that the salvation of the Church is mysteriously foreshadowed by the chosen people's exodus from the land of bondage. The Church, therefore, cannot forget that she received the revelation of the Old Testament through the people with whom God in His inexpressible mercy concluded the Ancient Covenant. Nor can she forget that she draws sustenance from the root of that well-cultivated olive tree onto which have been grafted the wild shoots, the Gentiles (cf. Rom. 11:17-24). Indeed, the Church believes that by His cross Christ, Our Peace, reconciled Jews and Gentiles, making both one in Himself (cf. Ep.h 2:14-16).

The Church keeps ever in mind the words of the Apostle about his kinsmen: "theirs is the sonship and the glory and the covenants and the law and the worship and the promises; theirs are the fathers and from them is the Christ according to the flesh" (Rom. 9:4-5), the Son of the Virgin Mary. She also recalls that the Apostles, the Church's mainstay and pillars, as well as most of the early disciples who proclaimed Christ's Gospel to the world, sprang from the Jewish people.

As Holy Scripture testifies, Jerusalem did not recognize the time of her visitation (cf. Luke 19:44), nor did the Jews in large number, accept the Gospel; indeed not a few opposed its spreading (cf. Rom. 11:28). Nevertheless, God holds the Jews most dear for the sake of their Fathers; He does not repent of the gifts He makes or of the calls He issues—such is the witness of the Apostle (cf. Rom. 11:28-29; cf. dogmatic Constitution, Lumen Gentium [Light of nations] AAS, 57 [1965] pag. 20). In company with the Prophets and the same Apostle, the Church awaits that day, known to God alone, on which all peoples will address the Lord in a single voice and "serve him shoulder to shoulder" (Soph. 3:9; cf. Isa. 66:23; Ps. 65:4; Rom. 11:11-32).

Since the spiritual patrimony common to Christians and Jews is thus so great, this sacred synod wants to foster and recommend that mutual understanding and respect which is the fruit, above all, of biblical and theological studies as well as of fraternal dialogues.

True, the Jewish authorities and those who followed their lead pressed for the death of Christ (cf. John 19:6.); still, what happened in His passion cannot be charged against all the Jews, without distinction, then alive, nor against the Jews of today. Although the Church is the new people of God, the Jews should not be presented as rejected or accursed by God, as if this followed from the Holy Scriptures. All should see to it, then, that in catechetical work or in the preaching of the word of God they do not teach anything that does not conform to the truth of the Gospel and the spirit of Christ.

Furthermore, in her rejection of every persecution against any man, the Church, mindful of the patrimony she shares with the Jews and moved not by political reasons but by the Gospel's spiritual love, decries hatred, persecutions, displays of anti-Semitism, directed against Jews at any time and by anyone.

Besides, as the Church has always held and holds now, Christ underwent His passion and death freely, because of the sins of men and out of infinite love, in order that all may reach salvation. It is, therefore, the burden of the Church's preaching to proclaim the cross of Christ as the sign of God's all-embracing love and as the fountain from which every grace flows . . .

SOURCE: *Declaration on the Relation of the Church to Nonchristian Religions, Vatican II, Nostra Aetate,* 28 October 1965, used by permission of the Vatican.

83

VLADIMIR LOSSKY

VLADIMIR LOSSKY (1903–1958), an Orthodox theologian, emphasized the place of mysticism in the practice of Christian faith. His *Mystical Theology of the Eastern Church* equated mysticism with doctrinal theology, both of which he argued were necessary for salvation. Devout Christian practice enables orthodox doctrine, and vice versa. In the selection below, Lossky addresses the ancient Eastern Orthodox idea of "theosis" (deification)—becoming like God in the spiritual journey toward God.

Theosis

Unlike Gnosticism, in which knowledge for its own sake constitutes the aim of the Gnostic, Christian theology is always in the last resort a means: a unity of knowledge subserving an end which transcends all knowledge. This ultimate end is union with God or deification, the [theosis] of the Greek Fathers. Thus, we are finally led to a conclusion which may seem paradoxical enough: that Christian theory should have an eminently practical significance; and that the more mystical it is, the more directly it aspires to the supreme end of union with God. All the development of the dogmatic battles which the Church has waged down the centuries appears to us, if we regard it from the purely spiritual standpoint, as dominated by the constant preoccupation which the Church has had to safeguard, at each moment of her history, for all Christians, the possibility of attaining to the fullness of the mystical union. So the Church struggled against the Gnostics in defense of this same idea of deification as the universal end: "God became man that men might become gods" . . . The main preoccupation, the issue at stake, in the questions which successively arise respecting the Holy Spirit, grace and the Church herself—this last the dogmatic question of our own time—is always the possibility, the manner, or the means of our union with God. All the history of Christian dogma unfolds itself about this mystical center, guarded by different weapons against its many and diverse assailants in the course of successive ages . . .

Adam did not fulfill his vocation. He was unable to attain to union with God, and the deification of the created order. That which he failed to realize when he used the fullness of his liberty became impossible to him from the moment at which he willingly became the slave of an external power. From the fall until the day of Pentecost, the divine energy, deifying and uncreated grace, was foreign to our human nature, acting on it only from outside and producing created effects in the soul. The prophets and righteous men of the Old Testament were the instruments of grace. Grace acted by them, but did not become their own, as their personal strength. Deification, union with God by grace, had become impossible. But the plan of God was not destroyed by the sin of man; the vocation of the first Adam was fulfilled by Christ, the second Adam. God became man in order that man might become god, to use the words of Irenaeus and Athanasius echoed by the Fathers and theologians of every age. However, this work, finished by the incarnate Word, is seen primarily by fallen humanity in its most immediate aspect, as the work of salvation, the redemption of a world captive to sin and death. Fascinated by the *felix culpa*, we often forget that in breaking the tyranny of sin, our Savior opens to us anew the way of deification, which is the final end of man. The work of Christ calls out to the work of the Holy Spirit (Luke 12:49) . . .

The deification or [theosis] of the creature will be realized in its fullness only in the age to come, after the resurrection of the dead. This deifying union has, nevertheless, to be fulfilled ever more and more even in this present life, through the transformation of our corruptible and depraved nature and by its adaptation to eternal life, If God has given us in the Church all the objective conditions, all the means that we need for the attainment of this end, we, on our side, must produce the necessary subjective conditions: for it is in this synergy, in this co-operation of man with God, that the union is fulfilled. This subjective aspect of our union with God constitutes the way of union which is the Christian life.

SOURCE: Vladimir Lossky, *The Mystical Theology of the Eastern Church* (London: James Clarke and Co., Ltd., 1973), 9–10, 133–34, 196. Reproduced by kind permission of James Clarke & Co., Ltd.

84

CLARENCE JORDAN

CLARENCE JORDAN (1912–1969) was a Baptist minister who founded an interracial commune, Koinonia Farm, near Americus, Georgia, in 1942. The commune was the subject of racial strife from segregationists, but its own house-building ministry served as inspiration for Millard Fuller's founding of Habitat for Humanity (1976). Jordan, a New Testament scholar, penned the *Cotton Patch Version* (1968–1969), a translation of several books of the New Testament. The biblical story was put in a Southern setting. The excerpt below is the story of the Good Samaritan (Luke 10:25-37) which, in Jordan's version, highlighted white/African American relations.

Cotton Patch Bible

One day a teacher of an adult Bible class got up and tested him with this question: "Doctor, what does one do to be saved?"

Jesus replied, "What does the Bible say? How do you interpret it?"

The teacher answered, "Love the Lord your God with all your heart and with all your soul and with all your physical strength and with all your mind; and love your neighbor as yourself."

"That is correct," answered Jesus. "Make a habit of this and you'll be saved."

But the Sunday school teacher, trying to save face, asked, "But . . . er . . . but . . . just who *is* my neighbor?"

Then Jesus laid into him and said, "A man was going from Atlanta to Albany and some gangsters held him up. When they had robbed him of his wallet and brand-new suit, they beat him up and drove off in his car, leaving him unconscious on the shoulder of the highway."

"Now it just so happened that a white preacher was going down that same highway. When he saw the fellow, he stepped on the gas and went scooting by."

"Shortly afterwards a white Gospel song leader came down the road, and when he saw what had happened, he too stepped on the gas."

"Then a black man traveling that way came upon the fellow, and what he saw moved him to tears. He stopped and bound up his wounds as best he could, drew some water from his water-jug to wipe away the blood and then laid him on the back seat. He drove on into Albany and took him to the hospital and said to the nurse, 'You all take good care of this white man I found on the highway. Here's the only two dollars I got, but you all keep account of what he owes, and if he can't pay it, I'll settle up with you when I make a pay-day,"

"Now if you had been the man held up by the gangsters, which of these three—the white preacher, the white song leader, or the black man—would you consider to have been your neighbor?"

The teacher of the adult Bible class said, "Why, of course, the nig—I mean, er . . . well, er . . . the one who treated me kindly."

Jesus said, "Well, then, *you* get going and start living like that!"

SOURCE: Clarence Jordan, *Clarence Jordan's Cotton Patch Gospel: Luke and Acts* (Macon, Ga.: Smyth & Helwys Publishing, 2004), 37–38. Used by permission.

85

GUSTAVO GUTIÉRREZ

GUSTAVO GUTIÉRREZ (b. 1928) is a Dominican priest from Peru regarded as the founder of liberation theology. His groundbreaking work was *A Theology of Liberation* (1971). The starting point of Gutiérrez' theology is the reality of life in Latin America, a life of poverty in an unjust sociopolitical structure. Thus, Gutiérrez' theology is rooted in practice (*praxis*) and viewed through the eyes of the poor. The selection below addresses the issue of praxis and liberation theology as social/political Christianity.

Liberation Theology

Theology must be critical reflection on humankind, on basic human principles. Only with this approach will theology be a serious discourse, aware of itself, in full possession of its conceptual elements . . . above all we intend this term to express the theory of definite practice. Theological reflection would then necessarily be a criticism of society and the Church insofar as they are called and addressed by the Word of God; it would be a critical theory, worked out in the light of the Word accepted in faith and inspired by a practical purpose—and therefore indissolubly linked to historical praxis.

By preaching the Gospel message, by its sacraments, and by the charity of its members, the Church proclaims and shelters the gift of the Kingdom of God in the heart of human history. The Christian community professes a "faith which works through charity." It is—at least ought to be—real charity, action, and commitment to the service of others. Theology is reflection, a critical attitude. Theology follows; it is the second step . . . Theology does not produce pastoral activity; rather it reflects upon it. Theology must be able to find in pastoral activity the presence of the Spirit inspiring the action of the Christian community.

But for some time now, we have been witnessing a great effort by the Church to rise out of this ghetto power and mentality and to shake off the ambiguous protection provided by the beneficiaries of the unjust order which prevails on the continent. Individual Christians, small communities, and the Church as a whole are becoming more politically aware and are acquiring a greater knowledge of the current Latin American reality, especially in its root causes. The Christian community is beginning, in fact, to read politically the signs of the times in Latin America. Moreover, we have witnessed the taking of positions which could even be characterized as daring, especially compared with previous behavior. We have seen a commitment to liberation which has provoked resistance and mistrust . . .

From this point of view the notion of salvation appears in a different light. Salvation is not something otherworldly, in regard to which the present is merely a test. Salvation—the communion of human beings with God and among themselves—is something which embraces all human reality, transforms it, and leads it to its fullness in Christ . . .Therefore, sin is not only an impediment to salvation in the afterlife. Insofar as it constitutes a break with God, sin is a historical reality, it is a breach of the communion of persons with each other, it is a turning in of individuals on themselves which manifests itself in a multifaceted withdrawal from others. And because sin is a personal and social intrahistorical reality, a part of the daily events of human life, it is also, and above all, an obstacle to life's reaching the fullness we call salvation.

SOURCE: Gustavo Gutiérrez, *A Theology of Liberation*, 15th anniversary ed. (Maryknoll, N.Y.: Orbis Books, 1988), 9, 58, 85. Used by permission.

$$\sim\!\!\stackrel{\circ}{\sim}\!\!\sim$$

86

ÓSCAR ROMERO

Ó SCAR ROMERO Y GALDÁMEZ (1917–1980) was an El Salvadoran arch-bishop in the Roman Catholic Church. While Romero opposed Libera-tion theology early in his ministry, he embraced much of its message after the assassination of his friend and fellow priest Rutilio Grande and Romero's experience of the political unrest in El Salvador, which was on the cusp of civil war. Romero became an outspoken opponent of governmental oppres-sion and an advocate for the poor. He was assassinated while giving mass. The Roman Catholic Church recognized him as a saint in 2015. The excerpts below come from Romero's speech upon receiving an honorary doctorate from the Catholic University of Louvain, Belgium. They highlight Rome-ro's understanding of the poor and oppressed as the primary object of the Church's mission.

A Church at the Service of the World

The church follows Jesus who lived, worked, battled and died in the midst of a city, in the polis. It is in this sense that I should like to talk about the political dimension of the Christian faith: in the precise sense of the reper-cussions of the faith on the world, and also of the repercussions that being in the world has on the faith.

We ought to be clear from the start that the Christian faith and the activ-ity of the church have always had socio-political repercussions. By commis-sion or omission, by associating themselves with one or another social group, Christians have always had an influence upon the socio-political makeup of the world in which they lived. The problem is about the "how" of this influ-ence in the socio-political world, whether or not it is in accordance with the faith. As a first idea, though still a very general one, I want to propose the intuition of Vatican II that lies at the root of every ecclesial movement of today. The essence of the church lies in its mission of service to the world, in its mission to save the world in its totality, and of saving it in history, here and now. The church exists to act in solidarity with the hopes and joys, the anxieties and sorrows, of men and women. Like Jesus, the church was sent "to bring good news to the poor, to heal the contrite of heart… to seek and to save what was lost" (Luke 4:18, 19:10).

The World of the Poor

To put it in one word—in a word that sums it all up and makes it con-crete—the world that the church ought to serve is, for us, the world of the poor. Our Salvadoran world is no abstraction. It is not another example of what is understood by "world" in developed countries such as yours. It is a world made up mostly of men and women who are poor and oppressed. And we say of that world of the poor that it is the key to understanding the Christian faith, to understanding the activity of the church and the political dimension of that faith and that ecclesial activity. It is the poor who tell us what the world is, and what the church's service to the world should be. It is the poor who tell us what the *polis* is, what the city is and what it means for the church really to live in that world. Allow me, then, briefly to explain from the perspective of the poor among my people, whom I represent, the situation and the activity of our church in the world in which we live, and then to reflect theologically upon the importance that this real world, this culture, this socio-political world, has for the church. In its pastoral work, our archdiocese in recent years has been moving in a direction that can only be described and only be understood as a turning toward the world of the poor, to their real, concrete world.

Incarnation in the World of the Poor

Just as elsewhere in Latin America, the words of Exodus have, after many years, perhaps centuries, finally resounded in our ears: "The cry of the sons of Israel has come to me, and I have witnessed the way in which the Egyptians oppress them" (Exod. 3:9). These words have given us new eyes to see what has always been the case among us, but which has so often been hidden, even from the view of the church itself. We have learned to see what is the first, basic fact about our world and, as pastors, we have made a judgment about it at Medellin and at Puebla. "That misery, as a collective fact, expresses itself as an injustice which cries to the heavens." At Puebla we declared, "So we brand the situation of inhuman poverty in which millions of Latin Americans live as the most devastating and humiliating kind of scourge. And this situation finds expression in such things as a high rate of infant mortality, lack of adequate housing, health problems, starvation wages, unemployment and underemployment, malnutrition, job uncertainty, compulsory mass migrations, etc." Experiencing these realities, and letting ourselves be affected by them, far from separating us from our faith has sent us back to the world of the poor as to our true home. It has moved us, as a first, basic step, to take the world of the poor upon ourselves.

. . .

Proclaiming the Good News to the Poor

Our encounter with the poor has regained for us the central truth of the gospel, through which the word of God urges us to conversion. The church has to proclaim the good news to the poor. Those who, in this-worldly terms, have heard bad news, and who have lived out even worse realities, are now listening through the church to the word of Jesus: "The kingdom of God is at hand; blessed are you who are poor, for the kingdom of God is yours." And hence they also have good news to proclaim to the rich: that they, too, become poor in order to share the benefits of the kingdom with the poor. Anyone who knows Latin America will be quite clear that there is no ingenuousness in these words, still less the workings of a soporific drug. What is to be found in these words is a coming together of the aspiration on our continent for liberation, and God's offer of love to the poor. This is the hope that the church offers, and it coincides with the hope, at times dormant and at other times frustrated or manipulated, of the poor of Latin America.

It is something new among our people that today the poor see in the church a source of hope and a support for their noble struggle for liberation. The hope that our church encourages is neither naive nor passive. It is rather a summons from the word of God for the great majority of the people, the poor, that they assume their proper responsibility, that they undertake their own conscientization, that, in a country where it is legally or practically prohibited (at some periods more so than at others) they set about organizing themselves. And it is support, sometimes critical support, for their just causes and demands. The hope that we preach to the poor is intended to give them back their dignity, to encourage them to take charge of their own future. In a word, the church has not only turned toward the poor, it has made of the poor the special beneficiaries of its mission because, as Puebla says, "God takes on their defense and loves them."

Commitment to the Defense of the Poor

The church has not only incarnated itself in the world of the poor, giving them hope; it has also firmly committed itself to their defense. The majority of the poor in our country are oppressed and repressed daily by economic and political structures. The terrible words spoken by the prophets of Israel continue to be verified among us. Among us there are those who sell others for money, who sell a poor person for a pair of sandals; those who, in their mansions, pile up violence and plunder; those who crush the poor; those who make the kingdom of violence come closer as they lie upon their beds of ivory; those who join house to house, and field to field, until they occupy the whole land, and are the only ones there.

Amos and Isaiah are not just voices from distant centuries; their writings are not merely texts that we reverently read in the liturgy. They are everyday realities. Day by day we live out the cruelty and ferocity they excoriate. We live them out when there come to us the mothers and the wives of those who have been arrested or who have disappeared, when mutilated bodies turn up in secret cemeteries, when those who fight for justice and peace are assassinated. . . .

In this situation of conflict and antagonism, in which just a few persons control economic and political power, the church has placed itself at the side of the poor and has undertaken their defense. The church cannot do otherwise, for it remembers that Jesus had pity on the multitude. But by defending the poor it has entered into serious conflict with the powerful who belong to the monied oligarchies and with the political and military authorities of the state.

Source: Archbishop Óscar Romero, "The Political Dimension of the Faith from the Perspective of the Option for the Poor: Address by Archbishop Romero on the Occasion of the Conferral of a Doctorate, Honoris Causa, by the University of Louvain, Belgium, February 2, 1980," in *Voice of the Voiceless: The Four Pastoral Letters and Other Statements*, trans. Michael J. Walsh (Maryknoll, N.Y.: Orbis, 1985), 178–79, 180–81.

87

JAMES H. CONE

JAMES H. CONE (b. 1938), theologian at Union Theological Seminary, New York, helped pioneer the field of black liberation theology—theology viewed through the experiences and perspectives of African Americans as an oppressed people—with his 1969 book *Black Theology and Black Power.* The selection below combines themes of oppression, the role of race in theologizing, and the intentional identification of Jesus with the oppressed: in other words, Jesus must be black.

Jesus Is Black

Before moving to the substance of the Black Christ issue, it is necessary to unmask the subjective interests of white theologians themselves. When the past and contemporary history of white theology is evaluated, it is not difficult to see that much of the present negative reaction of white theologians to the Black Christ is due almost exclusively to their *whiteness,* a cultural fact that determines their theological inquiry, thereby making it almost impossible for them to relate positively to anything black. White theologians' attitude toward black people in particular and the oppressed generally is hardly different from that of oppressors in any society. It is particularly similar to the religious leaders' attitude toward Jesus in first-century Palestine when he freely associated with the poor and outcasts and declared that the Kingdom of God is for those called "sinners" and not for priests and theologians or any of the self-designated righteous people. The difficulty of white theologians in recognizing their racial interest in this issue can be understood only in the light of the social context of theological discourse. They cannot see the christological validity of Christ's blackness because their axiological grid blinds them to the truth of the biblical story. For example, the same white theologians who laughingly dismiss Albert Cleage's "Black Messiah" say almost nothing about the European (white) images of Christ plastered all over American homes and churches. I perhaps would respect the integrity of their objections to the Black Christ on scholarly grounds, if they applied the same vigorous logic to Christ's whiteness, especially in contexts where his blackness is not advocated.

For me, the substance of the Black Christ issue can be dealt with only on *theological* grounds, as defined by Christology's source (Scripture, tradition, and social existence) and content (Jesus' past, present, and future). I begin by asserting once more that *Jesus was a Jew*. It is on the basis of the soteriological meaning of the particularity of his Jewishness that theology must affirm the christological significance of Jesus' present blackness. He *is* black because he *was* a Jew. The affirmation of the Black Christ can be understood when the significance of his past Jewishness is related dialectically to the significance of his present blackness. On the one hand, the Jewishness of Jesus located him in the context of the Exodus, thereby connecting his appearance in Palestine with God's liberation of oppressed Israelites from Egypt. Unless Jesus were truly from Jewish ancestry, it would make little theological sense to say that he is the fulfillment of God's covenant with Israel. But on the other hand, the blackness of Jesus brings out the soteriological meaning of his Jewishness for our contemporary situation when Jesus' person is understood in the context of the cross and resurrection . . .

The cross of Jesus is God invading the human situation as the Elected One who takes Israel's place as the Suffering Servant and thus reveals the divine willingness to suffer in order that humanity might be fully liberated. The resurrection means that God's identity with the poor in Jesus is not limited to the particularity of his Jewishness but is applicable to all who fight on behalf of the liberation of humanity in this world. And the Risen Lord's identification with the suffering poor today is just as real as was his presence with the outcasts in first-century Palestine. His presence with the poor today is not docetic; but like yesterday, today also he takes the pain of the poor upon himself and bears it for them. It is in the light of the cross and the resurrection of Jesus in relation to his Jewishness that Black Theology asserts that "Jesus is black" . . .

Christ's blackness is both literal and symbolic. His blackness is literal in the sense that he truly becomes One with the oppressed blacks, taking their suffering as his suffering and revealing that he is found in the history of our struggle, the story of our pain, and the rhythm of our bodies . . . The least in America are literally and symbolically present in black people. To say that Christ is black means that black people are God's poor people whom Christ has come to liberate. And thus no gospel of Jesus Christ is possible in America without coming to terms with the history and culture of that people who struggled to bear witness to his name in extreme circumstances. To say that Christ is black means that God, in his infinite wisdom and mercy, not only takes color seriously, he also takes it upon himself and discloses his will to make us whole—new creatures born in the spirit of divine blackness and redeemed through the blood of the Black Christ. Christ is black, therefore, not because of some cultural or psychological need of black people, but because and only because Christ *really* enters into our world where the poor, the despised, and the black are, disclosing that he is with them, enduring their humiliation and pain and transforming oppressed slaves into liberated servants. Indeed, if Christ is not truly black, then the historical Jesus lied. God did not anoint him "to preach good news to the poor" and neither did God send him "to proclaim release to the captives and recovering the sight to the blind, to set at liberty those who are oppressed" (Luke 4:18ff, RSV). If Christ is not black, the gospel is not good news to the oppressed, and Marx's observation is right: "Religion is the sign of the oppressed creature, and the heart of a heartless world . . . the spirit of a spiritless situation. It is the opium of the people."

SOURCE: James H. Cone, *God of the Oppressed*, rev. ed. (Maryknoll, N.Y.: Orbis Books, 1997), 123–26. Used by permission.

88

ROSEMARY RADFORD RUETHER

ROSEMARY RADFORD RUETHER (b. 1936) is a pioneer and leading theologian in feminist liberation theology—viewing theology through the experiences and perspectives of women as an oppressed people. According to feminist theologians, patriarchy (male-dominated social organization) is oppressive. Ruether's groundbreaking book was *Sexism and God-Talk: Towards a Feminist Theology* (1983). She is Roman Catholic and has criticized the church for its views on sexuality and reproduction.

Feminist Theology

The critical principle of feminist theology is the promotion of the full humanity of women. Whatever denies, diminishes, or distorts the full humanity of women is, therefore, appraised as not redemptive. Theologically speaking whatever diminishes or denies the full humanity of women must be presumed not to reflect the divine or an authentic relation to the divine, or to reflect the authentic nature of things, or to be the message or work of an authentic redeemer or a community of redemption.

This negative principle also implies the positive principle: what does promote the full humanity of women is of the Holy, it does reflect true relation to the divine, it is the true nature of things, the authentic message of redemption and the mission of redemptive community. But the meaning of this positive principle—namely, the full humanity of women—is not fully known. It has not existed in history. What we have known is the negative principle of the denigration and marginalization of women's humanity. Still, the humanity of women, although diminished, has not been destroyed. It has constantly affirmed itself, often in only limited and subversive ways, and it has been touchstone against which we test and criticize all that diminishes us. In the process we experience our larger potential that allows us to begin to imagine a world without sexism.

This principle is hardly new. In fact, the correlation of original, authentic human nature (*imago dei*/Christ) and diminished, fallen humanity provided the basic structure of classical Christian theology. The uniqueness of feminist theology is not the critical principle, full humanity, but the fact that women claim this principle for themselves. Women name themselves as subjects of authentic and full humanity . . .

The uses of this principle in male theology is perceived to have been corrupted by sexism. The naming of males as norms of authentic humanity has caused women to be scapegoated for sin and marginalized in both original and redeemed humanity. This distorts and contradicts the theological paradigm of *imago dei*/Christ. Defined as male humanity against or above women, as ruling-class humanity above servant classes, the *imago dei*/Christ paradigm becomes an instrument of sin rather than a disclosure of the divine . . .

This also implies that women cannot simply reverse the sin of sexism. Women cannot simply scapegoat males for historical evil in a way that makes themselves only innocent victims. Women cannot affirm themselves as *imago dei* and subjects of full human potential in a way that diminishes male humanity. Women, as the denigrated half of the human species, must reach for a continually expanding definition of inclusive humanity—inclusive of both genders, inclusive of all groups and races . . . In rejecting androcentrism (males as norms of humanity), women must also criticize all other forms of chauvinism: making white Westerners the norm of humanity, making Christians the norm of humanity, making privileged classes the norm of humanity. Women must also criticize humanocentrism, that is making humans the norm and crown of creation in a way that diminishes the other beings in the community of creation . . .

All the ways a woman has been taught to be "pleasing" and "acceptable" to men must be recognized as tools of her own seduction and false consciousness. Every woman has bought into some of these roles. We have been the pretty girl-child who is played with and praised for her cuteness; or the sexy lady who manipulates her physical attractiveness; or the good wife who wins the prize by her diligent housekeeping and attentive service to male needs—all these prevent a woman from asking herself who she is as a human person . . .

For Christian women, particularly in more conservative traditions, one of the most difficult barriers to feminist consciousness is the identification of sin with anger and pride, and virtue with humility and self-abnegation. Although this doctrine of sin and virtue supposedly is for "all Christians," it becomes, for women, an ideology that reinforces female subjugation and lack of self-esteem. Women become "Christ-like" by having no self of their own. They become the "suffering servants" by accepting male abuse and exploitation. Women are made to feel profoundly guilty and diffident about even the smallest sense of self-affirmation . . .

In this context, conversion from sexism is truly experienced as a breakthrough, as an incursion of power and grace beyond the capacities of the present roles, an incursion of power that puts one in touch with oneself as a self. *Metanoia* for women involves a turning around in which they literally discover themselves as persons, as centers of being upon which they can stand and build their own identity. This involves a willingness to get in touch with their own anger. Anger is liberating grace precisely as the power to break the chains of sexist socialization, to disaffiliate with sexist ideologies . . .

This creates a parting of the ways between feminists—those who are ready and willing to experience this deeper alienation and anger and those who draw back from it. Those who enter into deeper alienation become the "bad feminists," the separatists, lesbians, radicals. Those who take a more moderated stand are tempted to get "brownie points" for not being like those "bad feminists." Yet the depths of anger and alienation to which some women point are not inappropriate. It really has been "that bad." Unless one is willing to take the journey into that deeper anger, even to risk going a bit mad, one really will never understand the depths of the evil of sexism.

SOURCE: Rosemary Radford Ruether, *Sexism and God-Talk: Toward a Feminist Theology* (Boston: Beacon Press, 1993), 18–20, 185–87. Used by permission.

89

ADA MARÍA ISASI-DÍAZ

Ada María Isasi-Díaz (b. 1943) is a Cuban-born professor of ethics and feminist theologian at Drew University (New Jersey). Raised and trained in the Roman Catholic tradition, she is a pioneer in the arena of *mujerista* theology—feminist liberation theology viewed through the experiences and perspectives of Latinas. The selection that follows speaks to the disparity between the dominant culture and that of Hispanic women as they try to validate their world, their values, and their reality.

Mujerista Theology

In society, the dominant understandings and practices that are considered as having important religious significance, the ones that carry weight and impact societal norms, arise from the experience of the dominant culture, race, class and gender. Whether or not those of the dominant culture, class, race, and gender actually invest themselves in these understandings and practices, they abide by them, consciously or unconsciously, because they are elements of the structures that keep them in power. By using our lived-experience as the source of theology, Hispanic women start from a place outside those structures, outside the traditional theology which is controlled by the dominant group. This gives us an opportunity to be self-defining, to give fresh answers and, what is "most important, to ask new questions" . . .

A third reason for insisting on the lived-experience of Hispanic women as a source for *mujerista* theology has to do with our struggle for liberation of our sanity. As people who live submerged within a culture which is not ours, we often question our ability to comprehend "reality." In a very real way, as Hispanic women, we have to "go out of our minds" in order to survive physically. You can often hear Hispanic women, especially older women, respond to "that's the way things are done here," with the phrase, *En que cabeza cabe eso?*—In what kind of head does that fit? The reality that impacts our daily lives is often incomprehensible to us. What we say does not count; our cultural customs—dance, food, dress—are divorced from us and are commercialized; our values hardly count in society; our language is considered a threat, and millions have voted to have Spanish declared "not an official language"; our social reality is ignored. As a people we continue to slip into poverty, and suffer from the social ills prevalent in the culture of poverty.

By using our lived-experience as the source of *mujerista* theology we are trying to validate our world, our reality, our values. We are trying to reverse the schizophrenia that attacks our lives by insisting that who we are and what we do is revelatory of the divine. We ground our theology on the lived-experience of Hispanic women because it constitutes our common and shared reality. The "common sense" of Hispanic women is not wrong. We can trust it to inform and guide our day-to-day life. *Mujerista* theology wants to affirm the world-view of Hispanic women, shaped as it is by our lived-experience. For it is precisely in our world-view, in our paradigm of social reality, that we find "the categories and concepts through and by which we construct and understand the world." And understanding and constructing our world is a liberative praxis.

Source: Ada María Isasi-Díaz, "*Mujerista* Theology's Method," in Arturo J. Bañuelas, ed., "*Mestizo*" *Christianity: Theology from the Latino Perspective* (Maryknoll, N.Y.: Orbis Books, 1995), 184–86. Used by permission.

90

BILLY GRAHAM

WILLIAM FRANKLIN GRAHAM JR. (b. 1918), a native of Charlotte, North Carolina, began his itinerant preaching ministry in the late 1940s. He was the best-known evangelist of the twentieth century. His revival crusades and other preaching ministries have reached more than two billion people around the world. Graham embodied conservative evangelical preaching—people must be saved (born again) to get to heaven and each believer must have a personal relationship with Jesus Christ. He was also known as the unofficial chaplain for numerous American presidents. In the selections below are found modern revivalism's focus on hell and heaven and how to receive Christ through a series of steps (sometimes called "four spiritual laws") that culminates in the "sinner's prayer" for salvation.

Hell

Inquiring young people have asked me in a score of inquiry rooms, "How can a God of love send anyone to hell?" This is an honest question that arises often in the minds of thinking youth. My answer to this question is that God will never send anyone to hell. If you go to hell, it will be because of your own deliberate choice. Hell was never prepared for man but for the devil and his angels (Matt. 25:41). If you choose to follow Satan you will follow him to his ultimate destiny, but you will do it in spite of all that God has done to stop you. He sent His prophets. He gave you His Word. He has given you a faithful pastor and the prayers of a godly mother. He has sent His only Son. The Holy Spirit is constantly warning you. What more can a God of love do? You are a free moral agent! God did not create you as a machine to be compelled to love Him! You can choose either to obey or to disobey Him. You have the power of free choice. Never forget that God is a God of love. Only those who reject or forget Christ will be in hell. No man will go to hell because he lived an immoral life. Men go to hell because they reject God's plan of salvation in Christ . . .

The only way to salvation is acceptance of Christ as Savior. The only way to hell is rejection of Christ. In no other is there salvation, for "neither is there any other Name under heaven that is given among men whereby we must be saved" (Acts 4:12).

Just as heaven is prepared for those that accept Him, so hell is prepared for those that reject Him.

Get the picture! Two worlds are swinging in space throughout eternity. One is the world of the saved—paradise; salvation; glory; splendor; brilliant and dazzling beyond human comprehension or description; a place of joy and laughter, with gates of pearl, walls of jasper, palaces of ivory, streets of transparent gold, a river of life. The dwellers—who? All those who have been washing in the blood of the Lamb, those who have accepted Christ as Savior, whether they be Baptists, Methodists, Presbyterians or no church members at all, the redeemed of all ages who by faith accepted Christ!

The other world is the world of the damned. In that world through time without end, eternity, there will be weeping, wailing and gnashing of teeth. There is no love there because men by rejecting Christ have slain their own power to ever again feel His presence. Hell will be a place of tormenting memories.

My friend, you must make a choice. Life is but a vapor . . . it will soon be over. What you do with Christ here and now decides where you shall spend eternity.

How to Receive Christ

I do not believe that there is a tidy little formula, or a recipe which has the Good Housekeeping seal of approval. However . . . here are some guidelines

from the Bible which will help you to accept Christ as your Lord and Savior
. . .

First, you must recognize what God did: that He loved you so much He gave His son to die on the cross. Substitute your own name for "the world" and "whoever" in this familiar verse: "For God so loved the world, that He gave His only begotten Son, that whoever believes in Him should not perish, but have eternal life" (John 3:16) . . .

Second, you must repent for your sins. Jesus said, "Unless you repent, you will . . . perish" (Luke 13:3) . . . It's not enough to be sorry; repentance is that turnabout from sin that is emphasized.

Third, you must receive Jesus Christ as Savior and Lord. "But as many as received Him, to them He gave the right to become children of God, even to those that believe in His name" (John 1:12). This means that you cease trying to save yourself and accept Christ as your only Lord and your only Savior. Trust Him completely, without reservation.

Fourth, you must confess Christ publicly. This confession is a sign that you have been converted. Jesus said, "Every one therefore who shall confess Me before men, I will also confess him before My Father who is in heaven" (Matt. 10:32). It is extremely important that when you receive Christ you tell someone else about it just as soon as possible. This gives you strength and courage to witness.

Make it happen *now*. "Now is the accepted time . . .now is the day of salvation" (1 Cor. 6:2). If you are willing to repent for your sins and to receive Jesus Christ as your Lord and Savior, you can do it now. At this moment you can either bow your head or get on your knees and say this little prayer which I have used with thousands of persons on every continent:

O God, I acknowledge that I have sinned against You. I am sorry for my sins. I am willing to turn from my sins. I openly receive and acknowledge Jesus Christ as my Savior. I confess Him as Lord. From this moment on I want to live for Him and serve Him. In Jesus' name. Amen.

. . . If you are willing to make this decision and have received Jesus Christ as your own Lord and Savior, then you have become a child of God in whom Jesus Christ dwells. You do not need to measure the certainty of your salvation by your feelings. Believe God. He keeps His word. You are born again. You are alive!

Source: Selection on "Hell" from Billy Graham, *Calling Youth to Christ*, 2nd ed. (Grand Rapids: Zondervan, 1947), 129–30. Used by permission. "How to Receive Christ" is reprinted by permission from Billy Graham, *How to Be Born Again* (Nashville: Thomas Nelson, Inc., 1977). All rights reserved. See pp. 167–69.

91

JOHN HOWARD YODER

JOHN HOWARD YODER (1927–1997) was a Mennonite theologian and biblical scholar known for his Christian pacifism. He believed the mutually supportive relationship between the church and state, which he called Constantinianism, was a dangerous temptation for the church to use violence, coercion, and threat. He argued for the church to imitate Christ's radical pacifism as an alternative to society steeped in violence. The selection below speaks to the way of Christ and authentic pacifism.

The Work of Christ and the Powers

If our lostness consists in our subjection to the rebellious powers of a fallen world, what then is the meaning of the work of Christ? Subordination to these Powers is what makes us human, for if they did not exist there would be no history nor society nor humanity. If then God is going to save his creatures *in their humanity,* the Powers cannot simply be destroyed or set aside or ignored. Their sovereignty must be broken. This is what Jesus did, concretely and historically, by living a genuinely free and human existence. This life brought him, as any genuinely human existence will bring anyone, to the cross. In his death the Powers—in this case the most worthy, weighty representatives of Jewish religion and Roman politics—acted in collusion. Like everyone, he too was subject (but in his case quite willingly) to these powers. He accepted his own status of submission. But morally he broke their rules by refusing to support them in their self-glorification; and that is why they killed him. Preaching and incorporating a greater righteousness than that of the Pharisees, and a vision of an order of social human relations more universal than the Pax Romana, he permitted the Jews to profane a holy day (refuting thereby their own moral pretensions) and permitted the Romans to deny their vaunted respect for law as they proceeded illegally against him. This they did in order to avoid the threat to their dominion represented by the very fact that he existed in their midst so morally independent of their pretensions. He did not fear even death. Therefore his cross is a victory, the confirmation that he was free from the rebellious pretensions of the creaturely condition. Differing from Adam, Lucifer, and all the Powers, Jesus did "not consider being equal with God as a thing to be seized" (Phil. 2:6). His very obedience unto death is in itself not only the sign but also the firstfruits of an authentic restored humanity. Here we have for the first time to do with someone who is not the slave of any power, of any law or custom, community or institution, value or theory. Not even to save his own life will he let himself be made a slave of these Powers. This authentic humanity included his free acceptance of death at their hands . . .

This Gospel concept of the cross of the Christian does not mean that suffering is thought of as in itself redemptive or that martyrdom is a value to be sought after. Nor does it refer uniquely to being persecuted for "religious" reasons by an outspokenly pagan government. What Jesus refers to in his call to cross-bearing is rather the seeming defeat of that strategy of obedience which is no strategy, the inevitable suffering of those whose only goal is to be faithful to that love which puts one at the mercy of one's neighbor, which abandons claims to justice for oneself and for one's own in an overriding concern for the reconciling of the adversary and the estranged. I Peter 2 thus draws direct social consequences from the fact that Christ "when he suffered did not threaten but trusted him who judges justly."

This is significantly different from that kind of "pacifism" which would say that it is wrong to kill but that with proper nonviolent techniques you can obtain without killing everything you really want or have a right to ask for. In this context it seems that sometimes the rejection of violence is offered only because it is a cheaper or less dangerous or more shrewd way to impose one's will upon someone else, a kind of coercion which is harder to resist. Certainly any renunciation of violence is preferable to its acceptance; but what Jesus renounced is not first of all violence, but rather the compulsiveness of purpose that leads the strong to violate the dignity of others. The point is not that one can attain all of one's legitimate ends without using violent means. It is rather that our readiness to renounce our legitimate ends whenever they cannot be attained by legitimate means itself constitutes our participation in the triumphant suffering of the Lamb . . .

Accepting Powerlessness

We thus do not adequately understand what the church was praising in the work of Christ, and what Paul was asking his readers to be guided by, if we think of the cross as a peculiarly efficacious technique (probably effective only in certain circumstances) for getting one's way. The key to the ultimate relevance and to the triumph of the good is not any calculation at all, paradoxical or otherwise, of efficacy, but rather simple obedience. Obedience means not keeping verbally enshrined rules but reflecting the character of the love of God. The cross is not a recipe for resurrection. Suffering is not a tool to make people come around, nor a good in itself. But the kind of faithfulness that is willing to accept evident defeat rather than complicity with evil is, by virtue of its conformity with what happens to God when he works among us, aligned with the ultimate triumph of the Lamb.

SOURCE: John Howard Yoder, *The Politics of Jesus* (Grand Rapids: Wm. B. Eerdmans, 1994), 144–45. Used by permission.

92

LARRY NORMAN

Larry Norman (1947–2008) was one of the most influential pioneers in the field of Christian rock music and was considered by many to be the face of the "Jesus Movement" or "Jesus Revolution" that captivated many young people during the late sixties and early seventies. After leaving the secular rock group People! in 1968, Norman released his groundbreaking album of Christian music entitled *Upon This Rock* (1969). One of Norman's most popular and enduring songs during his career was "I Wish We'd All Been Ready" (selection below). The song was featured in the 1972 Christian themed movie about the end-times, "A Thief in the Night." The lyrics reflect the popularity of the dispensational emphasis in evangelical Christianity on an end-time rapture of the church before a time of tribulation that precedes the final triumph of Christ's victory over the devil. Christian contemporary music, indebted to pioneers like Norman, has extended its popularity beyond charismatic religion to more traditional Christian groups.

I Wish We'd All Been Ready

Life was filled with guns and war,
And everyone got trampled on the floor,
I wish we'd all been ready
Children died, the days grew cold,
A piece of bread could buy a bag of gold,
I wish we'd all been ready,

There's no time to change your mind,
The Son has come and you've been left behind.

A man and wife asleep in bed,
She hears a noise and turns her head, he's gone,
I wish we'd all be ready,
Two men walking up a hill,
One disappears and one's left standing still,
I wish we'd all been ready,
There's no time to change your mind,
The Son has come and you've been left behind.

Life was filled with guns and war,
And everyone got trampled on the floor,
I wish we'd all been ready,
Children died, the days grew cold,
A piece of bread could buy a bag of gold,
I wish we'd all been ready,
There's no time to change your mind,
How could you have been so blind,
The Father spoke, the demons dined,
The Son has come and you've been left behind.

SOURCE: Used by permission of www.larrynorman.com.

93

EMERGENT LEADERS

"RESPONSE TO RECENT CRITICISM" is a joint statement from a group of church leaders who were associated with an interdenominational movement known by various names including the Emerging Church, the Emergent Church Movement, the Emerging Conversation, etc. It intentionally had no formal statement of beliefs but, broadly speaking, the Emergent Church was a popular movement comprised mostly of Anglo-Protestants who associated themselves with a group of progressive church leaders and their attempt to reframe the Christian faith for a postmodern world, especially by focusing on dialogue, experience, community, and mission. Propelled by the internet's popularity, it came to prominence in 2000 but faded in the early 2010s. The Response was published online in 2005 and highlights the emergent church's emphases on decentralization, community, and conversation in addition to revealing their critics' fears of relativism, heterodoxy, and willingness to question traditional doctrine.

An Emergent Apologetic

We continue to be amazed by the enthusiastic interest in the work of emergent, a conversation and friendship of which we are a small part. This conversation is bringing together a wide range of committed Christians and those exploring the Christian faith in wonderful ways, and many of us sense that God is at work among us. As would be expected, there have also been criticisms.

A number of people have asked us to respond to these criticisms. These ten brief responses will, we hope, serve to clarify our position and suggest ways for the conversation to continue constructively for participants and critics alike. It is our hope and prayer that even our disagreements can bring us together in respectful dialogue as Christians, resulting in growth for all concerned.

First, we wish to say thanks to our critics for their honest feedback on our books, articles, speeches, blogs, events, and churches. We readily acknowledge that like all human endeavors, our work, even at its best, is still flawed and partial, and at its worst, deserves critique. We are grateful to those who help us see things we may not have seen without the benefit of their perspective. We welcome their input.

Second, we have much to learn from every criticism—whether it is fair or unfair, kindly or unkindly articulated. We pray for the humility to receive all critique with thoughtful consideration. Where we think we have been unfairly treated, we hope not to react defensively or to respond in kind, and where we have been helpfully corrected, we will move forward with gratitude to our critics for their instruction and correction. We especially thank those who seek to help us through cordial, respectful, face-to-face, brotherly/sisterly dialogue. As we have always said, we hope to stimulate constructive conversation, which involves point and counterpoint, honest speaking and open-minded listening. As a sign of good faith in this regard, we have invited and included the voices of our critics in some of our books, and as far as we know, have always treated these conversation partners with respect. We have also attempted to make personal contact with our critics for Christian dialogue. Even though most of these invitations have not been accepted, we hope that the friendly gesture is appreciated.

Third, we regretfully acknowledge that in our thought, writing, and speech, we have at times been less charitable or wise than we wish we would have been. Whenever possible we will seek to correct past errors in future editions of our books; when that is impossible, we will make other forms of public correction.

Fourth, we respect the desire and responsibility of our critics to warn those under their care about ideas that they consider wrong or dangerous, and to keep clear boundaries to declare who is "in" and "out" of their circles. These boundary-keepers have an important role which we understand and respect. If one of your trusted spiritual leaders has criticized our work, we encourage you, in respect for their leadership, not to buy or read our work, but rather to ignore it and consider it unworthy of further consideration. We would only ask, if you accept our critics' evaluation of our work, that in fairness you abstain from adding your critique to theirs unless you have actually read our books, heard us speak, and engaged with us in dialogue for yourself. Second-hand critique can easily become a kind of gossip that drifts from the truth and causes needless division.

Fifth, because most of us write as local church practitioners rather than professional scholars, and because the professional scholars who criticize our work may find it hard to be convinced by people outside their guild, we feel it wisest at this juncture to ask those in the academy to respond to their peers about our work. We hope to generate fruitful conversations at several levels, including both the academic and ecclesial realms. If few in the academy come to our defense in the coming years, then we will have more reason to believe we are mistaken in our thinking and that our critics are correct in their unchallenged analyses.

Sixth, we would like to clarify, contrary to statements and inferences made by some, that yes, we truly believe there is such a thing as truth and truth matters—if we did not believe this, we would have no good reason to write or speak; no, we are not moral or epistemological relativists any more than anyone or any community is who takes hermeneutical positions—we believe that radical relativism is absurd and dangerous, as is arrogant absolutism; yes, we affirm the historic Trinitarian Christian faith and the ancient creeds, and seek to learn from all of church history—and we honor the church's great teachers and leaders from East and West, North and South; yes, we believe that Jesus is the crucified and risen Savior of the cosmos and no one comes to the Father except through Jesus; no, we do not pit reason against experience but seek to use all our God-given faculties to love and serve God and our neighbors; no, we do not endorse false dichotomies—and we regret any false dichotomies unintentionally made by or about us (even in this paragraph!); and yes, we affirm that we love, have confidence in, seek to obey, and strive accurately to teach the sacred Scriptures, because our greatest desire is to be followers and servants of the Word of God, Jesus Christ. We regret that we have either been unclear or misinterpreted in these and other areas.

But we also acknowledge that we each find great joy and promise in dialogue and conversation, even about the items noted in the previous paragraph. Throughout the history of the church, followers of Jesus have come to know what they believe and how they believe it by being open to the honest critique and varied perspectives of others. We are radically open to the possibility that our hermeneutic stance will be greatly enriched in conversation with others. In other words, we value dialogue very highly, and we are convinced that open and generous dialogue—rather than chilling criticism and censorship—offers the greatest hope for the future of the church in the world.

We regret that some of our critics have made hasty generalizations and drawn erroneous conclusions based on limited and selective data. We would welcome future critics to converse with us directly and to visit our churches as part of their research. Of course, they would find weaknesses among us, as they would among any group of Christians, including their own. But we believe that they would also find much to celebrate and find many of their suspicions relieved when they see our high regard for the Scriptures, for truth, for worship, for evangelism, for spiritual formation, and for our fellow Christians—including our critics themselves.

Seventh, we have repeatedly affirmed, contrary to what some have said, that there is no single theologian or spokesperson for the emergent conversation. We each speak for ourselves and are not official representatives of anyone else, nor do we necessarily endorse everything said or written by one another. We have repeatedly defined emergent as a conversation and friendship, and neither implies unanimity—nor even necessarily consensus—of opinion. We ask our critics to remember that we cannot be held responsible for everything said and done by people using the terms "emergent" or "emerging church," any more than our critics would like to be held responsible for everything said or done by those claiming to be "evangelical" or "born again." Nobody who is a friend or acquaintance of ours, or who agrees with one of us in some points, should be assumed to agree with any of us on all points. Nobody should be held "guilty by association" for reading or conversing with us. Also, contrary to some uninformed reports, this conversation is increasingly global and cross-cultural, and because North Americans are only a small part of it, we urge people to avoid underestimating the importance of Latin American, African, Asian, European, and First Nations voices among us.

Eighth, we are aware that there is some debate about whether we should be considered evangelical. This is a cherished part of our heritage, but we understand that some people define this term more narrowly than we and in such a way that it applies to them but not to us. We will not quarrel over this term, and we will continue to love and respect evangelical Christians whether or not we are accepted by them as evangelicals ourselves. However others include or exclude us, we will continue to affirm an evangelical spirit and faith by cultivating a wholehearted devotion to Christ and his gospel, by seeking to join in the mission of God in our time, by calling people to follow God in the way of Jesus, and by doing so in an irenic spirit of love for all our brothers and sisters. (We hope that those who would like to disassociate us from the term evangelical will be aware of the tendency of some in their ranks toward narrowing and politicizing the term so that it only applies to strict Calvinists, conservative Republicans, people with specific views on U.S. domestic, foreign, military, or economic policy, single-issue voters, or some other subgroup. We pose no threat to these sincere people, nor do we wish to attack or discredit anyone, even though we do not wish to constrict our circle of fellowship to the parameters they propose.)

Ninth, we felt we should offer this encouragement to those who, like us, do not feel capable of living or explaining our faith in ways that would please all of our critics: if our work has been helpful to you, please join us in seeking to preserve the unity of the Spirit in the bond of peace by not becoming quarrelsome or defensive or disrespectful to anyone—especially those who you feel have misrepresented or misunderstood you or us. As Paul said to Timothy, "The Lord's servant must not be quarrelsome but must be kind to everyone, able to teach, patient when wronged." In addition he warned Timothy not to develop "an unhealthy interest in controversies and quarrels about words that result in envy, strife, malicious talk, evil suspicions, and constant friction." The apostle James also wrote, "the wisdom that comes from heaven is first of all pure; then peace-loving, considerate, submissive, full of mercy and good fruit, impartial and sincere. Peacemakers who sow in peace reap a harvest of righteousness." We believe it is better to be wronged than to wrong someone else; the Lord we follow was gentle and meek, and when he was reviled, he didn't respond in kind.

Instead of engaging in fruitless quarrels with our critics, we urge those who find our work helpful to pursue spiritual formation in the way of Christ, to worship God in spirit and truth, to seek to plant or serve in healthy and fruitful churches, to make disciples—especially among the irreligious and unchurched, to serve those in need, to be at peace with everyone as far as is possible, and to show a special concern for orphans and widows in their distress. We should keep careful control of our tongues (and pens or keyboards), and seek to be pure in heart and life, since this is "religion that God our Father accepts as pure and faultless."

With millions suffering from hunger, disease, and injustice around the world, we hope that all of us—including our critics—can renew our commitment to "remember the poor" (Gal. 2:10) rather than invest excessive energy in "controversies about words." "They will know you are my disciples," Jesus said, not by our excessive disputation, but by our love. Words and ideas are essential, for they often set the course for thought and action, and constructive dialogue is needed and worthwhile, but we cannot let less productive internal debates preoccupy us at the expense of caring for those in need.

Tenth, we should say that along with a few critiques, we are receiving many grateful and affirming responses to our work. Respected theologians and other leaders have told us, either in private or in public, that they are grateful for the emergent conversation and that they stand with us and support us. We are frequently told that people sense God graciously at work in the emergent community. We hope that those who see problems will not overlook the signs of

God's presence and activity among us, just as we do not overlook our many faults, including those pointed out by our critics. Only time will tell what the full outcome will be, but in the meantime, we welcome the prayers of both friends and critics.

We must once more thank both our critics and those who affirm our work, because we know that both are trying to help us in their respective ways, and both are trying to do the right thing before God—as we are. At the risk of redundancy, let us state once again that we welcome conversation with all who desire sincere and civil engagement over ideas that matter.

SOURCE: Tony Jones, Doug Pagitt, Spencer Burke, Brian McLaren, Dan Kimball, Andrew Jones, and Chris Seay, "Response to Recent Criticisms," June 2, 2005, http://www.patheos.com/blogs/tonyjones/2005/06/02/official-response-to-critics-of-emergent/.

§1. Ignatius of Antioch

Multiple Choice and Fill in the Blank

1. Ignatius instructed Christians to follow the _____, as Jesus Christ followed the Father.

    A. Leader

    B. Deacon

    C. Holy Spirit

    D. Bishop

2. Ignatius derided "unbelievers" who claimed what about Christ's suffering?

    A. It was ineffective for salvation.

    B. Christ did not physically suffer.

    C. It was not part of the plan of God.

    D. The Father suffered with the Son.

3. Ignatius claimed those "unbelievers" did not participate in Eucharist and prayer because they

    A. Denied the authority of bishops

    B. Had not received the Holy Spirit

    C. Were overzealous for martyrdom

    D. Denied that the eucharist is Christ's flesh

4. Ignatius hoped to be shown to "truly be a disciple of Jesus Christ" by

    A. Being completely devoured by beasts

    B. Raising himself up after death

    C. Winning converts through his death

    D. Miraculously escaping bondage

5. What was Ignatius's ultimate desire?

    A. The spread of the gospel

    B. Jesus Christ

    C. The destruction of his enemies

    D. Vindication of his innocence

---

§1. Ignatius of Antioch

Short Answer

1. What is the name given to the heresy Ignatius calls upon his followers to deny?

2. What three practices of the early church does Ignatius claim are valid only under a bishop?

3. Why is martyrdom so important to Ignatius?

§2. The *Didache*

Multiple Choice and Fill in the Blank

1. The *Didache* addressed the ways of
   A. Light and dark
   B. Life and death
   C. Good and evil
   D. Christian and non-Christian

2. The *Didache* said Christians should fast
   A. Sunday
   B. Two days a week
   C. Never, because fasting was not a Christian practice
   D. Every morning

3. The *Didache* instructed that only the _____ were allowed to participate in the Eucharist.
   A. Righteous
   B. Baptized
   C. Men
   D. Priests

4. The *Didache* said what was a sign of a false prophet?
   A. Predicts the end of the world
   B. Curses in Jesus' name
   C. Preaches for money
   D. Demands special treatment

§2. The *Didache*

Short Answer

1. What was the *Didache*'s purpose in the early church?

2. Summarize the *Didache*'s instructions concerning baptism, including the ideal baptismal conditions.

3. Compare the stipulations the *Didache* gave concerning the Eucharist with those of Ignatius.

§3. Justin Martyr

Multiple Choice and Fill in the Blank

1. According to Justin, non-Christians hated Christians "only" for
   A. Their generosity
   B. Their protest of injustices
   C. The name of Christ
   D. Ancestor veneration

2. Justin decried non-Christians principally for their inability to agree on
   A. Gods worthy of worship
   B. How to define "Logos"
   C. The question of the soul
   D. How to order society

3. The "Logos" in Justin is equated with universal
   A. Justice
   B. Reason
   C. Harmony
   D. Power

4. Justin claimed that the Greek writer _____ was dependent on Moses.
   A. Socrates
   B. Aristotle
   C. Heraclitus
   D. Plato

5. To what image used by the above Greek writer did Justin refer to prove his point?
   A. The shape of an X
   B. An everlasting fire
   C. A cosmic serpent
   D. The tabernacle

§3. Justin Martyr

Short Answer

1. Justin Martyr is considered one of the earliest Christian apologists. What does this term designate?

2. How does Justin define true "Christians"?

3. What is Justin Martyr's general view of Greek philosophy?

§4. *The Epistle to Diognetus*

Multiple Choice and Fill in the Blank

1. The author highlights how Christians
   A. Only follow their own laws and customs and live separately from non-Christians
   B. Only follow their own laws and customs and live among non-Christians
   C. Follow the customs and laws of the places where they live and live among non-Christians
   D. Follow the customs and laws of the places where they live and separate themselves from non-Christians

2. Those who help people who are in want are said to
   A. Receive their reward in helping their fellow Christians
   B. Become a god to those who they help, as an imitator of God
   C. Store up reward in heaven
   D. Rightly expect praise from others

3. For the author, the relationship between Christians and the world is the same as the relationship between
   A. The soul and the body
   B. The body and the brain
   C. The soul and the spirit
   D. The spirit and the soul

4. The author claims that the Greek gods are
   A. Senseless and deaf
   B. Made of common materials
   C. Perishable and temporary
   D. All of the above

5. Who does the author claim to have been a disciple of?
   A. Jesus
   B. Greek priests
   C. Jewish rabbis
   D. The Apostles

§4. *The Epistle to Diognetus*

Short Answer

1. What does the author say covered humanity's sins?

2. How do Christians relate to the countries in which they reside?

3. What advantage does the author say Jewish sacrifices have over Greek sacrifices?

§5. Perpetua

Multiple Choice and Fill in the Blank

1. Perpetua was a _____, a person learning the basic ideas and practices of Christianity.
   A. Catechumen
   B. Pagan
   C. Jew
   D. Martyr

2. The martyrdom of Perpetua took place in
   A. Rome
   B. Carthage
   C. Alexandria
   D. Jerusalem

3. Dinocrates was _____, who visited Perpetua in a dream.
   A. Perpetua's dead brother
   B. The emperor's dead son
   C. Felicitas' dead child
   D. Felicitas' dead brother

4. Felicitas became a _____ in her vision the day before her martyrdom.
   A. Man
   B. Lion
   C. Preacher
   D. Egyptian

5. Perpetua appeared to have no control over the manner of her death.
   A. True
   B. False

§5. Perpetua

Short Answer

1. What is the narrator's view of martyrdom?

2. Describe the actions of Perpetua's father. Briefly state the reason for his actions.

3. What reflections does this text incite about Christianity and gender? How does the author of the *Martyrdom of Perpetua and Felicitas* understand masculinity and femininity?

§6. Irenaeus of Lyons

Multiple Choice and Fill in the Blank

1. Irenaeus was a student of
   A. Ignatius
   B. Justin Martyr
   C. Tertullian
   D. Polycarp

2. Irenaeus claimed to be part of the developing tradition of
   A. Recapitulation theory
   B. Apostolic succession
   C. Martyrdom
   D. Gnosticism

3. According to Irenaeus, humanity is brought up to God by means of
   A. The incarnation
   B. Atonement
   C. The Divine Spirit
   D. The preaching of the gospel

4. What was the claim of "Valentinus' group"?
   A. The Spirit, not the Son, became human.
   B. Christ only appeared human.
   C. Mary was not a virgin.
   D. There could be no union between God and humanity.

5. Irenaeus calls upon the image of a fallen angel to describe the "Enemy."
   A. True
   B. False

§6. Irenaeus of Lyons

Short Answer

1. Against what broadly defined heresy is Irenaeus' *Against Heresies* directed?

2. Summarize the doctrine of recapitulation as Irenaeus articulates it. What does the phrase, "Thus gathering all into one, he was Himself gathered into one," mean?

3. Explain the relation that Irenaeus draws between the Virgin Mary and Eve.

§7. Tertullian of Carthage

Multiple Choice and Fill in the Blank

1. According to Tertullian, heresies are instigated by
   A. The Hebrew Bible
   B. Plato
   C. Philosophy
   D. The Rule of Faith

2. Tertullian claimed Valentinus was of the "school" of
   A. Plato
   B. Marcion
   C. The Stoics
   D. The Epicureans

3. Tertullian said that the _____ was taught by Christ.
   A. Didache
   B. Way of Life
   C. Analogy of Faith
   D. Rule of Faith

4. In Tertullian's analogy, the fruit of the tree represents the
   A. Father
   B. Son
   C. Holy Spirit
   D. Virgin

5. Which of these is not a term employed by Tertullian in discussing the Trinity?
   A. Monarchy
   B. *Tertium quid*
   C. Modalism
   D. Economy

§7. Tertullian of Carthage

Short Answer

1. What important theological term was Tertullian the first to use?

2. Explain what Tertullian meant by "What has Athens to do with Jerusalem?"

3. Summarize the content of the Rule of Faith.

§8. Cyprian of Carthage

Multiple Choice and Fill in the Blank

1. Cyprian's primary opponents were the schismatic
   A. Valentinians
   B. Platonists
   C. Epicureans
   D. Novationists

2. For Cyprian, reentry to the church is not possible without a vow of chastity.
   A. True
   B. False

3. The offense of an adulterer, Cyprian claims, is primarily against
   A. A spouse
   B. His or herself
   C. Christ
   D. Bishops and priests

4. Cyprian says there can be no salvation to any except in
   A. Virginity
   B. Christ
   C. Mary
   D. The church

5. Cyprian likens the church to a
   A. Bird
   B. Forest
   C. Mother
   D. Father

§8. Cyprian of Carthage

Short Answer

1. What is the principal aspect of the church that Cyprian stresses?

2. Describe Cyprian's process of church discipline.

3. How does Cyprian describe a person who was outside the church? What Old Testament story does he allude to in this connection?

§9. Origen of Alexandria

Multiple Choice and Fill in the Blank

1. Origen attributed the ultimate fate of souls to differences in
   A. Holiness
   B. Meritorious works
   C. Movement and will
   D. Wisdom

2. Origen claimed that "whole nations of souls" were stored somewhere beneath the earth.
   A. True
   B. False

3. According to Origen, a soul could ascend through the scale of being by means of
   A. Special knowledge
   B. Virtue
   C. Salvation in Christ
   D. Death and rebirth

4. Which of the following is not one of the three levels of biblical meaning/interpretation espoused by Origen?
   A. Body
   B. Spirit
   C. Soul
   D. Intelligence

5. Origen held that all of Scripture contains each of the three types of meaning.
   A. True
   B. False

§9. Origen of Alexandria

Short Answer

1. According to Origen, who will eventually have God in themselves, enjoying the benefits of salvation?

2. According to Origen, why are souls eventually embodied? Why would this be a problem for the church?

3. Why does Origen conceive of Scripture in a threefold way? Why is the "literal" interpretation inadequate to Origen?

§10. Edict of Milan

Multiple Choice and Fill in the Blank

1. The Edict was issued after the _____ persecution of Christians.
   A. Diocletian
   B. Constantinian
   C. Licinian
   D. Augustinian

2. The Edict only makes an allowance for the Christian religion.
   A. True
   B. False

3. The Edict makes reference to a "former edict" that had already granted Christians freedom.
   A. True
   B. False

§10. Edict of Milan

Short Answer

1. Which two emperors issued the Edict of Milan?

2. Explain the rationale given in the Edict for allowing "free liberty" in religion.

3. What additional stipulation is included for the benefit of Christians?

§11. Proceedings before the Consul Zenophilus

Multiple Choice and Fill in the Blank

1. Who did the Christians repeatedly say had the majority of the scriptural texts?
   A. The readers
   B. The bishop
   C. The subdeacons
   D. The priests

2. With what were the subdeacons threatened if they lied about giving over what they had?
   A. The anger of the mayor
   B. Death
   C. They would be shipped to Rome for trial
   D. Prison

3. What happened when the subdeacons were asked to identify the readers?
   A. There were no subdeacons.
   B. They refused and were arrested.
   C. Two refused and were arrested, the other two gave over everything and remained free.
   D. All four gave over everything and remained free.

4. Which of the following were found in the church?
   A. Large amounts of paper
   B. All of the church's copies of Scripture
   C. Large amounts of clothing
   D. All of the above

5. Who found a silver lamp and silver box after the church leaders had said they had brought out everything?
   A. The mayor's men
   B. Victor
   C. The bishop
   D. Silvanus

§11. Proceedings before the Consul Zenophilus

Short Answer

1. Name one of the emperors under whose orders the property was confiscated.

2. What did the two men say when they refused to name the readers?

3. What might a Donatist think about the actions of Silvanus?

§12. Arius of Alexandria

Multiple Choice and Fill in the Blank

1. The teaching of Arius was deemed heretical by the Council of
   A. Milan
   B. Rome
   C. Nicaea
   D. Alexandria

2. Which of the following is not a slogan of the Bishop of Alexandria?
   A. Always God always Son
   B. The Son ingenerably coexists with God
   C. The Son has a beginning, but God is without beginning
   D. Ever-begotten, ungenerated-created

3. Which of these views is a distinctively Arian one?
   A. The Son is distinct from the Father.
   B. The Son is subordinate to the Father in being.
   C. The Son is subordinate to the Father in function.
   D. The Son is superior to the Father.

4. Arius holds that the Son is begotten "from nothing."
   A. True
   B. False

5. Arius claims that the Son is subject to change.
   A. True
   B. False

§12. Arius of Alexandria

Short Answer

1. What theological concern leads Arius to deny the coeternity of the Son with the Father?

2. What are the "impieties" Arius complains about in attempting to justify himself as orthodox?

3. How does Arius describe the existence of the Son?

§13. Anthony of Egypt

Multiple Choice and Fill in the Blank

1. Anthony's biography belongs to the genre of hagiography, writings about
   A. Saints
   B. Bishops
   C. Ascetics
   D. Martyrs

2. Anthony was raised in a pagan (non-Christian) household.
   A. True
   B. False

3. What was Anthony's first act of asceticism?
   A. Flight to the desert
   B. Giving his family's inheritance to the poor
   C. A period of fasting and prayer
   D. Devoting himself to celibacy

4. Who attempted to deter Anthony from pursuing monastic discipline?
   A. His sister
   B. The villagers
   C. The devil
   D. His bishop

5. Anthony took up residence in
   A. Tombs
   B. A hut in the desert
   C. An abandoned church
   D. An old family estate

§13. Anthony of Egypt

Short Answer

1. What biblical passages encouraged Anthony to pursue monasticism?

2. Describe Anthony's practices of physical asceticism.

3. After what challenge did Anthony receive "more power in his body than before"?

§14. Athanasius of Alexandria

Multiple Choice and Fill in the Blank

1. Athanasius was at the forefront of opposition against
   A. Pelagianism
   B. Arianism
   C. Gnosticism
   D. Judaism

2. According to Athanasius, the Word of God was originally distant from creation.
   A. True
   B. False

3. Athanasius claims that the Son came to earth especially to
   A. Teach
   B. Heal
   C. Die
   D. Judge

4. In the Son, death is "annihilated" by virtue of
   A. The indwelling Word
   B. The power of the Father
   C. Jesus' faithfulness unto death
   D. The miraculous nature of Jesus' conception

5. Athanasius' canonical listing includes all the commonly accepted biblical books except
   A. Revelation
   B. The general epistles
   C. Esther
   D. Judith

§14. Athanasius of Alexandria

Short Answer

1. Summarize the various reasons Athanasius gives for the Word becoming flesh. Why is the incarnation "necessary" in Athanasius' understanding of salvation and redemption?

2. For Athanasius, what distinguishes the humanity and corporeality of Jesus from all other human beings?

3. What is the role of the canon in Athanasius' understanding? What supposed reason does he give for the writing of "apocryphal" writings?

---

§15. Gregory of Nyssa

Multiple Choice and Fill in the Blank

1. Gregory was one of the so-called Cappadocian Fathers, alongside
   A. Augustine of Hippo and Athanasius of Alexandria
   B. Basil the Great and Gregory of Nazianzus
   C. Eusebius of Caesarea and Cyprian of Carthage
   D. Benedict of Nursia and John of Damascus

2. With what philosophical school was Gregory associated?
   A. Aristotelianism
   B. Manicheism
   C. Platonism
   D. Stoicism

3. Gregory asserts that the terms used to describe the deity do not express the essence of the divine nature.
   A. True
   B. False

4. What is the "special passion" of the Enemy according to Gregory?
   A. Envy
   B. Pride
   C. Greed
   D. Hatred

5. Gregory holds that the Enemy had kept the spiritual nature of humanity in bondage through sin.
   A. True
   B. False

§15. Gregory of Nyssa

Short Answer

1. How does Gregory envision the actions of the Trinity? How do the Three relate to one another in acting?

2. Explain Gregory's reasoning in the illustration of those who sell themselves into slavery. What does he mean by "arbitrary method" of redemption?

3. Explain the "fishhook" metaphor. Who is the fish? What is the hook?

§16. Early Christian Creeds

Multiple Choice and Fill in the Blank

1. The current version of the Apostles' Creed dates to the eighth century, but it reflects earlier statements.
   A. True
   B. False

2. Which of the following was not a heretical movement against which the Symbol of Chalcedon was directed?
   A. Nestorianism
   B. Arianism
   C. Marcionism
   D. Apollinarianism

3. Which of the following does the Apostles' Creed assert about Jesus Christ?
   A. Created heavens and earth
   B. Descended into hell
   C. Consubstantial with the Father
   D. Forgives sins

4. The Symbol of Chalcedon gives Mary the title of
   A. Savior
   B. Only begotten
   C. Almighty
   D. Mother of God

5. The Symbol of Chalcedon emphasizes the distinction and division between the natures of Christ.
   A. True
   B. False

§16. Early Christian Creeds

Short Answer

1. What was the primary purpose of "rules of faith" and later creeds?

2. Describe some thematic resonances between these two credal statements. Who appears to be the focus of both? What might account for the different emphases of the two?

3. What, if anything, seems to be missing from the creeds as written? Why is it significant that those elements are not present?

§17. Augustine of Hippo

Multiple Choice and Fill in the Blank

1. Augustine addresses his *Confessions* to
   A. God
   B. His mother
   C. His friend
   D. Himself

2. Augustine thought God spoke through his mother's advice.
   A. True
   B. False

3. The sin Augustine most often struggled with in his youth was
   A. Slander
   B. Murder
   C. Pride
   D. Concupiscence

4. When Augustine experienced conversion in the garden, what did he "take up and read"?
   A. Gospel of Luke
   B. A letter from his mother
   C. Apostle Paul
   D. Cicero

5. What did Augustine and his friends do with the pears they took from the tree?
   A. Ate them
   B. Threw them to the hogs
   C. Sold them
   D. Destroyed them

§17. Augustine of Hippo

Short Answer

1. Summarize Augustine's conversion experience.

2. Describe how Augustine views the role of his study of the Platonists for his life as a Christian.

3. Summarize Augustine's analogy for the Trinity.

§18. Pelagius

Multiple Choice and Fill in the Blank

1. Pelagius was a Christian
   A. Apostate
   B. Priest
   C. Ascetic
   D. Martyr

2. The primary opponent of Pelagius' teaching was
   A. Maximus the Confessor
   B. John of Damascus
   C. Augustine of Hippo
   D. Pope Urban II

3. Pelagius argued for the goodness of human nature by reference to
   A. The eternal soul
   B. God the Creator
   C. Christ the Savior
   D. The indwelling Spirit

4. In Pelagius' view, human evil is a matter of nature, not habit.
   A. True
   B. False

5. Which of these terms or ideas does not feature in Pelagius' understanding of salvation?
   A. Christ as example
   B. Instruction
   C. Rebirth
   D. Ransom

---

§18. Pelagius

Short Answer

1. According to Pelagius, what is "good" about human nature? How does the capacity for evil factor in to this?

2. How does Pelagius distinguish rational from non-rational beings?

3. What distinction does Pelagius make between the period before Christ and the current age?

§19. Maximus the Confessor

Multiple Choice and Fill in the Blank

1. Maximus subscribed to dyothelitism, the belief that two _____ are present in the person of Christ.
   A. Natures
   B. Souls
   C. Wills
   D. Gods

2. Maximus "spiritualizes" the bread of the Lord's Prayer as the bread of life and
   A. Salvation
   B. Knowledge
   C. Power
   D. Glory

3. Maximus asserts that human nature, with its concern for "corruptible things," is to be overcome by
   A. Free will
   B. Grace
   C. Prayer and meditation
   D. Reason

4. Maximus envisions life as a preparation for death.
   A. True
   B. False

5. The body, according to Maximus, is to be a _____ of the soul.
   A. Slave
   B. Master
   C. Messenger
   D. Coequal

§19. Maximus the Confessor

Short Answer

1. Describe Maximus' view of the Christian's proper attitude toward matter.

2. What does Maximus mean by the phrase "man is a world"?

3. What is the distinction between "intelligible" and "sensible" things?

§20. Benedict of Nursia

Multiple Choice and Fill in the Blank

1. To dwell in God's kingdom or temple, Benedict says monks should focus on
    A. Good works
    B. Doctrine
    C. Preaching
    D. Traveling

2. Benedict calls the monastery an institute for
    A. Prayer
    B. Work
    C. Service of God
    D. Education

3. If monks persevered in the monastery until death, they were promised
    A. A burial in the monastery
    B. A share in the sufferings of Christ
    C. Access to heaven
    D. Less time in purgatory

4. Monks could own
    A. Only one book and one pen
    B. Only one table
    C. Personal belongings
    D. Nothing

5. What warranted the most severe discipline?
    A. Swearing
    B. Owning something
    C. Murmuring
    D. Concupiscence

§20. Benedict of Nursia

Short Answer

1. Discuss the guidelines for monastic living in Benedict's Rule.

2. Describe what Benedict identifies as conditions for dwelling in the shelter of God's kingdom.

3. Describe the distribution process in the Rule and the expected response from both those with more and less needs.

§21. John of Damascus

Multiple Choice and Fill in the Blank

1. John of Damascus received a traditional _____ education.
   A. Monastic
   B. Jewish
   C. Muslim
   D. Roman

2. In John's view, the injunctions against image-making were given because of the Jews' proneness to idolatry.
   A. True
   B. False

3. "Drawing a likeness" of God becomes acceptable when
   A. God reveals his glory
   B. God becomes incarnate
   C. Worshipers reach a certain level of wisdom
   D. Worshipers have the right state of heart

4. An "image" is defined as a _____ of the original.
   A. Shadow
   B. Replication
   C. Veneration
   D. Likeness

5. John of Damascus was adamant that Christian practices had nothing in common with "heathen" practices.
   A. True
   B. False

§21. John of Damascus

Short Answer

1. In what sense and why are Old Testament injunctions against image-making not applicable to Christians?

2. What are some examples of acceptable and suggested icons?

3. What point does John of Damascus make about "veneration"?

§22. Xi'an Monument

Multiple Choice and Fill in the Blank

1. In what languages was the text of the stele written?
   A. English and Chinese
   B. Chinese and Syriac
   C. Syriac and Nestorian
   D. Chinese and Nestorian

2. From which country was the first missionary to China according to the stele?
   A. Israel
   B. Syria
   C. China
   D. Persia

3. Which dynasty was ruling China when Christianity became prominent there?
   A. Tang
   B. Ming
   C. Han
   D. Chau

4. Which of the following Christian beliefs is not mentioned in the inscription?
   A. God is a Trinity.
   B. Jesus was God who came to earth as a man.
   C. Instigated by Satan, humanity fell from a pure state.
   D. Each person is assigned a guardian angel.

5. What is the name that the inscription gives to the religion it describes?
   A. Christianity
   B. Chinese Christianity
   C. Nestorianism
   D. The Illustrious Religion

§22. Xi'an Monument

Short Answer

1. What group of people does the tablet repeatedly celebrate as particularly holy Christians?

2. During which centuries does the stele describe Christianity flourishing in China?

3. What cleansing ritual do converts to this form of Christianity participate in?

§23. Pope Urban II

Multiple Choice and Fill in the Blank

1. The First Crusade was initiated in
   A. 1095
   B. 1042
   C. 1109
   D. 1200

2. Urban established the modern Roman _____ to facilitate administration of the church.
   A. Crusade
   B. Curia
   C. Clermont
   D. Cohort

3. By the time of Urban's sermon, Arab and Turkish forces had advanced as far West as
   A. Italy
   B. Spain
   C. France
   D. Romania

4. Which of the following is not a descriptor used by Urban for the Arabs and Turks?
   A. Degenerate
   B. Despised
   C. Pitiable
   D. Slave of demons

5. Urban urged Crusaders to make converts first, before seeking to kill the enemy.
   A. True
   B. False

§23. Pope Urban II

Short Answer

1. Whom did Pope Urban encourage to go on the Crusade?

2. What, in Urban's view, is at stake with the expanding presence of Muslim forces?

3. What promise does Urban make to those who pledged their lives to the Crusade?

§24. Anselm of Canterbury

Multiple Choice and Fill in the Blank

1. Anselm is known as the father of
   A. Intellectualism
   B. Ontology
   C. Ecclesiology
   D. Scholasticism

2. Anselm's ontological argument argued that God is
   A. That than which something greater can be conceived
   B. That than which a few things greater can be conceived
   C. That than which nothing greater can be conceived
   D. That which is inconceivable

3. Which prophet, according to Anselm, referred to Jesus having horns coming out of his hands?
   A. Isaiah
   B. Jeremiah
   C. Micah
   D. Habakkuk

4. Anselm taught that the atonement provided _____ to God's justice.
   A. Confession
   B. Satisfaction
   C. Neglect
   D. Love

5. According to Anselm, Jesus Christ suffered out of his own free will.
   A. True
   B. False

§24. Anselm of Canterbury

Short Answer

1. Describe how the painter and his painting demonstrated Anselm's ontological argument for God's existence.

2. Why did the devil have no just claim against God or people, according to Anselm?

3. According to Anselm, why could only the God-man resolve the problem created by humanity's sin?

§25. Peter Abelard

Multiple Choice and Fill in the Blank

1. Abelard is considered a representative of what medieval group?
   A. Scholastics
   B. Cistercians
   C. Benedictines
   D. Platonists

2. Abelard developed his view of the atonement in response to the
   _____ theory.
   A. Christus Victor
   B. Ransom
   C. Propitiation
   D. Expiation

3. Justification, or reconciliation, is effected in Abelard's view through
   A. Sacrifice
   B. Love
   C. Divine power
   D. Spiritual enlightenment

4. In Abelard's theory, fear of God is of paramount importance.
   A. True
   B. False

5. The Christian can only become more righteous through acts of
   penance, according to Abelard.
   A. True
   B. False

§25. Peter Abelard

Short Answer

1. Which theory of the atonement is Abelard famous for? What does it suggest, especially in contrast to previous theories?

2. Why does the Christian perform good works, according to Abelard? What does this say about his view of human nature?

3. Describe Abelard's understanding of God. What is unique about his perspective? How does his reading of Scripture inform this view?

§26. Bernard of Clairvaux

Multiple Choice and Fill in the Blank

1. Bernard was a member of what monastic order?

   A. Franciscans

   B. Benedictines

   C. Cistercians

   D. Jesuits

2. Bernard held that those who do not "know Christ" are sufficiently taught by

   A. Natural law

   B. Evangelism

   C. Their own religions

   D. Special revelation

3. According to Bernard, love of neighbor can exist even without love of God.

   A. True

   B. False

4. The word used for the most basic form of love, self-love, is

   A. Innate

   B. Reasonable

   C. Carnal

   D. Contemplative

5. What is the "joy" to be attained at the highest level of love?

   A. Perfection

   B. Illumination

   C. Divinization

   D. Contemplation

§26. Bernard of Clairvaux

Short Answer

1. Briefly describe each of the four stages of love. What is the highest, and why?

2. To what extent does nature teach us about God?

3. What is Bernard's view of the ultimate fate of human nature? Does he have a positive or negative understanding of humanity?

---

§27. Francis of Assisi

Multiple Choice and Fill in the Blank

1. The particular form of monasticism Francis modeled with his street-preaching and voluntary poverty is called
   A. Penitent
   B. Voluntary
   C. Mendicant
   D. Independent

2. Francis is now recognized as the patron saint of
   A. Hymnody
   B. The poor
   C. Stigmata
   D. Animals and creation

3. Brother _____ bears the likeness of the Most High.
   A. Bear
   B. Wind
   C. Stars
   D. Sun

4. God is said to sustain all life through
   A. His Spirit
   B. Clouds and weather
   C. Fire and water
   D. Love

5. Death is pictured as the ultimate enemy of creation.
   A. True
   B. False

§27. Francis of Assisi

Short Answer

1. What is striking and unusual about Francis' song?

2. Why do you think Francis chooses familial epithets for various elements of creation?

3. Suggest some implications of Francis' creation hymn for our own theology of creation and the environment.

§28. Clare of Assisi

Multiple Choice and Fill in the Blank

1. The Rule of Saint Clare evidences the central tenet of the mendicant orders, the vow of _____ poverty.
   A. Franciscan
   B. Apostolic
   C. Divine
   D. Blessed

2. Clare called Francis "our most blessed _____."
   A. Brother
   B. Sovereign
   C. Teacher
   D. Father

3. God's grace, Clare claimed, "enlightened" her to do what?
   A. Penance
   B. Make a pilgrimage
   C. Proclaim the gospel
   D. Contemplation

4. Francis' orders for the Poor Clares instructed them to "espouse themselves" to
   A. Their work
   B. The gospel
   C. Christ
   D. The Paraclete

5. The land that the Poor Clares owned for their monasteries could be used for a
   A. Commodity
   B. Garden
   C. Playground
   D. Festival

§28. Clare of Assisi

Short Answer

1. What does Clare emphasize as marks of the holy life which she and her sisters "of their own free will" entered into?

2. Describe the reasoning behind Clare's embrace of a life of poverty.

3. What does this life of poverty entail? Can the sisters "own" anything?

§29. Bonaventure

Multiple Choice and Fill in the Blank

1. Which of the following was not a major influence on Bonaventure's thought?
   A. Augustine
   B. Aristotle
   C. Platonism
   D. Gnosticism

2. Bonaventure advocated the view that knowledge could not come from reason alone, but from
   A. Virtue and fellowship with God
   B. Grace and faith
   C. Humility and penitence
   D. Mystical enlightenment

3. For Bonaventure, the words of Christ from the cross were the chief "witness" of his love.
   A. True
   B. False

4. "Rood" is a synonymous term for Christ's
   A. Tomb
   B. Wounds
   C. Crown of thorns
   D. Cross

5. According to Bonaventure, what should be your constant care and comrade?
   A. The cross
   B. Eucharist
   C. The sun and stars
   D. Virtue

§29. Bonaventure

Short Answer

1. What is Bonaventure's emotional response to contemplation of Christ's Passion?

2. The major theme of Bonaventure's two hymns was Christ crucified. Describe what Bonaventure believed the cross accomplished.

3. Why is the cross an ongoing source of comfort for Bonaventure? How does it equip the "saints" for the life of faith?

§30. Thomas of Celano

Multiple Choice and Fill in the Blank

1. Thomas of Celano authored the first biography of
   A. Thomas Aquinas
   B. Francis of Assisi
   C. Pope Gregory IX
   D. Bonaventure

2. Thomas' hymn is an example of popular piety in the Middle Ages.
   A. True
   B. False

3. According to both "saint and Sibyl," the earth is to end by
   A. A flood
   B. Darkness
   C. Fire
   D. Wasting away

4. God as Judge and King will freely save
   A. All souls
   B. The elect
   C. The worthy
   D. Those who "would" be saved

5. Thomas claims that Mary alone of all humans did not need to be saved.
   A. True
   B. False

§30. Thomas of Celano

Short Answer

1. Characterize the various events that Thomas of Celano believed would accompany the end of time.

2. What is Thomas' appraisal of his own sinfulness? When does he hope for the remission of sins?

3. How would you describe the tone of this hymn? Hopeful? Helpless? Would you say it is more concerned with the individual or with collective humanity?

§31. Thomas Aquinas

Multiple Choice and Fill in the Blank

1. If there are effects, it is necessary that a preceding _____ exists.
    A. Cause
    B. Effect
    C. Personal Creator
    D. Natural law

2. Aquinas argued that God's existence could be proven in how many ways?
    A. 3
    B. 7
    C. 5
    D. 1

3. Aquinas believed people could know God perfectly through observance of the world.
    A. True
    B. False

4. Aquinas said it pertains to the _____ of God that God permits evil to exist.
    A. Goodness
    B. Evil
    C. Freedom
    D. Justice

5. Aquinas's hymn for Corpus Christi discusses which sacrament?
    A. Baptism
    B. Ordination
    C. Eucharist
    D. Marriage

§31. Thomas Aquinas

Short Answer

1. List the reasons that some people give for believing God's existence is not demonstrable. What Scripture does Aquinas present to make the point that God's existence is demonstrable? What is the significance of his point about "natural reason"?

2. Explain Aquinas' concept of God as first mover, as described in his first proof for God's existence.

3. Describe the various ways Aquinas portrays Jesus in the hymn for Corpus Christi.

§32. Pope Boniface VIII

Multiple Choice and Fill in the Blank

1. *Unam Sanctum* was issued in response to conflicts with
   A. The king of France
   B. The poet Dante
   C. Theologians
   D. Bishops

2. Outside of the "one holy Catholic and apostolic Church," Boniface claimed, there is neither salvation nor
   A. Grace
   B. Knowledge
   C. Security
   D. Remission of sins

3. The universal church is likened to all of the following except
   A. A bride
   B. The ark
   C. A rock
   D. A mystic body

4. Who is "Christ's vicar"?
   A. The king
   B. Peter
   C. Moses
   D. St. Dionysius

5. In Boniface's understanding of universal law, the temporal and spiritual always work hand-in-hand.
   A. True
   B. False

§32. Pope Boniface VIII

Short Answer

1. What claims does Boniface make about the nature of the church? How does this serve to bolster his claims of his own authority?

2. Summarize Boniface's illustration of the "two swords."

3. What is the scope of papal authority as Boniface envisions it?

§33. Marsilius of Padua

Multiple Choice and Fill in the Blank

1. Marsilius of Padua was a champion of, and was protected by, the
   A. Ottoman Empire
   B. Holy Roman Empire
   C. City of Florence
   D. King of France

2. According to Marsilius, the primary lawgivers in society are
   A. Kings
   B. Judges
   C. Citizens
   D. Merchants

3. Marsilius allowed for kings, but argued that they should be elected.
   A. True
   B. False

4. What did Marsilius identify as the source of "civil discord and dissension"?
   A. Papal overreach
   B. Unjust courts
   C. Theological confusion
   D. Secularization

5. Marsilius accepted _____ as "true and essential to salvation."
   A. Scripture alone
   B. Scripture and conciliar interpretation
   C. Scripture and church tradition
   D. Scripture and reason

§33. Marsilius of Padua

Short Answer

1. Characterize this document's attitudes toward the state. Is the state superior to the church? What is the issue with the church attaining "secular" power? To what do both state and church answer?

2. What grounding of papal authority and superiority does Marsilius undermine in this document?

3. List some of the restraints Marsilius imposes on the authority of bishops. What does he call for the church to do with its wealth?

§34. Council of Constance

Multiple Choice and Fill in the Blank

1. Who or what does the council claim to be the source of its authority?
   A. Christ
   B. Previous church councils
   C. The Apostles
   D. The pope

2. Who has to obey the council's decisions?
   A. Everyone, including the pope
   B. Everyone who was not at the council
   C. Everyone, except the pope
   D. Everyone who was at the council

3. How can the timing of a church council be changed according to *Frequens*?
   A. It cannot change, it has to happen every 10 years.
   B. It can only be delayed.
   C. It can only be moved up.
   D. It can be moved up or delayed.

4. According to *Frequens*, who can change the location of a church council?
   A. Only the cardinals
   B. Only the pope
   C. The pope with the approval of his brothers, the cardinals
   D. Only another council

5. What phrase (which would often be picked up by the 16th-century Reformations) do the declarations use to describe the extent of reform needed in the church?
   A. Reform in head and members
   B. Reform from head to toe
   C. Reform from pope to plebe
   D. Reform in body and soul

§34. Council of Constance

Short Answer

1. According to *Haec Sancta*, who is the final authority for the church?

2. What does the council say will happen to those who disobey the judgments of a general council?

3. What (nonmetaphorical) reasons does the council state for holding general councils?

§35. Desiderius Erasmus

Multiple Choice and Fill in the Blank

1. Foremost among Erasmus' humanist achievements was his printed edition of
   A. Aristotle
   B. Augustine
   C. The Greek New Testament
   D. The Hebrew Old Testament

2. Unlike Luther, Erasmus was unwilling to break with the Catholic Church.
   A. True
   B. False

3. What is the meaning of the Latin phrase *Dulce bellum inexpertis*?
   A. "War is sweet to those who know it not"
   B. "Youth breeds boldness"
   C. "Faith arises from experience"
   D. "Bravery lies with the wise"

4. In what group does Erasmus locate the ideal of human friendship?
   A. The community of faith
   B. Families
   C. Companies of soldiers
   D. The learned

5. According to Erasmus, Christ's ultimate gift to his Apostles was
   A. Knowledge
   B. Peace
   C. Boldness
   D. Friendship

§35. Desiderius Erasmus

Short Answer

1. Describe Erasmus' view of ideal human nature. What is humanity's role in creation? In what way does Erasmus' Renaissance humanism influence his thinking here?

2. How would you characterize Erasmus' diagnosis of his society?

2. How does Erasmus depict the relation of Christ to war and violence?

§36. Martin Luther

Multiple Choice and Fill in the Blank

1. In the "95 Theses," Luther attacked
   A. Baptism
   B. Marriage
   C. The sale of indulgences
   D. Mass

2. Luther argued that the teaching that _____ was one of the three "walls" of the Romanists.
   A. Spiritual power is over temporal power
   B. Only the pope can interpret Scripture
   C. Only the pope can call a council
   D. All of the above

3. Luther said Christ gave the keys to
   A. John
   B. Peter
   C. Bishops and priests
   D. The whole community

4. Luther used _____ as the primary source to support his arguments.
   A. Scripture
   B. Church Fathers
   C. The Holy Spirit
   D. Aquinas

5. Luther said that people are justified by
   A. The sacraments
   B. Works
   C. Faith
   D. All of the above

§36. Martin Luther

1. Discuss reasons Luther gave for attacking the pope.

2. For Luther, what made someone a priest?

3. Explain what Luther meant when he said, "Good works do not make a good man, but a good man does good works."

§37. Anne Askew

Multiple Choice and Fill in the Blank

1. What was Anne Askew arrested for before escaping?
   A. Stealing
   B. Distributing literature
   C. Preaching
   D. Possessing banned books

2. Who examined Anne Askew at Saddler's Hall?
   A. Steven Dare
   B. Christopher Dare
   C. Paul Dare
   D. Henry Dare

3. "I answered that I would not throw pearls among swine, for
   _____ were good enough."
   A. Rocks
   B. Seeds
   C. Acorns
   D. Apples

4. When asked about her views on confession, Anne Askew cites St. Paul.
   A. True
   B. False

5. "Then I asked, how many women he had seen go into the pulpit and
   preach. He said he _____."
   A. Never saw one
   B. Saw one
   C. Saw three
   D. Saw many

§37. Anne Askew

Short Answer

1. What was Anne Askew's reasoning supporting her claim that she would rather read five lines in the Bible than hear five masses in the temple?

2. What was Anne Askew's reasoning for "uttering Scripture"?

3. Why was Anne Askew ultimately burned at the stake?

§38. Act of Supremacy

Multiple Choice and Fill in the Blank

1. The Act of Supremacy recognizes the king or queen of England as what?
   A. The leader of the Church of England
   B. The leader of the Church of England along with the pope
   C. The leader of the Church of England second only to the pope
   D. The leader of the Church of England second only to the Archbishop of Canterbury

2. The language of the Act of Supremacy implies what?
   A. The king always was head of the English church.
   B. The king had not been the head of the English church before but he is now.
   C. The pope can still overrule the king, but otherwise the king is the head of the English church.
   D. The king can only act as head of the church in cooperation with the Archbishop of Canterbury.

3. To whom does the Act of Supremacy apply explicitly?
   A. All of the churches in the world
   B. The Church of England and all of the other realms of the British Empire
   C. All of the churches in Europe
   D. The Church of England only

4. According to the Act of Supremacy, who is responsible for carrying out church discipline and dealing with heresy?
   A. Parliament
   B. God
   C. The church as a whole
   D. The king

5. Given the context, what "foreign authority" do the writers of the Act of Supremacy most likely have in mind?
   A. Other kings and queens
   B. The pope
   C. The bishops of the church
   D. The Holy Roman emperor

§38. Act of Supremacy

Short Answer

1. What title does the Act of Supremacy recognize as belonging to the monarch of England?

2. Who will be the head of the church after King Henry VIII dies?

3. What relationship does the act recognize between the church and state?

§39. John Calvin

Multiple Choice and Fill in the Blank

1. Calvin's _____ was one of the most influential systematic exposi-
   tions of Protestantism.
   A. *To the Christian Nobility of the German Nation*
   B. New Testament
   C. *Institutes of the Christian Religion*
   D. *The City of God*

2. Calvin said that everything happening in the world was
   A. Governed by God
   B. Happening by chance
   C. Not governed by God
   D. Governed by human decisions

3. Calvin used _____ as analogous to the way Scripture clarified
   human notions of God.
   A. Spectacles
   B. Creation
   C. A mirror
   D. Children

4. Calvin argued that the spiritual promise given to Christians in
   _____ was the very same as that given to the Hebrew people in
   circumcision.
   A. The Eucharist
   B. The Bible
   C. The Spirit
   D. Baptism

5. What was to be experienced rather than understood?
   A. Baptism
   B. Circumcision
   C. Eucharist
   D. Government

§39. John Calvin

Short Answer

1. What was Calvin's basic definition of "predestination"?

2. Explain civil government's role in religious beliefs and practices, according to Calvin.

3. What did Calvin mean by God's providence? Why did he think people opposed it?

§40. Westminster Confession

Multiple Choice and Fill in the Blank

1. According to the Westminster Confession, the infallible rule of interpretation of Scripture is
    A. The word of clergy
    B. Scripture itself
    C. Found through intense reading
    D. There is none

2. When was the covenant of grace established?
    A. Under the rule of Henry VIII
    B. Under the rule of King David
    C. At the death of Jesus
    D. At the creation of the world

3. The outward element to be used in the sacrament of baptism is water.
    A. True
    B. False

4. According to the Westminster Confession, infants do not have to be baptized.
    A. True
    B. False

5. The Westminster Confession was drafted in
    A. 1800
    B. 1544
    C. 1320
    D. 1646

§40. Westminster Confession

Short Answer

1. What kind of covenant was the first covenant? With whom was it made? Why was a second covenant necessary?

2. Summarize the differences between the understanding of covenant in the time of the law and in the time of the gospel.

3. How did the Westminster Confession shape the Puritan/Calvinist understanding of the sacrament of baptism?

§41. Menno Simons

Multiple Choice and Fill in the Blank

1. Menno's followers were known as
   A. Believing Baptists
   B. Mennonites
   C. Simonites
   D. Radical pacifists

2. According to the text, which of the following is not a prerequisite for baptism?
   A. Preaching of the gospel
   B. Belief
   C. Repentance
   D. The gift of the Holy Spirit

3. According to Menno Simons, the Lord's Supper is intended only as a memorial of Jesus' sacrifice.
   A. True
   B. False

4. Which of the following does Simons not identify as a "weapon" of the followers of Christ?
   A. Prophetic resistance
   B. Patience
   C. Hope
   D. God's word

5. Who does Simons exclude from the "ban"?
   A. Pastors
   B. Spouses
   C. Widows
   D. No one is excluded from the ban

§41. Menno Simons

Short Answer

1. What reasoning does Simons give for refusing baptism to infants and small children?

2. Discuss the political element of Simons' view of baptism; what is his point about "tyranny" and "persecution"?

3. Give some reasons someone might fall under the ban.

§42. Council of Trent

Multiple Choice and Fill in the Blank

1. The Council of Trent decreed this edition of the Scripture as authentic.
   A. Textus Receptus
   B. The Vulgate
   C. Any Latin edition
   D. Luther's Bible

2. According to the Council of Trent, who ultimately had the responsibility of judging the true sense and interpretation of Scripture?
   A. Individuals
   B. Priests
   C. Preachers
   D. Holy Mother Church

3. The Council of Trent anathematized anyone who said Adam's sin injured himself alone and not his
   A. Friends
   B. Wife
   C. Posterity
   D. Family

4. Baptism was for _____, since that which infants contracted by generation could be cleansed away by regeneration.
   A. A clean conscience
   B. The remission of sins
   C. A symbol
   D. A constitution

5. Baptized persons no longer struggled with concupiscence or sin.
   A. True
   B. False

§42. Council of Trent

Short Answer

1. To what was the Council of Trent a response? At what twentieth-century council were the decisions of Trent revisited?

2. Where does the church believe the "unwritten traditions" originate? How did they get transmitted to the current church?

3. Who does the Catholic Church baptize? Why is this necessary?

§43. Ignacio of Loyola

Multiple Choice and Fill in the Blank

1. When was Ignacio of Loyola canonized by the Roman Catholic Church?
    A. 1619
    B. 1620
    C. 1621
    D. 1622

2. According to the Sixth Rule, a person should do what?
    A. Praise the relics of saints
    B. Hear mass often
    C. Praise religious orders
    D. Obey God

3. According to the Eleventh Rule, Christians should avoid scholastic learning.
    A. True
    B. False

4. According to the Seventeenth Rule, Christians "ought not to speak so much with insistence on _____ that _____ be poisoned."
    A. free will; minds
    B. grace; free will
    C. grace; minds
    D. free will; grace

5. According to the Eighteenth Rule, which fear is one with divine love?
    A. Mortal fear
    B. Servile fear
    C. Filial fear
    D. Pious fear

§43. Ignacio of Loyola

Short Answer

1. Rules 1, 9, 10, and 13 of Ignacio de Loyola's Spiritual Exercises advised obedience to the Catholic Church. Describe what Ignacio advised and why he advised it.

2. Why did Ignacio instruct readers to avoid speaking much about predestination?

3. Why are people to avoid making comparisons between the living and the dead?

§44. Teresa of Avila

Multiple Choice and Fill in the Blank

1. Teresa is best known for her explorations of mental ascent through acts of physical labor.
   A. True
   B. False

2. According to Teresa, what has the soul lost that is reclaimed through inward prayer?
   A. Divinity
   B. Immortality
   C. Senses
   D. Beauty

3. Who does Teresa mention who claimed to have found God internally?
   A. Ignacio of Loyola
   B. St. Augustine
   C. Francis of Assisi
   D. Martin Luther

4. Teresa claims that God is found "in our interior" not through _____ but through the help of God's favor.
   A. Penitence
   B. Understanding
   C. Grace
   D. Epiphany

5. The external senses, Teresa suggests, help guide us deeper into the "interior castle."
   A. True
   B. False

§44. Teresa of Avila

1. Why does Teresa describe the Prayer of Recollection as "supernatural"?

2. What does Teresa say about meditation? How does it differ from "recollection"?

3. Explain what the whistle and the guards represent in Teresa's analogy which described the process of the prayer of recollection.

§45. Racovian Catechism

Multiple Choice and Fill in the Blank

1. Socinians believed that Jesus Christ is divine by _____ and not by nature.
   A. Office
   B. Procession
   C. Adoption
   D. Belief

2. The Racovian Catechism was first written in Polish.
   A. True
   B. False

3. By what event did Jesus "particularly" become like God immortal?
   A. His conception by the Spirit
   B. His sinless and holy life
   C. His obedient death
   D. His being raised from the dead

4. The Racovian Catechism claims that Jesus was not merely the only begotten Son of God, but also a
   A. Man
   B. God
   C. Savior
   D. Priest

5. The Catechism claims that "next after God," no one had a higher degree of divinity that Christ.
   A. True
   B. False

§45. Racovian Catechism

Short Answer

1. The Racovian Catechism, like other catechisms, is written in the form of questions and answers. Why might this be helpful in introducing the faith to others?

2. What are the biblical passages cited to support the Socinian view that Jesus was a "real man?"

3. The belief that Christ shared in the very essence of God was, to the Socinians, in opposition to what two things?

§46. Thomas Helwys

Multiple Choice and Fill in the Blank

1. Along with John Smyth, Thomas Helwys established the first
   _____ church in the city of Amsterdam.
   A. Lutheran
   B. Baptist
   C. Methodist
   D. Episcopalian

2. Helwys did not think the people should be forced to believe against
   their will.
   A. True
   B. False

3. What book does Helwys quote when he uses Paul as an example?
   A. Thessalonians
   B. Colossians
   C. Philippians
   D. Acts

4. Helwys believed in
   A. Voluntary faith
   B. Local church independence
   C. Congregational polity
   D. All of the above

5. Helwys states that his argument for free will in faith does not apply to
   heretics.
   A. True
   B. False

§46. Thomas Helwys

Short Answer

1. What arguments against the king (in particular) did Helwys use to establish that the king should not force his people to follow any religion?

2. Why is it so important that a person is able to choose his or her own faith?

3. What is the role of the earthly judiciary system when it comes to faith?

§47. John Winthrop

Multiple Choice and Fill in the Blank

1. Winthrop argued that the care of the _____ must oversway _____ respects.
   - A. Individual; public
   - B. Public; private
   - C. Church; public
   - D. American; British

2. Winthrop said his hearers had to follow _____ counsel, to do justly, love mercy, and to walk humbly with God.
   - A. Jonah's
   - B. Micah's
   - C. Nahum's
   - D. Isaiah's

3. Winthrop said New England was to be
   - A. As a city upon a hill
   - B. The New Israel
   - C. Just like Old England
   - D. A haven for all types of Christians

4. Winthrop argued that if his hearers turned away from God's commandments and laws, they would surely succeed.
   - A. True
   - B. False

5. Winthrop's diary entry refers to the trial of which pioneer of religious liberty?
   - A. John Mayhew
   - B. Jonathan Edwards
   - C. Roger Williams
   - D. John Locke

§47. John Winthrop

Short Answer

1. Why should the colony be like "a city on a hill?"

2. List the ways that the colonists can keep their covenant with God.

3. Briefly explain why Roger Williams was banished.

§48. Roger Williams

Multiple Choice and Fill in the Blank

1. What image does Williams use to illustrate his idea of liberty of conscience in a commonwealth?

    A. Kite

    B. Sled

    C. Ship

    D. Carriage

2. For Williams, what does freedom of conscience mean for the religious practice in the colony?

    A. Everyone must be a Christian, especially the civic leaders.

    B. Everyone must be a Baptist, especially the civic leaders.

    C. People have to attend the colony's official religious service but can continue their private practices how they choose.

    D. People do not have to attend particular religious services or give up their own practices.

3. Who is the "commander" of the ship in Williams' letter?

    A. The colony's civic leaders

    B. Jesus

    C. The colony's religious leaders

    D. The king of England

4. What must a person do regardless of their religion in Providence?

    A. Obey the civic leaders

    B. Participate in the colony's defense

    C. Pay colonial taxes

    D. All of the above

5. How does Williams feel about infinite liberty of conscience?

    A. He disapproves of it.

    B. He approves of it.

    C. He thinks it is the wisest option.

    D. He thinks it is the safest option.

§48. Roger Williams

Short Answer

1. To what area of life does William's freedom of conscience apply?

2. What limitation, if any, does Williams place on freedom of conscience?

3. What does Williams think should be done to someone who does not support the colony?

§49. Robert Barclay

Multiple Choice and Fill in the Blank

1. What is the guide by which the saints are led into all truth?
    A. The Scriptures
    B. The Spirit
    C. The Light
    D. The Church

2. The Spirit of God is the principal or primary rule of faith and Scriptures are the secondary rule.
    A. True
    B. False

3. For as in _____ all die, even so in _____ all shall be made alive.
    A. Sin; salvation
    B. Eve; Mary
    C. Adam; the Spirit
    D. Adam; Christ

4. Which is a biblical figure for the Lord's Supper?
    A. Christ multiplying the loaves and fishes
    B. Christ healing the sick
    C. Christ breaking bread with his disciples
    D. Moses delivering the Israelites from the tyranny of Pharaoh

5. From whose spirit does the forced coercion of conscience proceed?
    A. The Spirit of Cain
    B. The Spirit of Abel
    C. The Spirit of Solomon
    D. The Spirit of God

§49. Robert Barclay

Short Answer

1. What does Barclay list as the forms that the "revelations of God by the Spirit" take?

2. What event is considered the figure for the Christian practice of baptism? By contrast, what does Barclay claim is a "mere human tradition"?

3. Who has power over the human conscience? Who does not have power over it?

§50. John Wesley

Multiple Choice and Fill in the Blank

1. Where was Wesley when his "heart was strangely warmed"?
   A. Moravia
   B. Aldersgate Street Chapel
   C. Georgia
   D. Aboard ship to the colonies

2. In the 2 Kings story, there was no inquiry about Jehonadab's
   A. Heart
   B. Opinions
   C. Hair
   D. Prayer

3. Wesley said disagreements over interpretations of Scripture among Christians was proof that
   A. People were not infallible.
   B. His interpretation was the correct one.
   C. Christianity was not legitimate.
   D. The Bible was not reliable.

4. Christian perfection is another term for
   A. Salvation
   B. Holiness
   C. Right doctrine
   D. The afterlife

5. What was Wesley's view of human will?
   A. Aristotelian
   B. Arminian
   C. Augustinian
   D. Calvinist

§50. John Wesley

Short Answer

1. Wesley acknowledged that a variety of opinions concerning Christian worship existed. How did he instruct his readers to choose from such variety?

2. Describe what Wesley means by Christian perfection.

3. Describe the differences between Calvinists and Arminians, according to Wesley.

§51. Charles Wesley

Multiple Choice and Fill in the Blank

1. How is Charles Wesley related to John Wesley?
   A. They were first cousins.
   B. John is Charles' father.
   C. Charles is John's grandfather.
   D. They were brothers.

2. Which of these names for Jesus does not appear in the hymn?
   A. Messiah
   B. Alpha and Omega
   C. Joy of Heav'n
   D. Almighty

3. The hymn writer believes that human beings can be the dwelling place and temples of Jesus.
   A. True
   B. False

§51. Charles Wesley

Short Answer

1. For what hymns is Charles Wesley most famous?

2. Does Charles Wesley think that humans can stop sinning?

3. What lines from this hymn support your answer to question 2?

§52. Jonathan Edwards

Multiple Choice and Fill in the Blank

1. What was the First Great Awakening?
   A. The development of the scientific method
   B. The return to classical learning that ended the Dark Ages
   C. The first major revival movement in America
   D. The period of reconstruction that began after the American Civil War

2. What does Edwards believe started the awakening?
   A. The Spirit of God began to work among the people.
   B. The church changed its policies.
   C. The people began to think differently.
   D. The people grew tired of their sinfulness.

3. The moment a person is converted is a sudden and total act, so we should be able to identify when it occurred.
   A. True
   B. False

4. Which of the following, according to Edwards, is not responsible for keeping us from hell?
   A. The hand of God
   B. The power of God
   C. The pleasure of God
   D. Our own bodily health

5. God's creatures are good, and were made for humans _____ and for no other purpose.
   A. To enjoy
   B. To satisfy us
   C. To serve God
   D. To respect

§52. Jonathan Edwards

Short Answer

1. What are some of the signs that Edwards points to as evidence of an "extraordinary dullness" in the religious life of Americans?

2. What are the various ways that people become awakened, according to Edwards?

3. How is God characterized in the second sermon excerpt from *Sinners in the Hands of Angry God*?

§53. Immanuel Kant

Multiple Choice and Fill in the Blank

1. The categorical imperative can be described as the ethical theory that absolute moral commands are rooted in
   A. Righteousness and goodness
   B. Universal duty
   C. Laws and punishments
   D. Common decency

2. When considering a question of duty, ethics should eliminate the question of ends altogether.
   A. True
   B. False

3. According to Kant, the law is the _____ the use of freedom.
   A. Formal condition of
   B. Final condition of
   C. Correct exercise of
   D. Best measure of

4. After a person has done everything he or she can to exercise the latent capacities for good, what happens next?
   A. Nothing. That is as good as it gets.
   B. We hope and pray for God to make us better.
   C. The goodness that lies beyond our power can be supplied by a higher cooperation.
   D. We make better laws.

5. For Kant, praying should be central to all forms of religion.
   A. True
   B. False

§53. Immanuel Kant

Short Answer

1. Kant argues that humans cannot be said to be good by nature. Instead, how can they be deemed good?

2. What are the categories of religion for Kant?

3. Which of these does he consider the Christian religion to be? Why?

§54. Friedrich Schleiermacher

Multiple Choice and Fill in the Blank

1. What is the authoritative basis for religious truth, according to Schleiermacher?

   A. Reason

   B. Divine revelation

   C. Personal religious experience

   D. Church teaching and instruction

2. Schleiermacher's treatise "On Religion" is written to a cultured and cultivated audience who no longer values religion.

   A. True

   B. False

3. What term most accurately corresponds to the human self-consciousness?

   A. Receptivity

   B. Reciprocity

   C. Relevance

   D. Relation

4. What does Christ alone mediate?

   A. All existence of God in the world

   B. All revelation of God through the world

   C. Both A and B

   D. Neither A nor B

5. The beginning of the life of Jesus can be seen as the completed creation of human nature.

   A. True

   B. False

§54. Friedrich Schleiermacher

Short Answer

1. How does Schleiermacher's description of Christ differ from the Christology of Nicaea (Nicene orthodoxy)?

2. Schleiermacher hopes to establish a certain concept of "religion." What does that concept include?

3. What did the appearance of the first man constitute? What did the appearance of the "Second Adam" add?

§55. Søren Kierkegaard

Multiple Choice and Fill in the Blank

1. What is Kierkegaard known as the father of?
    A. Philosophy
    B. Paradox
    C. Pseudonymous writing
    D. Existentialism

2. To claim that there is an absolute duty toward God is another way of expressing what concept?
    A. The individual nature of faith
    B. The paradox of faith
    C. The knight of faith
    D. The institutional church

3. Outside "the universal," what is the path like?
    A. Solitary
    B. Narrow
    C. Steep
    D. All of the above

4. A person can be both an "individual" and a "knight of faith" at the same time.
    A. True
    B. False

5. How is the knight of faith viewed by others?
    A. As brave
    B. As confused
    C. As holy
    D. As crazy

§55. Søren Kierkegaard

Short Answer

1. To whom does Abraham have an absolute relation? To whom does he have an ethical relation?

2. How does the individual become the knight of faith?

3. Does Kierkegaard believe it is better to belong to the universal or to be outside of it? Give support for your answer.

§56. Ludwig Feuerbach

Multiple Choice and Fill in the Blank

1. Which of the following does not correctly describe Feuerbach?

   A. Scientist

   B. German

   C. Philosopher

   D. Atheist

2. What kind of approach did Feuerbach provide for the study of religion?

   A. Revelation-centered approach

   B. Human-centered approach

   C. Creation-centered approach

   D. Christ-centered approach

3. It is our task to show that the antithesis of divine and human is

   A. Altogether illusory

   B. Utterly illuminating

   C. Another illustration

   D. Alone illustrious

4. Feuerbach claims that in religion humans give up certain things. Which of the following does he say that we do?

   A. Deny our reason

   B. Deny our own knowledge

   C. Give up our dignity

   D. All of the above

5. God acts, that man may be

   A. Punished and rewarded

   B. Saved and redeemed

   C. Good and happy

   D. Good and redeemed

§56. Ludwig Feuerbach

Short Answer

1. What does Feuerbach say constitutes the historical progress of religion?

2. What, according to Feuerbach, is the Christian religion?

3. What, according to Feuerbach, is the mystery of religion?

§57. Peter Cartwright

Multiple Choice and Fill in the Blank

1. American frontier religion in the time of the Second Great Awakening prized formal ministry training and learned, studious sermons.
   A. True
   B. False

2. According to Cartwright, who put forth a mighty effort to stop the work of God in the revival?
   A. Predestinarians
   B. Free Willinarians
   C. Episcopalians
   D. Cartwright

3. Cartwright had seen more than 500 people with the jerks at one time in his congregation.
   A. True
   B. False

4. Eventually, the drunken man who involuntarily experienced the jerks
   A. Praised God
   B. Prayed for forgiveness
   C. Expired
   D. Jumped for joy

5. What does Cartwright recommend as a remedy for the jerks?
   A. Dancing
   B. Whiskey
   C. Fervent prayer
   D. Utter repentance

§57. Peter Cartwright

Short Answer

1. Describe how Cartwright thought God worked through the jerks.

2. Did Cartwright acknowledge that the jerking exercise could be abused or misused? Who might fall prey to this temptation?

3. Given Cartwright's descriptions, give some impressions of what the atmosphere must have been like at these meetings.

§58. Charles G. Finney

Multiple Choice and Fill in the Blank

1. What is required to change those who are reluctant to obey God?
   A. Coerce them
   B. Punish them
   C. Excite them
   D. Ignore them

2. Finney argued that a revival was not
   A. A good thing
   B. A miracle
   C. Godly
   D. Possible

3. How many people did Finney guess had gone to hell because the church did not use appropriate means?
   A. None
   B. One million
   B. Five thousand millions
   D. One trillion

4. Finney acknowledges that one of the dangers of revivals is that once Christians are brought to see the full extent of their sins, they will abandon all hope.
   A. True
   B. False

5. Revivals are partly for the conversion of sinners but Finney argues that they are first aimed at:
   A. Thieves and villains
   B. The state in need of reform
   C. The backslidden church
   D. Lazy magistrates

§58. Charles G. Finney

Short Answer

1. What are some of the ways that the Second Great Awakening differed from the First Great Awakening?

2. Explain Finney's analogy that seed/grain was like the means of revival.

3. What does Finney claim are the steps of repentance?

§59. Richard Furman

Multiple Choice and Fill in the Blank

1. On whose behalf did Furman pen this defense of slavery?
   A. The Triennial Convention
   B. All Christians
   C. South Carolina Baptists
   D. Abolitionists

2. The right of holding slaves, according the Furman, is clearly established by
   A. Reason
   B. Power
   C. Law
   D. Scripture

3. Furman cites numerous groups and civilizations that held slaves as evidence of his argument for the practice of slavery. Which of the following does he not list?
   A. Hebrew people
   B. Christian church
   C. Roman Empire
   D. Hittites

4. What condition does Furman suggest must be met before slaves are given freedom?
   A. They must be qualified to enjoy it.
   B. They must obtain it without harming the community's interest.
   C. They must obtain it without disturbing the peace of the community.
   D. All of the above

5. Slavery, argues Furman, when tempered with humanity and justice, is a state of
   A. Lamentable suffering
   B. Ignorant sinfulness
   C. Tolerable happiness
   D. Understandable necessity

§59. Richard Furman

1. List the Old Testament and New Testament passages that Furman used to argue that slavery was a right given by the Divine Law.

2. Explain how he used them to support his argument.

3. What does Furman think can and ought to be done to those who abuse their just authority? What, on the other hand, should not be done?

§60. Civil War Religion

Multiple Choice and Fill in the Blank

1. In his 1861 letter, Robert Ryland gives detailed advice about how his son can make a Christian profession among his fellow soldiers. Which of the following does he not advise?

    A. Avoid strong drink

    B. Do not use profanity

    C. Lead prayer-meetings with other soldiers

    D. Preach whenever possible

2. Ryland tells his son that in the hour of conflict he should

    A. Hate the enemy

    B. Show mercy to the enemy

    C. Follow his conscience

    D. Not cherish personal rage against the enemy

3. Robert Ryland said Providence sometimes used war to

    A. Chastise proud and wicked nations

    B. Kill off evil people

    C. Show power

    D. Control the population

4. Ryland tells his son that if he knew some of the men he was fighting, he might love them; nevertheless, he writes: the laws of war do not forbid you to pity them, even in the act of

    A. Destroying them

    B. Saving them

    C. Fighting them

    D. Protecting them

5. Ryland believes that Providence has surrounded his son with unsaved soldiers and exhorts him to share the gospel with his fellow soldiers and to teach them about Jesus.

    A. True

    B. False

§60. Civil War Religion

Short Answer

1. What were the markers of the "Lost Cause"?

2. How does Ryland argue that the Civil War is defensive?

3. Describe the instructions Robert Ryland gave to his son about how, when, and why he could participate in winning soldiers to Christ.

§61. Frederick Douglass

Multiple Choice and Fill in the Blank

1. Frederick Douglass was a former slave who had been freed by his master.
    A. True
    B. False

2. Frederick Douglass thought
    A. Christians could be slaveholders
    B. Christians should be slaveholders
    C. Christians should not be slaveholders
    D. Slavery was in accord with the New Testament

3. The _____ and the church-going bell chime in with each other.
    A. Stately church organ
    B. Minister's loud voice
    C. Congregation's lovely singing
    D. Slave auctioneer's bell

4. What sound does Douglass imagine is competing against the sound of the church's psalm reading and prayers?
    A. Cries of children
    B. Rattling of slave chains
    C. Shouts of auctioneers
    D. Singing of slave spirituals

5. Douglass makes clear that in this passage he is describing his view of all American religions, whether Christian or not.
    A. True
    B. False

§61. Frederick Douglass

1. Douglass writes about two kinds of Christianity. What are those two? How does he describe each one?

2. Douglass notes many inconsistencies to be found in those whose religious convictions and teachings do not align with their actions against slaves. List three of those.

3. Do you think Christians at this time would have been persuaded by this writing? Why or why not?

§62. Peter Randolph

Multiple Choice and Fill in the Blank

1. Randolph was a freed slave who worked to free and protect others fleeing slavery.
   A. True
   B. False

2. The slave auctioneer refers to the young boy as a piece of merchandise and as property. How does Randolph refer to him?
   A. As a fine youth
   B. As a hard worker
   C. As a free person
   D. As the image of God

3. Slaveholders carried what upon their back and in their pockets, according to Peter Randolph?
   A. Satan
   B. Eternal punishment
   C. The price of blood
   D. Sin

4. Which of the following biblical texts does Randolph not point to as evidence against slavery?
   A. Gospel passages about preaching deliverance to the captive
   B. Old Testament passages about freeing the Israelites from captivity in Egypt
   C. New Testament passages about loving your neighbor
   D. The "golden rule" found in Matthew

5. The anti-slavery cause is the cause of humanity, the cause of religion, and the cause of
   A. God
   B. Good people everywhere
   C. White Christians
   D. Northerners

§62. Peter Randolph

1. What evidence does Randolph offer to show that there is an inconsistency to the sale of a slave and the claim of the slave master to be a Christian?

2. What does the story reveal about the portrayal of black women in slavery?

3. Explain why Peter Randolph said that the sin of slaveholding was against the whole world. What grounds did he give for this claim?

§63. First Vatican Council

Multiple Choice and Fill in the Blank

1. Who convened the First Vatican Council?
    A. Pope Innocent III
    B. The Roman Curia
    C. Pope Pius IX
    D. Martin Luther

2. What evidence is offered in support of the church's belief in Apostolic Primacy?
    A. The Holy See has always held this belief.
    B. The practice of the church has always attested to it.
    C. The previous ecumenical councils have affirmed it.
    D. All of the above

3. How did the Council of Florence define the pope's role?
    A. The true vicar of Christ
    B. The head of the whole Church
    C. The father and teacher of all Christians
    D. All of the above

4. The pope has been given the gift of truth and never-failing faith so that the flock of Christ might be kept away from poisonous food of error and instead be nourished with the
    A. Food of true faith
    B. Manna from heaven
    C. Ppasture of heavenly doctrine
    D. Fount of wisdom

5. The First Vatican Council claims that the infallible teaching of the pope is a divinely revealed dogma.
    A. True
    B. False

§63. First Vatican Council

Short Answer

1. What authority is claimed for the pope in this document?

2. What does this document claim is Peter's appointed role? From whom did Peter receive this role? Who is Peter's successor?

3. Does the pope speak infallibly every time he speaks? If not, what are the conditions necessary to be considered infallible speech or teaching?

§64. Charles Hodge

Multiple Choice and Fill in the Blank

1. Which of the following is not true of the "Princeton theologians"?

    A. They taught in the nineteenth-century.

    B. They were strongly influenced by Eastern Orthodoxy.

    C. They were in line with the Calvinist or Reformed tradition.

    D. They were central in developing the doctrine of inerrancy.

2. The sacred writers were the organs of God, so that what they taught

    A. Was truth

    B. God taught

    C. Was believed

    D. Did not err

3. Hodge's doctrine of plenary inspiration asserted that authors of Scripture were

    A. Imbued with plenary knowledge

    B. Infallible human beings

    C. Infallible in matters on science

    D. Infallible only in the special purpose for which they were employed

4. Hodge contends that it is in the very nature of inspiration for God to use human language, even to express divine truths.

    A. True

    B. False

5. Which of the following is not a biblical example that Hodge employs to illustrate his point?

    A. Paul could not remember how many people he baptized, but still could not err in his teachings.

    B. Isaiah was a product of his time and its knowledge of the universe, but he was infallible in his predictions.

    C. Peter made mistakes in conduct, but not in teaching.

    D. Pharaoh had a hardened heart, but still ultimately let the Israelites go.

§64. Charles Hodge

Short Answer

1. Describe Hodge's doctrine of plenary inspiration. What did he claim the authors of Scripture were and were not?

2. What are some images that Hodge employs as metaphors to illustrate his claims about how God did and did not inspire the writers of Scripture?

3. This passage on the Protestant doctrine of inerrancy and the previous passage on the Roman Catholic doctrine of papal infallibility both suggest that these doctrines developed in response to modernism. From these two doctrines, what conclusions can you draw about what kind of "threat" modernism was seen to be? What might have been at stake for the church?

§65. Charles A. Briggs

Multiple Choice and Fill in the Blank

1. What did Briggs call the superstition that some Protestants exhibited toward the Bible?

   A. Inerrancy

   B. Bibliolatry

   C. Infallibility

   D. White Magic

2. Briggs believed that miracles should not be viewed as occurrences that could violate the laws of nature.

   A. True

   B. False

3. Briggs believed the only authenticity we are concerned with is divine authenticity.

   A. True

   B. False

4. What barrier does inerrancy confront?

   A. Religious criticism

   B. Historical criticism

   C. Natural criticism

   D. Higher criticism

5. Those who profess the dogma of verbal inspiration must reckon with what kind of errors found in the text of the Bible?

   A. Errors of authenticity

   B. Errors of translation

   C. Errors of truth

   D. Errors of transmission

§65. Charles A. Briggs

Short Answer

1. List the five barriers that Briggs said obstructed the way to the Bible.

2. Explain what Briggs meant by verbal inspiration.

3. Explain why Briggs argues that inerrancy is a barrier keeping people from the Bible?

§66. Elizabeth Cady Stanton

Multiple Choice and Fill in the Blank

1. Cady Stanton, an early feminist, advocated for all of the following except
   A. Abolition
   B. Temperance
   C. Women's rights
   D. Immigration reform

2. Cady Stanton said Christians should address prayers to
   A. Only a heavenly Father
   B. Only a heavenly Mother
   C. Jesus Christ
   D. Both a heavenly Father and Mother

3. Cady Stanton thought the Bible taught
   A. The equality of the sexes
   B. The superiority of women
   C. The superiority of men
   D. Nothing, because she did not care what the Bible said

4. According to Cady Stanton, the Bible makes no claim about
   A. Evolution
   B. Man's dominion over women
   C. Sexuality
   D. A literal six-day creation

5. For Cady Stanton, the biblical notion of the Fall is preferential to the Darwinian theory of gradual growth.
   A. True
   B. False

§66. Elizabeth Cady Stanton

Short Answer

1. What does Cady Stanton claim is suggested about the Godhead from the language used in the account of the creation of woman?

2. What point does Cady Stanton make about the "two contradictory accounts" of creation in Genesis and their use in contemporary Christianity?

3. According to Cady Stanton, with what did the tempter lure Eve? Why was that a temptation for her?

§62. Russell H. Conwell

Multiple Choice and Fill in the Blank

1. Conwell said Christians should spend their time
    A. Feeding the poor
    B. Reading the Bible
    C. Helping the outcast
    D. Getting rich

2. Conwell said that money was the root of all evil if a person squeezed the dollar till
    A. The person's hand went numb
    B. The dollar crumbled
    C. The eagle squealed
    D. The fingers broke

3. Conwell says that it is absurd to disconnect
    A. Wealth and philanthropy
    B. Poverty and power
    C. Love and power
    D. Suffering and wealth

4. If a man is poor when he could have been rich, he
    A. Has done some great wrong
    B. Has been untruthful to himself
    C. Has been unkind to his fellow man
    D. All of the above

5. According to the Bible, what is the root of all evil?
    A. Money
    B. Love of money
    C. Lack of money
    D. Hoarding money

§62. Russell H. Conwell

Short Answer

1. Explain the theological student and Conwell's conversation. What nuance did Conwell emphasize?

2. For Conwell, why is being poor sometimes the wrong thing to do?

3. What does "the love of money" mean to Conwell?

§68. Walter Rauschenbusch

Multiple Choice and Fill in the Blank

1. Rauschenbusch urged Christians to focus on
   A. Heaven
   B. Sunday morning worship
   C. Hell
   D. This earth

2. Rauschenbusch thought Christians should work to transform
   A. Creeds
   B. Social institutions
   C. Science
   D. Literature

3. Rauschenbusch argued the most pressing task is
   A. The self
   B. Earning money
   C. Reforming the economic system
   D. Women's suffrage

4. According to Rauschenbusch, in the past, the Christian church has focused on the salvation of individuals.
   A. True
   B. False

5. In the words of Rauschenbusch, "we need a _____ to serve as a spiritual basis for the tremendous social task before us."
   A. Political power
   B. Great faith
   C. Strong president
   D. Moving sermon

§68. Walter Rauschenbusch

Short Answer

1. What type of love does Rauschenbusch argue that Christians need now?

2. Summarize Rauschenbusch's argument for how the doctrine of stewardship is "not enough for our modern needs."

3. In what ways did Rauschenbusch's location influence his ideology?

§69. Charles Sheldon

Multiple Choice and Fill in the Blank

1. Charles Sheldon's novel, _____, was translated into more than a dozen languages.
   A. *Imitating Jesus*
   B. *The Social Gospel*
   C. *The Cost of Discipleship*
   D. *In His Steps*

2. Sheldon's novel was largely responsible for the popular evangelical slogan, "What Would Jesus Do?"
   A. True
   B. False

3. Before becoming unemployed, the man in the novel was a
   A. Painter
   B. Carpenter
   C. Preacher
   D. Salesman

4. Who is the only person in the city who had been kind to the unemployed man?
   A. The minister
   B. The mayor
   C. A church deacon
   D. No one

5. In Sheldon's novel, what happened to the man three days after he interrupted the service?
   A. He became a Christian.
   B. He got a job.
   C. He was baptized.
   D. He died.

§69. Charles Sheldon

Short Answer

1. In the selection from Sheldon, what four steps does the minister say Christians are to follow? Which one does the man raise questions about?

2. What aspects of Christianity does the unemployed man in the story challenge?

3. What does following Jesus mean to him?

§70. William J. Seymour

Multiple Choice and Fill in the Blank

1. Under Seymour's preaching, the Pentecostal movement erupted from a revival in
    A. Times Square
    B. New Orleans
    C. Azusa Street
    D. International Church of the Foursquare Gospel

2. Which of these did Seymour not mention as an effect of the atonement?
    A. Forgiveness of sin
    B. Sanctification
    C. Security from all harm
    D. Healing

3. Seymour said God provided _____ as confirmation of Seymour's preaching of the full gospel.
    A. Fire and water
    B. Miracles and theophanies
    C. Tongues and snakes
    D. Signs and wonders

4. Sickness is comparable in Seymour's mind to
    A. Ignorance
    B. Original sin
    C. The sufferings of Jesus
    D. Baptism

5. What is the ultimate effect of "baptism with the Holy Ghost?"
    A. The power to forgive sins
    B. Perfect knowledge
    C. A contrite and humble heart
    D. The ability to speak all languages

§70. William J. Seymour

Short Answer

1. Describe Seymour's understanding of how the atonement influenced healing.

2. Explain what Seymour means by the term "sanctification."

3. How does the focus of Seymour's spirituality differ from the "social gospel" of Rauschenbusch?

§71. Aimee Semple McPherson

Multiple Choice and Fill in the Blank

1. McPherson said the immediate result and the outward evidence of being filled with the Spirit was
    A. Feeling of drunkenness
    B. A warming of the heart
    C. Speaking in other tongues
    D. A pillar of fire

2. What two groups did McPherson identify as existing in the first century as well as in her own time?
    A. Mockers and thinkers
    B. Prophets and prophetesses
    B. Wealthy and poor
    C. Upper class and lower class

3. The first-century scenario McPherson based her argument on was from
    A. Acts
    B. Luke
    C. Romans
    D. Matthew

4. In what particular scandal was McPherson involved?
    A. Kidnapping
    B. Murder
    C. Arson
    D. Treason

5. McPherson says that there is no longer any Holy Spirit for the twentieth-century Christian.
    A. True
    B. False

§71. Aimee Semple McPherson

Short Answer

1. Explain the reasoning of the "thinkers," according to McPherson.

2. Recount the question McPherson posed to Peter, Paul, James, and John, and the answer they gave.

3. Why was the sign of speaking in tongues so unique and important?

§72. Adam Clayton Powell Sr.

Multiple Choice and Fill in the Blank

1. Which judge(s) does Powell encourage his listeners to appeal to?

    A. God

    B. The Supreme Court

    C. The owners of the land they are share-cropping

    D. Themselves

2. What was the ironic result of the improvement in African Americans' educational and economic situation?

    A. Instead of making their lives better, they became spiritually impoverished.

    B. Instead of more respect, it earned them more opposition.

    C. Instead of merely improving the social standing of African Americans, they had overtaken whites in terms of social influence.

    D. Instead of threatening African Americans' spiritual lives, money, the "root of all evil," had improved their spiritual lives.

3. What does Powell say will happen if African Americans try to achieve their goals through physical force?

    A. African Americans will prevail if they keep the faith.

    B. All African Americans will be killed.

    C. African Americans will force a stalemate with the government, and force it to act.

    D. African Americans will bring in the kingdom of God.

4. Who or what does Powell mean by "Ethiopia?"

    A. Africa

    B. African Americans

    C. The United States

    D. The country in Africa

5. How does Powell view violence?

    A. When in self-defense, it can be acceptable.

    B. Violence should be our last resort, but is acceptable.

    C. Violence is always acceptable.

    D. Violence is never acceptable.

§72. Adam Clayton Powell Sr.

Short Answer

1. What does Powell say is the only hope of African Americans?

2. What biblical story does Powell use as an extended metaphor for African Americans and their situation in the United States?

3. How would African Americans' reaching out to God benefit white people in Powell's mind?

§73. Helen Barrett Montgomery

Multiple Choice and Fill in the Blank

1. Helen Barrett Montgomery was the first woman to be elected president of the National Baptist Convention.
    A. True
    B. False

2. Helen Barrett Montgomery argues that the Old Testament legislation sets forth the liberation of women.
    A. True
    B. False

3. "The great _____ of the mother and child must be known in every dark corner of earth."
    A. Liberator
    B. Sovereign
    C. Emancipator
    D. Enslaver

4. Helen Barrett Montgomery argues that the Spirit of Jesus has created a
    A. Man's world
    B. Woman's world
    C. Small world
    D. New world

5. Helen Barrett Montgomery argues that there are warring theories of life between which two lands?
    A. The Land of Good and the Land of Evil
    B. The Land of Ladies First and the Land of Ladies Last
    C. The Land of Equality and the Land of Discrimination
    D. The Land of Feminism and the Land of Christianity

§73. Helen Barrett Montgomery

Short Answer

1. List the four reasons why Helen Barrett Montgomery argues that the Christian Scriptures contain teachings of women and equality.

2. Did Helen Barrett Montgomery believe that Jesus taught equality? Give an example from the text in support of your answer.

3. Describe the "new world" created by the Spirit of Jesus.

§74. Edgar Y. Mullins

Multiple Choice and Fill in the Blank

1. Mullins was an influential leader in which denomination?
   A. Methodism
   B. Presbyterian
   C. Southern Baptist
   D. Anglican

2. Mullins' most well-known and lasting book was
   A. *The Axioms of Reason*
   B. *The Baptist World Alliance*
   C. *The Axioms of Religion*
   D. *The Historical Significance of Baptists*

3. Mullins believes that the principle of soul competency originated in
   A. The Old Testament
   B. The New Testament
   C. The teaching of the church
   D. Early Baptist preaching

4. Which of the following can interfere with soul competency?
   A. Episcopacy
   B. Infant baptism
   C. Religion by proxy
   D. All of the above

5. Religion, according to Mullins, is
   A. A church matter because we must first be taught what to believe
   B. A personal matter between the soul and God
   C. A matter of right worship
   D. A matter between individual believers and their pastors

§74. Edgar Y. Mullins

Short Answer

1. What are two Baptist principles that Mullins considers to be distinctive but not "the" distinguishing Baptist principle?

2. What does he believe is "the" distinguishing Baptist principle and what does he mean by it?

3. What system of church governance logically follows from the doctrine of soul competency?

§75. William B. Riley

Multiple Choice and Fill in the Blank

1. What "menace" did Riley strongly oppose?
   A. Fundamentalism
   B. Modernism
   C. Moral relativism
   D. Heresy

2. According to Riley, this "menace"
   A. Is an enemy
   B. Has rejected Jesus
   C. Repudiated the Bible
   D. All of the above

3. Riley desired to be harsh and uncharitable.
   A. True
   B. False

4. William B. Riley was a leader during which controversy?
   A. Debates between Catholics and Protestants about church governance
   B. The fundamentalist-modernist controversy
   C. The debate over female ordination
   D. Interdenominational controversies over slavery

5. According to Riley, the greatest enemy of any church of Jesus Christ is the person
   A. Who remains in the church
   B. Who assumes to be one of the church's teachers
   C. Who disputes the authority of the Book upon which the church has rested its every contention
   D. All of the above

§75. William B. Riley

1. What are three examples Riley gives to support his claim that "modern thinkers make the interpretation of the Bible a matter of mental and personal convenience?"

2. What does Riley mean by "physical manifestations?" Whose "physical manifestations" is he referring to? Name two of the physical manifestations that he mentions specifically.

3. Describe Riley's George Washington metaphor and how it supports his point about Jesus.

§76. Rudolf Bultmann

Multiple Choice and Fill in the Blank

1. How many stories is the cosmological structure of the New Testament?
    A. Two
    B. Three
    C. Four
    D. Five

2. A modern person can accept a prescientific, mythical view of the world as true.
    A. True
    B. False

3. According to Bultmann, what is the best way for myth to be interpreted?
    A. Existentially
    B. Anthropologically
    C. Cosmologically
    D. Astronomically

4. _____ is not to be tied down to the imagery of New Testament mythology.
    A. Existence
    B. Truth
    C. Justice
    D. Faith

5. Why can spirits no longer be believed in?
    A. They never existed to begin with.
    B. Satan is tricking us.
    C. Laws and forces of nature have been discovered.
    D. The Bible tells us otherwise.

§76. Rudolf Bultmann

Short Answer

1. Describe Bultmann's view of myth and mythology for the modern
   man.

2. How should humans understand faith?

3. Why is the cosmology of the Bible no longer correct in Bultmann's
   eyes?

§77. Paul Tillich

Multiple Choice and Fill in the Blank

1. Paul Tillich was forced out of his teaching position for
    A. Teaching heresies
    B. Opposing the Third Reich
    C. Losing his faith
    D. Gross incompetence

2. Which of the following is not given by Tillich as a description of religious concern?
    A. It is ultimate.
    B. It is unconditional.
    C. It is total.
    D. It is indefinite.

3. The content of our ultimate concern can be an object.
    A. True
    B. False

4. Nothing can be of ultimate concern for us which does not have the power of _____ our being.
    A. Determining
    B. Moving and shaping
    C. Threatening and saving
    D. Harming or helping

5. The human is ultimately concerned about
    A. Being and time
    B. Being and meaning
    C. Meaning and existence
    D. Existence and life

§77. Paul Tillich

Short Answer

1. What method is Tillich known for? What two things does it correlate?

2. What biblical commandment does Tillich cite as the heart of ultimate concern?

3. What is the first formal criterion of theology?

§78. Karl Barth

Multiple Choice and Fill in the Blank

1. Why should the members of the Lutheran, Reformed, and United churches not keep silent?
   A. In order not to be seen as sinners
   B. In order to remain faithful to their various confessions
   C. Because they are suicidal
   D. In order to separate themselves from the state

2. What task does the state have by divine appointment?
   A. Providing for justice and peace
   B. Punishing sinners
   C. Eliminating poverty
   D. Killing enemies of the state

3. Jesus is both the electing God and the elected man.
   A. True
   B. False

4. Part of being God is that God is able to forgive himself.
   A. True
   B. False

5. According to Barth, righteousness means
   A. Eliminating wrong
   B. Establishing right
   C. Correcting wrong
   D. To set right

§78. Karl Barth

Short Answer

1. How can God both forgive and be in need of forgiveness, according to Barth?

2. How does Barth explain how Jesus can be both the electing God and the elected man?

3. Why is Barth able to reject German Nazism if the Christian is supposed to obey the state?

§79. Reinhold Niebuhr

Multiple Choice and Fill in the Blank

1. Niebuhr argued that sin was _____ but not _____.
   A. terrible; inescapable
   B. powerful; consuming
   C. inevitable; necessary
   D. wrong; unavoidable

2. According to Niebuhr, where is moral pride revealed?
   A. Through prayer
   B. Through sermons
   C. On social media
   D. In self-righteous judgments

3. The sin of moral pride also results in the sin of spiritual pride.
   A. True
   B. False

4. What fuels moral pride in humans?
   A. God
   B. Self-love
   C. Social status
   D. Reading the Bible daily

5. Niebuhr argues that spiritual pride makes every virtue "the very vehicle of sin."
   A. True
   B. False

§79. Reinhold Niebuhr

Short Answer

1. How does Niebuhr define Christianity as a religion?

2. What is the difference between moral and spiritual pride?

3. What, according to Niebuhr, is the "worst form" of class dominion? The worst form of intolerance? The worst form of self-assertion?

§80. Dietrich Bonhoeffer

Multiple Choice and Fill in the Blank

1. Which of the following happened to Dietrich Bonhoeffer?
    A. He was arrested and accused of plotting to assassinate Hitler.
    B. He was imprisoned in a military prison and a concentration camp.
    C. He was executed.
    D. All of the above

2. Cheap grace means justification of sin but not of
    A. Sinfulness
    B. The sinner
    C. The unpardonable sin
    D. Evil

3. Cheap grace is
    A. Baptism without the discipline of community
    B. Absolution without personal confession
    C. Preaching forgiveness without repentance
    D. All of the above

4. According to Bonhoeffer, which of the following does not miss the blessing of visible fellowship?
    A. Those who are imprisoned.
    B. Those who sin.
    C. Those who are sick.
    D. Those who proclaim the gospel in heathen lands.

5. What is a source of "incomparable joy and strength" to Christian believers?
    A. The Lord's Supper
    B. Gathering in worship
    C. Personal prayer and thanksgiving
    D. The physical presence of other Christians

§80. Dietrich Bonhoeffer

Short Answer

1. Why did Bonhoeffer write against German Christianity?

2. Bonhoeffer compares costly grace to a hidden treasure and to a pearl. How is costly grace like these two things?

3. What three biblical examples does Bonhoeffer give to support his view that being with other believers is a joy?

§81. Dorothy Day

Multiple Choice and Fill in the Blank

1. What was happening in the world when Day wrote this piece?
   A. The Great Depression
   B. The First World War
   C. The Second World War
   D. The Great Influenza Epidemic

2. What does Day argue is always the charge leveled against pacifists?
   A. They are traitors.
   B. They do not understand politics.
   C. They are weak.
   D. They are too sentimental and afraid of suffering and war.

3. In this excerpt, Day quotes from the novel
   A. *War and Peace*
   B. *The Brothers Karamazov*
   C. *Crime and Punishment*
   D. *Doctor Zhivago*

4. The victims of the class war that Day mentions are
   A. Seel workers
   B. Coal miners
   C. Agricultural workers
   D. All of the above

5. What does Day say about love?
   A. It is a breaking of bread not the starving of whole populations.
   B. It is not the bombardment of open cities.
   C. It is not killing, but the laying down of one's life for one's friend.
   D. All of the above

§81. Dorothy Day

Short Answer

1. Day argues that the hardships of the slum are not easy. How does she describe what it is like there?

2. What are the two wars that Day argues are going on "side by side" with the world war? Why can they not keep silent in the face of these wars?

3. Describe what happened to the African American man in Missouri that Day mentions.

§82. Second Vatican Council

Multiple Choice and Fill in the Blank

1. The Catholic Church "rejects nothing of what is _____" in the world religions.
   A. Godly and upright
   B. Christian and holy
   C. Sound and wise
   D. True and holy

2. Which religion receives the most attention and the most positive assessment?
   A. Judaism
   B. Islam
   C. Hinduism
   D. Buddhism

3. This document encourages
   A. Parents to teach their children the basics of religious faith
   B. Participation in dialogue with persons of other religions
   C. Prayer and fasting
   D. A new crusade in the Holy Lands

4. According to Vatican II, other religions often have
   A. A ray of truth
   B. More truth than Christianity
   C. No truth because they are evil
   D. An equal amount of truth as Christianity

5. With reference to Christian-Muslim relations, which of the following does Vatican II not encourage?
   A. Liberty
   B. Peace
   C. Joint worship
   D. Social justice

§82. Second Vatican Council

Short Answer

1. Discuss the reasons the Catholic Church has a high regard for Muslims.

2. Discuss what this document identifies as positive ideas in Judaism.

3. In what specific ways does the Catholic Church encourage interaction with other religions, and for what ends?

§83. Vladimir Lossky

Multiple Choice and Fill in the Blank

1. Lossky emphasizes the place of _____ in the practice of Christian faith.
   A. Mysticism
   B. Orthodoxy
   C. Nihilism
   D. Witchcraft

2. Lossky says that the more mystical Christian theory is, the more directly it aspires to the supreme end of union with God.
   A. True
   B. False

3. According to Lossky, Adam did what he was called to do and formed a union with God.
   A. True
   B. False

4. When was the divine energy foreign to human nature?
   A. From Jesus' death until His resurrection
   B. From Noah until Moses
   C. From the Fall until Pentecost
   D. From Joseph until Jesus

5. According to Lossky, Christ is the second
   A. Moses
   B. Adam
   C. Elijah
   D. Joseph

§83. Vladimir Lossky

Short Answer

1. How did God create a way for the deification of humanity to still occur, even after the Fall?

2. What is the final end for the human being?

3. Why is mysticism compatible with Christianity, according to Lossky?

§84. Clarence Jordan

Multiple Choice and Fill in the Blank

1. What biblical parable does Jordan retell in this excerpt?
   A. Good Samaritan
   B. Prodigal Son
   C. Mustard Seed
   D. Faithful Servant

2. What happens to the traveler in Jordan's story?
   A. Gangsters hold him up on the road from Atlanta to Albany.
   B. He is mugged while walking in downtown Birmingham.
   C. The traveler is a high school student attacked by his peers between classes.
   D. He is robbed while going from Jerusalem to Jericho.

3. What does the Sunday school teacher in the story want to know?
   A. What he must do to be saved
   B. Who is his neighbor
   C. Which of the Ten Commandments is most important
   D. Both A and B

4. What does the man who stops do for the wounded traveler?
   A. Holds him while he dies
   B. Takes him to the hospital, but can't pay his bill
   C. Takes him to the hospital and pays his bill
   D. Takes him to the morgue after he dies

5. Clarence Jordan founded an interracial community.
   A. True
   B. False

§84. Clarence Jordan

Short Answer

1. What was Koinonia Farm and why was it significant?

2. What changes does Jordan make to the story in order to focus on racial tension?

3. According to Jordan's version of the story, how should people treat individuals with different racial backgrounds?

§85. Gustavo Gutiérrez

Multiple Choice and Fill in the Blank

1. Gutiérrez says theological reflection must be linked to
   A. Children
   B. America
   C. Praxis
   D. The university

2. Gutiérrez's theology grew out of experience in
   A. Portugal
   B. Spain
   C. Romania
   D. Latin America

3. Gutiérrez is the founder of what type of theology?
   A. Soteriology
   B. Christology
   C. Feminist theology
   D. Liberation theology

4. According to Gutiérrez, what is an obstacle to salvation?
   A. The Devil
   B. Sin
   C. Lack of reflection
   D. Secular culture

5. Gutiérrez claims the church is becoming more politically aware.
   A. True
   B. False

§85. Gustavo Gutiérrez

Short Answer

1. What kinds of things does Gutiérrez want theology to reflect on?

2. What changes does Gutiérrez see in Christian community, especially in regards to Latin America?

3. Describe Gutiérrez's understanding of salvation.

§86. Óscar Romero

Multiple Choice and Fill in the Blank

1. What experience does Romero identify as the source of his new understanding of the gospel?
   A. The civil war in El Salvador
   B. Studying in Rome
   C. Encountering the poor
   D. Encountering the powerful and wealthy

2. What biblical sources does Romero use to explain his position?
   A. The Gospels
   B. Exodus
   C. The prophetic books of Amos and Isaiah
   D. All of the above

3. According to Romero, what should be "a source of hope and support" in the poor's struggle for liberation?
   A. All of the churches in the world
   B. The Church of England and all of the other realms of the British Empire
   C. Private charities
   D. The government of El Salvador

4. According to Romero, the church has _____ had social and political implications.
   A. Never
   B. Always
   C. Only recently
   D. Sometimes

5. According to Romero, defending the poor has led to conflict with whom?
   A. The wealthy and powerful
   B. The people
   C. The bishops of the church
   D. Liberation theologians

§86. Óscar Romero

Short Answer

1. What or who constitutes the "world" which the church should be serving for Romero?

2. What "dimension" of the Christian faith does Romero claim to be addressing in his speech?

3. What has oppressed and repressed the poor in El Salvador?

§87. James H. Cone

Multiple Choice and Fill in the Blank

1. Black Liberation Theology can be defined as
   A. Theology viewed through the experiences of African Americans
   B. Theology viewed through the perspectives of African Americans
   C. Theology that includes identification of Jesus with the oppressed
   D. all of the above

2. Cone says it is in light of the cross and the resurrection in relation to Jesus' _____ that Black Theology asserts that "Jesus is black."
   A. Jewishness
   B. Humility
   C. Power
   D. Poverty

3. Cone argues that the Black Christ issue must be dealt with on _____ grounds.
   A. Political
   B. Theological
   C. Historical
   D. Ecumenical

4. Which of the following events from Jesus' life does Cone discuss as part of Jesus' blackness?
   A. The way in which he was treated by religious leaders
   B. His death on the cross and resurrection
   C. His childhood
   D. Both A and B

5. Cone argues that Christ must be black for the gospel to be good news.
   A. True
   B. False

§87. James H. Cone

wer

1. List a few of the reasons Cone gives for Jesus' blackness.

2. Why, according to Cone, do white theologians have a negative response to the Black Christ?

3. What does Cone mean when he says Christ's blackness is literal?

§88. Rosemary Radford Ruether

Multiple Choice and Fill in the Blank

1. With which denomination does Rosemary Radford Ruether identify?
   A. Roman Catholicism
   B. Presbyterian
   C. Lutheran
   D. Baptist

2. Feminist Theology promotes the _____ of women.
   A. Equality
   B. Full humanity
   C. Sovereignty
   D. Blessed nature

3. Which of the following, according to Radford Ruether, happens as a result of men being named the norm of authentic humanity?
   A. Women are scapegoated for sin
   B. Women are marginalized in redeemed humanity
   C. Women cannot achieve full salvation
   D. Both A and B
   E. All of the above

4. Women can reverse the sin of sexism by diminishing male humanity.
   A. True
   B. False

5. There are no divisions between feminists.
   A. True
   B. False

§88. Rosemary Radford Ruether

Short Answer

1. According to Radford Ruether, what must women do in order to claim their full humanity?

2. What barriers to feminist consciousness does Radford Ruther identify?

3. What role does Radford Ruether argue anger plays in feminist theology?

§89. Ada María Isasi-Díaz

Multiple Choice and Fill in the Blank

1. Who Latina women are and what they do, according to Isasi-Díaz, is revelatory of the
   A. Latin culture
   B. Latin femininity
   C. Divine
   D. Majority view

2. What is the source of *mujerista* theology?
   A. Spanish-speaking church
   B. Lived-experience of Hispanic women
   C. Political needs of Hispanic women
   D. Writing of Latina saints

3. In *mujerista* theology, Hispanic women step outside dominant understandings and practices.
   A. True
   B. False

4. Which of the following are challenges faced by Hispanic women?
   A. Divorce from their cultural customs
   B. Poverty
   C. Their language is viewed as a threat
   D. All of the above

5. The dominant culture, class, and race in a society determine the societal norms, understandings, and practices.
   A. True
   B. False

§89. Ada María Isasi-Díaz

Short Answer

1. What does Isasi-Díaz mean by "lived-experience"?

2. How and why does beginning with "lived-experience" differ from other, dominant forms of doing theology?

3. According to Isasi-Díaz, what are the goals of *mujerista* theology?

§90. Billy Graham

Multiple Choice and Fill in the Blank

1. According to Billy Graham, what type of relationship must someone have with Jesus Christ in order to be saved?
    A. Collective
    B. Personal
    C. Distant
    D. A relationship is not necessary

2. Billy Graham claims that God will never send anyone to hell.
    A. True
    B. False

3. Which of the following statements accurately describe Billy Graham's career?
    A. He was the unofficial chaplain for multiple American Presidents.
    B. His preaching ministry began in the twentieth century.
    C. He embodied liberal evangelical preaching.
    D. Both A and B.

4. According to Graham, who resides in heaven?
    A. Everyone who accepted Christ as their Savior
    B. Only Baptists and Methodists
    C. Anyone who attends church
    D. Those whom God foreordained

5. Graham's sermons include Scripture references.
    A. True
    B. False

§90. Billy Graham

1. According to Graham, what role does individual choice play in whether a person goes to heaven or hell?

2. How does Graham describe heaven and hell? What does he say these two worlds are like?

3. In "How to Receive Christ," Graham articulates four things you must do in order to be saved. List two of the steps.

§91. John Howard Yoder

Multiple Choice and Fill in the Blank

1. Constantinianism is
    A. The mutually supportive relationship between the church and state
    B. The law separating the church and state
    C. Emperor Constantine's stance on how the church should interact with the state
    D. None of the above

2. Yoder believed in war and the necessity of violence.
    A. True
    B. False

3. According to Yoder, Jesus' call to cross-bearing includes
    A. Abandoning claims of justice for oneself
    B. A deep concern for reconciliation
    C. Being at the mercy of one's neighbor
    D. All of the above

4. Jesus' death on the cross is a
    A. Tragedy
    B. Symbol of the necessity of violence
    C. Triumphant victory
    D. Effective method of getting your own way

5. In Jesus' context, how does Yoder define "the Powers"?
    A. All forms of government
    B. Representatives of Jewish religion and Roman politics
    C. Satan
    D. Both A and C

§91. John Howard Yoder

Short Answer

1. How was Jesus' relationship with the Powers (the Romans and the Jewish leaders, laws, customs, institutions, etc.,) different from all other human relationships with the Powers?

2. According to Yoder, what makes the type of pacifism embodied by Christ different from a pacifism that still lets you get everything you want?

3. How does Yoder define obedience?

§92. Larry Norman

Multiple Choice and Fill in the Blank

1. Larry Norman's music is written in which genre?
   A. Classical
   B. Christian rock
   C. Contemporary worship
   D. Traditional hymns

2. "I Wish We'd All Been Ready" was one of Norman's most popular songs.
   A. True
   B. False

3. Norman was the face of which of the following movements?
   A. Great Awakening
   B. Jesus Movement (also known as the Jesus Revolution)
   C. Christian Rock Movement
   D. Contemporary Crusade Movement

§92. Larry Norman

Short Answer

1. What images does Norman use to describe the world in "I Wish We'd All Been Ready?"

2. What significant event does Norman's song discuss?

3. What role does repetition play in the song?

§93. Emergent Leaders

Multiple Choice and Fill in the Blank

1. Who does the Response claim to be the spokesperson for the Emerging Church?

    A. Jesus

    B. Brian McLaren

    C. The authors of the Response as a group

    D. There is no central spokesperson

2. What occupation do the authors claim for themselves?

    A. Theologians

    B. Scholars

    C. Local church practitioners/leaders

    D. Philosophers

3. What is the relationship between the Emerging Church and evangelicalism according to the Response?

    A. The Response does not mention evangelicalism.

    B. They have an evangelical heritage and continue to affirm an evangelical spirit.

    C. They have an evangelical heritage but try to distance themselves from the group.

    D. They view themselves as truer evangelicals than their critics.

4. Who do the authors of the Response think should respond to scholarly critique of their movement?

    A. Scholars who are friendly to the movement

    B. Each and every believer, since we are all equal

    C. Pastors of churches

    D. No one, they should be ignored and dismissed

5. What is one of the authors' recurring frustrations throughout the Response?

    A. They are being characterized by one member's views.

    B. They are not being referred to by the correct name.

    C. They are only being criticized by scholars.

    D. They are not being taken seriously.

§93. Emergent Leaders

Short Answer

1. What central metaphor(s) does the Response use to describe the Emergent movement?

2. Who do the authors of the Response say should not read their work?

3. How does the Emerging Church view the ancient Christian creeds and Trinitarianism?